Indiana
USA

Silver Burdett Ginn
Parsippany, NJ • Needham, MA
Atlanta, GA   Deerfield, IL   Irving, TX   Santa Clara, CA

PROGRAM AUTHORS

Juan R. García
Associate Professor of History and Associate Dean
  of the College of Social and Behavioral Sciences
University of Arizona
Tucson, AZ

Daniel J. Gelo
Associate Professor of Anthropology, Division of
  Behavioral and Cultural Sciences
University of Texas at San Antonio
San Antonio, TX

Linda L. Greenow
Associate Professor and Acting Chair,
  Department of Geography
S.U.N.Y. at New Paltz
New Paltz, NY

James B. Kracht
Professor of Geography and Educational
  Curriculum and Instruction
Texas A&M University
College Station, TX

Deborah Gray White
Professor of History
Rutgers University
New Brunswick, NJ

CONTRIBUTING AUTHORS

Dr. Claudia Crump
Professor of Elementary Social Studies Education
Indiana University Southeast
New Albany, IN

Dr. Rick Bein
Professor of Geography
Indiana University—Purdue University
  at Indianapolis
Indianapolis, IN

Silver Burdett Ginn
A Division of Simon & Schuster
299 Jefferson Road, P.O. Box 480
Parsippany, NJ 07054-0480

CONTENTS

REFERENCE 340

MAPS

*Found in Summing Up, Geography and You

ATLAS MAPS

MAP ADVENTURES

*Found in Summing Up, Geography and You

TIME LINES

GRAPHS, TABLES, CHARTS, AND DIAGRAMS

SKILLS

LITERATURE

The following books are recommended for optional reading and research.

Map Handbook
CONTENTS

INDIANA
★ State capital
● Major cities

How Do You Make a MAP From a PHOTO?

Would it be hard to take a long car trip without a road map? How many words would it take to tell where Indiana is located if you couldn't show it on a map? With the right map, you can quickly find the information you need to take a trip or describe a location.

A map shows what a place would look like if you were looking down from a hot-air balloon. The higher you went, the more you would see. But as you went higher, the features of the land would get smaller.

Look for the details.
- Study the photograph.
- Make a list of the things that you see.

Here is how a mapmaker shows the same scene as the photograph. The mapmaker picks out the most important features of the photograph. The map has **symbols**, or signs, that stand for these features. Sometimes the symbols are colors. The symbols are explained in the **map key**.

Now Try This!

Think of a place you know well, such as a room in your home or school. Then draw a map that shows how the place would look if seen from above. Make up symbols for important features on the map. Explain these symbols in a map key.

Use the symbols in the key.

Find the lake in the photograph.

◆ What color on the map stands for the lake? Find the lake on the map.

◆ Now find the main streets, the houses, and the swimming pools. Does the map show these in the same spots as the photograph?

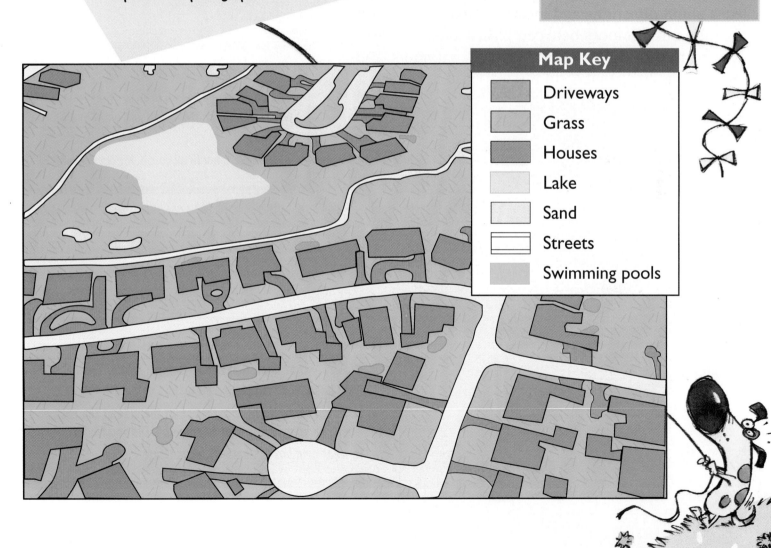

Map Key

- Driveways
- Grass
- Houses
- Lake
- Sand
- Streets
- Swimming pools

How Much Can You Learn About

MAPS?

Lee and Kim had just heard the good news! Their family was going to travel across Indiana this summer. They had always wanted to visit Spring Mill State Park and the Hoosier National Forest, but they wondered exactly where these places were.

The two looked at a map of Indiana showing some state parks, like the one on the next page. To plan the trip, Lee and Kim decided that they had to learn to understand the symbols on the map. They needed to learn about directions and **locator maps**. Lee wanted to figure out distances between places. Finally, they decided to learn how to use the letters, numbers, and crisscrossed lines that form the map grid.

The Scale

The scale lets you tell the actual distances between places.

- How many miles are represented on this scale?

The Compass Rose

The compass rose is a drawing that tells where north, south, east, and west are on the map.

- Is Muncie north or south of Fort Wayne?

The Grid

A grid is a set of lines that cross to form boxes. The grid system helps you find places on maps.

- Look for Terre Haute. Find row C at the side of the map. Then run your finger over to column 1. Did you find it?
- In what grid box is Chain O'Lakes State Park?

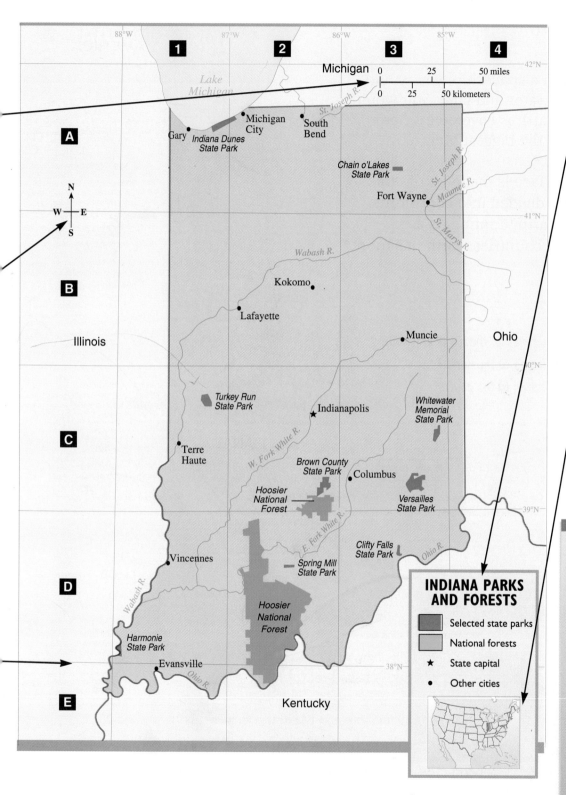

1 **2** **3** **4**

Michigan

0   25   50 miles

0   25   50 kilometers

42°N

Lake Michigan

88°W   87°W   86°W   85°W

A

Gary   Michigan City   South Bend
Indiana Dunes State Park

St. Joseph R.

Chain o'Lakes State Park

Maumee R.

Fort Wayne

St. Joseph R.

B

St. Marys R.

41°N

Wabash R.

Kokomo

Lafayette

Illinois

Muncie   Ohio

40°N

C

Turkey Run State Park

Indianapolis

Whitewater Memorial State Park

Terre Haute

W. Fork White R.

Brown County State Park

Columbus

Hoosier National Forest

Versailles State Park

D

E. Fork White R.

Clifty Falls State Park

Ohio R.

39°N

Vincennes

Spring Mill State Park

Wabash R.

Hoosier National Forest

Harmonie State Park

Evansville   38°N

Ohio R.

E

Kentucky

INDIANA PARKS AND FORESTS

- ▢ Selected state parks
- ▢ National forests
- ★ State capital
- • Other cities

N / W–E / S

The Title

In this book you will find a map title at the top of the key. The title tells what kind of information is on the map.

◆ What is the title of this map?

The Key

On most maps, a box called a key, or legend, explains the symbols or colors.

◆ What color on the map stands for state parks?

The key sometimes includes a locator map. This helps you locate a place in relation to a larger area.

◆ What area is shown on the main map? What larger area is shown on the locator map?

Now Try This!

Draw a map of your neighborhood or town.

◆ Draw in the major streets, and put in the major places of interest.

◆ Make a grid for the map. Use numbers along the top and letters running down the left side.

Save this map. You'll use it later on!

Can You Count the CONTINENTS?

If you traveled around Earth in a spaceship, you would see below you a huge ball of water and land. You would see that about three fourths of Earth is covered by water. Much of that water is in **oceans**, the biggest bodies of water on Earth. Earth has four oceans.

The other fourth of Earth's surface is made up of large land areas. These land areas are divided into **continents**. There are seven continents on Earth. Continents are divided into smaller areas called countries. Earth has more than 170 countries.

Say "Hi, neighbor!"

The United States has neighboring countries to the north and south.

- ◆ What country borders the United States to the north?
- ◆ What country borders the United States to the south?

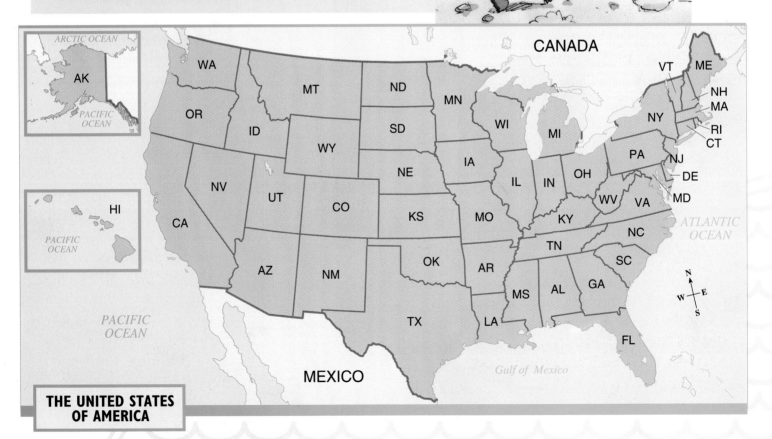

THE UNITED STATES OF AMERICA

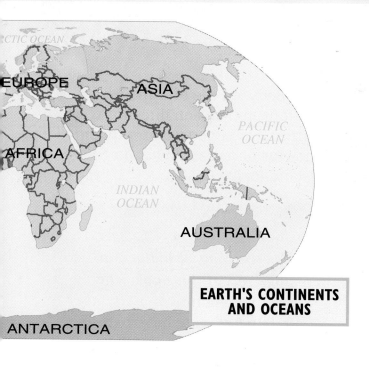

EUROPE

ASIA

PACIFIC OCEAN

AFRICA

INDIAN OCEAN

AUSTRALIA

EARTH'S CONTINENTS AND OCEANS

ANTARCTICA

Now Try This!

Find a map of North America in an atlas. Trace it on a piece of tracing paper.

◆ Outline the continent in blue pen or pencil. Outline the United States in red. Outline Indiana in black.

◆ Now place an orange star on the map for Indianapolis, the capital of Indiana. Place a brown dot for the name of the community in which you live.

◆ Finally, complete this statement: I live in the community of _____, in the state of _____, in the country of _____, on the continent of _____, on the planet known as _____.

Give it a name.

The names of Earth's oceans and continents are shown on this map.

◆ Name the oceans and the continents.

◆ On what continent is the United States of America?

◆ Which continent lies south of Europe?

Think about Indiana.

The United States is divided into 50 parts. Each part is called a state. You live in the state of Indiana. Its nickname is the Hoosier State.

◆ What other states share boundaries with Indiana?

◆ What lake borders Indiana?

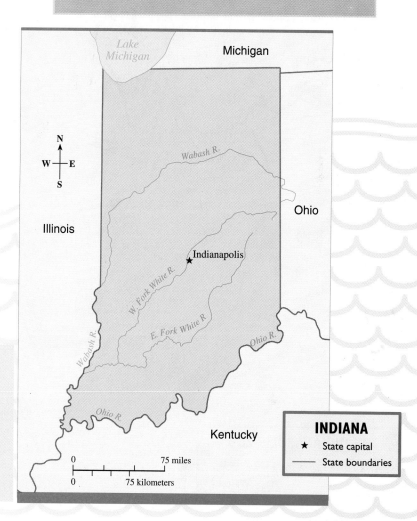

Lake Michigan

Michigan

N
W — E
S

Illinois

Wabash R.

Ohio

★ Indianapolis

W. Fork White R.

E. Fork White R

Ohio R.

Wabash R.

Ohio R.

Kentucky

0   75 miles
0   75 kilometers

INDIANA
★ State capital
— State boundaries

What Can a COMPASS ROSE Do for Me?

Many maps have a drawing that shows where north, south, east, and west are on the map. The drawing is called the **compass rose**. On the compass rose, the letters *N*, *S*, *E*, and *W* stand for north, south, east, and west. Between the four main directions are four in-between directions. For example, northeast is in between north and east. *NE* stands for northeast. What do *NW*, *SE*, and *SW* stand for?

Go see some sights.

You are at the Dolphin Show. You want to see mammals of the African Plains.

- Should you go south or west?

Next you visit the Encounters section.

- In what in-between direction should you travel?

Now Try This!

Use the map of Indiana on page M5 of this book. Find your community or a city near it. In what main or in-between directions are the following places from your community?

- **Lake Michigan**
- **Versailles State Park**

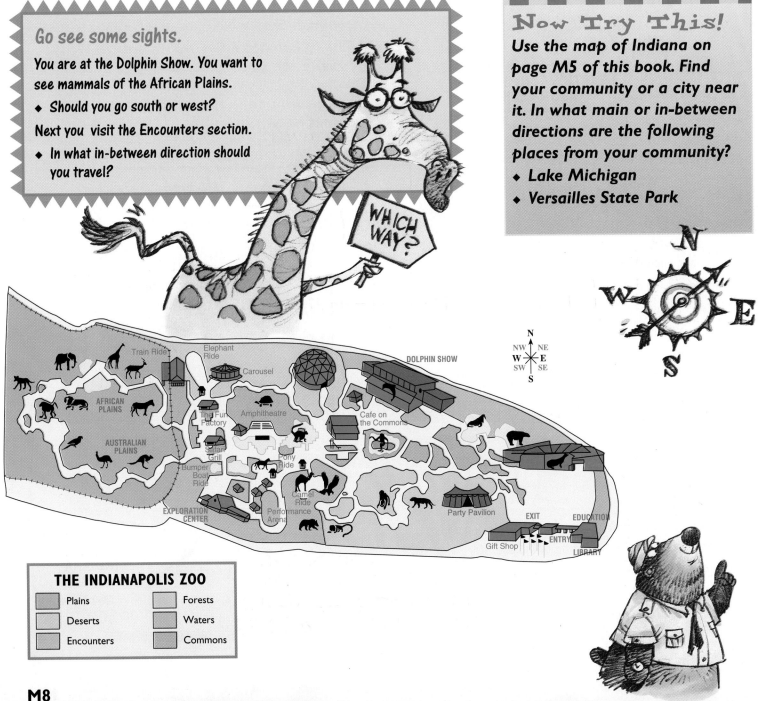

THE INDIANAPOLIS ZOO

- Plains
- Deserts
- Encounters
- Forests
- Waters
- Commons

What Doors Does a MAP KEY Open?

All maps have their own language. You need to "read" that language to understand the map. The "words" of this map language are the symbols on the map. A mapmaker gathers all the symbols together in one place on the map, called the key. Another term for the key is the **legend**.

This map is a **precipitation map**. It shows the amount of rain, snow, hail, and sleet that falls in the Midwest and Great Plains region in an average year.

Use the key to unlock meaning.

- Name three states in this region.
- What does color show on this map?
- Which state receives more precipitation in an average year, Minnesota or Indiana?

Keep on traveling!

- What could you say about precipitation in this region when traveling from east to west?

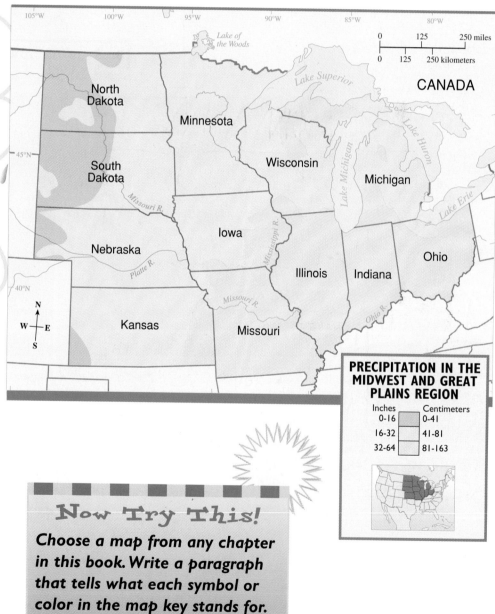

PRECIPITATION IN THE MIDWEST AND GREAT PLAINS REGION

Inches		Centimeters
0-16		0-41
16-32		41-81
32-64		81-163

Now Try This!

Choose a map from any chapter in this book. Write a paragraph that tells what each symbol or color in the map key stands for.

Why Use a SCALE That Can't Weigh Anything?

How far is it from your home to your school? How big is a soccer field? How far is it from Gary to Evansville? You can use a map to find all these distances. All you need is a piece of paper and knowledge of a **distance scale**.

Distances on maps are always smaller than the real distances on Earth. The distance scale tells us how much smaller. A certain number of inches on a map stands for a certain number of feet, yards, or miles on Earth.

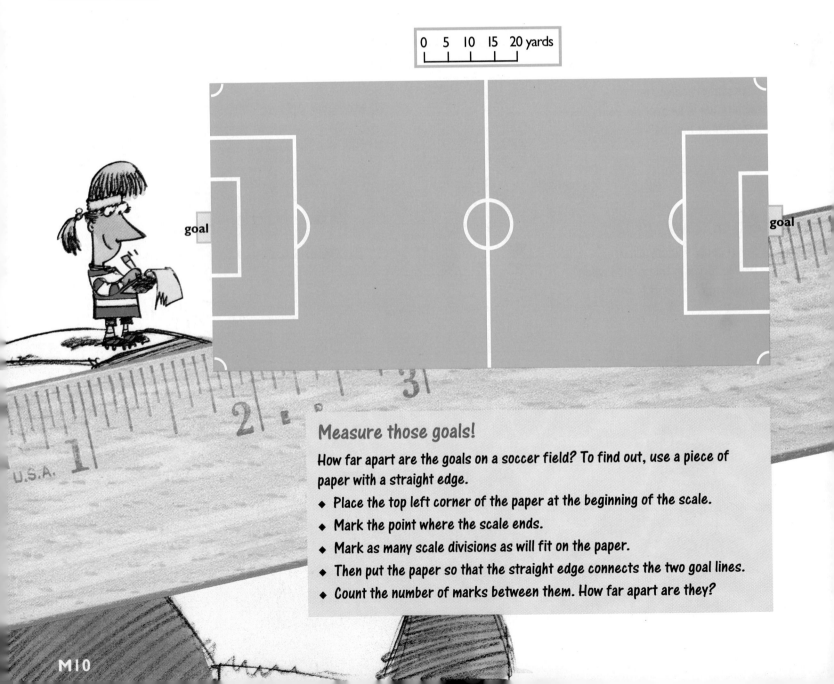

0 5 10 15 20 yards

goal

goal

Measure those goals!

How far apart are the goals on a soccer field? To find out, use a piece of paper with a straight edge.

- ◆ Place the top left corner of the paper at the beginning of the scale.
- ◆ Mark the point where the scale ends.
- ◆ Mark as many scale divisions as will fit on the paper.
- ◆ Then put the paper so that the straight edge connects the two goal lines.
- ◆ Count the number of marks between them. How far apart are they?

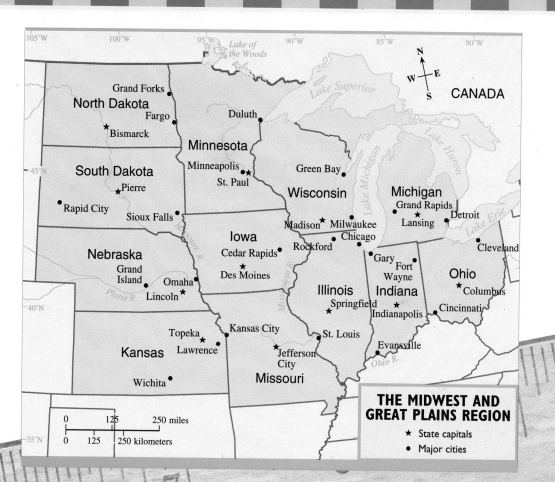

THE MIDWEST AND GREAT PLAINS REGION

★ State capitals
• Major cities

Scale:
0   125   250 miles
0   125   250 kilometers

Inches sometimes stand for miles.

◆ Look at the scale on the map of the Midwest and Great Plains region of the United States. How many miles does one inch stand for? About how far is it from Indianapolis, Indiana, to St. Paul, Minnesota?

◆ Look at the scale on the map of Indiana. About how many inches are there in a straight line between Evansville and Gary? About how far is it from Evansville to Gary?

INDIANA

★ State capital
• Major cities

Scale:
0   25   50 miles
0   25   50 kilometers

Now Try This!

Find the map of your neighborhood or town that you drew for page M5 of this Handbook.

◆ Pace out the distance between any two points on your map by walking from one place to the other.

◆ Then create a scale that shows how many steps apart the two places are.

◆ Finally, complete the statement below.
I inch equals _____ steps on my map.

LATITUDE and LONGITUDE
Learn All About Them!

In order to locate a place, you need its **latitude** and its **longitude**. Latitude and longitude provide the "address" for any place you want to locate.

Latitude and longitude are part of a special kind of grid system for Earth. This system uses two sets of lines that crisscross. All the east–west lines that run across the map are latitude lines. The latitude line that circles Earth at its center is called the **equator**. It is numbered 0°. (You say this number as "zero degrees.")

Lines of latitude measure distance north and south of the equator. These lines never meet. Because they run parallel around Earth, another name for them is **parallels**.

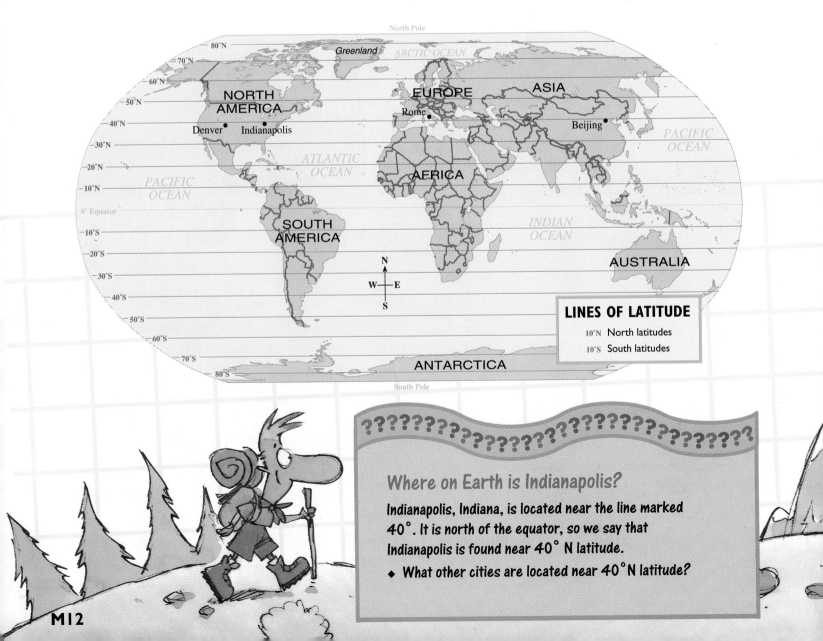

LINES OF LATITUDE

10°N North latitudes
10°S South latitudes

Where on Earth is Indianapolis?

Indianapolis, Indiana, is located near the line marked 40°. It is north of the equator, so we say that Indianapolis is found near 40° N latitude.

♦ What other cities are located near 40°N latitude?

Mapmakers also use another set of lines, called lines of **longitude**. Longitude lines run north–south on maps. The most important line of longitude is the **prime meridian**. It is numbered 0° longitude. (Say "zero degrees.")

All other lines of longitude measure distance east and west of the prime meridian.

Any line located east of the prime meridian is called east longitude. It is marked 15°E, 30°E, and so on. Lines west of the prime meridian are called west longitude. Lines of longitude are not parallel. They meet at the North Pole and the South Pole.

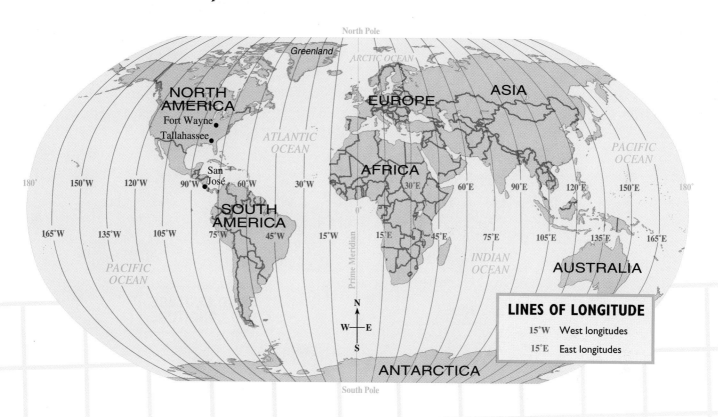

LINES OF LONGITUDE

| 15°W | West longitudes |
| 15°E | East longitudes |

??????????????????????????????????

Where on Earth is Fort Wayne?

Fort Wayne, Indiana, lies near the 85° meridian west of the prime meridian. We call its longitude 85°W.

◆ What other cities lie near the 85°W meridian?

Latitude and longitude make it possible to find places on a map quickly. Use the map on this page to find Indianapolis, Indiana. Notice its latitude—40° north latitude. This is written as 40°N. But Indianapolis does not fall exactly on a line of longitude. It is near 86° west longitude. This is written as 86°W. So, Indianapolis is located at 40°N latitude, 86°W longitude. This is written as 40°N/86°W. No other place on Earth has that location.

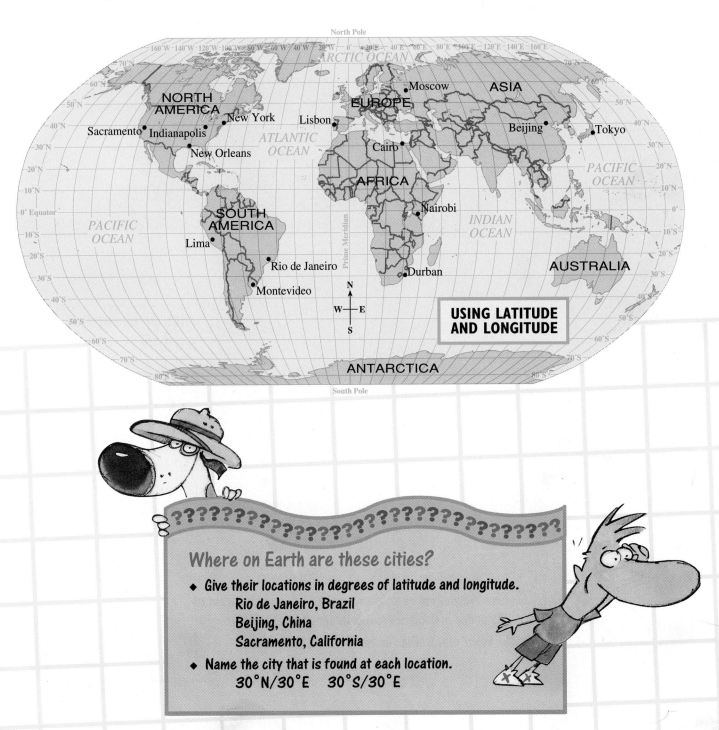

USING LATITUDE AND LONGITUDE

Where on Earth are these cities?

◆ Give their locations in degrees of latitude and longitude.
   Rio de Janeiro, Brazil
   Beijing, China
   Sacramento, California

◆ Name the city that is found at each location.
   30°N/30°E   30°S/30°E

The equator divides Earth into **hemispheres**, or two equal halves. Any place north of the equator is in the **Northern Hemisphere**. Any place south of the equator is in the **Southern Hemisphere**. Do you live in the Northern Hemisphere or in the Southern Hemisphere?

The map on page M13 shows the location of the prime meridian at 0° longitude. Any place located east of the prime meridian is in the **Eastern Hemisphere**. Any place west of the prime meridian is in the **Western Hemisphere**. Do you live in the Eastern Hemisphere or in the Western Hemisphere?

Northern Hemisphere

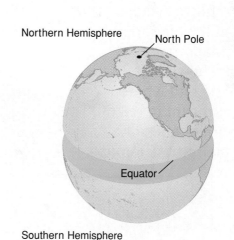
Northern Hemisphere
North Pole
Equator
Southern Hemisphere

Southern Hemisphere

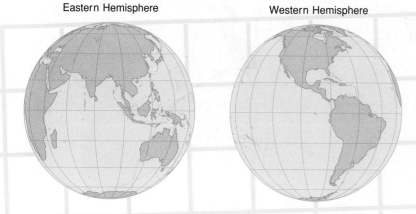
Eastern Hemisphere
Western Hemisphere

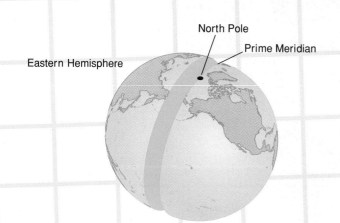
Eastern Hemisphere
North Pole
Prime Meridian

Now Try This!

A message crawls across the bottom of the TV screen.

WARNING: A tornado watch is out for people living in the area of 40°N/100°W. The warning zone extends east to 40°N/80°W.

Should you prepare to take cover, or should you watch another comedy rerun? To find out, look up the locations on the map of the United States on pages 346–347. Make a list of some of the communities that might be affected.

What's So Special About SPECIAL-PURPOSE Maps?

Maps can show many things besides where places are and how far apart one place is from another. Maps can tell about the history of places. They can tell what kinds of work people do and where. Because these maps are not meant to tell us about the land features or boundaries of a region, they are called **special-purpose maps**.

The map below is a **time zone map**. It shows the different time zones in the United States. A time zone map is helpful to people who are planning to travel to a place in a different time zone or to communicate with others across time zones by telephone or fax machine.

The color is the code.

- What does each color in the map key stand for?

What time is it?

- In what time zone is Indianapolis?
- When it is 10:00 A.M. in New York City, what time is it in Denver, Colorado?
- When it is 3:00 P.M. in San Francisco, what time is it in Indianapolis?

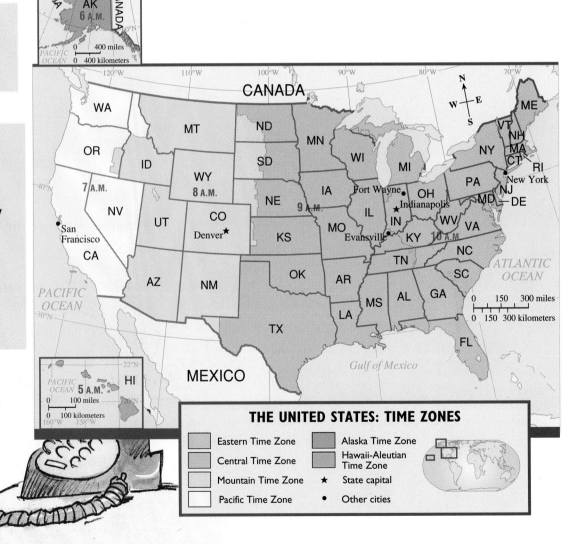

THE UNITED STATES: TIME ZONES

Eastern Time Zone
Central Time Zone
Mountain Time Zone
Pacific Time Zone
Alaska Time Zone
Hawaii-Aleutian Time Zone
★ State capital
● Other cities

Some special-purpose maps are called **climate maps**. They show what the weather is like most of the time in certain places. The map below shows the different climates in the United States.

Think About Weather Patterns.

◆ Describe the climate in most of Indiana.

◆ How does the climate in Indiana compare with the climate in FL? WA? SC?

Now Try This!

◆ **Look at the two maps of the United States. Choose a state that you would like to visit this summer. Is that state in a different time zone than your state? Did the climate in the state help you make your choice? Why?**

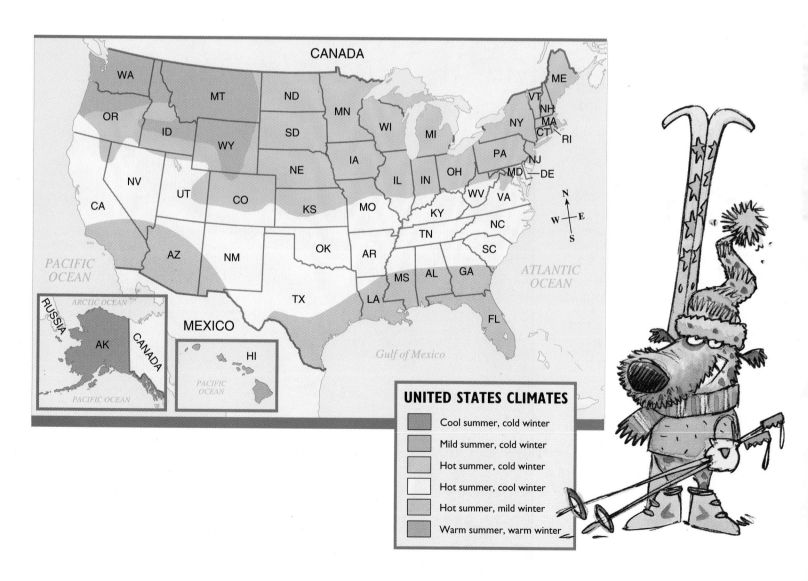

UNITED STATES CLIMATES

- Cool summer, cold winter
- Mild summer, cold winter
- Hot summer, cold winter
- Hot summer, cool winter
- Hot summer, mild winter
- Warm summer, warm winter

Which GEOGRAPHIC TERMS
Should You Know?

The diagram on these pages shows important forms of land and water. All of these are natural forms that are found on Earth's surface. To see what a form looks like, check the number next to its description. Then find the form on the diagram.

1 **bay** A bay is a part of an ocean or lake that is partly enclosed by land.

2 **canyon** A canyon is a deep, narrow valley with steep sides.

3 **coast** A coast is land that borders on a sea or ocean.

4 **glacier** A glacier is a huge body of ice that moves slowly across land.

5 **gulf** A gulf is a part of an ocean or sea that reaches into land. It is larger than a bay.

6 **island** An island is an area of land that is surrounded by water.

7 **lake** A lake is a body of water that is almost completely surrounded by land.

8 **marsh** A marsh is low land that is wet and soft.

9 **mountain range** A mountain range is a group of connected mountains, or steep, high land areas.

10 **mouth of a river** A river mouth is the place where a river flows into a larger body of water.

11 **ocean** The oceans are the entire body of salt water that covers almost three fourths of Earth's surface.

12 **plain** A plain is a broad stretch of level or nearly level land.

13 **plateau** A plateau is a large level area of high land.

14 **tributary** A tributary is a stream or river that flows into a larger river.

15 **valley** A valley is a long, low area of land, usually between mountains or hills.

UNIT 1

Welcome TO A Great State

What Makes Indiana a Special State?

What is the land of Indiana like? Who are the people of our state and how did they live in the past? Discover the answers to these questions by using the tools of geography and history.

INDIANA'S REGIONS

HOOSIER STATE

Great Lakes Plain

Southern Hills and Lowlands

Geography

1

CHAPTER 1

THE GEOGRAPHY

In this chapter you will learn about the regions of Indiana and about some of the many people and places that make our state great.

CONTENTS

◀ Find out on page 23 what this tool has to do with geography.

OF INDIANA

The following books give you information about geography in general and the geography of Indiana in particular. Read one that interests you and fill out a book-review form.

READ AND RESEARCH

Indiana by Dennis Brindell Fradin and Judith Bloom Fradin (Children's Press, 1994)
Tour exciting places in Indiana, meet some special Hoosiers, and learn lots of facts about your state. *(nonfiction)*

Scholastic Environmental Atlas of the United States by Mark Mattson (Scholastic, 1993)
The fascinating photos, maps, charts, and graphs in this book will make you an environmental expert in no time. *(nonfiction)*

Let's Investigate Marvelously Meaningful Maps by Madelyn Wood Carlisle (Barron's, 1992)
Maps often hold the keys to true tales of adventure. Learn how to unlock their secrets and how to make your own maps. *(nonfiction)*

Dinosaurs Walked Here and Other Stories Fossils Tell by Patricia Lauber (Aladdin Books, 1992)
Discover what fossils teach us about dinosaurs, saber-toothed tigers, and other creatures who walked the earth thousands of years ago. *(nonfiction)*

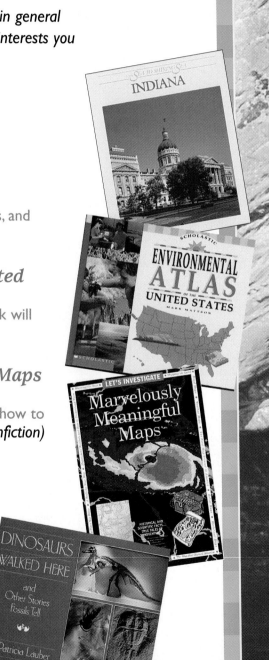

Skill POWER

Using Special-Purpose Maps

Knowing how to use special-purpose maps helps you learn interesting facts about places.

UNDERSTAND IT

Long ago, people grew most of their own food. So Hoosiers couldn't get foods that didn't grow in Indiana, such as oranges. There weren't any trucks, planes, or trains to bring them in!

Today, you can find almost any kind of food at any time of the year. Foods are shipped into Indiana from all over the country. A special-purpose map, such as the one on the next page, can help you see where the foods you eat are grown.

EXPLORE IT

You can use a special-purpose map to find out which food crops grow in Indiana and which ones have to be shipped in. The first thing you need to do when you look at a special-purpose map is to read the title to see what the map shows. What is the title of the map on the next page?

The next thing to check is the map key. It tells what the symbols on the map mean. Use the map to answer these questions.

- Name three states that grow apples.

- Which crop grows in both Maine and Alaska?

- What crop is grown in Ohio, Indiana, Illinois, Iowa, Nebraska, and Minnesota?

- What other crop is grown in Indiana?

◀ Hoosiers can enjoy fresh foods from all over the country throughout the year.

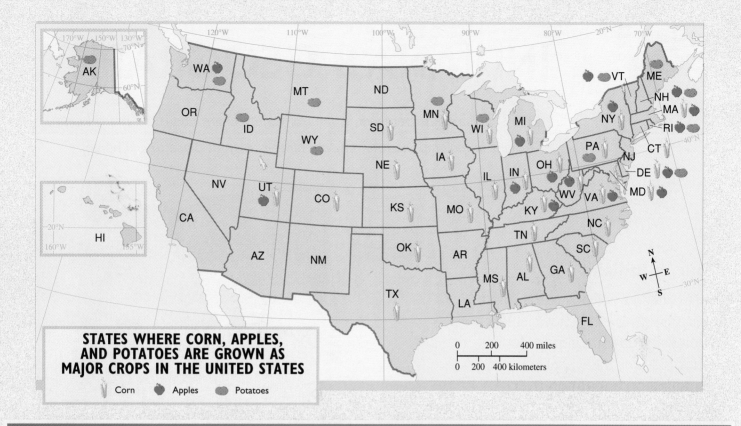

STATES WHERE CORN, APPLES, AND POTATOES ARE GROWN AS MAJOR CROPS IN THE UNITED STATES

Corn   Apples   Potatoes

TRY IT

Work with a group of your classmates to make a special-purpose map. Think of something you are curious about or interested in, such as any of the following examples:

• The ten largest lakes in Indiana

• The locations of state and national parks in Indiana

• Children's museums in Indiana

• The locations of colleges and universities in Indiana

After you have the information you need on your subject, decide on symbols for your map. For example, to represent a state or a national park, you could draw a tree. Then make your map and place the symbols in the state where they belong. Share your finished map with the class.

SKILL POWER SEARCH How many different kinds of special-purpose maps can you find in this chapter? What does each map show?

Setting the Scene

★ **KEY TERMS**

region
geography
climate
precipitation
economy
population

INDIANA'S GEOGRAPHY

FOCUS *Indiana has tremendous natural variety. Learn about the many kinds of regions in Indiana. Discover why our state is a great place to call home.*

A Tour of Indiana

This collection of postcards might surprise you. One shows skiers snowplowing down a gentle slope. Another pictures a kayaker (KYE ak-ur) paddling on a foaming river. A third postcard shows city streets with many buildings.

The postcards all come from one state—Indiana. On a tour of our state, you would see forests, prairies, farmland, and hills. You might swim in a lake or canoe down a river. You could cheer with people from big cities and small towns at a basketball game. At the end of your tour, you would agree that Indiana is a state with great variety.

▲ These postcards show three different views of Indiana.

The Idea of a Region

How would you describe the particular part of Indiana where you live to someone who has never been there? If you live in a town, you might tell about its different areas. You might start by describing the downtown area with its large buildings. Then you might write about the area around your home. Next you might describe areas that you visit that are outside your town. You could include a park, a shopping mall, or one of the forests or rivers shown on the map.

In your description you would have talked about three different areas—your downtown, your neighborhood, and the area outside your town. Each area is a region. A region is an area of land whose parts have one or more common characteristics.

Many Kinds of Regions

In order to study geography, it is helpful to divide the area you're studying into regions. We can divide Indiana into many different kinds of regions.

Sports fans might be interested in Indiana's high

---

region A part of the earth's surface that has common characteristics
geography The study of the earth and how people use it

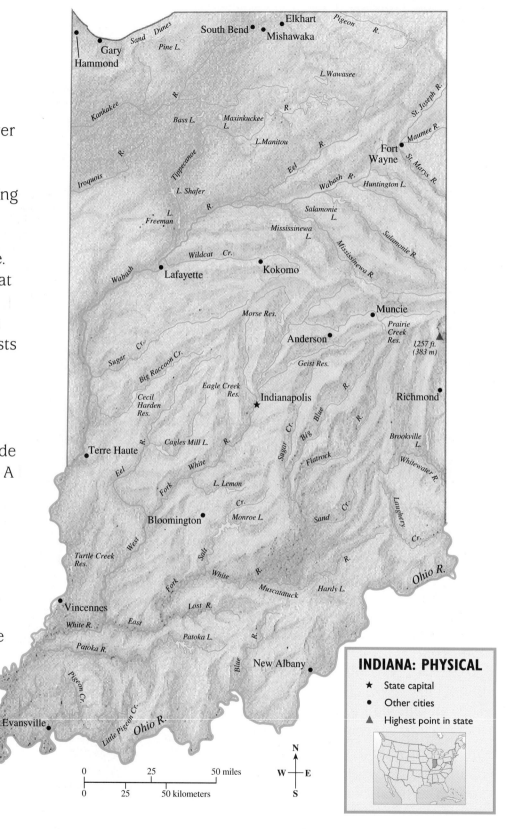

INDIANA: PHYSICAL

★ State capital
● Other cities
▲ Highest point in state

0   25   50 miles
0   25   50 kilometers

N
W—E
S

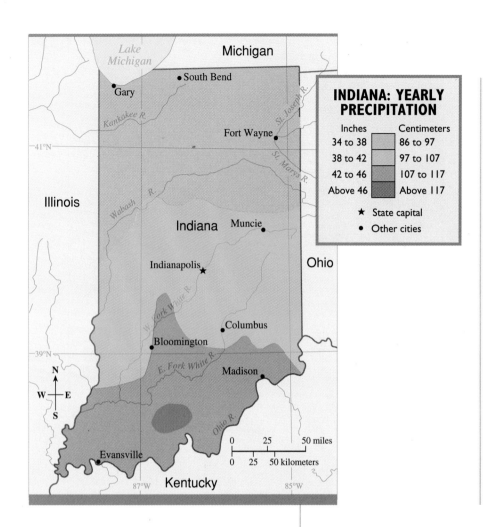

INDIANA: YEARLY PRECIPITATION

Inches		Centimeters
34 to 38		86 to 97
38 to 42		97 to 107
42 to 46		107 to 117
Above 46		Above 117

★ State capital
• Other cities

Climate Regions

Climate is another way to divide our state. **Climate** is different from weather. Weather may change from day to day. It can be rainy or sunny, hot or cold. Climate is the kind of weather that a place has over many years. The climate of Indiana, for example, is hot in the summer and cold in the winter.

Precipitation is a part of both weather and climate. Precipitation is rain, sleet, hail, and snow. The map on this page shows how precipitation varies from place to place in Indiana.

Climate also varies from place to place. In the summer, if you put your toes in a river in southern Indiana, the water could be

climate   The general weather conditions of an area over a long period of time
precipitation   Water that falls to the earth as rain, snow, sleet, or hail

school basketball regions. Bird lovers enjoy learning about regions where certain kinds of birds nest. Rock collectors divide the state into regions by the kind of rocks they can find.

Other people might want to know how land is used in Indiana. They might want to learn about Indiana's forest regions, its farm regions, or its many cities. The chart shows how Hoosiers use the land of Indiana.

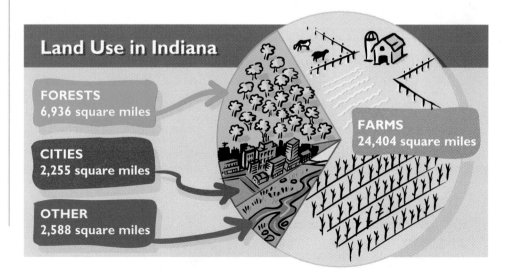

Land Use in Indiana

FORESTS
6,936 square miles

CITIES
2,255 square miles

OTHER
2,588 square miles

FARMS
24,404 square miles

70 degrees Fahrenheit. On the same day, Lake Michigan might be only 60 degrees.

Many factors influence an area's climate. Oceans keep the nearby land from getting very hot or very cold. Indiana is in the middle of North America. So, its seasons tend to be hotter and colder than in states along the oceans. It sometimes gets colder in Indiana than it does in parts of Alaska!

Economic Regions

We can also divide Indiana into regions to show the state's **economy**—the way people produce and distribute goods and services. Hoosiers have many different jobs. They farm, mine, and manufacture. Hoosiers also provide services, such as banking, selling, and teaching.

Some parts of our state are known for special kinds of work. In parts of Indiana, for example, workers quarry, or dig, for limestone. Indiana sells more limestone than any other place in the world.

Farming is a major business in flat parts of our state. Most Indiana farmers grow corn and soybeans. Other farmers raise hogs, dairy cows, or poultry, or grow vegetables and fruit such as apples.

Cities and Work

Cities have workers, customers, and transportation. As a result, cities have many kinds of businesses.

Some cities are known for one kind of work. For example, the city of Gary is part of a major steel-making region. Factories there

Some farmers use sprinklers to water their fields.

School buses are made in Richmond, Indiana.

economy The production and distribution of goods and services

This picture map is one way of showing where people live in Indiana and other states.

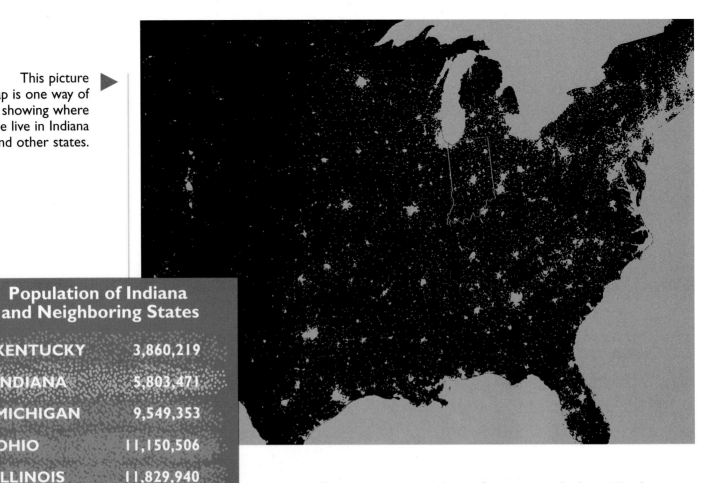

Population of Indiana and Neighboring States

KENTUCKY	3,860,219
INDIANA	5,803,471
MICHIGAN	9,549,353
OHIO	11,150,506
ILLINOIS	11,829,940

buy iron from Minnesota. Workers from Gary and other nearby cities help turn the iron into steel. Ships carry this steel across Lake Michigan to other parts of the country and the world.

Population of Indiana

The population of Indiana is about 5.8 million people. The picture map above shows part of the United States including the state of Indiana. Each speck of light shows where a group of people live. The dark parts of the map show

where fewer people live. Find Indiana on the picture map.

Where Hoosiers Live

Most Hoosiers live in cities. People settle where there is work, and most jobs are in cities. The cities on this picture map stand out as larger patches of light. Try to locate the light patch that shows Indianapolis.

The chart on this page gives another kind of information about where people live. It compares Indiana's population with that of its neighboring states.

population   The number of people who live in an area

United States Regions

You have learned that Indiana can be divided into many kinds of regions. Maybe you've figured out that Indiana can be part of larger regions, too.

The map below shows one way to divide the United States into regions. Locate all seven regions. Indiana is part of the Midwest and Great Plains region. Name the other states in this region.

Our state has several things in common with our closest neighbors. We share a similar climate, similar soils, similar histories, and similar people. Maybe you know of other similarities as well.

When you think about it, you may realize that Indiana is a part of many regions. For example, it's part of the corn- and soybean-growing region of the United States.

Our state also fits into a coal-mining region, with our neighbors Kentucky and Illinois. Indiana is a part of the Great Lakes region and the Ohio River Valley region. Learning about regions Indiana belongs to helps us understand the geography of our state.

SHOW WHAT YOU KNOW!

REFOCUS
COMPREHENSION

1. What is a region?

2. Name five kinds of regions.

THINK ABOUT IT
CRITICAL THINKING

Explain why Indiana is more like Illinois than Hawaii.

WRITE ABOUT IT
ACTIVITY

In your Indiana journal, write a letter to a friend describing the area in which you live.

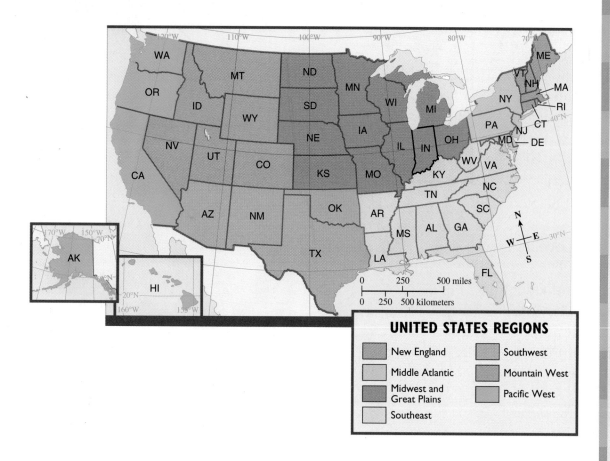

| 0 | 250 | 500 miles |
| 0 | 250 | 500 kilometers |

UNITED STATES REGIONS

- New England
- Middle Atlantic
- Midwest and Great Plains
- Southeast
- Southwest
- Mountain West
- Pacific West

11

Spotlight

KEY TERMS

landform
glacier
till
silt

INDIANA'S REGIONS

FOCUS *Indiana has three main landform regions. Each region has landforms that make it special—and different from every other region.*

Three Landform Regions

Geographers sometimes divide Indiana into three **landform** regions. Landforms include hills, plains, caves, lakes, and rivers. Each region has different landforms. These features make each region different from the other two.

The map on this page shows Indiana's three regions. In the north is the Great Lakes Plain region. Across the middle of the state is the Tipton Till Plain region. The Southern Hills and Lowlands region is in the southern third of the state. Each region's name includes an important landform in that region.

The Southern Hills and Lowlands region has a wide variety of landforms. So geographers divide it into four smaller parts. They are the Wabash Lowland, the Caves and Limestone area, the Knobs, and the Ancient Glacier area.

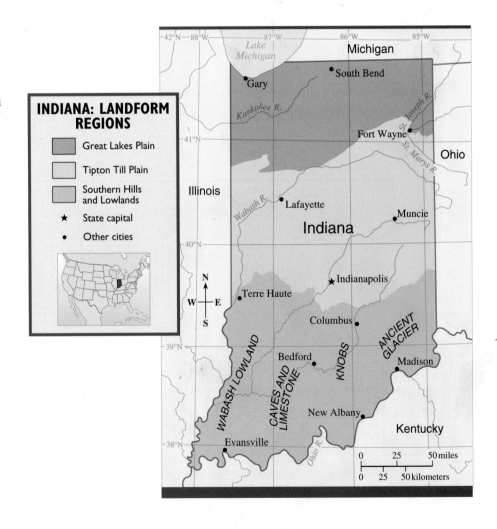

INDIANA: LANDFORM REGIONS

- Great Lakes Plain
- Tipton Till Plain
- Southern Hills and Lowlands
- ★ State capital
- • Other cities

---

 landform A feature of the earth's surface created by nature

The Ice Age

Over 2 million years ago, an Ice Age began. Ice and snow covered part of North America. During this period, ice came and went, each time covering Indiana for thousands of years.

The climate changed from hot to cold several times during the Ice Age. During the long cold periods, snow and ice built up. Around the North Pole, the ice was miles thick.

The weight of the ice caused it to move. Masses of slowly moving ice, called **glaciers** (GLAY shurz), spread

---

⭐ *glacier* A huge mass of ice that moves across land until it melts

out from the North Pole. In North America, they moved as far south as Indiana. Sliding along the ground, these gigantic blankets of ice scraped up soil and rocks and anything else in the way. They carried these materials for thousands of miles to the south.

Glaciers Change the Land

Along the way, the glaciers flattened the land. They pushed off the tops of hills. They filled in valleys with soil and rocks. They also dug out holes. The diagram below shows how a melting glacier left behind material that it

▼ This is the front edge of a glacier.

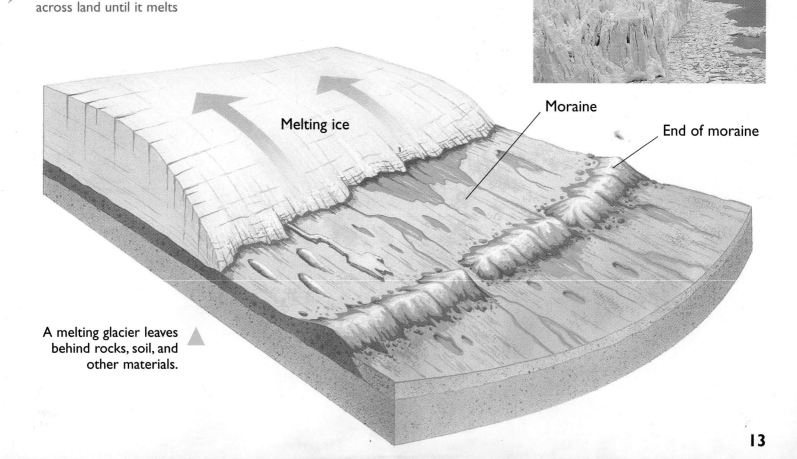

Melting ice

Moraine

End of moraine

A melting glacier leaves behind rocks, soil, and other materials. ▲

scraped off lands in the north. The mass of rocks, sand, and gravel left behind is called a moraine (muh RAYN). Where the glacier stopped moving forward, and began to melt, it dropped a ridge of heavy rock and stone. This ridge marks the end of the moraine.

Great Lakes Plain

Lake Michigan sits on the northwest border of the Great Lakes Plain region. Find it on the map. Like all the Great Lakes, Lake Michigan was formed by glaciers.

When the ice melted, five huge holes carved by the glaciers filled with water. They became the largest group of freshwater lakes in the world—the Great Lakes.

Glaciers also changed the plains, or flatlands, located around the Great Lakes. Glaciers scooped out many small lakes and left moraines on these plains.

The last melting glaciers left behind a layer of sand. Along the southern edge of Lake Michigan, winds blew the sands into dunes. In some parts of north central Indiana, the last glacier left a layer of thick soil, or **till**.

Today, ships move easily through the Great Lakes to the Atlantic Ocean. They bring goods and products to Indiana. Ships also transport products made in Indiana to many parts of the world. In this way, the waters of Lake Michigan have helped Indiana grow.

till Soil made of clay, sand, gravel, and other materials left by a glacier

GREAT LAKES PLAIN REGION

87°W · 86°W · 85°W · 42°N · Lake Michigan · Gary · Hammond · South Bend · Angola · Warsaw · 41°N · Indiana · 40°N · 0 25 50 miles · 0 25 50 kilometers · N W E S

▼ Hoosiers fish on a lake at Chain O'Lakes State Park in northeastern Indiana.

Farmers harvest corn in Parke County in the Tipton Till Plain.

TIPTON TILL PLAIN REGION

Tipton Till Plain

The last glacier to affect Indiana scraped soil from Canada, Michigan, and northern Indiana as it moved southward. When it melted 11,000 years ago, the glacier left the soil behind.

This thick blanket of soil, called till, formed the Tipton Till Plain. The plain is named after Tipton County in the north-central part of the region.

Because the Tipton Till Plain is so flat, water doesn't drain easily from this region. When pioneers arrived almost 200 years ago, they found many swamps. Great forests also covered the plain.

Settlers drained the water and cleared the forests for farmland. This farmland holds some of the world's richest soil.

Cities of the Tipton Till Plain

Indiana's two largest cities are found in the Tipton Till Plain region. They are Fort Wayne and Indianapolis. Fort Wayne is located in the northern part of the region. This city is named for an American general.

Indianapolis lies in the southern part of the region. It became a center for trade. Canals, roads, and railways crossed through the flat land around Indianapolis. They connected the city to the rest of the state, the country, and the world.

Southern Hills and Lowlands

The Southern Hills and Lowlands region is very hilly compared to the Tipton Till Plain. The last glacier did not reach southern Indiana. As a result, the surface of the land was not flattened out.

The wide Ohio River forms the southern border of this region. Within this region, the landscape varies from place to place. So, geographers divide it into several smaller regions. The map shows the four small regions that make up the Southern Hills and Lowlands.

The Wabash Lowland is covered with **silt** deposits from the Wabash River. This rich soil is great for farming. You can see the river in the photograph below. Two large Indiana cities, Terre Haute and Evansville, are located here.

A Varied Land

Glaciers did not affect the Caves and Limestone area. But water did affect the way this area looks. Limestone is a soft rock. It formed in shallow seas from the skeletons of shellfish millions of years ago.

Water formed holes in the soft limestone. Over time, these holes grew larger and larger. Eventually, they became caves. The photo on the next page shows one of these caves. Limestone is quarried near Bloomington and Bedford.

 silt Small pieces of soil left by water or wind

SOUTHERN HILLS AND LOWLANDS REGION

Indiana

Terre Haute • Columbus • Bedford • New Albany • Evansville •

WABASH LOWLAND • CAVES AND LIMESTONE • KNOBS • ANCIENT GLACIER

0   25   50 miles
0   25   50 kilometers

INDIANA FACTS

The Indiana General Assembly named the Wabash River the official state river in 1996.

The Wabash River snakes through southern Indiana.

▲ Over many centuries, water cut caves into the limestone of southern Indiana.

The Knobs is a row of shale hills that runs north and south. Shale is a dark, flat rock, formed long ago from clay in the bottom of ancient seas. The glaciers never passed through the Knobs, so the hills remained. As a result, the Knobs are higher than nearby areas.

Most of the hilly Knobs area is not good for farming, so settlers let its forests grow. Today people enjoy visiting Brown County to see the beautiful trees. The city of New Albany is located in this region.

The Ancient Glacier area gets its name from a glacier that plowed through there and melted one hundred thousand years ago. After that glacier melted, streams cut deep valleys into the area near Ohio. The cities of Columbus and Madison are located here.

The Ohio River

The Ohio River is one of the country's longest rivers. It forms the boundary between Indiana and Kentucky at the southern end of the Southern Hills and Lowlands region. It begins in Pennsylvania and flows west into the Mississippi River in Illinois.

SHOW WHAT YOU
KNOW!

REFOCUS
COMPREHENSION

1. What are the three major landform regions of Indiana?

2. What are the four smaller regions of the Southern Hills and Lowlands region?

THINK ABOUT IT
CRITICAL THINKING

Compare the way glaciers changed the Great Lakes Plain region with the way they changed the Tipton Till region.

WRITE ABOUT IT
ACTIVITY

In your Indiana journal, write a letter describing one of Indiana's regions to someone who has never been there.

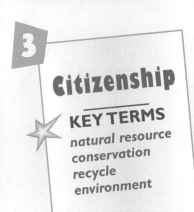

Citizenship

KEY TERMS
natural resource
conservation
recycle
environment

CONSERVATION

FOCUS *Indiana's citizens have demonstrated that protecting our state's land and resources is everyone's responsibility.*

A Citizen Gets Involved

In the early 1900s, the steel mills on Lake Michigan brought money into Indiana. They also provided many jobs. But the factories created a problem. Factory smoke polluted the air and water.

The steel industry expanded eastward along the beautiful Lake Michigan shore. The factory owners planned to flatten some more sand dunes to build more factories.

But Bess Sheehan, who had moved to Gary, Indiana, in 1909, loved the dunes. She did not want this unusual natural resource to be destroyed. She joined with other local women who hoped to save the dunes. They held meetings and got people interested in their cause. They also went to the Indiana State Legislature for help.

Their efforts paid off. In 1925, Indiana Dunes State Park opened. Later, the U. S. government set up the Indiana Dunes National Lake Shore in a nearby area.

natural resource Any useful material from the earth, such as water, oil, or minerals

▼ Many people visit the beautiful Lake Michigan dunes every year.

Many plants and animals, such as prickly pear cacti, great blue herons, and lake trout, live in the dunes.

Our Natural Resources

What are natural resources? Natural resources are things from nature that we use for food, recreation, protection, and comfort. Dunes are natural resources. So are forests, mountains, water, and shores. Plants and animals are natural resources, too.

People use many natural resources in everyday living. Gas and oil, needed for heating and running machines, are natural resources. So are the rocks and metals we use for building. Which resources do you use?

Saving Resources

Conservation means saving and protecting natural resources, so that we will always be able to use them.

conservation Protecting resources

Bess Sheehan and others who worked to save the dunes believed that conservation is an important responsibility.

Today, Americans practice conservation in many ways. We keep rivers and lakes clean, remove our trash, and recycle materials, such as paper, plastics, and metals. We also conserve by turning off lights when we do not need them and by not wasting our running water.

As more and more people are born and live on our planet, the need for resources increases. Yet, our resources are not as plentiful as they once were.

recycle To reuse resources

Many fossils are found in the riverbed at the Falls of the Ohio State Park.

This exhibit is at the museum at the Falls of the Ohio State Park.

Conservation Today

Today, many groups in Indiana work to protect the **environment**. Some groups work for the government. Others are made up of citizens.

At the state level, two departments have the job of looking after the environment. The Department of Natural Resources is in charge of state parks. The Department of Environmental Management helps to control pollution and other misuses of the environment.

Many citizens' groups do their share to save our land and resources, too. Some groups work to protect endangered species.

Some groups are concerned with preserving rivers and other waterways. Other groups use donations to buy land. They make sure that people will not build on this land or use its resources.

In Indiana, citizens have bought and donated land to the state. One citizens' group even gave money that helped buy a state park. This happened at the Falls of the Ohio State Park in Clarksville. The community also contributed toward a museum at the park.

Protecting the Environment

You, too, can help protect our environment. Above all, learn everything you can about nature and how it works. Ask questions, spend time outdoors, read about nature, and watch nature programs on television. Become an informed "citizen of the environment."

There are many other things you can do to practice conservation. Take shorter showers or use less water in the bathtub. Keep the doors closed, if you are using air conditioning or heating. Reuse paper products, such as paper bags or writing paper. Saving these resources will also save money!

environment   Things that surround us

▲ This poster, made by a fourth grader, gives examples of many recycling projects that young people do.

Recycle, Reuse, Reduce

Everybody can practice conservation by remembering the three Rs: recycle, reuse, reduce. Many things that get thrown away can be reused. By using bottles, cans, paper bags, and plastic containers again, you conserve natural resources.

When you recycle paper, you save trees and forests. Used metals, plastics, and glass can be melted down and recycled. Recycling means less trash.

You can reduce the amount of paper, gas, and water you use. For example, you can stop using paper plates or napkins. Carry home things from the store in cloth bags. For short trips, walk or bike instead of riding in a car.

Getting Involved

There are many other ways you can help—alone or with a group. Some volunteers donate their time to clearing road sites of litter. Others get involved in trying to stop pollution, adopting a tree, or beautifying a park. Scout troops, 4-H clubs, and school groups can take on a project. Your efforts to protect our environment make a difference. Conservation is everybody's responsibility.

SHOW WHAT YOU KNOW!

REFOCUS
COMPREHENSION

1. What are natural resources?

2. Name five natural resources.

THINK ABOUT IT
CRITICAL THINKING

Which form of conservation do you think is most important? Explain.

WRITE ABOUT IT
ACTIVITY

Create a brochure showing students in your school ways to practice the three Rs in the classroom.

CAREERS IN GEOGRAPHY

FOCUS *Weather forecasters, forest rangers, travel agents, surveyors, and many other people can't do their jobs without geography.*

Why Study Geography?

When we study geography, we learn more than just where places are on a map. Studying geography teaches us many things about the earth. It tells us about our environment and about how people use land and resources.

Geography is also a part of many careers. Geographers, of course, use geography in their work. They help us understand how places on earth are similar and how they are different. However, lots of other people need to understand geography for their jobs as well. It's obvious why a mapmaker needs geography, but you may be surprised by other workers who do also.

Weather forecasters help people to prepare for all kinds of weather.

Weather Forecasters

Weather forecasters use geography all the time. Wind brings our weather from places outside Indiana. So weather forecasters must understand the geography of those places. They need to know where storms are coming from and how fast the wind is carrying them. They also have to know how strong the wind and rain may be when they get here. All this information helps them to predict what the weather is going to be.

Forest Rangers

Forest rangers can't do their work without geography. Geography helps them understand the climate, the soil, and the **vegetation** of many kinds of forests.

Forest rangers also use maps to keep track of different parts of forests. During emergencies, such as fires or floods, they have to be able to read these maps.

vegetation   Plant life

Surveyors use special instruments to map boundaries.

Surveyors

Surveyors use geography for **surveying**, or measuring the size and shape of land. They need to be able to read maps and understand what the land is like. To collect important information about the land, they use special instruments and maps. People use this information to build tunnels, roads, and bridges.

Surveyors also help cities, states, and countries figure out boundaries. Boundaries mark where one place starts and another ends. Using geography, surveyors do many important jobs.

 survey To measure the size, shape, boundaries, or other features of an area

Travel Agents

Travel agents use geography to arrange trips for people. They make travel plans between different parts of the country and the world. Customers have many questions about the weather, the land, the cities, and the people in places they want to visit. Travel agents use their knowledge of geography to give them this information. Good travel plans mean happy customers!

Travel agents use geography to help customers plan what to see on a trip. ▶

SHOW WHAT YOU KNOW!

REFOCUS
COMPREHENSION

1. How does geography involve more than just studying places on a map?

2. Name some jobs that use geography.

THINK ABOUT IT
CRITICAL THINKING

Compare how a travel agent and a surveyor use geography.

WRITE ABOUT IT
ACTIVITY

Choose another kind of worker such as a mapmaker, geologist, city planner, pilot, or truck driver. Write about how geography is a part of that career, too.

SUMMING UP

1 DO YOU REMEMBER...
COMPREHENSION

1. What kind of climate do we have in Indiana?

2. In what region of the United States is Indiana located?

3. Why is the Tipton Till Plain region well suited for farming?

4. Name three ways to conserve natural resources.

5. Choose one career described in the chapter and tell how it involves geography.

2 SKILL POWER
USING SPECIAL-PURPOSE MAPS

Look at the facts below. Which three facts could be used to create a special-purpose map? What would be the subject of the map?

a. Indiana is the leading producer of steel in the United States.

b. Fort Wayne is Indiana's second-largest city.

c. The Great Lakes Plain region is in northern Indiana.

d. The manufacture of electrical equipment is the state's second-largest industry.

e. The Ohio River forms the southern border of Indiana.

f. The production of cars and trucks is an important industry in Indiana.

3 WHAT DO YOU THINK?
CRITICAL THINKING

1. How does Indiana's climate affect things that Hoosiers can do for a living?

2. Why did manufacturing develop in the region around Lake Michigan?

3. How did the early settlers influence the geography of the Tipton Till Plain?

4. If factories had been built where the dunes are, what might have happened to the blue herons in Indiana?

5. Why is the work of weather forecasters important?

4 SAY IT, WRITE IT, USE IT
VOCABULARY

Suppose that you are a travel agent writing to a person in New England who plans to visit Indiana. Write a letter in which you tell the visitor all about your state, using as many of the vocabulary terms as possible.

climate	population
conservation	precipitation
economy	recycle
environment	region
geography	silt
glacier	survey
landform	till
natural resource	vegetation

5 GEOGRAPHY AND YOU
MAP STUDY

1. In what region is Indianapolis located?

2. What region is in the northern part of the state? How did this region get its name?

3. Name the four areas of the Southern Hills and Lowlands region.

4. In what region of Indiana do you live?

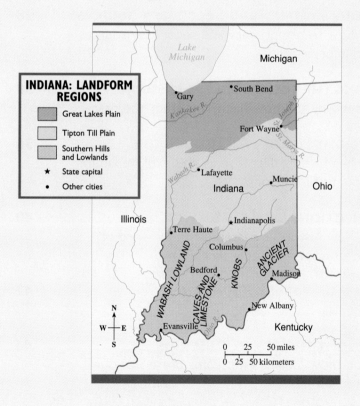

INDIANA: LANDFORM REGIONS

- Great Lakes Plain
- Tipton Till Plain
- Southern Hills and Lowlands
- ★ State capital
- • Other cities

Lake Michigan

Michigan

Gary • South Bend

Kankakee R.

Fort Wayne

St. Joseph R.

St. Marys R.

Wabash R.

Lafayette

Muncie

Illinois

Indiana

Ohio

Terre Haute

• Indianapolis

Columbus

WABASH LOWLAND

CAVES AND LIMESTONE

KNOBS

ANCIENT GLACIER

Bedford

Madison

New Albany

Evansville

Kentucky

N W E S

0   25   50 miles
0   25   50 kilometers

6 TAKE ACTION
CITIZENSHIP

You have read about how Bess Sheehan worked to save the dunes, and how other Indiana citizens donated land and money for a state park. Discuss the efforts of people who work to protect the environment in your region today. Look in your local newspaper or talk to a community member to learn about any projects or other efforts. Then look at the recycling poster on page 21. With a group of classmates, draw a poster to show what you would do to help one of these efforts.

7 GET CREATIVE
LANGUAGE ARTS CONNECTION

Make a brochure that will attract tourists to your region of Indiana. List the features that visitors might enjoy. Illustrate your brochure with images that "capture" your region in a special way.

LOOKING AHEAD
Find out in the next chapter what history is and why it is important to you.

BECOMING A

Historians try to find out how and why things happened in the past. They also explore how events that happened in earlier times can help people understand events today.

CONTENTS

◀ See page 40 to learn how a tape recorder can help you find out about history.

HOOSIER HISTORIAN

These books give you information for learning about history through folklore, for finding your ancestors, and for making records of your own life. Choose one that interests you and fill out a book-review form.

READ AND RESEARCH

Johnny Appleseed A Tall Tale Retold and Illustrated by Steven Kellogg (Morrow Junior Books, 1988)

John Chapman, known as Johnny Appleseed, spent his life planting apple trees throughout the eastern United States. This folk tale tells about Johnny Appleseed, about the early days of the United States, and about Indiana's first settlers. *(fiction)*

• *You can read a selection from this book on page 42.*

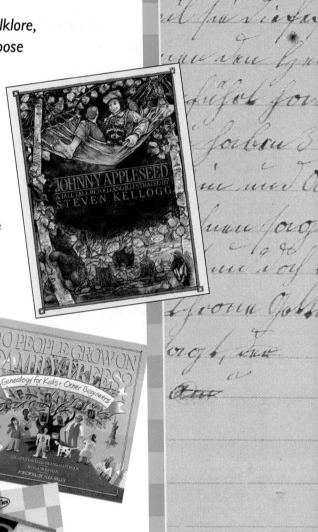

Do People Grow on Family Trees? by Ira Wolfman, illustrated by Michael Klein (Workman Publishing, 1991)

Ever wonder where your great-great grandfather lived? This book tells you how to trace your family back 100 or even 200 years. It also tells you how to host a family reunion and how to keep records of your own history. *(nonfiction)*

Melting Pots: Family Stories & Recipes by Judith Eichler Weber, illustrated by Scott Gubala (Silver Moon Press, 1994)

Read about the many families in America who celebrate their special days with recipes passed down from generation to generation. *(nonfiction)*

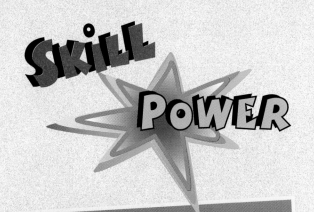

Skill Power

Using Primary and Secondary Sources

Studying primary and secondary sources can help you learn about the past.

UNDERSTAND IT

There are many ways to find out about the past, but one of the best sources you can use is a *primary source*. Primary sources are sources of information created by people who were present at an event. Primary sources include diaries, letters, photographs, and drawings.

Secondary sources are sources of information created by people who were not present at an event, but who read or studied about it. Secondary sources include encyclopedia articles and textbooks.

Has anyone in your family saved old letters? If so, what could you learn from these primary sources?

EXPLORE IT

The page below comes from a diary written by an Indiana resident in 1902. It tells about a holiday, an illness, the weather, and a shopping trip. It is a good example of a primary source.

. . . This morning 16 degrees below freezing, without wind and most cloudy but not so sharp cold as yesterday. It snowed a little bit during last night. Flora went to market on car [trolley] at morning and bought different things to live on. I done all kinds of [odd jobs] about home & got 5 gallons of coal oil from grocery for 60 cents.

With a group of your classmates, go on a search for primary sources. Find old photographs in books in your library and make photocopies of them. Write the date of the photo next to each one. Try to find different kinds of photos, such as city streets, country scenes, family portraits, and news photos.

When you have finished, share your primary sources with another group. Carefully study each group of photographs. Then make a list of the things you can learn from them.

Indiana farm, 1915

Indianapolis, 1901

SKILL

POWER SEARCH Look through this chapter to find examples of primary and secondary sources.

Setting the Scene

KEY TERMS
research
document
artifact
archaeologist
culture

WHAT IS HISTORY?

FOCUS *Historians study people and events from the past. They use many tools and the work of many different people to do their jobs.*

Why We Study the Past

History is the study of what has happened in the past. Many people are interested in finding out about the past. Many of these people are not professional historians. They may want to know their family history. They may be interested in the history of a town or city. Or they may just wonder how and why things happened in the past.

Other people are professional historians. They make their living studying the past. Historians want to know what happened in the past and what life was like then. Knowing what happened in earlier times can also help people understand events today. We can learn how people faced problems similar to our own.

Historians Look for Clues

Professional historians actively look for clues and facts about the past. Then they put this information together to tell a story.

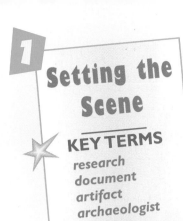

▼ Historians use many tools to study the past.

Historians who study government might visit the Indiana State Capitol. Military historians might examine war medals.

write articles or books about what they have discovered.

A historian may also write a biography—the life story of a famous person in history. A historian's story of why and how something happened in the past can be very exciting to read.

Different Kinds of History

Most of the history you read in school is political history. It is mainly about different countries, rulers, and governments.

Historians study other kinds of history, too. Some concentrate on wars and how generals planned and fought battles. They look at how these battles changed the course of history.

Some historians look at businesses and the economy. Historians who study economic history research how the economies of different countries have changed over time.

Other historians study how ordinary people lived in the past—what their homes, food, and clothing were like. These historians are called social historians. They also find out what people did for fun. They look at family life, sports, music, games, dance, and the hobbies people once enjoyed.

Historians usually choose a certain part of history to study. Then they do **research**. They study old papers, books, and letters. They read what other historians have written about the subject. They may travel to the place where a historical event happened.

Most historians share what they have learned about people and events in the past with others. They become teachers in schools or professors at colleges. Often they

research Careful study to find out facts about a subject

This diploma is from a school in Indianapolis.

Studying Objects

The farther back in history you go, the harder it is to find written sources. Many people in the past could not read or write. Documents are important to historians, but objects from the past can also tell fascinating stories.

To learn more about the past, historians look at things people made. These are called **artifacts**.

This washing machine is from the early 1900s.

Using Written Sources

Written sources, or **documents**, are important to historians. Historians look at old newspapers and other records stored in libraries. They look up records that show when people were born, married, and died.

Historians also look at official documents. These documents include passports, diplomas, and papers that tell when a person came to this country.

Historians particularly like to find personal documents, such as letters and diaries. Sometimes these documents have been hidden away in attics and drawers for many years until historians find them. These documents tell historians how ordinary people lived in the past.

document A written record
artifact An object made by humans

Some artifacts, such as pieces of pottery and spear points, are thousands of years old. Others, such as clothing and toys, are more recent. Artifacts from any time are clues that tell historians how people used to live.

Studying Pictures

Even before people could write, they could draw pictures. Some of the oldest known works of art are paintings found in caves or on rocks. To historians, these pictures tell how ancient people lived and what they believed.

Later, people made paintings, drawings, and statues that showed life around them. In early America, for example, traveling painters painted family portraits that

This Indiana couple had their portraits painted in the 1800s.

showed parents, children, and even pets. Looking at these pictures gives you an idea of how people lived several hundred years ago.

About 150 years ago, inventors made the first photographs. At first only professionals knew how to use the heavy cameras and glass plates necessary for photography. People had to sit very still for minutes at a

These team photos were taken 100 years apart.

sculpture. Or they might investigate a campsite where hunters made a fire thousands of years ago.

Often the places that archaeologists study have been buried by many layers of soil over hundreds of years. Archaeologists dig carefully to find artifacts and other clues to history. An archaeological site is called a "dig."

▲ Indiana students on a dig learn how to sift soil so that no artifacts are lost.

time while their pictures were taken. Later, faster cameras were invented. Today anyone can take a photograph in just a few seconds. Photographs are an excellent way for historians to see how people and places used to look.

Digging for History

Historians often depend on scientists to help them study the past. The work of scientists is especially useful to historians who research ancient history or study people without a written language.

Scientists who study artifacts from the past are called **archaeologists** (ahr kee AHL uh jihsts). They explore places where people lived long ago. They might study ancient cities that were once filled with pottery, paintings, and

Help From Other Scientists

Scientists who study the bones of ancient people also help historians. By studying bones, scientists can tell what people looked like, what they ate, and how long they lived.

Historians also use the work of scientists who study ancient and modern **cultures**. These scientists discover information about the language, traditions, and beliefs of people today and in the past.

Other scientists study the rocks and soil of the earth. They can tell the age of a long-buried fossil. Or they can trace how the course of a river has changed over many years. Clues like these help historians study an ancient civilization. By using the help of scientists, historians are able to piece together the stories of the past.

 archaeologist A scientist who studies ancient times and people

 culture The ideas, skills, arts, tools, and way of life of certain people at a certain time

The Old State Capitol still stands in Corydon. ▶

History in Our State

Indiana is filled with places where both historians and people curious about history can look for clues to the past. Much of this history has been preserved at historic sites around the state. Some of these sites are shown on the map on this page.

Some state sites were the scene of important events in Indiana history. Corydon was Indiana's first state capital. Famous battles took place at Tippecanoe Battlefield and at the site of the George Rogers Clark Memorial.

History in People and Places

Other sites freeze a historic moment in time. At Conner Prairie, Spring Mill Village, and Chellberg Farm, you can see what life was like when the first settlers came to Indiana. In Madison you can walk through homes built when Madison was a bustling river town in the early 1800s.

INDIANA HISTORIC SITES

★ State capital
● Other cities
■ Historic sites

Some places in Indiana are important because famous people lived there. Abraham Lincoln grew up in a cabin in Little Pigeon Creek, Indiana. The Lincoln Boyhood Memorial marks this spot today.

Johnny Appleseed planted apple trees throughout Indiana. He is buried in Fort Wayne, where Johnny Appleseed Memorial Park honors this midwestern hero.

SHOW WHAT YOU KNOW!

REFOCUS
COMPREHENSION

1. Describe four kinds of history that people can study.

2. Briefly describe the work of the scientists who help historians.

THINK ABOUT IT
CRITICAL THINKING

Why are primary source documents important to historians?

WRITE ABOUT IT
ACTIVITY

Choose a photo that is important to you. Write an entry in your Indiana journal describing what a historian might learn about you from this photo.

2

Spotlight

KEY TERMS
family tree
ancestor

HISTORY ALL AROUND YOU

FOCUS *Every person and place has a history. A family's history is recorded in journals, family trees, and letters. Clues to a community's history can be seen in street signs, buildings, and cemeteries.*

Everyone Has a History

History is not just the story of leaders and governments. It is also the story of people, families, and communities.

Even if you are only 10 or 11 years old, you have a history. It includes where you were born, where you live now, and all the things you have seen and done. Your parents and grandparents have longer histories, but they include the same kinds of things.

▲ This family tree is from the 1800s.

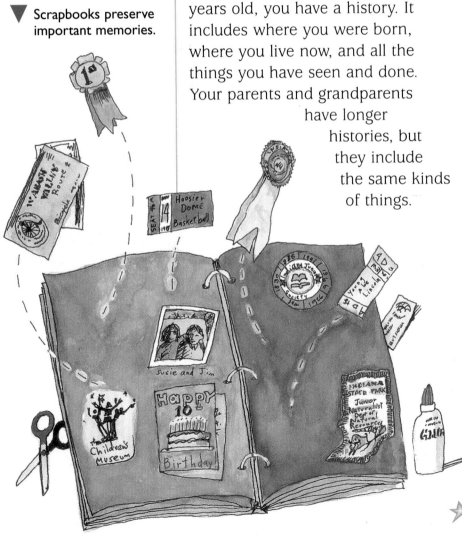

▼ Scrapbooks preserve important memories.

Family Trees

Your personal history is part of a family history. A **family tree** is a simple drawing of that history. If you draw a chart that shows you, your parents, your grandparents, and the relatives that came before them, it will look like a huge tree. You are at the base of the tree. Your parents and other **ancestors** are on higher and higher branches that spread out to the sides.

⭐ **family tree** A chart of family members
ancestor A family member from the past

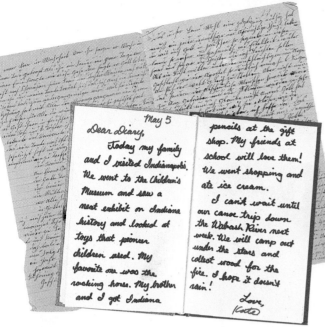

May 5

Dear Diary,
   Today my family and I visited Indianapolis. We went to the Children's Museum and saw a neat exhibit on Indiana history and looked at toys that pioneer children used. My favorite one was the rocking horse. My brother and I got Indiana pencils at the gift shop. My friends at school will love them! We went shopping and ate ice cream.
   I can't wait until our canoe trip down the Wabash River next week. We will camp out under the stars and collect wood for the fire. I hope it doesn't rain!
              Love,
              Kate

▲ A German settler who came to Indiana in the 1800s and a present-day fourth grader wrote these diaries.

Family trees often give birth and death dates. They also can show where each person lived and what he or she did for a living.

Personal History on Paper

Maybe you keep a journal for a class. Or you have a diary where you record your private thoughts. Diaries and journals help people record their own history on paper.

Many families also take photographs. Photos record birthdays, holidays, vacations, and other events. Letters also provide family records. Family records are exciting sources for historians. They show what ordinary people did and thought at certain times in history.

History in Communities

By now you can see that clues to your family history are all around you. Clues to your community history are everywhere too.

One place to look for community history is in the names of streets, towns, and buildings. Names may reflect what Native American groups lived in your area or what heroes were popular when your town was founded.

A road may be named for where it once went—Canal Street or Mill Road. The town of Youngstown, in western Indiana, was named for William Young, an early settler. Names like Twin Lakes in northern Indiana and Riverside on the Wabash River describe local geography.

▼ Signs on buildings and along roads give clues to local history.

This simple Indiana house was built with logs and stone in 1720.

This 1806 Indiana house has glass windows and a porch.

History in Buildings

Buildings also give clues about community history. When people first settled Indiana communities in the 1700s, they built rough houses. You can see a picture of this kind of house on this page.

Early settlers used building materials like wood and stone that were easy to find. They had little time and money to spend on building a large, fancy house. Settlers had more important needs. They had to plant crops, hunt, and feed their families.

Once crops were planted and their lives more settled, people had more time and money. They were able to replace their rough log houses with larger, more comfortable homes. They started to add decorations to their houses.

The photograph above shows a house built in the early 1800s in Indiana. It is built of smooth boards cut at a sawmill. Most people who lived in log houses hung animal skins or oiled paper over their windows. Glass was too expensive. By the early 1800s, people were able to afford glass for their windows. Many added front porches and painted the outsides of their houses.

As time passed, building styles changed. New building materials—including plastics, metal, and concrete—became available. Many people could afford larger houses with many decorations. All of these houses tell a story.

History in Cemeteries

You might be surprised to learn that a cemetery is one of the best places to learn about history. A cemetery can give you clues about the people of a community and the times in which they lived.

Gravestones often have messages and poems carved on them. Some gravestones list a person's children or parents. They can help historians understand family history. In some cemeteries, beautifully carved statues or gravestones show that rich people lived in the town.

Finding many gravestones from the same year is a clue that a community suffered widespread sickness, or a disaster like a flood.

▲ Markers on soldiers' graves tell about wars.

FRANCOIS RIDAY BUSSERON

CAPT CONTINENTAL TROOPS REV WAR

1748   1791

The large number of children's gravestones from the 1800s tell that many people died of disease before they became adults.

Preserving History

In some communities, only a few very old buildings, artifacts, and cemeteries still exist. Many people want to save the historic objects that are still left in their communities. They hope to preserve history so that everyone can learn how people lived and worked in the past.

History belongs to everyone and should be preserved for all to enjoy. Never touch artifacts without permission. Share what you learn about history to help others appreciate the history of your town and state.

▼ A worker uses a small brush to clean a gravestone.

SHOW WHAT YOU KNOW!

REFOCUS
COMPREHENSION

1. Describe the ways that families record their history.

2. How can you find out about your community's history?

THINK ABOUT IT
CRITICAL THINKING

Why do many communities try to save their historic buildings?

WRITE ABOUT IT
ACTIVITY

Describe a place or building in your community where you can learn about history.

3

Connections

⭐ **KEY TERMS**
oral history
folk tale

📖 **LITERATURE**
Johnny Appleseed

ORAL HISTORY

FOCUS *People often pass on stories and traditions by word of mouth. This kind of history helps historians learn more about the past.*

▲ This boy is recording oral history.

Oral History

Until about 150 years ago, many Americans did not have a chance to learn to read and write. To keep their history and traditions alive, people told stories aloud. History told through the spoken word is called **oral history**.

You have probably heard oral history in your own family. Maybe a grandparent or an older friend tells stories about what life was like many years ago. Perhaps these relatives also know stories from their older friends. To be your own family historian, you can save these stories by using a tape recorder or a video camera.

Folk Tales and Folk Songs

Old stories and beliefs also appear in **folk tales**. In Europe, the word *folk* meant ordinary people rather than kings and queens or lords and ladies. Folk tales are the stories ordinary people told each other. Sometimes stories were set to music as folk songs.

Some folk tales and folk songs were based on events that really happened. Some were meant to teach a lesson. Others were told just for fun. Different storytellers told folk tales in many different ways. Later these stories were written down.

Historians study folk tales because these stories show many

 oral history Information about the past passed down by word of mouth

 folk tale A story passed down by word of mouth

things about how people lived and thought long ago. You probably know some stories that began as European folk tales, such as "Beauty and the Beast." Other familiar tales are from other parts of the world.

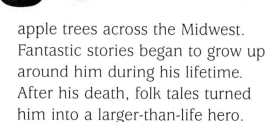

American Folk Tales

The United States has its own folk tales and songs. Many are stories about the men and women who helped the country grow.

On pages 42–43, you can read a folk tale about Johnny Appleseed. Johnny Appleseed was a real person named John Chapman, who planted apple trees across the Midwest. Fantastic stories began to grow up around him during his lifetime. After his death, folk tales turned him into a larger-than-life hero.

How Hoosiers Came to Be

People often use words that come from folk history and can't really be explained. One of these words is *Hoosier*.

People tell different stories to explain the word *Hoosier*. In one, a riverboat captain named Sam Hoosier hired workers from Indiana. They came to be known as "Hoosier's men." Some people like a humorous explanation for the word *Hoosier*. Early settlers had rowdy fights. One might bite off the ear of another. When someone found the ear the next day, the person would ask, "Whose ear?"

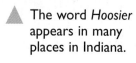

▲ The word *Hoosier* appears in many places in Indiana.

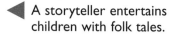

◀ A storyteller entertains children with folk tales.

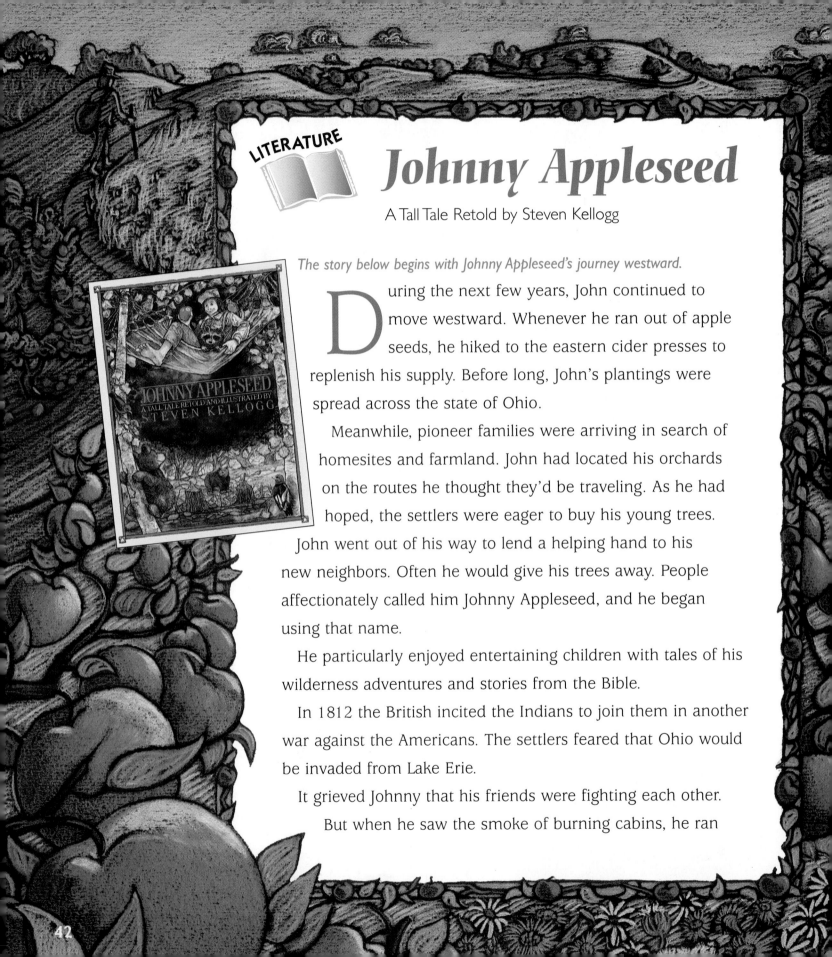

Johnny Appleseed

A Tall Tale Retold by Steven Kellogg

The story below begins with Johnny Appleseed's journey westward.

During the next few years, John continued to move westward. Whenever he ran out of apple seeds, he hiked to the eastern cider presses to replenish his supply. Before long, John's plantings were spread across the state of Ohio.

Meanwhile, pioneer families were arriving in search of homesites and farmland. John had located his orchards on the routes he thought they'd be traveling. As he had hoped, the settlers were eager to buy his young trees.

John went out of his way to lend a helping hand to his new neighbors. Often he would give his trees away. People affectionately called him Johnny Appleseed, and he began using that name.

He particularly enjoyed entertaining children with tales of his wilderness adventures and stories from the Bible.

In 1812 the British incited the Indians to join them in another war against the Americans. The settlers feared that Ohio would be invaded from Lake Erie.

It grieved Johnny that his friends were fighting each other. But when he saw the smoke of burning cabins, he ran

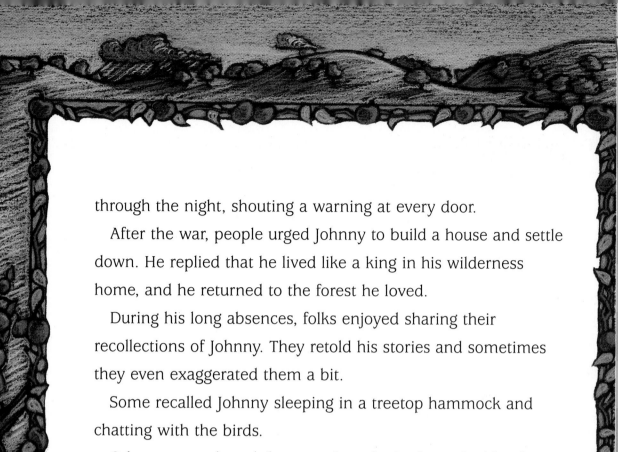

through the night, shouting a warning at every door.

After the war, people urged Johnny to build a house and settle down. He replied that he lived like a king in his wilderness home, and he returned to the forest he loved.

During his long absences, folks enjoyed sharing their recollections of Johnny. They retold his stories and sometimes they even exaggerated them a bit.

Some recalled Johnny sleeping in a treetop hammock and chatting with the birds.

Others remembered that a rattlesnake had attacked his foot. Fortunately, Johnny's feet were as tough as elephant's hide, so the fangs didn't penetrate.

It was said that Johnny had once tended a wounded wolf and then kept him for a pet.

An old hunter swore he'd seen Johnny frolicking with a bear family.

The storytellers outdid each other with tall tales about his feats of survival in the untamed wilderness.

As the years passed, Ohio became too crowded for Johnny. He moved to the wilds of Indiana, where he contined to clear land for his orchards.

You can find out about Johnny Appleseed's life in Indiana by checking the book out of your school or public library.

HISTORY IN MUSEUMS

FOCUS *Museums tell the story of Indiana's past. Hoosier museums contain displays about cars, astronauts, sports, and many other interesting subjects.*

Museums Preserve History

Indiana has many museums that preserve your state's past. In these museums you can explore things that already interest you or learn something new.

Museums hold collections that include artifacts, paintings, scientific samples, and even race cars and basketballs. **Exhibits** display these collections to visitors. People called **curators** plan the exhibits, set them up, and take care of them. Some exhibits change every few months. Others are on permanent display.

The map on this page shows where some of Indiana's museums are located. Several are located in or near Indianapolis. Other museums are located throughout the state.

Some Indiana museums, such as the Howard Steamboat Museum, preserve artifacts from Indiana's past. Others focus on famous people and events. The Grissom Air Museum includes displays about Hoosier astronaut Gus Grissom.

House museums show how people used to live. They preserve houses as they would have looked in the past. Grouseland was once the home of President William Henry Harrison. It contains many of Harrison's possessions.

Art Museums

Indiana has many museums of art such as the Museum of Art at Indiana University. One of the most famous art museums is the Eiteljorg (EYE tul jorg) Museum. The Eiteljorg displays art by Native

INDIANA MUSEUMS

★ State capital

• Other cities

■ Museums

Map labels:
- Lake Michigan
- 88°W   86°W   42°N
- Studebaker National Museum
- South Bend
- Auburn-Cord-Duesenberg Museum
- Fort Wayne
- Grissom Air Museum
- 40°N
- Motor Speedway Hall of Fame
- Children's Museum
- Eiteljorg Museum
- Indianapolis
- Bloomington
- Indiana University Art Museum
- Grouseland
- Howard Steamboat Museum
- Indiana Baseball Hall of Fame
- New Albany
- Evansville
- 38°N
- 0 25 50 miles
- 0 25 50 kilometers

---

exhibit   A show open to the public
curator   A person in charge of a museum

American and other artists who painted pictures of the American West. The Eiteljorg also includes displays of clothing, pottery, jewelry, and crafts.

The museum's paintings and artifacts were collected by Harrison Eiteljorg, an Indianapolis businessman, beginning in the 1940s. His collection forms the basis for the museum's displays.

Sports Museums

Sports museums are Hoosier favorites. These museums display the uniforms and equipment used in sports like basketball and football. They also display photographs and exhibits about famous athletes.

The Speedway Hall of Fame is a popular Hoosier sports museum.

◀ This Native American dress is at the Eiteljorg Museum.

Displays show the history of the world-famous Indy 500 auto race, which began in 1911. The museum also contains many trophies from past races.

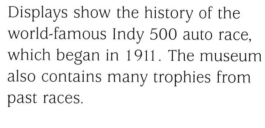
This car won the first Indy 500 race.

SHOW WHAT YOU KNOW!

REFOCUS
COMPREHENSION

1. Name two kinds of museums in Indiana.

2. Describe what you might see if you visited the Eiteljorg Museum.

THINK ABOUT IT
CRITICAL THINKING

Describe a new type of museum that you might plan for your state.

WRITE ABOUT IT
ACTIVITY

Write an advertisement in your Indiana journal that encourages people to visit one of Indiana's museums.

SUMMING UP

1 DO YOU REMEMBER . . .
COMPREHENSION

1. Name four kinds of written sources that historians use in their research.

2. When written sources are unavailable, what other kinds of sources do historians use?

3. What are some ways that street signs may give clues to a community's history?

4. What are folk tales? Why do historians study them?

5. What do curators do?

2 SKILL POWER
USING PRIMARY AND SECONDARY SOURCES

Read the excerpt below and decide whether it is a primary or a secondary source. Then make a list of the information that a historian might learn from the selection.

Our family, consisting of father, mother, two brothers, and one sister, left this morning for that far and much talked of country, California. . . . Our train numbered fifty wagons. The last hours were spent in bidding good-bye to old friends. My mother is heartbroken over this separation of relatives and friends. . . . Our carriage upset at one place. All were thrown out, but no one was hurt.

—Sallie Hester's diary (March 20, 1849)

3 WHAT DO YOU THINK?
CRITICAL THINKING

1. Is it easier for a historian to learn about ordinary people or famous people from the past? Explain your answer.

2. Why is it important that a historian be able to work well with others?

3. What might historians be able to learn from the diary of a family member that they could not learn from a family photo album?

4. What can historians learn about frontier life from the folk tale about Johnny Appleseed?

5. What can you learn from visiting a museum that you cannot learn from reading about its exhibits?

4 SAY IT, WRITE IT, USE IT
VOCABULARY

Suppose that you are the curator of a museum in Indiana. Think of a display you might include in an exhibit titled "Hoosier History." Then write a brief description of the display. Use as many vocabulary terms as possible in your descriptions.

ancestor	exhibit
archaeologist	family tree
artifact	folk tale
culture	oral history
curator	research
document	

5 GEOGRAPHY AND YOU
MAP STUDY

Create a poster map of historic sites in Indiana, using the map below and the map on page 35 as models. On a large sheet of paper trace an outline map of Indiana. Include the historic sites that are labeled, and find out about other sites to add to the map. Title your poster "Historic Sites in Indiana."

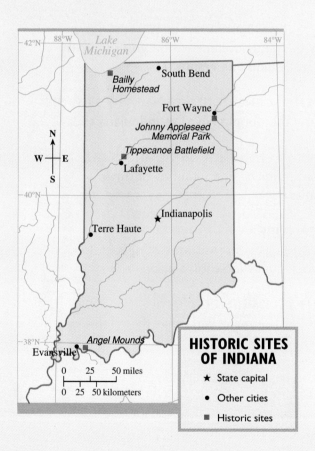

HISTORIC SITES OF INDIANA

★ State capital
● Other cities
■ Historic sites

Labels on map: Lake Michigan, 42°N, 88°W, 86°W, 84°W, Bailly Homestead, South Bend, Fort Wayne, Johnny Appleseed Memorial Park, Tippecanoe Battlefield, Lafayette, 40°N, Indianapolis, Terre Haute, Angel Mounds, Evansville, 38°N

0 25 50 miles
0 25 50 kilometers

N W E S

6 TAKE ACTION
CITIZENSHIP

History is all around you. It is in your family album, in the names of streets and towns, and in buildings and monuments. Find out about a historic event that happened in or near your community. Use books or talk to adults to learn more about this event. Draw a scene to illustrate the event. Write a paragraph describing the scene. Share your illustration with your classmates.

7 GET CREATIVE
LANGUAGE ARTS CONNECTION

In this chapter you learned that folk tales are important sources of historical information. Visit the library and find an American folk tale. Read the folk tale and prepare to read it to your class. Try to find out if the folk tale was based on events that really happened, as the folk tale of Johnny Appleseed was.

LOOKING AHEAD

In the next chapter, explore the backgrounds, surroundings, and occupations of the people of Indiana.

CHAPTER 3

INDIANA'S

Hoosiers have come to Indiana from all over the world. Read about where they came from, where they live, and how they make their living.

CONTENTS

▼ See someone who grows and sells popcorn on page 66.

PEOPLE TODAY

These books can help you learn more about the people of Indiana. Read one that interests you and fill out a book-review form.

READ AND RESEARCH

Indiana (America the Beautiful series) by
R. Conrad Stein (Children's Press, 1994)
Find out about Indiana's people and their history as you read this informative book. *(nonfiction)*

Indiana by **Gwenyth Swain** (Lerner Publications Company, 1992)
Explore Indiana from the dunes to the hills and learn interesting facts about its people and geography. *(nonfiction)*

Eastern Great Lakes: Indiana, Michigan, Ohio by
Thomas G. Aylesworth and Virginia L. Aylesworth
(Chelsea House Publishers, 1996)
Compare the people and attractions of Indiana with those of its two neighboring states in the Great Lakes region. *(nonfiction)*

Immigrants by **Martin W. Sandler** (HarperCollins, 1995)
Using photographs and documents, this book tells the story of the many immigrants who came to this country between 1870 and 1920. *(nonfiction)*

SKILL POWER Using Bar Graphs and Line Graphs

Bar graphs help you compare information. Line graphs help you see how things have changed over time.

UNDERSTAND IT

A graph is a kind of drawing that uses pictures, circles, bars, or lines to make comparisons. Graphs can compare information about people, places, objects—almost anything!

A graph usually has a title to tell what the graph is comparing. It also has labels to identify the kinds of information being shown.

Look at the *bar graph* on page 51. What is the title? What are the labels? You can see that the states are named along the left side of the graph. And you can see that the numbers along the bottom stand for millions of people.

The second graph on page 51 is a *line graph*. A line graph often compares things by showing how they change over a period of time. Has the population of the United States become larger or smaller over time?

EXPLORE IT

Using the bar graph on page 51, compare the number of people in Indiana and in Florida. Which of these states has the larger population? To find out, put your finger on the bar for Florida. Now move your finger to the right. The bar reaches almost to the 15. Florida has about 14,000,000 people. About how many millions of people are in Indiana?

Now look at the line graph on page 51. How many people were living in the United States in 1900? In 1920? During what years did the United States population grow the fastest?

TRY IT

On a sheet of paper, write two questions that can be answered by reading the bar graph and two questions that can be answered by reading the line graph. Use the questions asked in Understand It and Explore It to help you.

Trade your paper with a partner. Use the graphs to answer your partner's questions.

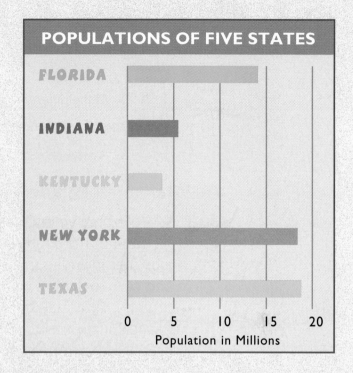

POPULATIONS OF FIVE STATES

FLORIDA

INDIANA

KENTUCKY

NEW YORK

TEXAS

0   5   10   15   20

Population in Millions

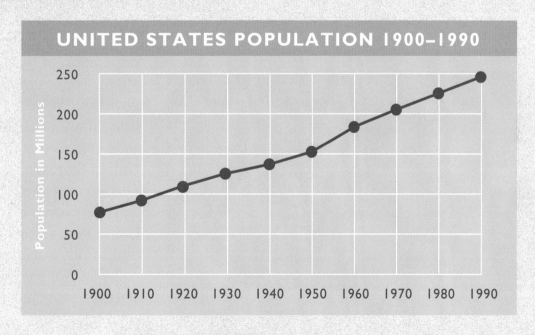

UNITED STATES POPULATION 1900–1990

Population in Millions

250

200

150

100

50

0

1900 1910 1920 1930 1940 1950 1960 1970 1980 1990

SKILL POWER SEARCH *Search the chapter for other graphs. What are they comparing? Be sure to read the titles and labels.*

1 Setting the Scene

⭐ **KEY TERMS**
census
population density
rural
urban
suburb
immigrant

YOUR HOOSIER NEIGHBORS

FOCUS *Many different people live in your state. Some live in small towns, but most live in cities. They work at many different kinds of jobs.*

Indiana's People

Hoosiers live in cities, in towns, and in the country. They have jobs that include growing soybeans and corn, teaching people who are disabled, and making and selling musical instruments.

Your Hoosier neighbors have come to Indiana from all over the world. They have all made valuable contributions to your state.

▼ Hoosiers of many ages and backgrounds run in a road race.

The Population of Indiana

About 5,800,000 people live in Indiana. Here's one way to think of Indiana's population. The RCA (Hoosier) Dome seats 60,500 people. It is one of the largest indoor sports stadiums in the United States. If every Hoosier came to the dome, we would need 96 RCA Domes to seat everyone.

Many people need to know the population of Indiana and of other states. For example, the federal government needs to know exactly how many people live in each state.

To obtain this information, the United States government takes a **census** every ten years. In a census, every person in the country is counted. Information about jobs and family background is also collected for the census.

The census lets officials keep track of how state populations have changed over time. The line graph on the next page shows how the population of Indiana has changed since 1900.

⭐ **census** An official count of the number of people living in a place

INDIANA POPULATION
1900–1990

Number of People (in millions)

6
5
4
3
2
1

1900 1910 1920 1930 1940 1950 1960 1970 1980 1990

Population Density

In addition to telling how many people live in Indiana, the census tells where people live. Information about location lets you know the state's **population density**.

In areas where people are crowded together, we say that the population is dense. In areas with few people, we say that the population is sparse.

Look at the map on this page. The colors show which regions are most crowded and which regions are less crowded. Which color represents the area where you live?

⭐ **population density** The average number of people living in an area

Notice that the areas around Indiana's largest cities are the most densely populated. Indianapolis, located in the geographical middle of the state, is Indiana's largest population center.

Another densely populated area is located along the shores of Lake Michigan. It is called the Calumet region, after a river and lake called Calumet in Illinois. Many Hoosiers simply call it "the Region." Some cities of the Calumet region are East Chicago, Gary, and Hammond.

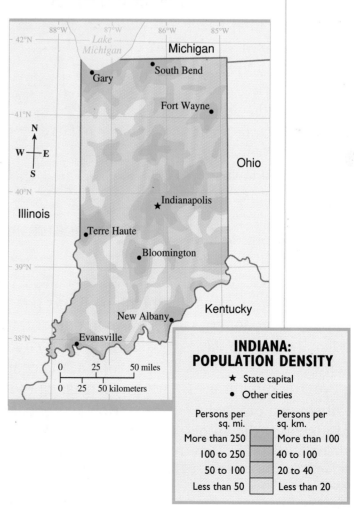

INDIANA: POPULATION DENSITY

★ State capital
• Other cities

Persons per sq. mi.	Persons per sq. km.
More than 250	More than 100
100 to 250	40 to 100
50 to 100	20 to 40
Less than 50	Less than 20

Fort Wayne and its surrounding area in northeastern Indiana also have a high population density.

Rural, Suburban, and Urban

A **rural** area has a low population density. Rural communities are far apart and surrounded by open land. This land includes farms, forests, and recreational areas like forests and parks. Rural areas in Indiana are mostly found in the western and southern regions of the state. These regions are where most of the state's agricultural products are grown or raised.

A city is called an **urban** area. It has tall buildings, factories, and many streets. Areas outside cities are called **suburbs**. These are areas with shopping centers, small factories, and houses with lawns. People in suburbs often travel to nearby cities to work.

Beech Grove, located southeast of Indianapolis, is a typical Indiana suburb. Businesses such as grain storage and train repair are located in Beech Grove. But most people commute to Indianapolis each day to work in the city.

Perhaps you live in a rural or a suburban area. If so, you probably live near one of the cities shown on the map on this page. Or perhaps you live in one of the state's largest cities. Find your city on the map. Then look at the chart of Indiana's twenty largest cities on the next page. How many people live in the city you have named?

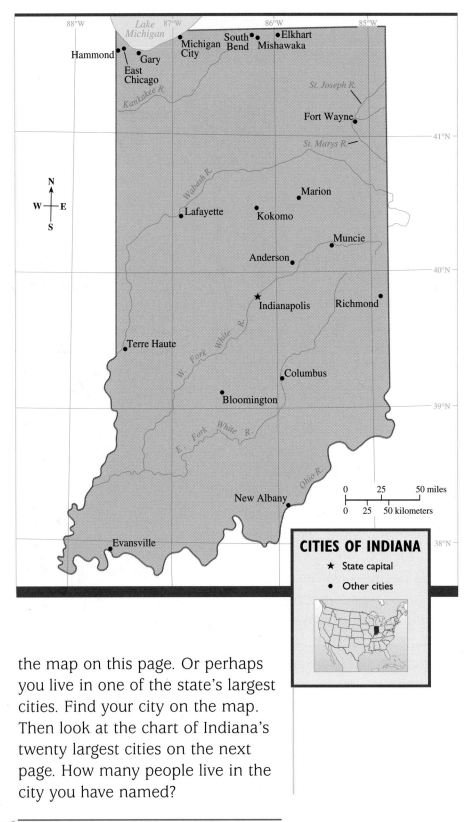

CITIES OF INDIANA
★ State capital
● Other cities

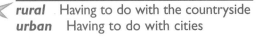

★ **rural** Having to do with the countryside
urban Having to do with cities

★ **suburb** A town on the outskirts of a city

Why People Live in Cities

In the 1800s, most Hoosiers lived in rural areas. Today, most people live in or near cities. Two reasons help explain the growth of cities. First, with the help of modern machinery, fewer people are needed on farms. Second, people come to cities to find work in the many businesses located in urban areas.

Cities also offer many activities. Residents do not need to travel far to go to museums and restaurants. They can shop in nearby stores and easily attend movies, concerts, or sports events.

Life in Cities

Hoosier cities share many characteristics. In Indianapolis, as in many other cities, the main business section lies in the center of the city. It is also called the downtown.

The downtown is the busiest part of the city. People from the city and the suburbs work in offices and stores there. A city's downtown may contain thousands of people because

INDIANA'S TWENTY LARGEST CITIES

City	Population
Indianapolis	762,844
Fort Wayne	183,359
Evansville	129,452
Gary	114,256
South Bend	105,092
Hammond	82,837
Muncie	71,407
Bloomington	62,560
Anderson	60,846
Terre Haute	60,200
Kokomo	46,027
Lafayette	45,877
Elkhart	44,840
Mishawaka	43,843
Richmond	38,810
New Albany	37,920
Columbus	35,689
Michigan City	33,899
East Chicago	32,592
Marion	32,312

INDIANA FACTS

The city of Carmel, Indiana, is believed to be the site of the nation's first automatic stoplight. It was installed in 1923.

many offices are located in tall buildings. One of Indiana's most beautiful tall buildings is the all-glass NBD Bank building. This tower rises 37 stories over Indianapolis.

An area of factories usually lies near a city's downtown. This section is known as the industrial area. Highways and shipping docks are located near this area. They are used to transport the city's industrial goods and products.

Residential neighborhoods are found beyond the industrial area. These neighborhoods are where most people live, since many people prefer to live away from the noise and bustle of the downtown area.

Lockerbie Square and Woodruff Place are two well-known neighborhoods in Indianapolis. Another neighborhood, Broad Ripple, is home to many artists.

Italian pizza

Middle Eastern salad

Japanese sushi

German sausage

French croissant

Indian spices

Mexican burrito

Hoosiers enjoy foods from many different countries.

Hoosier Ancestors

Most Hoosiers living in the state today were born in Indiana. Many of their great-grandparents came from Kentucky, North Carolina, Virginia, and Tennessee.

These early residents settled throughout the south central part of Indiana. Southern speech patterns can still be heard in southern regions of Indiana today. Later settlers came from Pennsylvania, New York, and the New England states. Many of these residents settled in northern Indiana.

Suppose we looked at a group of 100 Hoosiers and asked them where their ancestors lived before they came to the United States. About 90 out of 100 would claim that their ancestors came from Europe. Many Hoosier ancestors once lived in England, Germany, Ireland, Sweden, and Scotland. Others came from Hungary, Greece, Italy, and Poland.

Recent Newcomers

About 8 out of every 100 Hoosiers are African American. Recently Indiana has also attracted many newcomers from Latin America. People from North Africa, the Middle East, Japan, India, China, and many other countries have also come to Indiana to live, study, and work.

Like all **immigrants**, these newcomers came to their new home looking for a better life. They also brought their special ways of doing things to Indiana.

---

immigrant Person from one country who moves to another country to live

Many Contributions

When people move to new homes, they bring the things they own in suitcases and boxes. They also bring things that don't need a suitcase. These are their memories and skills—important parts of their culture, or way of living.

Immigrants bring memories of the places where they lived to their new homes. Many towns in Indiana are named after the places that immigrants came from. These include the towns of Scotland, Peru, and New Paris.

Immigrants often cook foods from their home countries. Sometimes they open restaurants to serve this food to others. Look under "Restaurants" and "Groceries" in the yellow pages of your telephone book. There you will find many clues about the origins of the immigrants in your community.

Celebrations

Indiana has many festivals in which people celebrate the cultures of their homelands. For example, German Oktoberfests celebrate the fall harvest. Italian Americans celebrate the Little Italy Festival. African Americans enjoy the Indiana Black Expo each summer.

These and many other groups share their foods, stories, music, dance, and dress with the rest of the community. They also share traditional crafts and games.

The International Festival in Indianapolis is one of Indiana's largest celebrations. This festival includes jewelry from Mexico, art from India, dances from Hungary, and food from all over the world.

▼ Japanese immigrants bring their traditional music to Indiana.

SHOW WHAT YOU KNOW!

REFOCUS
COMPREHENSION

1. What information can you learn from a census?

2. Where are three of Indiana's most densely populated areas?

THINK ABOUT IT
CRITICAL THINKING

In what ways might people who live in suburbs benefit from living near cities?

WRITE ABOUT IT
ACTIVITY

Write an entry in your Indiana journal describing the foods and customs you would take with you if you moved to another country.

PAOLI, SOUTH BEND, AND INDIANAPOLIS

FOCUS *Hoosiers live in both towns and cities. Towns provide quiet and a chance to know everyone in the community. Cities offer excitement and many activities.*

Hoosier Towns

Many Hoosiers live in towns. Towns are smaller than cities and have fewer businesses and stores. Houses in towns usually have more open space and trees between them.

Many people like living in a town because the pace of life is more relaxed than in a city. People also like life in a town because most residents are able to greet each other by name.

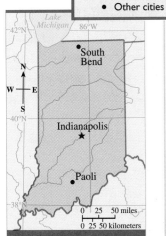

THREE HOOSIER COMMUNITIES
★ State capital
● Other cities

Lake Michigan 86°W
42°N
South Bend
N
W—E
S
40°N
Indianapolis ★
Paoli
38°
0 25 50 miles
0 25 50 kilometers

▲ The Orange County Courthouse in Paoli

Paoli

Paoli (pay OH lee) is a small town located in one of southern Indiana's green valleys. Its population numbers about 4,000 people. Find Paoli on the map on this page.

Like many towns, Paoli is built around a **town square**. Public buildings and shops grew up around the square as the town expanded in the early 1900s. One

of these buildings is the famous Orange County **Courthouse**.

During the late 1800s and early 1900s, visitors flocked to Paoli and other towns in southern Indiana. Many came to drink the mineral waters that bubble up from the earth in this part of the state.

 town square   A park or green in the center of a town

courthouse   A building with law courts and government offices

These kayakers are racing on South Bend's St. Joseph River.

People thought these salty waters could cure illness. We know now that the waters do not possess any special medical powers. Today visitors come for other reasons, such as skiing at Paoli Peaks.

South Bend

With a population of about 105,000, South Bend is a medium-sized city. Locate South Bend on the map on page 58.

A medium-sized city has more attractions than a small town. These include movie theaters, museums, universities, and restaurants. Cities also offer more jobs than small towns. They have several kinds of industries.

Beginning in the 1800s, South Bend was home to many important industries. Studebaker (STOO duh bay kur) Company, famous for making some of the earliest cars, was located there. The Singer Company made wooden cabinets for the country's sewing machines.

As South Bend enters the twenty-first century, industry is still important. But more people are finding other sorts of jobs, such as computer programming and sales.

South Bend has many interesting places to visit. Century Center features exhibits that tell about the city's industrial past. It also houses buggies, wagons, and early cars made by Studebaker.

South Bend is also home to the University of Notre Dame. Since 1842, people from all over the world have come to study here.

Studebaker made this convertible in 1950.

Notre Dame is well known for excellence in teaching and for outstanding football teams. The College Football Hall of Fame is also located in South Bend.

Indianapolis

Two hundred years ago, Indianapolis was just a small clearing in the wilderness. Today Indianapolis is Indiana's biggest city. As the state's capital, it is the location of the state's government. Find Indianapolis on the map on page 58.

Since the early days of train travel, the Indianapolis economy has relied on the transportation industry. The medical industry has also been important to the city's growth. Videotape production, computer software design, and electronics companies have recently moved to Indianapolis.

▲ Notre Dame football games draw huge crowds.

Over the years, people from all over the world have moved to Indianapolis. These newcomers have brought a great variety of new foods and celebrations to the city.

Attractions and Events

Indianapolis is often called the sports capital of the country. The city hosts bicycle races, swimming meets, and other events. It is also home to the Indianapolis Colts football team and the Indiana Pacers basketball team.

Children in Indianapolis like the things they can do in the city. For example, they can visit the cageless Indianapolis Zoo. There the animals roam freely through areas that look like their natural environments.

In Indianapolis, children can visit the zoo and the Children's Museum.

Children can also explore the Children's Museum. This museum has nine galleries filled with hands-on displays. Visitors can explore a cave, sift through an archaeological dig for artifacts, or sit inside the jawbones of an enormous shark.

Indianapolis is also home to the Indiana State Fair. Every August thousands of people from all over the state crowd into the fairgrounds. There they enjoy carnival rides, music, and competitions where judges select champion livestock.

Cities like Indianapolis also have many chances for people to enjoy the performing arts. One of the newest places to see these events in Indianapolis is the Artsgarden. Here audiences can enjoy music, dance, theater, and films.

The Indianapolis skyline rises above the city's streets.

SHOW WHAT YOU KNOW!

REFOCUS
COMPREHENSION

1. What are three attractions you could see if you visited Indianapolis?

2. Describe two early industries in South Bend.

THINK ABOUT IT
CRITICAL THINKING

What are some of the advantages and disadvantages of living in a city?

WRITE ABOUT IT
ACTIVITY

Write a brochure for the Paoli tourist bureau explaining why Paoli is a good place to visit.

Map Adventure

KEY TERM

diverse

LET'S MOVE TO INDIANA!

FOCUS The people who have settled in Indiana have come from nearby states and faraway countries. They have come to find jobs, to attend universities, and to live near family members. Explore some of the places Hoosiers have chosen to live.

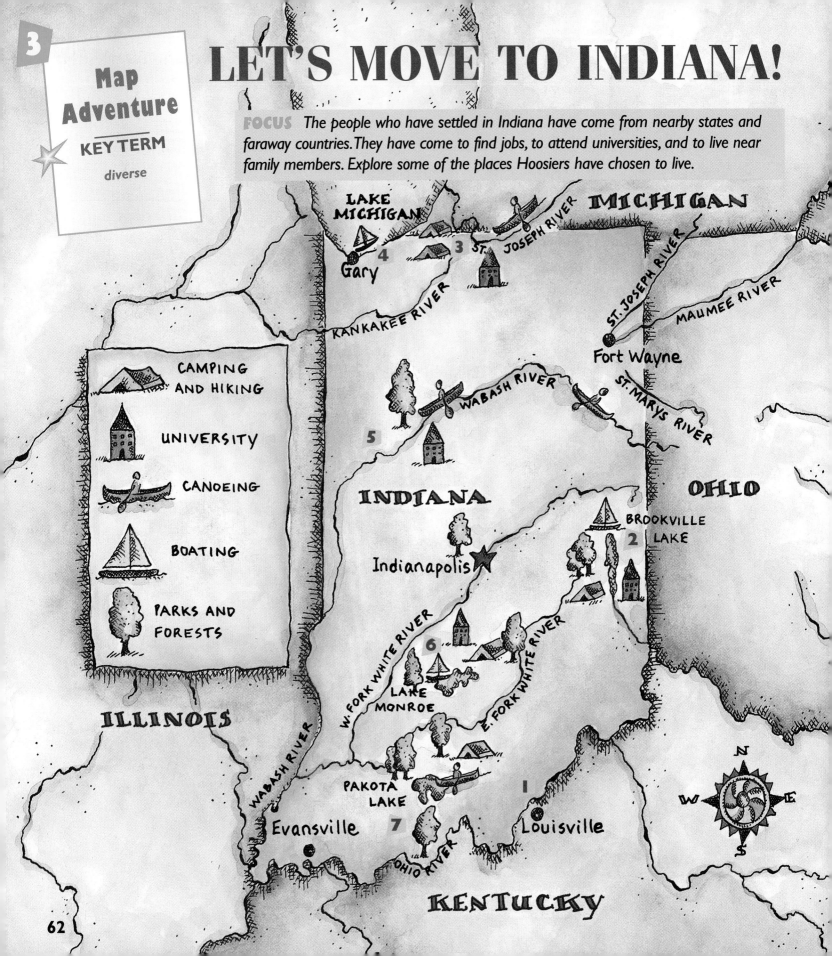

Where to Move?

It's moving day! Your family is leaving Kentucky for a new home in Indiana. Your mother wants to live in a river town, your father wants to be near a university, and you'd like to be near a lake. Let's take a tour to find the Hoosier city that best suits everyone.

Map Key

1 New Albany Founded in 1813 as a shipbuilding center, this city is located on the Ohio River. Indiana's Knobs overlook it.

2 Richmond The Quakers founded Earlham College here in 1847. This city has many historical sites. A short drive will take you to a state recreation area and a state park.

3 South Bend This is Indiana's fifth-largest city. It is home to the University of Notre Dame and its famous golden dome.

4 Indiana Dunes National Lakeshore and State Park You can swim, fish, and camp along the lakeshore. The dunes are home to **diverse** types of plants and animals.

5 West Lafayette This city was originally a French fur-trading fort and is now the site of Purdue University.

6 Bloomington Indiana University was founded here in 1820. The city is close to many parks and to Lake Monroe, the largest lake in Indiana.

7 Hoosier National Forest Some of Indiana's original forests still exist in this 172,000-acre park. Here you can go horseback riding and hiking.

★ *diverse* Different from one another

MAP IT

1. You drive from Louisville, Kentucky, into Indiana. Which river do you cross to reach New Albany? Why might your mother wish to settle there?

2. As you head northeast, you stop in Richmond to ask for directions to South Bend. In which direction should you travel? What could you visit?

3. In South Bend, you hear people talking about Indiana Dunes National Lakeshore and State Park. In which direction do you travel to get there? What are some things you might do at the park?

4. You head southwest to West Lafayette. Why might your father like to live in this city?

5. Your final stop is Bloomington. Why does this city appeal to you?

EXPLORE IT

Your tour of Indiana is complete. Help your family make a decision. Match everyone's interests with what you have learned about Indiana during your trip. Where do you decide to live? Why?

HOOSIERS AT WORK

FOCUS *Hoosiers work at many different kinds of jobs. They grow food, make products, and offer useful services.*

Many Workers

About 3 million people in Indiana have jobs. That's almost two thirds of all the adults in the state. Look at the graph on this page. It shows the different kinds of industries that employ workers in Indiana.

One large group of people works in manufacturing. They work for companies that make

▲ The Hoosier farmers in this parade are proud of their work.

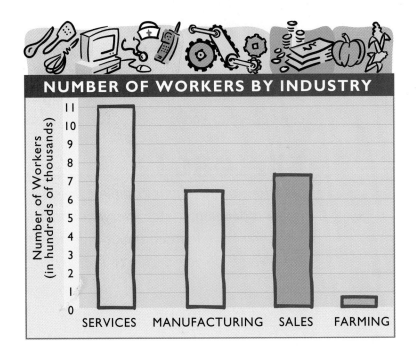

NUMBER OF WORKERS BY INDUSTRY

Number of Workers (in hundreds of thousands)

SERVICES MANUFACTURING SALES FARMING

products such as car engines. Other Indiana manufacturers prepare and pack food products like bread, milk, tomatoes, cheese, and popcorn.

Another large group of Hoosiers works in sales. Some have jobs in stores. Others sell the goods made by factories.

The largest number of workers works in **service industries**. Instead of making products, they work in businesses that provide services. These services include banking and computer repair.

 service industry A business that employs people who help others

Farming was once Indiana's main source of work. Fewer people are farmers today, but farming still provides many Hoosiers with jobs.

Indiana Products

The map on this page shows the areas of Indiana where various products are grown or made. As you can see, people in many parts of the state grow food, such as corn and soybeans.

Some of the state's first large steel and chemical factories were located in northern Indiana along the shore of Lake Michigan. The Calumet region, which includes Gary and Hammond, is still one of the nation's great industrial centers. Limestone is mined in several areas of the state, including south central areas and the northeast.

Jobs in Agriculture

Popcorn, peppermint, pork, and pickles—these are just a few of the foods that come from Indiana farm products. Some people with jobs in agriculture work on farms growing crops or raising animals. Other jobs provide services to agriculture. Veterinarians keep farm animals healthy. Truck

INDIANA PRODUCTS

sales

The Gettelfinger Popcorn Company, owned by Irvin Gettelfinger, grows and sells popcorn.

Indiana farmers grow many fruits and vegetables.

drivers carry vegetables to markets throughout the state and the nation. Government agents help farmers use the most up-to-date planting methods.

Manufacturing

People who work in manufacturing do many kinds of jobs. Some workers run machines, pack boxes, or plan new products. Others check products to make sure they are made correctly.

Automobiles are an important industry in Indiana. Workers at Indiana companies make cars, trucks, and automobile parts. In other Indiana factories, workers make chemicals and medicines. In many smaller Hoosier businesses,

skilled craftspeople turn out special products like fine furniture and pottery made from Indiana clay.

Selling Products

The people in the state who make manufactured goods or grow food need people to sell their products. More than 700,000 Hoosiers work in sales jobs.

Many people sell directly to the public. They work in supermarkets, gas stations, and bookstores. They sell everything from marshmallows to tires.

Other salespeople sell goods to stores or to other companies. For example, the salesperson for a cheese factory tries to convince supermarkets and grocery stores to

Bett Etenohan (right) teaches about nature.

A teacher helps a student at Earlham College.

carry the company's products. Some salespeople work in other countries. They sell Hoosier goods to people around the world.

Providing Services

More and more Hoosiers work in jobs that provide services. They include doctors, teachers, mail carriers, government workers, and lawyers. New kinds of service jobs open up every day. Many new jobs today are in computer science and **telecommunications**.

Hoosiers make, grow, and sell many different products. They also work in the state's many services. The people of Indiana work hard to make a difference in your state and in the nation.

---

telecommunications The exchange of information by computer, telephone, and satellite

Many musical instruments are manufactured in Indiana.

SHOW WHAT YOU KNOW!

REFOCUS
COMPREHENSION

1. Describe three kinds of jobs in manufacturing.

2. What are three jobs that provide services to farmers?

THINK ABOUT IT
CRITICAL THINKING

Look at the graph on page 64. Which bar might have been the tallest 100 years ago? Explain why.

WRITE ABOUT IT
ACTIVITY

Choose a job in the service industry. Write three questions in your Indiana journal that you would like to ask someone who works at that job.

SUMMING UP

1 DO YOU REMEMBER . . .
COMPREHENSION

1. Name the three largest population centers in Indiana.

2. What advantages does city life offer to its residents?

3. Why might some people prefer to live in a town rather than a big city?

4. Which city is the fifth largest in Indiana? Why might you want to visit this city?

5. List four things that are manufactured in Indiana.

2 SKILL POWER
USING BAR GRAPHS AND LINE GRAPHS

Conduct a poll to find out whether the students in your school would rather live in an urban, a suburban, or a rural area. Ask ten people this question. Then use their responses to create a bar graph comparing the answers of your schoolmates. One bar on your graph will represent "Urban," another "Suburban," and another "Rural." Label the bottom and side of your graph and give your graph a title.

3 WHAT DO YOU THINK?
CRITICAL THINKING

1. How might an International Festival like the one held in Indianapolis help draw a community closer together?

2. Why might families choose to visit Indianapolis on their summer vacation?

3. What industry was important in New Albany's early days? Why, do you think, did this industry develop here?

4. How might Indiana's economy be affected if people stopped driving cars?

5. What field of work, do you think, will be most important to Indiana in the future?

4 SAY IT, WRITE IT, USE IT
VOCABULARY

Suppose that you and your family have just moved to Indiana. Write a letter to a friend in your old hometown that describes your new hometown and new state. Use as many vocabulary terms as possible in your letter.

census	service industry
courthouse	suburb
diverse	telecommunications
immigrant	town square
population density	urban
rural	

5 GEOGRAPHY AND YOU
MAP STUDY

Use the map below to answer the following questions.

1. What city is the capital? Where is it located in the state?

2. Based on the map, would you say that Gary is urban, suburban, or rural?

3. What is the southernmost city shown on this map of Indiana?

4. Which city shown on this map is closest to the Ohio border?

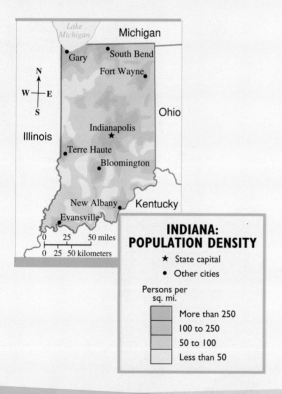

INDIANA: POPULATION DENSITY

★ State capital
• Other cities

Persons per sq. mi.

More than 250
100 to 250
50 to 100
Less than 50

6 TAKE ACTION
CITIZENSHIP

In this chapter, you read about the different cultural backgrounds of Indiana's citizens. Find out about the different cultural backgrounds of the students in your school. With your class, plan a school "International Festival" similar to the one that is held in Indianapolis. Invite all students and their families to prepare food, crafts, clothing, or other items that reflect their cultural backgrounds.

7 GET CREATIVE
MUSIC CONNECTION

Write a song that celebrates the people of Indiana. Start by choosing a tune that you like. Then, with a group of classmates, put new words to the music. Use the information in the chapter and your creative ideas. Your song might tell about the farms, cities, and suburbs of Indiana. It might also describe the kinds of work people in Indiana do every day. Perform your song for the class.

LOOKING AHEAD In the next chapter, learn about the people who first settled in Indiana.

Indiana's
EARLY History

How Was Indiana Settled?

Go back in time to learn about the lives of early peoples of Indiana. Share the challenges faced by the pioneers. You will learn how they changed Indiana and helped it grow.

1836

1876

1818

1866

INDIANA'S

Long ago, people crossed a land bridge that connected Asia and North America. Eventually, their descendants reached Indiana! In this chapter you will read about Indiana's first residents.

CONTENTS

▲ Find out on page 90 what crops early Native Americans planted.

FIRST PEOPLE

These books can help you learn more about Native American life in Indiana and the United States. Read one that interests you and fill out a book-review form.

READ AND RESEARCH

From Abenaki to Zuni: A Dictionary of Native American Tribes **by Evelyn Wolfson**
(Walker and Company, 1988)
This dictionary of 68 American Indian tribes offers fascinating details about the housing, diet, clothing, beliefs, and ceremonies of each group. *(nonfiction)*

Mounds of Earth and Shell **by Bonnie Shemie**
(Tundra Books, 1993)
Learn more about the mound builders. Discover what the mysterious mounds tell us about the earliest Native Americans. *(nonfiction)*

The Trees Stand Shining: Poetry of the North American Indians **edited by Hetti Jones**
(Dial Books, 1971)
Reading the beautiful poems in this collection will help you understand Native Americans' respect for nature. *(poetry)*

SKILL POWER Reading a Time Line

Knowing how to read a time line will help you keep track of the order in which important events happened.

UNDERSTAND IT

How good is your memory? You can probably remember almost everything that happened to you two days ago. But chances are you've forgotten a great deal of what happened two years ago.

How do historians keep track of time? A time line is a tool for organizing historical facts. A time line lists important events in the order in which they happened. It is divided into equal periods of years. The time line on this page is divided into time periods of ten years each.

EXPLORE IT

The time line below shows some events that took place in Indiana in the 1900s. To read the time line, find the event farthest to the left. This is the earliest event. Continue to read the events and dates from left to right. What is the most recent event? What happened in 1930? Which two similar events happened 50 years apart?

1902
The Studebaker Company produces its first car

1916
Hoosiers celebrate 100 years of statehood

1930
Indiana Mounds State Park is established

1949
Indiana's first two television stations begin broadcasting

1966
Hoosiers celebrate 150 years of statehood

1989
Hoosier Dan Quayle becomes Vice President of the United States

1900 1910 1920 1930 1940 1950 1960 1970 1980 1990 2000

TRY IT

A time line may cover a long period of time, or a shorter period. Try making a time line like the one shown on this page. Start with the year you were born and end with the present year. Then make a list of seven or eight events in your life and the years they happened. Place these events on the time line. Then decorate your work with photographs, drawings, or anything else that illustrates the events you've listed.

When you're finished, share your time line with a partner. Have the two of you chosen similar events? Why are these events important to you?

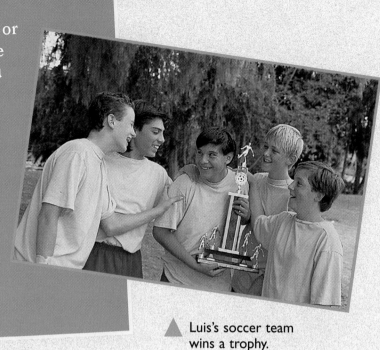

▲ Luis's soccer team wins a trophy.

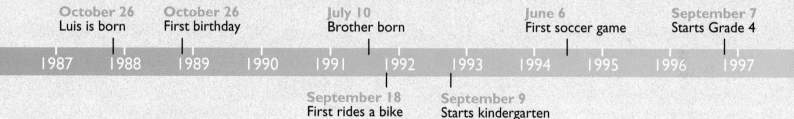

| October 26 Luis is born | October 26 First birthday | | July 10 Brother born | | June 6 First soccer game | September 7 Starts Grade 4 |

1987   1988   1989   1990   1991   1992   1993   1994   1995   1996   1997

September 18 First rides a bike   September 9 Starts kindergarten

◄ Many young people still remember when they first learned to read.

SKILL

POWER SEARCH *How many other time lines can you find in this book? What does the other time line in this chapter show?*

75

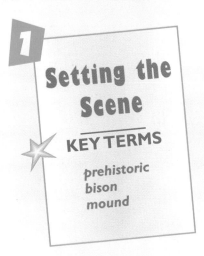

EARLY PEOPLE IN INDIANA

FOCUS *The first people in Indiana were hunters who came here thousands of years ago. Over time, their ways of living changed. Later, other groups of Native Americans moved into Indiana.*

A Land Bridge

Before the Ice Age, the Americas were a wilderness filled with trees, grasslands, and other plants and animals. Most archaeologists believe that no people lived there.

During the Ice Age, glaciers covered large parts of the earth. These glaciers held a lot of the oceans' water as ice. As a result, the water level of the oceans dropped by hundreds of feet. Some land that had been under water was uncovered.

One place where this happened was between eastern Asia and Alaska. The map on this page shows how uncovered land formed a "bridge" there. (Today, that land is covered by the shallow waters of the Bering Strait.)

People Arrive

Bands of hunters lived in eastern Asia. When animal herds wandered onto this new land bridge, some of these hunters probably followed them. Over time, they likely followed the animals onto the new continent. Archaeologists believe

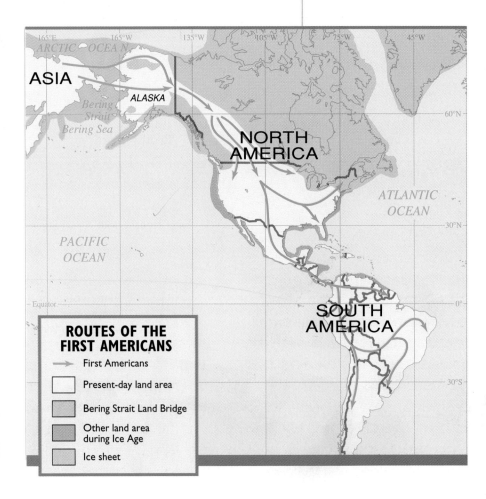

ROUTES OF THE FIRST AMERICANS

→ First Americans

Present-day land area

Bering Strait Land Bridge

Other land area during Ice Age

Ice sheet

ca. 11,000–8,000 B.C.
**Paleo-Indians
live in Indiana**

ca. 8,000–1,000 B.C.
**Archaic Indians
live in Indiana**

ca. 1,000 B.C.–A.D. 900
**Woodland Indians
live in Indiana**

ca. A.D. 900–A.D. 1600
**Mississippians
live in Indiana**

11,000 B.C.

7,000 B.C.

3,000 B.C.

1,000 A.D.

ca. 1680
Miamis settle
in Indiana

they were the first people in North America. They are called the Paleo-Indians (PAY lee oh IHN dee unz.)

No one is sure how long ago the Paleo-Indians came to North America. Many experts think they arrived between 12,000 and 20,000 years ago.

Following the Herds

On the new continent, the Paleo-Indians found many new plants and animals. Other animals, such as caribou (KAR uh boo), had come from Asia like the Paleo-Indians.

Gigantic animals that have now died out lived in North America during the Ice Age. Many were grazing animals, such as woolly mammoths. One kind of beaver grew as large as a modern bear!

The Paleo-Indians also met huge, dangerous creatures, like the saber-toothed tigers. Fortunately, these early people knew how to hunt for food and defend themselves.

Leaving Clues

The Paleo-Indians were **prehistoric**. They did not write about themselves. So how do we know anything about these people from long ago?

Archaeologists study clues left from the past. They use these clues to learn how prehistoric people lived. For example, they study evidence from ancient campsites to find out what foods they ate.

▲ Prehistoric people hunted the woolly mammoth.

prehistoric Of the time before written history

77

Artifacts—objects made by humans—also provide important clues. These objects tell us how skillful these people were, what tools they used, and even where they traveled. A grinding stone, for example, shows that they pounded nuts or seeds for food.

Even with such clues, our knowledge of these early prehistoric people is far from complete. Many items they used were made of wood. With time, these items decayed. So, many clues have been lost. Archaeologists can only guess about many parts of their lives.

Wandering Paleo-Indians

Over many centuries, the Paleo-Indians spread across the Americas. They broke up into different groups. Over time, they spoke different languages. They developed different ways of living.

These early people first came to what is now Indiana about 13,000 years ago. They didn't settle in one place. They camped where their prey grazed or drank. They may have returned to the same spots year after year.

Like other Paleo-Indians in North America, early people in Indiana probably hunted **bison**.

bison The American buffalo

Archaic Indians found wild hazelnuts, elderberries, mussels, opossums, and ducks.

They used long spears with stone points as their weapons. Paleo-Indians did not rely only on large animals for food. They probably gathered nuts and berries from the forests and shellfish from the rivers. They likely hunted small animals, too.

Archaic Indian Hunters and Gatherers

About 10,000 years ago, the Ice Age ended. Indiana's climate warmed up. New trees and plants took root. The huge Ice Age animals died out.

As the land changed, the prehistoric people found new ways of doing things. They still hunted and gathered berries and nuts. But many groups lived a more settled life. Archaeologists call the Native Americans of this time the Archaic (ahr KAY ihk) Indians.

Their population increased. Groups of Archaic Indians spread across Indiana. Many groups settled in valleys along the Wabash, Ohio, and White rivers. Some Archaic people may have had a main camp and used other small camps for hunting and gathering.

Archaic people also used slightly different kinds of spear points to hunt smaller forest animals. They caught fish with bone hooks and gathered mussels from streams.

Woodland Indian Farmers

About 3,000 years ago, people in southern Indiana began to plant corn, squash, and sunflowers. Growing food crops changed the way Native Americans lived. These early farmers are known as Woodland Indians.

The Woodland Indians had less trouble getting food. They didn't have to chase after their food, as the early hunters did. Instead, they settled in one spot.

Mississippian farmers dug with this stone tool.

The Woodland Indians were different from the Archaic people in other ways, too. They built special **mounds**—great piles of earth. Some mounds were for burying important people. Other, more mysterious mounds may have been meeting places for trade or ceremonies. Because of these earthworks, the Woodland Indians are sometimes called "Mounds Builders."

Mississippian Mounds Builders

Another group of American Indians, known today as Mississippians, also built mounds in Indiana. These mounds builders were probably newcomers who settled here about 1,000 years ago.

They lived in southwest Indiana and along the Ohio River. They are called Mississippians because they were so much like other groups living along the Mississippi River at the same time.

New Ways of Living

Mississippians differed from the Woodland people. They had several large towns. Some of their towns held a few thousand people.

Woodland people made pottery, like this jar.

INDIANA FACTS

Indiana's first recorded archaeological dig happened in 1898 in Posey County near the Wabash River.

mound A heap or bank of earth

NATIVE AMERICAN NATIONS OF INDIANA AROUND 1790

- Town
- Present-day boundaries

In Indiana their main settlement, now called Angel Mounds, was near present-day Evansville.

Mississippians hunted and grew many crops, including corn, beans, squash, and melon. They ate better than the Woodland Indians, because they had more tools—and perhaps better farming methods, too.

Mississippian mounds were also different. These mounds were flat-topped platforms. On top of the platforms sat important buildings.

The Next Migrations

Strange as it may seem, almost no Native Americans lived in Indiana during the 1500s. No one is sure why they left.

Starting around 1680, however, new groups migrated and settled in Indiana. They were attracted to Indiana's rich land, thick forests, and clear rivers. Their ways of living were different from those of Indiana's prehistoric residents.

The Potawatomis (paht uh WAHT uh meez), Miamis, Kickapoos, and others came from the Great Lakes region in Wisconsin and Michigan. The map at the left shows where they settled.

Others groups, such as the Delawares and Shawnees, migrated from the East. Settlers from Europe had taken up land there and were pushing westward. They forced Native Americans off their original lands. Some came to Indiana.

We have records about these Native Americans who migrated to Indiana. French traders and early settlers wrote about them.

Miamis and Potawatomis

The Miamis and the Potawatomis were Indiana's most important Native American groups. The

Weas (WEE ahz) and Piankashaws (pee AHNGK ah shahz) were related to the Miamis.

The Potawatomis settled in the northern part of present-day Indiana. The Miamis settled in the middle part. The main Miami settlement was Kekionga (kihk ee AHNG guh). The Miami tribal council met at this busy spot. Locate Kekionga on the map on page 80. Other Native American groups claimed areas south of the Miami and Potawatomi lands.

Many Similarities

The Miami and Potawatomi people lived in scattered villages. They had many things in common with each other—and with other Native Americans. Both groups farmed the land. Of all their crops, corn was the most important. They also hunted, fished, and gathered nuts and berries in the forests, rivers, and streams. They treated the land with care, and they used its resources wisely.

▲ Native Americans carved out trees to make dugout canoes.

SHOW WHAT YOU KNOW!

REFOCUS
COMPREHENSION

1. Name the four groups of prehistoric people who lived in Indiana.

2. What Native American groups lived in Indiana around 1700?

THINK ABOUT IT
CRITICAL THINKING

Compare the life of the Woodland Indians with that of the Mississippians.

WRITE ABOUT IT
ACTIVITY

In your Indiana journal, write about a day in the life of a group of Paleo-Indians.

CLUES TO THE PAST

FOCUS *Indiana's earliest residents left no written history. But archaeologists have been able to put together an idea of what their lives may have been like. They have used artifacts and other clues these ancient people left behind.*

Paleo-Indians

Archaeologists know that the first people in the Americas were hunters. They have learned this from studying many stone spear points made by the Paleo-Indians. Archaeologists use special equipment to figure out the age of these spear points.

They found that the spear points are sharp enough to pierce tough animal hides. They've discovered these weapons along with the bones of mastodons, elk, bears, mammoths, and other large animals. Finding these things together helped archaeologists determine that early people hunted for their food.

An **artisan** used tools of stone and bone to form the long, sharp point pictured on this page. Making grooved points from very simple tools took skill and practice.

▲ Paleo-Indians made spear points like this one to hunt for food.

This birdstone was found in western Indiana. ▼

Archaic Indians

Archaeologists think that the Archaic Indians probably traded goods. At Archaic campsites, they have found copper beads from Michigan. They have also found spear points made from stones found in faraway places.

Archaeologists think that the Archaic Indians probably traded for these beads and stones. They also believe that these Native Americans traded for birdstones. But they aren't sure what the birdstones, carved to look like birds' heads, were for.

Some Archaic Indians likely settled in one place—at least for a time. We know this from their garbage! Some groups built up mounds of shells from a favorite food—mussels. For this reason, these Archaic Indians are sometimes called "Shell Mounds Builders."

artisan A person who makes objects using great skill

This shard from a Woodland pot was discovered in central Indiana.

Woodland Indians

As centuries passed, Native Americans in Indiana learned new skills. The Woodland Indians had a steady food supply. Their way of living changed.

Archaeologists know this from studying artifacts, such as pottery and utensils, found in burial mounds. Making such items required new skills. These items also meant that the Woodland Indians had new things to make their lives easier.

The **shard** pictured above came from a pot that took a lot of time to make. Archaeologists believe that farming allowed more time for activities like making pots. Unlike earlier people, Woodland Indians didn't have to rely on hunting for food.

★ **shard** · A broken piece of pottery

Mississippians

Archaeologists tell us that Mississippians lived in large towns and had an organized government and religion. Archaeologists have learned this from studying the sites of Mississippian towns at Angel Mounds and other places.

Archaeologists can tell about how large these towns were, how many people lived there, and what kinds of buildings they had. They have discovered that some of the buildings were probably used for religious and government activities.

Archaeologists also know that skilled artisans lived in these towns. They have found jewelry, painted pottery, fine tools, bottles, and statues—like the one shown here—at the sites where Mississippian people once lived.

Archaeologists discovered this owl statue at Angel Mounds.

SHOW WHAT YOU KNOW!

REFOCUS
COMPREHENSION

1. Who were the "Shell Mounds Builders"?

2. What information did archaeologists learn about the Woodland Indians from studying their pottery?

THINK ABOUT IT
CRITICAL THINKING

How do the artifacts left by Mississippians differ from the artifacts left by the Archaic Indians?

WRITE ABOUT IT
ACTIVITY

Suppose you are the archaeologist who found the spear point shown on page 82. Write a description of your find.

83

INDIANA MOUNDS

FOCUS *Building mounds was important—for different reasons—to two groups of Native Americans in Indiana. The mounds that remain today are a source of interest and pride to people all over the state.*

The Mound Builders

The Woodland and Mississippian Indians built hundreds of mounds in Indiana. As you can see from the map on this page, there are mounds all over our state.

Indiana's mounds come in many sizes and shapes—round, square, rectangular, cone-shaped, u-shaped, guitar-shaped. Some mounds measure only six or seven feet across. Others are over a thousand feet across.

You can visit some of these mounds in parks. Others are on private property.

The mounds meant different things to the Woodland and Mississippian Indians. Woodland Indians built the mounds that are found in Mounds State Park. They probably held religious ceremonies at their mounds. At the park's circular Great Mound, prehistoric astronomers may have studied the sun and stars.

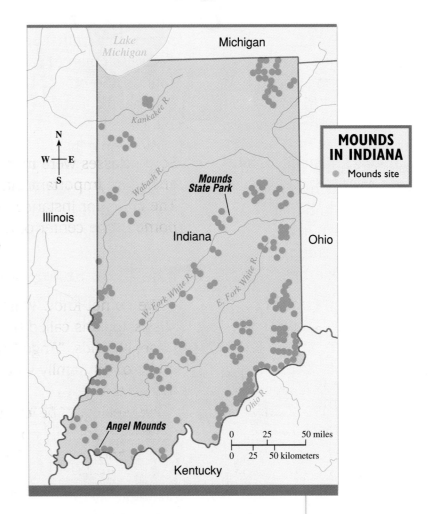

MOUNDS IN INDIANA
● Mounds site

The Mississippian mounds were large platforms. Their main purpose was to elevate important buildings. The largest Mississippian town was

at Angel Mounds, near the Ohio River. Other Mississippian villages were located in the Wabash and Ohio river valleys.

Mississippian Culture

For many years, teams of modern archaeologists have worked at Angel Mounds to piece together the story of the Mississippians. They have learned that the Mississippian culture—or way of life—was well developed.

Mississippians traded with other groups. Skilled craftspeople made beautiful objects. Farmers planted new crops and used new farming tools. Religion was also important.

Mississippian communities were divided into a few social classes. Some classes were more powerful and more important than others. The chief, for instance, had a large home in the center of town.

The Town at Angel Mounds

We do not know what the Mississippians called their town at Angel Mounds. "Angel" was the name of the family who later owned this land.

Archaeologists believe that the settlement held about 200 houses and nearly 1,000 people. Mississippians probably built it about 700 to 900 years ago.

Around the town was a thick stockade made of mud and sticks. It kept out their enemies and wild animals.

The mounds are now covered with grass.

The statue below was found at Angel Mounds.

⭐ **stockade** A wall of tall stakes built around a place for defense

85

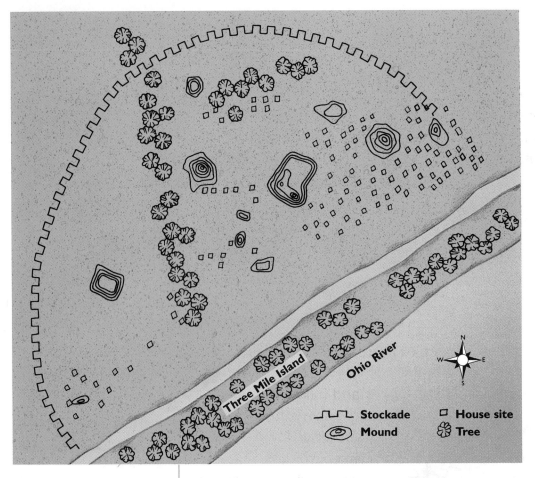

Stockade 〰   **House site** ▱

Mound ◎   **Tree** ✿

▲ This layout of Angel Mounds shows its stockade, mounds, and house sites.

Building a Giant Mound

To build the huge mound in the center of town, workers probably hauled thousands of baskets of dirt to the site. Mississippian chiefs must have been strong rulers to organize and carry out this job. They would have needed many people to get the task done.

Archaeologists think that the chief's house stood on top of this huge, central mound. Locate this mound on the map. When a chief died, his or her house was burned and another one was built on the same spot.

Life at Angel Mounds

At Angel Mounds, archaeologists have found darkened soil left by rotting posts, or poles, that the Mississippians used for building ordinary houses. Their summer houses had roofs but were open on all sides. In the winter, they lived in houses with four walls. The walls were made of sticks and mud. A hole in the roof let out smoke from a fire pit.

Like other Mississippian Indians, the people of Angel Mounds planted

Within the stockade were mounds and buildings, including houses.

At the town center was a huge, flat-topped mound with three different terraces, or levels. It was 44 feet high—taller than a three-story building! Its base measured 650 feet by 300 feet.

On top of a nearby mound was a temple. People were buried in this mound along with artifacts. Between these two large mounds was a big open plaza. People probably met here for public ceremonies and games.

corn, squash, and pumpkins. They gathered wild berries, grapes, and nuts from the forests. They also collected mussels from the Ohio River. Later, they used the mussel shells for bowls, scrapers, and jewelry. Nearby streams and forests supplied other foods, too, such as fish, deer, and turkey.

Protecting the Mounds

Today, you can visit the museum and reconstructed town at Angel Mounds. You can pass through

A Mississippian potter used his or her fingernails to create the design on this bowl found at Angel Mounds.

rebuilt houses that look much like Mississippian houses probably looked. You can see Mississippian fire pits. You can view the giant mounds and walk through the great temple. You can look out across the land where these Native Americans once hunted, farmed, and gathered food from the forests and streams.

Visiting a mound site brings you closer to the past. The state parks that hold the mounds are special places. They belong to all people. Therefore, when you visit the mounds, it's important to remember and follow this rule:

Take only photographs. Leave only footprints!

Keep in mind that, for many Native Americans, the mounds stand for the deep beliefs of their ancestors. To honor their **heritage**, visitors to the mounds should be quiet and respectful. They should follow the rules of the park. The mounds have been in Indiana for hundreds of years. It's up to all of us to make sure that they last far into the future.

⭐ **heritage** Something handed down from one's ancestors or the past

SHOW WHAT YOU KNOW!

REFOCUS
COMPREHENSION

1. What two groups of Native Americans built mounds?

2. What were some of the buildings at Angel Mounds?

THINK ABOUT IT
CRITICAL THINKING

What might Mississippian astronomers have learned from studying the sky and the stars?

WRITE ABOUT IT
ACTIVITY

Suppose you visited Angel Mounds. What would you expect to see? Write about it in your Indiana journal.

You Are There

⭐ **KEY TERMS**

wigwam
sapling

LIFE IN A MIAMI VILLAGE

FOCUS *The Miamis moved into northern and central Indiana in the late 1600s, settling along rivers. Turn the clock back 300 years to find out what everyday life was like for the largest Native American group in Indiana.*

▼ The Miamis lived in wigwams of saplings covered with bark.

Your Village

You are proud to be one of the Miami people. You also call yourselves the Twightwees (TWYE tweez) after the call of a bird. Another name you go by is the Beaver People, after an animal you hunt. You are the largest and most powerful Native American group in Indiana.

Your village stretches for nearly a mile beside a river.

It's not far from the main Miami settlement of Kekionga, in northern Indiana.

To go from village to village, you follow a narrow trail marked by cuts on the trees. To go on longer journeys or to travel a distance to trade, your people paddle dugout canoes on the rivers.

Actually, your people have more than one home. In the summer, you all live together in the village until crops are harvested. In the winter, only elders—the older people—remain. The rest of you go off in small groups to hunt and trap. In the forest, you set up hunting camps.

Your House

Because your land has thick forests, there is plenty of wood for building comfortable **wigwams**. Large families—parents, children, aunts, uncles, grandparents—share a home. Among the Miamis, women and girls, like yourself, build the wigwams.

⭐ **wigwam** A round, bark-covered house

To build a wigwam, you make the frame first. You use **saplings** that are about 2 inches wide. In a circle 16 to 20 feet across, you stick these saplings deep into the ground. You bend the saplings to make a rounded or cone-shaped frame and tie them at the top.

In the winter, you cover the frame with overlapping slabs of elm bark. This covering keeps out cold winds and keeps in warmth from your fire. Only the piece of bark at the top of the wigwam is not tied down. You can open it to let smoke from your fire escape.

In the summer, woven mats replace some of the bark. These mats, made from reeds or cattails, can be rolled up to let in cool air.

Time for Work

For women and girls in the village, summertime is when you plant a garden. You hoe the ground, drop in the seeds, and water the soil. As the summer goes on, the corn grows tall, and bean vines grow up the corn stalks. Bright yellow blossoms form on the squash and pumpkin

▲ This Miami skirt is made of wool, silver beads, and silk ribbon.

▼ These Miami moccasins were decorated with silk ribbon, glass beads, and porcupine quills.

vines. In the fall, you harvest your crops.

For boys, summer is the time for learning to hunt. Men and boys supply the village with meat from bear, deer, bison, and other forest animals. They also learn to catch wild ducks and fish. Women go along on the hunt to prepare the meat and skins.

Men and boys also practice to become brave and noble warriors. Your people are prepared to defend their hunting grounds!

To keep meat until winter, you hang up long strips that dry into jerky. This dried meat is good to eat. Sometimes you cook deer or buffalo meat with tasty wild onions. Or you grind corn into a fine meal to make flat cakes you bake on a hot stone.

When spring comes and sap is running in the maple trees, you collect it by tapping into the tree trunks. Then you boil the thin sap over the fire until it thickens. Squash cooked with maple sugar is delicious! Young girls also learn to weave bison fur into soft cloth and to treat animal

sapling A young tree

skins. They make the skins soft and clean for clothing and blankets. Buffalo skins make warm blankets, while deerskins make fine leggings and skirts. Some furs, especially beaver, are valuable for trade.

Trading for Goods

Men, who are traders, travel the swift rivers in dugout canoes. They trade with other villages. Miami men make these canoes. They hollow out and smooth tree trunks. Your cousins in a nearby village have told you about the French traders who come there to trade for furs. People in that village now use the goods they got from the French. Your mother's sister has an iron cooking pot. The heavy metal does not break easily like clay pots do. Somehow, though, the food cooked in that pot doesn't taste quite the way you like it. But you do like the beautiful trade beads on your cousin's clothes!

Time for Play

Of course, you don't work all the time. At the end of the day, your people gather around the fire. They dance to the sounds of drums and rattles. Later, as the moon rises, people tell stories.

▲ The Miami Indians grew corn, squash, and beans.

THE MIAMI MOONS

March
Ma-kon-sa Moon
Month of the Young Bear

April
An-da-kwa
Moon of the Crow

May
Tca-tca-qua Moon
The Sandhill Crane's Time

June
Wi-ko-wi
Whippoorwill's Moon

July
Pap-sa-ka-wi-pin-wi-ki
Midsummer Time

August
Ki-cin-gwi-a
Green Corn Time

September
Mi-ci-wi-a
Elk's Moon

October
Ca-ca-ka-yol-ia Moon
Grass Burns in Streaks

November
Ki-ol-i-a Moon
Smoky Burning Time

December
Ai-a-pan-sa
Young Buck Moon

January
Ai-a-pi-a
Full Grown Buck Time

February
Ma-qua
Bear Moon

Two important holidays bring feasts, dancing, and games. One holiday celebrates the harvest in the fall. The other comes when the men return from the winter hunt.

Love for the Earth

Everyone in your village understands how important the earth is to your lives. The elders pass on what they have learned about the importance of clean water and the many uses of plants.

Looking after each other is an important part of village life. Villagers help care for one another. They also share what they get from the earth with children and elders who can't care for themselves.

Some of your people have learned to make medicines from certain plants. They use these herbal medicines to help cure people who are sick.

The earth gives you plants and animals for food, shelter, and medicine. These things are

A modern Miami artist works with beads, following the traditional style.

important, not just to you but to all the people who will be born after you. You know that it is not wise to waste food or kill things you do not need. You want to be sure that future people in your village are able to enjoy the same rich life that you do.

SHOW WHAT YOU KNOW!

REFOCUS
COMPREHENSION

1. Name eight foods that the Miamis ate.

2. How did the Miamis travel long and short distances?

THINK ABOUT IT
CRITICAL THINKING

Why did life among the Miamis change from season to season?

WRITE ABOUT IT
ACTIVITY

Make a poster that illustrates and explains the steps for building a wigwam.

SUMMING UP

1 DO YOU REMEMBER . . .
COMPREHENSION

1. Where did the first people to live in Indiana come from?

2. Name three of the first crops grown by the Native Americans who lived in what is now Indiana.

3. Why do archaeologists think that Native Americans in Indiana traded goods with people from other places?

4. Briefly describe what Mississippian culture was like.

5. Name five skills that Miami women possessed.

2 SKILL POWER
READING A TIME LINE

The Skill Power lesson on page 74 shows a time line. It lists some events that took place in Indiana in the 1900s. Use encyclopedias and other history books to find three other events that happened in Indiana during those years. Put the events in the correct order on a time line of your own.

3 WHAT DO YOU THINK?
CRITICAL THINKING

1. How did growing food crops change the lives of Native Americans?

2. Why do you think Archaic Indians settled near rivers?

3. Why do archaeologists believe that Mississippian chiefs were strong rulers?

4. What evidence best supports the belief that the Mississippian culture was well developed?

5. What items were the Miami Indians able to make because they lived in a land of thick forests?

4 SAY IT, WRITE IT, USE IT
VOCABULARY

Suppose that you are the director of a historic Mississippian site. Create an advertisement that you might put in the newspaper to encourage people to visit. Use as many of the vocabulary terms as possible in your advertisement.

artisan	sapling
bison	shard
heritage	stockade
mound	wigwam
prehistoric	

5 GEOGRAPHY AND YOU

MAP STUDY

Use the map below to answer the following questions.

1. Where in Indiana is Angel Mounds located?

2. Near which river is Mounds State Park located?

3. Why were many of the mounds in Indiana built near rivers?

4. In which direction would you travel to get from Angel Mounds to Mounds State Park?

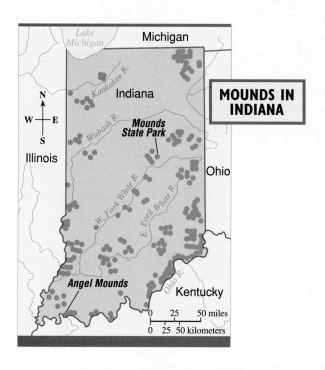

MOUNDS IN INDIANA

6 TAKE ACTION

CITIZENSHIP

As you read on page 87, we must honor the heritage of Native Americans when visiting a mound site. Think about the meaning of the word *heritage*. What buildings, traditions, or artifacts would you want to be preserved to show people in the future what life in your community was like? With a group of students, discuss ways to help preserve those items. Draw a plan that shows how you might preserve important parts of your community's heritage. Share your plan with the other students in your class.

7 GET CREATIVE

LANGUAGE ARTS CONNECTION

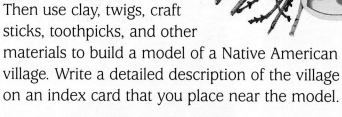

Do research in your library to find pictures of mounds and prehistoric American Indian villages in Indiana. Then use clay, twigs, craft sticks, toothpicks, and other materials to build a model of a Native American village. Write a detailed description of the village on an index card that you place near the model.

LOOKING AHEAD In the next chapter, find out about the exciting days that led up to the American Revolution.

EXPLORING AND

The resources and location of present-day Indiana drew newcomers from Europe. Who would own the land? Native Americans were there first. The French and English followed. After the American Revolution, American settlers claimed the land as their own.

CONTENTS

Find out on page 99
who used a paddle in
Indiana's early days.

SETTLING INDIANA

The following books give you information about people, places, and events of interest at the time of European settlement of Indiana. Read one that interests you and fill out a book-review form.

READ AND RESEARCH

Scholastic Atlas of Exploration by Dinah Starkey
(Scholastic, 1993)
Find out more about explorers in North America and other parts of the world. This book contains many interesting details about explorers and the cultures they encountered. *(nonfiction)*

The French in America by Virginia Brainard Kunz
(Lerner Publications, 1990)
French explorers were among the first Europeans to see North America. Learn more about the many French contributions to the United States and Canada. *(nonfiction)*

Brown Paper School USKids History: Book of the American Revolution by Howard Egger-Bovet and Marlene Smith-Baranzini, illustrated by Bill Sanchez (Little, Brown and Company, 1994)
This lively account of the Patriot revolt against the British contains stories, primary sources, cartoons, and speeches. *(nonfiction)*

Skill Power

Recognizing Fact and Opinion

Knowing the difference between a fact and an opinion can help you evaluate information that you hear and read.

UNDERSTAND IT

When you listen to people talk, watch television, or read books, you encounter facts and opinions. A fact can be proven true. For example, if you say that "A buffalo appears on the state seal of Indiana," you can prove your statement by showing a picture of the seal.

Opinions show how a person thinks or feels about something. Opinions cannot be proven, and people may have very different opinions about the same topic. For example, you might say, "I think the prettiest spot in Indiana is at the dunes." However, another person might say, "Indiana's prettiest spot is the Knobs of Brown County." Opinions may vary from one person to another. Facts do not vary from person to person.

EXPLORE IT

Look at the postcard below. Decide if the statement "Lake Monroe is the most beautiful lake in Indiana" is a fact or an opinion. First, ask yourself if you can prove the statement. Can you look for proof in an encyclopedia, an almanac, or your textbook? You will not be able to find proof of the statement because it is an opinion. Your opinion on the subject may be different from someone else's.

Now look at another statement about Lake Monroe. Is the statement "Lake Monroe is located southeast of Bloomington" a fact or an opinion? You may use the map on page 97 to prove this statement. The statement is a fact.

Lake Monroe
Indiana

TRY IT

Use the map on this page to help you decide whether the statements below are facts or opinions:

Lake Monroe is located in the Hoosier National Forest.

To reach Paynetown State Recreation Area, travel south from Bloomington.

The road around Lake Monroe is the most scenic route in Indiana.

There are two state recreation areas pictured on the map.

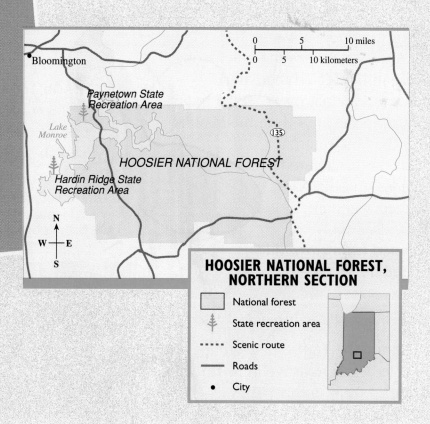

HOOSIER NATIONAL FOREST, NORTHERN SECTION

- National forest
- State recreation area
- ···· Scenic route
- —— Roads
- • City

SKILL POWER SEARCH As you read this chapter, list five interesting facts that you find.

1

Setting the Scene

★ **KEY TERMS**
colony
trading post
rebellion
proclamation
tax
treaty

TRADERS AND SETTLERS

FOCUS *In the 1600s the French and English arrived in Indiana. Each group used the land differently and had different relationships with Native Americans.*

Native Americans in 1650

For hundreds of years, Native Americans were the only people living in the region that later became Indiana. By 1650 the main groups in the area were the Miamis and the Potawatomis.

Living in scattered villages, these groups farmed and hunted. They used tools chipped from stone and traded among themselves.

◄ The Potawatomis in Indiana made spoons like this one.

Europeans Arrive

During the 1600s, new groups of people began to arrive in North America from Europe. They included the English, Spanish, and French. Some came looking for riches, land, or trade. Some hoped to find a route that would let them sail through North America to Asia. Many wanted more freedom than they had in Europe.

The British established their first permanent settlement in Jamestown, Virginia, in 1607. Soon they had 13 **colonies** on the east coast of North America. The Spanish settled in southern

▼ This painting by George Winter shows Native Americans on the Wabash River.

★ **colony** An area of land settled by people from a distant country and controlled by that country

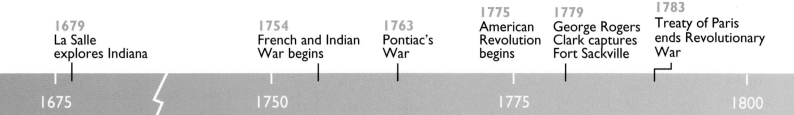

| 1679 La Salle explores Indiana | 1754 French and Indian War begins | 1763 Pontiac's War | 1775 American Revolution begins | 1779 George Rogers Clark captures Fort Sackville | 1783 Treaty of Paris ends Revolutionary War |

1675   1750   1775   1800

and western regions of the continent. You can see the lands claimed by the British and the Spanish on the map on this page.

La Salle in North America

At first the French settled in the region that is now Canada. Then in 1679 a group of French explorers traveled south by way of the Great Lakes. They were led by René-Robert Cavelier (kah vul YAY), who was known as La Salle. Sometimes canoeing and sometimes carrying their canoes, they reached the Mississippi River. Then they explored all the way to the Gulf of Mexico. La Salle claimed a large part of North America west of the Appalachian Mountains for France. You can see this claim on the map.

La Salle may have been the first European to set foot on the land that later became Indiana. He wanted to explore new lands and to

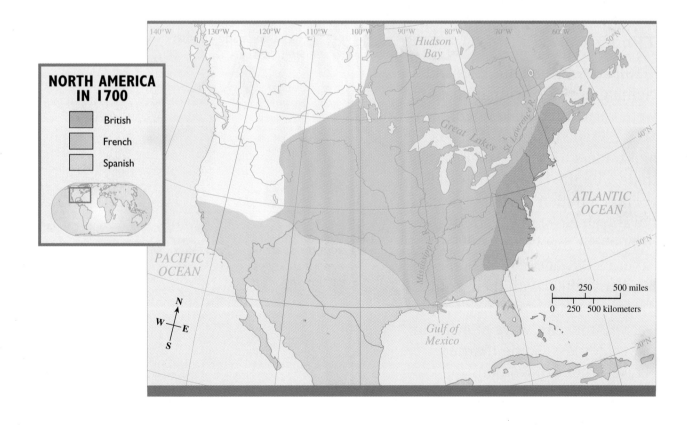

NORTH AMERICA IN 1700

- British
- French
- Spanish

plan for French settlement. He also hoped that the French could trade with the Native Americans who lived on these lands.

In the early 1680s La Salle met with the Native Americans and promised peace. The tree under which La Salle spoke was called the Council Oak. It stood in South Bend until 1991, when it was felled by storms.

With La Salle was Father Louis Hennepin (HEN uh-pihn), a Catholic priest who kept a diary of La Salle's journey. It includes the first known history written about Indiana.

The French

During this time, fur hats and clothing trimmed with animal fur were very fashionable in Europe. So the French sent fur trappers and traders to North America to trade with the Native Americans.

French traders, called *voyageurs* (vwah yah ZHUR), traveled throughout many parts of North America. Voyageurs and hunters lived peacefully with their Native American neighbors. They adopted Native American ways of living in the wilderness. Some married Native American women.

▲ French traders adopted Native American styles of clothing.

The Fur Trade

The French wanted beaver and raccoon furs from the Native Americans. In exchange they offered goods from Europe. Some of these goods are shown on the chart on page 101. They were exchanged at French **trading posts** scattered along the region's rivers and lakes.

To protect their trade from the British, the French built forts. In Indiana they built Fort Ouiatenon (wee AHT uh nahn), Fort Miami, and Fort Vincennes (vihn SENZ). The map on page 101 shows where these forts were located.

▼ Beaver skins were stretched on a rack and shipped to Europe to be made into hats.

⭐ **trading post** A store where goods are bought, sold, and traded

BRITISH AND FRENCH TRADE GOODS

Clothing and Jewelry	Tools and Weapons	Food and Supplies
shirts	scissors	kettles
coats	needles	grain
shoes	hoes	blankets
rings	shovels	salt
bells	guns	tea
beads	knives	dishes
leggings	axes	candles
hats	hatchets	pans
stockings	nails	spices
mirrors		

The French and Native Americans

At first, Native Americans welcomed the French and their European trade goods. But Native Americans soon came to depend too much on European trade.

Native American men now spent their time trapping animals and selling furs. Animals that they had once used for food began to disappear as more and more were killed for their skins. Some groups were forced to move away from their lands in search of food.

Native Americans also began to fight with one another over valuable trading areas. Diseases like smallpox, brought by the French and other Europeans, also killed many Native Americans.

The British and Native Americans

Native Americans fared even worse under the British than under the French. Like the French, the British traded with Native Americans for furs. But the British

FRENCH FORTS IN INDIANA

🏰 French forts
● Present-day cities
— Present-day boundaries

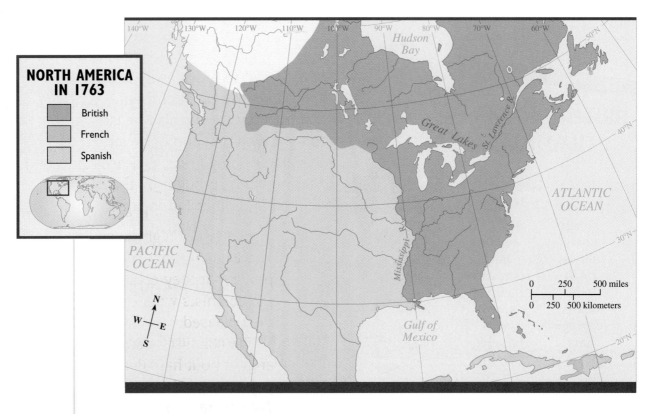

NORTH AMERICA IN 1763

- British
- French
- Spanish

British soldiers fought with the French over control of North American lands.

wanted more than just trade—they wanted to push Native Americans off the land. Unlike the French, the British wanted to settle on the land and build houses and farms.

The French and Indian War

British plans to settle in the Ohio Valley alarmed the French. In 1754 the two countries began fighting the French and Indian War. Most Native Americans sided with the French.

Despite American Indian help, the French lost the war in 1763. As a result, France lost

most of its claims in North America, including Canada and all lands east of the Mississippi. The map above shows European claims after the French and Indian War. Notice that Great Britain claimed the land that became Indiana.

Pontiac Goes to War

Even before the French and Indian War, Native Americans feared losing land to the British. During the 1760s a leader from the Ottawa nation named Pontiac tried to unite Native Americans against the British.

In 1763 Pontiac led a **rebellion**. He captured nine British forts. Two

⭐ **rebellion**   A fight or struggle against a government or authority

▲ Pontiac persuaded Native Americans to join in a war against the British.

of those forts were in Indiana—Forts Miami and Ouiatenon. But Pontiac faced great odds against the powerful British. He finally had to give up in defeat.

Native Americans did, however, win something from Pontiac's War. After so many years of war, the British were tired of fighting. So the British government issued a **proclamation**. The Proclamation of 1763 closed Native American lands to settlers. The Native Americans were pleased, but the settlers were not pleased at all.

The American Revolution

The French and Indian War left the British with a huge debt. To raise money to pay this debt, the British made the colonists pay high **taxes**. The British also wanted to prove that they could tax the colonists whenever they pleased.

The colonists were angry about having to pay taxes to the British. They were also angry about the Proclamation of 1763. Many wanted to declare their independence from Great Britain.

War broke out between Great Britain and the colonies in 1775. The fighting reached Indiana in 1779. The most important American in the battle for the West was George Rogers Clark.

In 1779 Clark captured Fort Sackville, the British name for Fort Vincennes. His victory helped the Americans claim the Ohio Valley—including Indiana—as their own.

The war ended in 1781. In 1783 the **Treaty** of Paris declared freedom for the American colonists. The United States was an independent nation at last!

 proclamation An official announcement

 tax Money paid to the government
treaty An agreement between nations

THE REVOLUTIONARY SPIRIT

FOCUS *George Rogers Clark fought the Revolution in the West. In the 13 colonies, other important events took place in the battle for independence.*

BOSTON TEA PARTY

The British forced the American colonists to buy their tea. They also added a tax on tea. The people of Boston, Massachusetts, were angry.

In 1773 a group of Boston citizens dressed in costumes sneaked onto British ships. They tossed 342 big boxes of tea into the sea. This event came to be known as the Boston Tea Party.

PAUL REVERE'S RIDE

On the night of April 18, 1775, Bostonian Paul Revere quietly crossed the Charles River to Charlestown, Massachusetts, where he began his famous horseback ride. He needed to warn colonists that British soldiers were marching toward Concord.

Paul Revere and another messenger, William Dawes, rode different routes to Lexington, a town near Concord. They got word to colonists that the British were coming.

When the British arrived in Lexington, townspeople waited for them. Shots were fired. The American Revolution had begun!

THE DECLARATION OF INDEPENDENCE

As the war continued, a committee was formed to write a Declaration of Independence. Thomas Jefferson was asked to be its author.

The Declaration stated that the colonies were "free and independent states." On July 4, 1776, the Continental Congress, meeting in Philadelphia, Pennyslvania, adopted the document.

1773
Boston
Tea Party

1775
Paul Revere's ride
signals the beginning
of the Revolution

1776
Declaration of
Independence
is signed

1777
Washington's troops
settle in for winter
at Valley Forge

1781
British surrender
at Yorktown

1773   1775   1777   1779   1781

WASHINGTON AT VALLEY FORGE

In 1777 General George Washington and his troops settled in for the winter at Valley Forge, Pennsylvania. The winter was bitterly cold, and the temperature often fell below zero. Most soldiers had no shoes or warm clothing.

Day after day, the food was the same. Breakfast, lunch, and dinner was a thick paste made of flour and water cooked over an open fire. The soldiers called it "fire cake." Many soldiers grew sick and many died of disease.

SURRENDER AT YORKTOWN

In 1781 British General Charles Cornwallis moved his army to Yorktown, near the York River in Virginia. Helped by the French, American forces attacked the British at Yorktown on both land and water. They trapped British General Charles Cornwallis and his army and blocked their escape routes. Cornwallis was forced to surrender.

The Battle of Yorktown led to the end of the war. A peace pact ending the war was signed two years later in Paris, France. Then the American colonies were officially free.

REFOCUS
COMPREHENSION

1. What was the Boston Tea Party?

2. What was the importance of the Battle of Yorktown?

THINK ABOUT IT
CRITICAL THINKING

Why is July 4, 1776, considered the birthday of the United States?

WRITE ABOUT IT
ACTIVITY

In your Indiana journal, describe how you might have felt as a colonist first hearing that the Revolution had begun.

GEORGE ROGERS CLARK

FOCUS *George Rogers Clark is one of Indiana's best-known heroes. During the American Revolution, he led a daring capture of a key British fort for the Americans.*

Clark Goes West

As a small boy in Virginia, George Rogers Clark dreamed of going west of the Appalachian Mountains. His grandfather taught him to be a surveyor—a person who measures land. This was a good skill to have in the colonies. Land had to be measured and marked before settlers could claim it.

Despite British rules against settlement west of the Appalachian Mountains, many colonists traveled there anyway in search of land and adventure. At age 19, the tall, young George Rogers Clark went west to the Ohio Valley. There he surveyed the land and learned how to live in the wilderness. He also learned about the growing conflict between the British and the Americans.

▲ This portrait of Clark was painted after the American Revolution.

Henry Hamilton Arrives in the West

At the same time that Clark went to the Ohio Valley, British General Henry Hamilton traveled west to command the British forts there. Fort Detroit was a large fort located on Lake Erie. Fort Vincennes, located in present-day Indiana, was a small fort with very few soldiers.

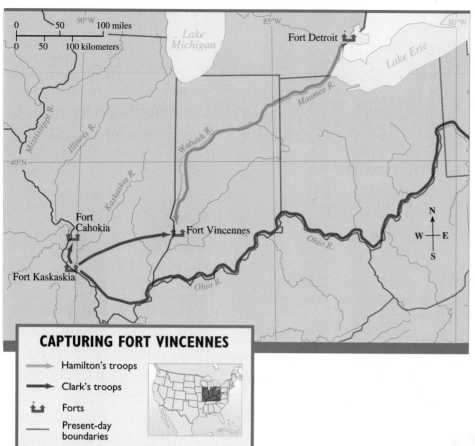

CAPTURING FORT VINCENNES

→ Hamilton's troops
→ Clark's troops
⛫ Forts
— Present-day boundaries

the governor. Governor Henry believed in Clark and gave orders for Clark to receive soldiers and supplies. Clark returned to the West with 175 soldiers.

In June 1778, Clark's small army set out to capture Forts Vincennes, Cahokia, and Kaskaskia. British soldiers at these forts were so surprised that they **surrendered** after firing only a few shots.

Hamilton Hears the News

At Fort Detroit, British General Hamilton heard the news that Clark had captured the three forts. He could hardly believe what this small band had done!

During the winter, Hamilton recaptured the forts. He reached Fort Vincennes in 1778 and took it for the British. He renamed it Fort Sackville. He did not plan to fight again until good weather returned in the spring, so he sent many of his soldiers home for the winter.

Now Clark needed to make a decision. Should he march his soldiers across icy, flooded land between Forts Kaskaskia and Sackville and surprise Hamilton? Or should he wait until the weather improved in the spring when travel would be easier?

Forts Kaskaskia (kas KAS kee uh) and Cahokia (kuh HOH kee uh) were located in the region that would later become Illinois. These forts were also small and had few soldiers to guard them. You can find these forts on the map above.

Clark Attacks

When the American Revolution started, Clark was sure that winning the West was the key to winning the war. Luckily, Clark had powerful friends such as Governor Patrick Henry of Virginia. Clark went to Virginia to share his opinion with

▲ Clark used a measuring chain and compass to conduct his surveys.

 surrender To give up

107

The March to Fort Sackville

Clark decided that he had to march to Fort Sackville right away, when no one would expect an attack. His small band trudged on day after day, for 240 miles. They had no tents and very little food. Sometimes the flood waters reached all the way to the neck of the tallest soldier.

At last Clark reached Fort Sackville. He had only about 130 weak, tired, and hungry men. They had little gunpowder. But Clark had a plan. He led his soldiers to a spot behind the hills close to Fort Sackville. Then Clark had his soldiers march back and forth carrying many banners. Only the banners could be seen from the fort. The British were fooled into thinking that Clark's army numbered 650 or 700 men!

Clark's soldiers held their weapons above the flood waters.

Clark Takes the Fort

Clark then had his soldiers sneak up close to the fort walls. The British soldiers opened their gunports—small doors in front of the cannons. When the cannons boomed, the cannon balls sailed over the heads of Clark's soldiers. Then the Americans shot their rifles through the gunports into the fort.

Clark demanded that Hamilton surrender the fort. Hamilton refused. Clark demanded surrender again. Finally, on February 25, 1779, Hamilton and his soldiers marched out of the fort under a white flag of surrender. Picture their surprise when they saw that they had been defeated by such a small, ragged army!

Clark's bravery helped the American colonists defeat the British in the Ohio Valley. The colonists could now claim the land that would later become the states of Ohio, Illinois, Wisconsin, Michigan, and Indiana. The Americans could settle in the West.

▲ This painting shows Hamilton's surrender to Clark.

Honoring a Leader

Today the George Rogers Clark Memorial honors the man who helped win the West. It stands in Vincennes on the spot where the fort was once located. Paintings inside the Memorial tell the story of the capture of Fort Sackville.

Clark had spent his own money and borrowed money from friends to win the West. Virginia gave him only a sword and land in southern Indiana for his service. Clark and his soldiers settled on the land and started the town of Clarksville on the Ohio River.

George Rogers Clark School, Clark Boulevard, and Clark Bridge in Clarksville are named for Clark. Many other places in Indiana also bear his name.

Residents of Vincennes celebrate the surrender of Fort Sackville every year. They also honor Clark by celebrating his birthday each year in November.

▼ Clark's statue stands in Vincennes.

SHOW WHAT YOU KNOW!

REFOCUS
COMPREHENSION

1. Why did Clark first go West?

2. Why did Clark attack Fort Sackville in the winter?

THINK ABOUT IT
CRITICAL THINKING

What might have happened if Clark had failed to capture Fort Sackville?

WRITE ABOUT IT
ACTIVITY

Write an entry in your Indiana journal in which you describe what it was like to march with Clark to Fort Sackville.

Map Adventure

Exploring With La Salle

FOCUS *La Salle traveled from the Great Lakes down the Mississippi River to the Gulf of Mexico. An important part of his journey involved finding an overland route between the St. Joseph and Kankakee rivers in Indiana.*

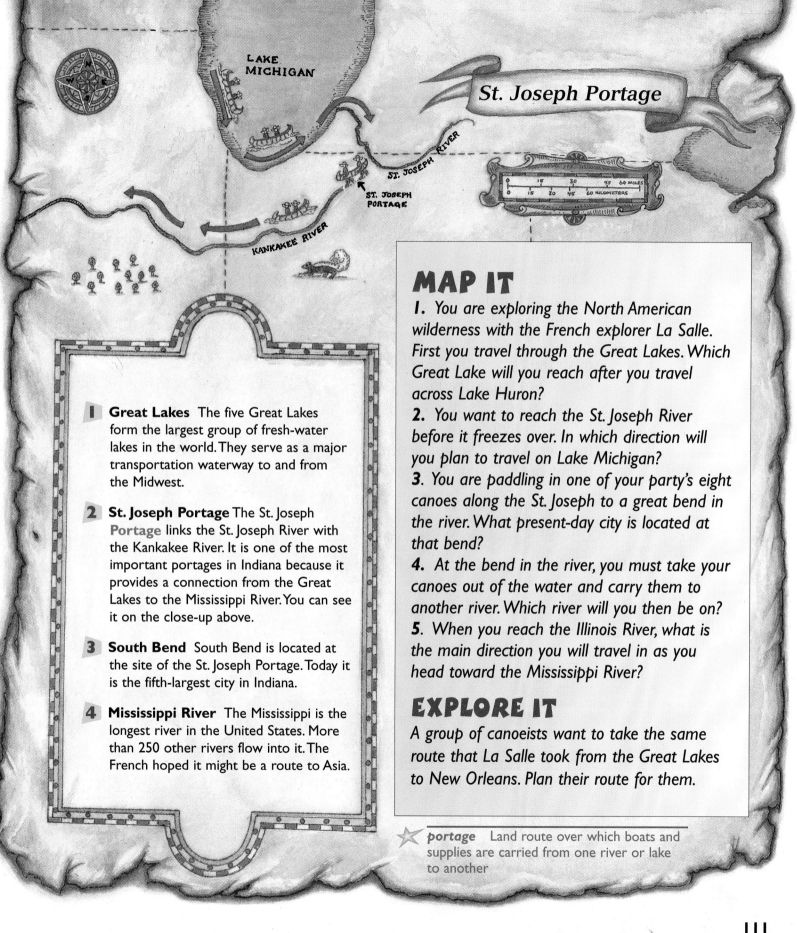

LAKE MICHIGAN

ST. JOSEPH RIVER

ST. JOSEPH PORTAGE

KANKAKEE RIVER

St. Joseph Portage

0 15 30 45 60 MILES
0 15 30 45 60 KILOMETERS

1 **Great Lakes** The five Great Lakes form the largest group of fresh-water lakes in the world. They serve as a major transportation waterway to and from the Midwest.

2 **St. Joseph Portage** The St. Joseph Portage links the St. Joseph River with the Kankakee River. It is one of the most important portages in Indiana because it provides a connection from the Great Lakes to the Mississippi River. You can see it on the close-up above.

3 **South Bend** South Bend is located at the site of the St. Joseph Portage. Today it is the fifth-largest city in Indiana.

4 **Mississippi River** The Mississippi is the longest river in the United States. More than 250 other rivers flow into it. The French hoped it might be a route to Asia.

MAP IT

1. You are exploring the North American wilderness with the French explorer La Salle. First you travel through the Great Lakes. Which Great Lake will you reach after you travel across Lake Huron?
2. You want to reach the St. Joseph River before it freezes over. In which direction will you plan to travel on Lake Michigan?
3. You are paddling in one of your party's eight canoes along the St. Joseph to a great bend in the river. What present-day city is located at that bend?
4. At the bend in the river, you must take your canoes out of the water and carry them to another river. Which river will you then be on?
5. When you reach the Illinois River, what is the main direction you will travel in as you head toward the Mississippi River?

EXPLORE IT

A group of canoeists want to take the same route that La Salle took from the Great Lakes to New Orleans. Plan their route for them.

⭐ **portage** Land route over which boats and supplies are carried from one river or lake to another

111

LIFE AT A FRENCH FORT

FOCUS *What would it have been like to live at a French fort? Your days would be filled with preparing food, visiting your friends, and celebrating.*

Life at the Fort

In the morning you wake up early. You are happy that you will be spending the day with your Wea friend, Pac-kah. The Wea are Native Americans who live across the river from the fort. In the Wea language, *pac-kah* means "beautiful."

Your mother is Wea and your father is French. Your mother teaches you the language and skills of her people. You have learned to prepare animal skins for clothing and **moccasins**. You help cook strips of deer meat over the open fire so that they have a pleasant, smoky flavor. You know where to hunt for berries and nuts to store for the long winter ahead.

You are looking forward to the voyageurs coming home soon. Your father is a voyageur who has been away trading for six months. You can't wait to see him!

Gathering Food

Frost is near and you must gather vegetables from the garden. Today Pac-kah will help you carry the pumpkins, squash, and potatoes to the **root cellar** for storage. You will also collect the last herbs and ears of corn.

Your mother gathers herbs for teas, seasonings, and medicines. She will hang the herbs and corn to dry. You will share with Pac-kah. You also hope to exchange dried herbs with the voyageurs for the beads and cloth you asked them to bring home for you.

▼ Voyageurs return from a trading journey.

★ *moccasin*   A shoe made of soft leather
root cellar   An underground storage room

Forts were protected by a high fence, called a stockade.

Inside the Fort

On most days you walk by the tall stockade of the fort and through the wide gates. Inside, you pass the well where your family gets its water. You wave to the blacksmith making horseshoes. At the far end of the fort, you see the row of houses where soldiers and their families live.

This morning you help bake bread in the outdoor oven inside the fort. This is one of your favorite jobs. You watch your mother mix the wheat flour and shape the loaves. How good this bread will taste after eating so much corn bread each day!

You also help make your father's favorite molasses cookies. Just as the eight-pound bread loaves come out of the oven, you place the pan of cookies inside. Your mouth waters as you smell the odors from the oven!

Finally, you fill a large iron pot with potatoes, beans, water, and deer meat. The stew will cook for many hours. Tomorrow everyone living near the fort will celebrate the harvest with the Feast of the Hunter's Moon. You hope that the voyageurs will arrive in time to celebrate, too.

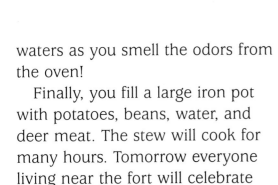
On feast days, settlers made stews in large pots.

Life With the Wea

Sometimes you paddle your birch canoe across the river to visit the Wea village. You are welcomed into Pac-kah's large wigwam. It is built of bent saplings covered with bark. Several family members have sleeping benches around the room.

The center fire pit is a good place for sharing food and stories. The Wea gardens and platforms for drying meat look like those of the French. After all, the Wea taught the French settlers how to grow and prepare food.

They Are Coming!

At noon you dash outside at the sound of a rifle. A soldier shouts, "They are coming! The voyageurs are coming!" Soon six long, slender canoes glide ashore. You race toward Papa. He looks grand in his **buckskins** and beaver hat.

From his pack, Papa pulls out a hunting knife for your brother, Pierre. He gives fine cloth to your mother. To you he gives a silver necklace.

You know that the other items— weapons, gunpowder, jewelry, and food—will be

⭐ **buckskins** Deerskin clothing

These people celebrate the Feast of the Hunter's Moon with traditional crafts.

traded for more beaver and raccoon skins from the Wea.

Soon Papa will be leaving for another voyage to the West or the North. But for tonight, you are happy to celebrate the return of Papa and the other voyageurs.

Feast of the Hunter's Moon

Early in the evening, the Wea cross the river with deer meat for roasting. The French settlers bring onions, carrots, and potatoes from their root cellars to make a delicious stew. The voyageurs share their gifts from their long travels.

And not a crumb of your molasses cookies is left over from the Feast of the Hunter's Moon!

Later that night you write about the day's many events in your diary. The last flames of your candle have already begun to flicker. Outside, the music and dancing can still be heard. You are glad that the French and Wea are such good friends and enjoy having so many wonderful feasts.

SHOW WHAT YOU KNOW!

REFOCUS
COMPREHENSION

1. Name three foods that people living in a French fort might have eaten.

2. What skills did the Wea teach the French?

THINK ABOUT IT
CRITICAL THINKING

How might life have been different for the French if they had not been friendly with the Wea?

WRITE ABOUT IT
ACTIVITY

Write an entry in your Indiana journal describing what you see in the French fort on page 113.

SUMMING UP

1 DO YOU REMEMBER . . .
COMPREHENSION

1. What was the result of the French and Indian War for the French?

2. How did George Rogers Clark fool the British into thinking his army was large?

3. What were the beginning and ending points of La Salle's 1679 journey?

4. List four items that the voyageurs traded.

5. Why was the winter at Valley Forge difficult for General Washington and his troops?

2 SKILL POWER
RECOGNIZING FACT AND OPINION

Use the picture on page 112 to help you decide whether the statements below are fact or opinion.

1. Some Native Americans lived in wigwams on the banks of rivers.

2. The voyageurs were the smartest of the French settlers.

3. The land near the Native American villages was the most beautiful in all of Indiana.

4. The voyageurs used rivers to travel to and from Native American villages.

3 WHAT DO YOU THINK?
CRITICAL THINKING

1. How did French fur trapping and trading affect Native Americans' lives?

2. How might Native Americans have felt about the surveying work of George Rogers Clark?

3. Why is the portage joining the Mississippi River with the Great Lakes important?

4. How might life in Indiana have been different if the British held Fort Sackville and Fort Vincennes?

5. Why did British General Cornwallis surrender at Yorktown?

4 SAY IT, WRITE IT, USE IT
VOCABULARY

Write a children's story that tells about the settlers in Indiana and the struggles among the Native Americans, the French, and the British. Use as many of the vocabulary terms as you can. Illustrate your story.

buckskins	root cellar
colony	surrender
moccasin	tax
portage	trading post
proclamation	treaty
rebellion	

CHAPTER 5

5 GEOGRAPHY AND YOU
MAP STUDY

1. What present-day city grew up near old Fort Ouiatenon?

2. In what direction would you travel from Fort Miami to reach Fort Vincennes?

3. Which French fort was located on the present-day border between Indiana and Illinois?

4. Which French forts are located on a river? Why do you think this is the case?

FRENCH FORTS
- French forts
- Present-day cities
- Present-day boundaries

6 TAKE ACTION
CITIZENSHIP

Starting a new life in a new place can be difficult. In this chapter you learned how the Native Americans got along with the French in North America. Discuss ways in which you welcome newcomers to your school or community. Interview a newcomer. Share what you learned with a group of your classmates. Make a list of helpful things that you do. Then see if you can think of other ways to help new members of your community feel welcome and become involved in community life.

7 GET CREATIVE
LANGUAGE ARTS CONNECTION

In 1863 the poet Henry Wadsworth Longfellow published the poem "Paul Revere's Ride." Find this poem in the library and read it. Then write your own poem about Indiana hero George Rogers Clark and his daring adventures during the American Revolution.

LOOKING AHEAD

In the next chapter, learn about the steps Indiana took to become a state.

CHAPTER 6

THE BIRTH

After the American Revolution, settlers began streaming west. Their push westward made Native Americans fear—and then fight—for their way of life. By 1816, Indiana was at peace, and it had become the nation's nineteenth state.

▼ Read pages 134–135 to find out when Indiana was ready to become a state.

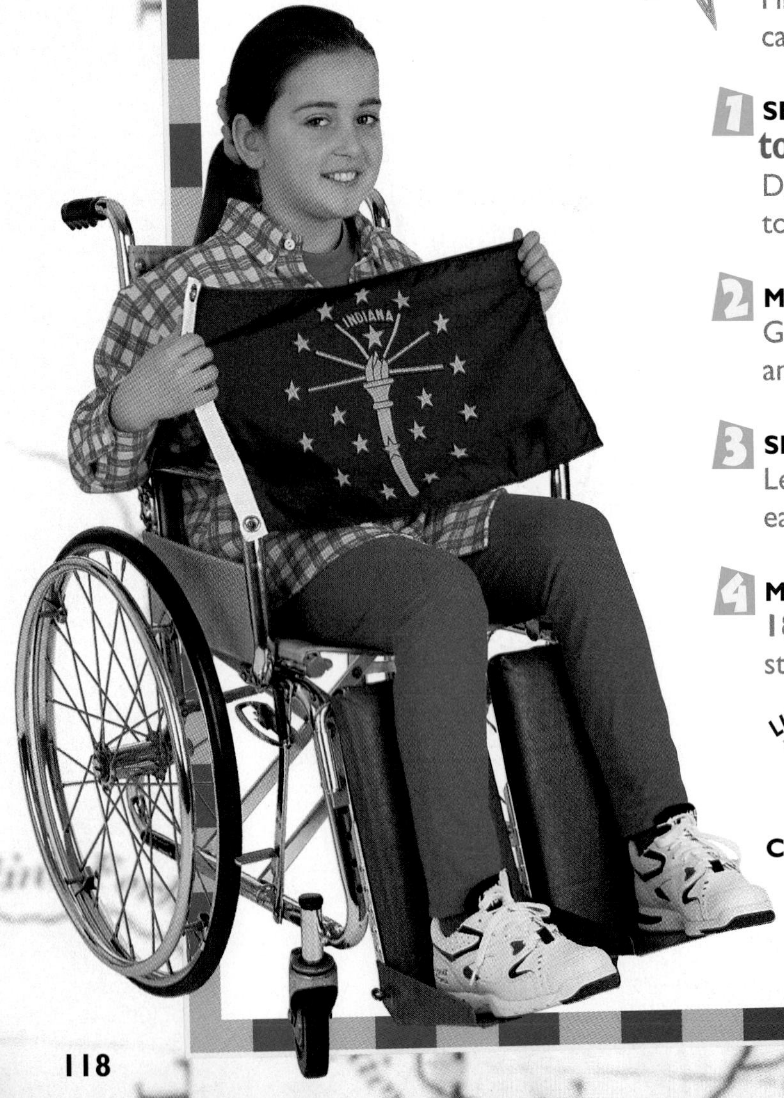

CONTENTS

OF A STATE

The following books give you more information about some of the people, places, and events in the history of the Indiana Territory. Read one that interests you and fill out a book-review form.

READ AND RESEARCH

The Floating House by Scott Russell Sanders
(Macmillan, 1995)

Join the McClure family on a flatboat as they travel to Jeffersonville, Indiana, the site of their new home. *(fiction)*
• *You can read a selection from this book on page 136.*

In a Circle Long Ago: A Treasury of Native Lore from North America by Nancy Van Laan
(Apple Soup Books, 1995)

This beautifully illustrated book contains stories, poems, and proverbs that show similarities and differences among Native American groups. *(fiction)*

Tecumseh and the Dream of an American Indian Nation by Russell Shorto
(Silver Burdett Press, 1989)

Learn more about the great Shawnee leader Tecumseh and his efforts to unite the Native Americans of the Northwest Territory. *(nonfiction)*

Skill POWER

Understanding Cause and Effect

Finding connections between cause and effect helps you understand why and how things happen.

UNDERSTAND IT

Have you ever heard about an earthquake on the news? If you have, you know what can happen. Buildings, houses, and trees can break or fall to the ground. The earthquake and the damage have a cause-and-effect relationship. One thing (the earthquake) causes another thing (the damage) to happen.

EXPLORE IT

By asking yourself what happened (the effect) and why it happened (the cause), you can better understand what you read. Watch for words such as *because, therefore, so,* and *as a result.* These words may be clues that there are cause-and-effect relationships in what you are reading.

Use what you know about cause and effect to understand the paragraph below. Then answer the questions.

After the French and Indian War, the British controlled the land of the Ohio Valley. Native Americans feared that many British settlers would soon move into their lands. The great Ottawa leader Pontiac believed that Native Americans had to take a stand to save their lands from the British. So he worked to unite his people.

• What clue words did you find to tell you that there were cause-and-effect relationships?

• What caused Pontiac to try to unite his people?

◀ An earthquake in Northridge, California (cause), made this parking garage collapse (effect).

With a group of your classmates, try playing the Cause-and-Effect Game. In one sentence, write down a funny or an interesting event that has happened to you. Read the sentence to your group. Ask the group to guess the cause of your event. Could the event have more than one cause?

THE CAUSE AND EFFECT GAME

I practiced the saxophone.

I made the band.

oops...

I left my homework at home.

grrrr

My dog ate it.

hmmm...

I studied hard for my test.

I got an A!

Cynthia slept late (cause), so she missed the school bus (effect).

SKILL POWER SEARCH Pick a few paragraphs in this chapter. What cause-and-effect relationships can you find in them?

Setting the Scene

★ **KEY TERMS**

territory
legislature
ordinance
civil rights
confederacy
constitution

FROM TERRITORY TO STATEHOOD

FOCUS *Find out how the settlement of the Northwest Territory led first to conflict between settlers and Native Americans—and later to statehood.*

A New Territory

The American Revolution added a giant chunk of land to the new nation. Under the Treaty of Paris, the United States gained control of the **territory** east of the Mississippi River. You can see on the map the area known as the Northwest Territory. Present-day Indiana was part of that territory.

Many Americans were eager to settle in this territory. But the United States had to find a way to sell the land and to govern it. After the war, the United States set up a new government. The **legislature** was called Congress.

Congress passed several land **ordinances** (ORD un uns ihz) and acts. These ordinances spelled out the rules for how people could buy land and how the territory would be governed. The most important was the Northwest Ordinance of 1787.

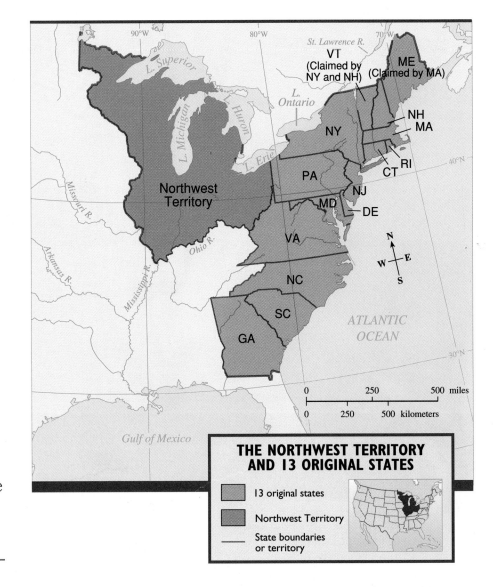

THE NORTHWEST TERRITORY AND 13 ORIGINAL STATES

- 13 original states
- Northwest Territory
- State boundaries or territory

★ **territory** Land ruled by a nation or state
legislature A group that makes laws
ordinance An official order or rule

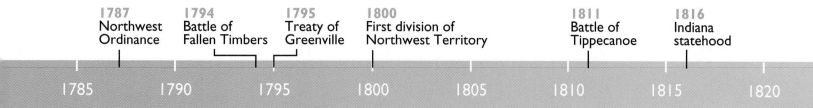

| 1787 | 1794 | 1795 | 1800 | | 1811 | 1816 |
| Northwest Ordinance | Battle of Fallen Timbers | Treaty of Greenville | First division of Northwest Territory | | Battle of Tippecanoe | Indiana statehood |

1785　　1790　　1795　　1800　　1805　　1810　　1815　　1820

The Northwest Ordinance set up rules for creating states from the territory. It guaranteed American settlers their civil rights. It also prohibited slavery in the territory.

New Settlements and Forts

Settlers slowly moved into the territory. They were attracted by the cheap price of land, the rich soil, and the opportunity for a new life in the West.

The first Indiana towns sprouted along rivers—the Ohio, the Wabash, and the Whitewater. There was a sprinkling of forts, too. These forts offered the settlers little protection.

Clash of Cultures

In 1800, Native Americans still held most of the land north of the Ohio River. To them, the Treaty of Paris meant nothing. The land had never belonged to the British or the French. And it didn't belong to the Americans now. It was Native American land—and always had been. For hundreds of years, they had hunted and farmed this land.

★ *civil rights*　The rights of all citizens to life, liberty, property, and equal protection under the law

Settlers believed that one person could own a piece of land. But Native Americans felt that the land belonged to all people. It was everyone's to use for food, water, clothing, and shelter. This difference between Native Americans and settlers would cause conflicts in years to come.

▼ Settlers cut down forests and fenced off land on their new farms.

123

Native Americans Take a Stand

Native Americans were determined to keep the settlers from moving deeper into the land. At first, they had been friendly to the pioneers. But, in time, their attitude changed. Clearly, these newcomers wanted to own the land, not to share it.

American Indians needed to protect their way of life. As a result, they sent out war parties and raided pioneer settlements. The settlers, in turn, called on the national government for help.

The Battle of Fallen Timbers marked the end of the Miamis' fight against the settlers.

The Miamis Lead the Way

The most important group in the area was the Miamis. The Miamis joined other groups in a **confederacy**. Under Chief Little Turtle, the Miami Confederacy tried to stop the settlers from taking over more of its land.

The United States government responded by sending forces to fight the confederacy. Starting in 1787, they attacked Miami villages and burned their cornfields.

Over the next eight years, the Americans fought several battles with the confederacy. The United States sent thousands of troops to fight. Their leader was General Anthony Wayne.

The Battle of Fallen Timbers

On August 20, 1794, the Miami Confederacy made its last stand near what is now Toledo, Ohio, in a spot where a tornado had passed. Fallen trees were all over the ground. Outnumbered, the Native Americans fought bravely for three hours. Finally, they were defeated.

---

confederacy A union of people, groups, or states united for a certain purpose

124

▲ Chief Little Turtle and General Anthony Wayne meet after the Battle of Fallen Timbers.

Soon afterward, General Wayne built a new fort near Kekionga, the great Miami village. He meant to send the confederacy a message that the United States Army was not leaving. Wayne's fort later became the city of Fort Wayne.

Following their defeat at Fallen Timbers, members of the Miami Confederacy signed the Treaty of Greenville on August 3, 1795. They were forced to give up most of their land in what is now Ohio and southeastern Indiana. They also agreed to leave the settlers in peace.

▼ A copy of the Treaty of Greenville

The Indiana Territory

By 1800, so many people had moved into the Northwest Territory that it was cut into smaller parts. One part was still called the Northwest Territory. The other part was called the Indiana Territory. It was a large area that included the present-day state of Indiana.

The governor of the new Indiana Territory was 27-year-old William Henry Harrison. He set out to buy more land from the Native Americans. Using threats, he succeeded in getting them to turn over the lower third of what is now Indiana and most of Illinois.

125

![Portrait of Tecumseh]

Tecumseh was "a bold, active, sensible man, daring in the extreme," according to Harrison.

This compass was a gift to Tecumseh from a British general.

To Tecumseh from "Brock" Aug. 1812

Two Shawnee Heroes

For several years after the Treaty of Greenville, Native Americans did not resist the settlers. However, they continued to be pushed from their homes and off their land.

At that time, two leaders appeared on the scene. One was Tenskwatawa (ten SKWAH tah wah), also known as "the Shawnee Prophet." He called for all Native Americans to give up the ways of settlers and to return to their old ways.

The Prophet's brother, Tecumseh (te KUM se), was a great political leader. He planned to unite all the Native American groups in the territories. He hoped that the United States might deal fairly with a strong, united people.

Together these brothers offered a message of hope to American Indians. However, the settlers began to worry about raids again.

Harrison and Tippecanoe

Governor Harrison met several times with Tecumseh. He warned Tecumseh that the United States would send more and more Americans to fight against his people. But Tecumseh didn't give in. The Shawnee leader set out to get the support of more Native American groups.

On November 7, 1811, while Tecumseh was away, Harrison marched on Prophetstown. This village was located on the Tippecanoe River. Warriors attacked Harrison's forces in what became known as the Battle of Tippecanoe. Then the warriors retreated.

The War of 1812

After the Battle of Tippecanoe, Tecumseh continued to resist the Americans. When Britain went to

THE BATTLE OF TIPPECANOE
November 7, 1811
Here, on this site, military forces commanded by General William Henry Harrison, engaged in battle with the Indians of the Wabash country led by The Prophet, brother of the great Indian leader, Tecumseh. This battle destroyed forever the hope of Tecumseh for a complete Indian Confederacy, launched Harrison toward the Presidency of the United States twenty-nine years later, and is considered one of the primary events leading to conflict between the United States and Great Britain in the War of 1812.

This sign near present-day Lafayette marks the site of the Battle of Tippecanoe.

Steps to Indiana Statehood

STEP 1   **First Government of Northwest Territory**

- Congress chose a governor and three judges.
- The governor and judges made laws.
- Over time, the territory was divided into states.

STEP 2   **Second Stage of Government**

When Indiana had 5,000 free men:
- They elected a legislature.
- The legislature made laws.
- The legislature elected a delegate to the U.S. Congress.

STEP 3   **Final Steps to Statehood**

When Indiana had 60,000 free people:
- The legislature asked Congress for statehood.
- Congress told Indiana to create a constitution and a state government.
- The legislature set up a constitutional convention.
- The constitutional convention wrote a constitution and planned a state government.
- Congress admitted Indiana into the Union.

war with the United States again in the War of 1812, Tecumseh joined the British forces. During a final battle with Harrison's troops in 1813, Tecumseh died. With him, the dream of a great Native American confederacy died as well.

The March to Statehood

The end of the War of 1812 brought peace to the Indiana Territory. Both the British and the Native Americans there stopped fighting the American settlers—once and for all. Now the pioneers could concentrate on building their homesteads and towns.

They could also get to the business of writing a state constitution and forming a state government. These events would allow Indiana to become a state. The chart above shows the different steps that led to statehood. On December 11, 1816, Indiana became the nineteenth state in the Union.

 constitution A document with the basic laws and rules of a government

BUILDING STATES

2

FOCUS The Northwest Ordinance of 1787 set up the rules for dividing the Northwest Territory. By 1800, so many people had moved into the territory that it was divided into the Indiana and Northwest Territories.

Indiana and Northwest Territories, 1800

Grand Portage

Lake Superior

CANADA

Sault Ste. Marie

Michilimackinac

Lake Huron

Lake Ontario

Wisconsin R.

Ft. La Baye

Lake Michigan

Mississippi R.

Rock R.

5

Lake Erie

PA

Ft. St. Joseph

Ft. Dearborn

Ft. Sandusky

Ft. Crèvecoeur

Ft. St. Louis

Ft. Wayne

Illinois R.

White R.

Chillicothe

1

4

Miami R.

Kaskaskia R.

Ft. Washington

Cahokia

2

Ohio R.

VA

Wabash R.

Clarksville

3

KY

Vincennes

Louisville

Kaskaskia

Lexington

Settlements

Forts

Native American villages

☐ **Indiana Territory**

☐ **Northwest Territory**

Dividing the Land

The year is 1800. A census shows that about 2,500 settlers live in the Indiana Territory. As a representative in the legislature, you will help decide if the capital should move from Vincennes to a new location. You will also help divide the territory into states. A tour of the territory is planned.

Map Key

1 Marietta The first government of the Northwest Territory was located here.

2 Clark's Grant The soldiers of George Rogers Clark's army received this land for their victories.

3 Corydon The capital of the Indiana Territory was moved here in 1813.

4 Ouiatenon Approximately a dozen French people lived here.

5 Detroit The British still held control here after the American Revolution.

MAP IT

1. You start your tour in Marietta and travel westward on the Ohio River. What kinds of places do you find along this river? Whom do you meet?

2. Why might you want to locate your capital along the Ohio River? What other things do you look for in a capital?

3. You continue west along the Ohio River. You travel north on the Mississippi River, and northeast by land to Grand Portage. Then you cross Lake Superior to Sault Ste. Marie. Why not locate your capital in the north?

4. You return to Marietta. In which direction do you travel?

5. Where do you choose to locate the capital? Explain your choice.

EXPLORE IT

The legislature will divide the Northwest and Indiana Territories into three to five states. How many states would you make? Where would you divide them? Explain why you think your plan would be the best.

★ ***grant*** Something given, such as a piece of land

INDIANA'S EARLY LEADERS

FOCUS *Learn about some people who helped to determine the course of Indiana's history.*

A Great Leader

Little Turtle understood that the Americans—and their new President, George Washington—meant to drive the Miamis off their lands. "Hold the line at the Ohio," was Little Turtle's cry.

By this, he meant to keep American settlers from moving north of the Ohio River. Little Turtle knew that if his people did not **resist**, they would be forced to move. He hoped to drive out the Americans before this happened. He led many raids against settlers.

Little Turtle was not only a great leader. He was also a great war chief. The Americans had a larger army and many more guns. But Little Turtle knew when to strike and when to leave. He knew when to catch the Americans by surprise and when to hide.

Little Turtle united the Miamis, the most powerful group in the Indiana Territory.

Little Turtle's Victories

To protect American settlers, Washington sent General Josiah Harmar in 1790 to fight the Miami Confederacy. But the American troops were poorly prepared and not well supplied.

Harmar and his army of young boys and old men marched on Kekionga, the Miami village. However, Little Turtle knew that Harmar's army was coming. By the time the troops got there, the village was nearly deserted.

When Harmar sent troops to look for the Miami, Little Turtle ambushed them. Then he returned to Kekionga. In a battle outside the village, the American forces were defeated.

The next year, President Washington sent General Arthur St. Clair to battle Little Turtle. With a force of about 2,000 men, St. Clair's army

⭐ **resist** To fight or work against; oppose

Little Turtle called General Wayne "the chief who never sleeps."

outnumbered Little Turtle's men by two to one. But the general and his untrained troops were no match for the clever Miami leader.

At breakfast time, Little Turtle struck St. Clair's fort, catching everyone by surprise. When the fighting was over, Little Turtle had won another victory.

"Mad Anthony" Wayne

Some members of Congress wanted to give up and leave the Northwest Territory to Little Turtle and his people. But not President Washington. He decided to send a general who would be a better match for Little Turtle. He chose General "Mad Anthony" Wayne.

Wayne had earned his nickname because of his reckless bravery during the American Revolution. The general had proven he'd do anything to win.

Washington's fearless general also knew how to train soldiers. He drilled his men until they were ready to fight the Miami. Then he moved his army toward Kekionga, building forts along the way.

Little Turtle believed that the Miamis' best bet was to cut off the general's supplies. He wanted to do this over time. His men, however, were impatient. They chose to fight. As Little Turtle had suspected, they did not have enough

General Wayne presented this flag to a Native American chief during the signing of the Treaty of Greenville.

▲ Tecumseh's belt

men to win a big open battle against Wayne's forces. The Miamis lost at Fallen Timbers in 1794.

The Prophet's Message

About ten years passed before new leaders succeeded in uniting the Native American people again.

Tenskwatawa, the Shawnee Prophet, called on Native Americans to give up the ways of settlers and to return to their old methods and customs. He also spoke out against Harrison's land treaties. Tenskwatawa's message drew many followers. Some of his followers even moved to Prophetstown.

Tecumseh's Confederacy

The Prophet's brother, Tecumseh, joined the Shawnee Prophet in resisting Harrison's treaties. He told the Native Americans that a strand of hair can be broken. But a braid cannot. Standing alone, each individual group was weak. Together, Tecumseh told them, Native Americans could be powerful.

Toward this goal, Tecumseh worked tirelessly to unite many Native American groups into a new confederacy. As you can see from the map, Tecumseh's travels through the Northwest Territory led to a large confederacy.

Warriors from many nations heard him and understood his message. They joined Tecumseh's

Map

90°W 85°W 80°W

0   50   100 miles
0   50   100 kilometers

Lake Superior

OTTAWAS

N
W   E
S

45°N

CHIPPEWAS   MENOMINEES

Lake Huron

Lake Michigan

Lake Ontario

WINNEBAGOS

CHIPPEWAS POTAWATOMIS   WYANDOTTES

Lake Erie

SACS AND MESQUAKIES

IOWAS

SHAWNEES

Wabash R.   ● Kekionga

● Prophetstown

40°N

Mississippi R.

KICKAPOOS

DELAWARES

Ohio R.

THE AREA OF TECUMSEH'S CONFEDERACY

● Towns

— Present-day boundaries

confederacy. They agreed not to sell any more land to the Americans. They vowed to fight for their villages and land.

Harrison Strikes

Governor William Henry Harrison, pictured on the right, understood that the Shawnee confederacy was a threat to the Americans. So, in 1811, he marched on the Prophet's village while Tecumseh was away.

The Prophet was a religious leader, not a soldier. He told the warriors that the bullets of the American troops would be as soft as rain. But his statements proved false.

The warriors attacked Harrison's troops, but the Shawnees were defeated at the Battle of Tippecanoe. Later, this victory helped Harrison to become President in 1840.

Harrison's Strategies

As governor of the Indiana Territory, Harrison made the area safer for settlers by winning battles and by persuading Native Americans to sign land treaties. Harrison warned the Native Americans that he would send soldiers "as numerous as the mosquitoes on the shores of the Wabash" if they did not sign his treaties.

When Tecumseh met with Harrison, he argued that such treaties were not legal. The land, he said, belongs to all Native Americans. Therefore, no one leader could sell Native American land to the United States government.

The Battle of Tippecanoe was the last great battle fought by Indiana's Native Americans. In 1813, Tecumseh died in Canada fighting with the British during the War of 1812. Native Americans had lost their land and a great leader.

SHOW WHAT YOU KNOW!

REFOCUS
COMPREHENSION

1. How did Little Turtle succeed against the Americans at first?

2. What messages did Tenskwatawa and Tecumseh bring to Native Americans?

THINK ABOUT IT
CRITICAL THINKING

Why did Governor Harrison succeed against Tecumseh's Confederacy?

WRITE ABOUT IT
ACTIVITY

What questions would you like to ask Tecumseh? Write three questions. Then answer them as he might have.

THE ROAD TO STATEHOOD

FOCUS *How did Indiana move from territorial government to statehood? Find out about some key moments in Indiana's march toward becoming a state.*

CORYDON MADE TERRITORIAL CAPITAL

March 11, 1813—This was a sad day for Vincennes. The legislature of the Indiana Territory voted to move the capital to Corydon. Vincennes' small capitol building was no longer the center of government for the territory.

"Center" was a key to the legislature's vote. Vincennes was once at the center of the Indiana Territory. But that changed. The center of population had shifted to Corydon and other settlements along the Ohio River.

INDIANA'S POPULATION TOPS 60,000

January 5, 1816—The census figures arrived in December 1815. All the free people were counted. The population of the Indiana Territory stood at 63,897. This was great news for the citizens of the territory. It meant that the territory could soon become a state—the new state of Indiana.

The next step was to ask Congress to pass an Enabling Act. As representative of the territory, Jonathan Jennings brought this request to Washington on January 5, 1816.

March 11, 1813
Corydon named
new capital

January 5, 1816
Indiana asks Congress
for statehood

April 19, 1816
Enabling Act signed

June 29, 1816
Indiana delegates sign
new constitution

December 11, 1816
Indiana becomes
nineteenth state

1813   1816   1817

JONATHAN JENNINGS BATTLES FOR INDIANA

April 19, 1816—On this day, President James Madison signed the Enabling Act. This act enabled the people of Indiana Territory to create a constitution and a state government.

Only one important question remained: How long would it be before Indiana became a state? Jonathan Jennings led the effort to make sure that it happened quickly.

HOOSIERS MEET UNDER ELM

June 29, 1816—In Corydon, 43 delegates signed a new state constitution—the result of 18 days of hard work. Nothing could stop Indiana's determined delegates—not the hot sun or the stuffy room of the small capitol building. When the heat grew unbearable, they simply moved to the shade of a huge elm—and finished the job. Thanks to their efforts under the "Constitutional Elm," Indiana was now ready to become a state.

INDIANA BECOMES A STATE

December 11, 1816—On this day, President Madison signed the new Indiana constitution. And Indiana became the nineteenth star on the American flag.

At last, the citizens of the Indiana Territory would have a say in both their state and national governments. They would share the rights and responsibilities of all United States citizens.

It was a great day for all Hoosiers when the other eighteen states welcomed Indiana into the Union.

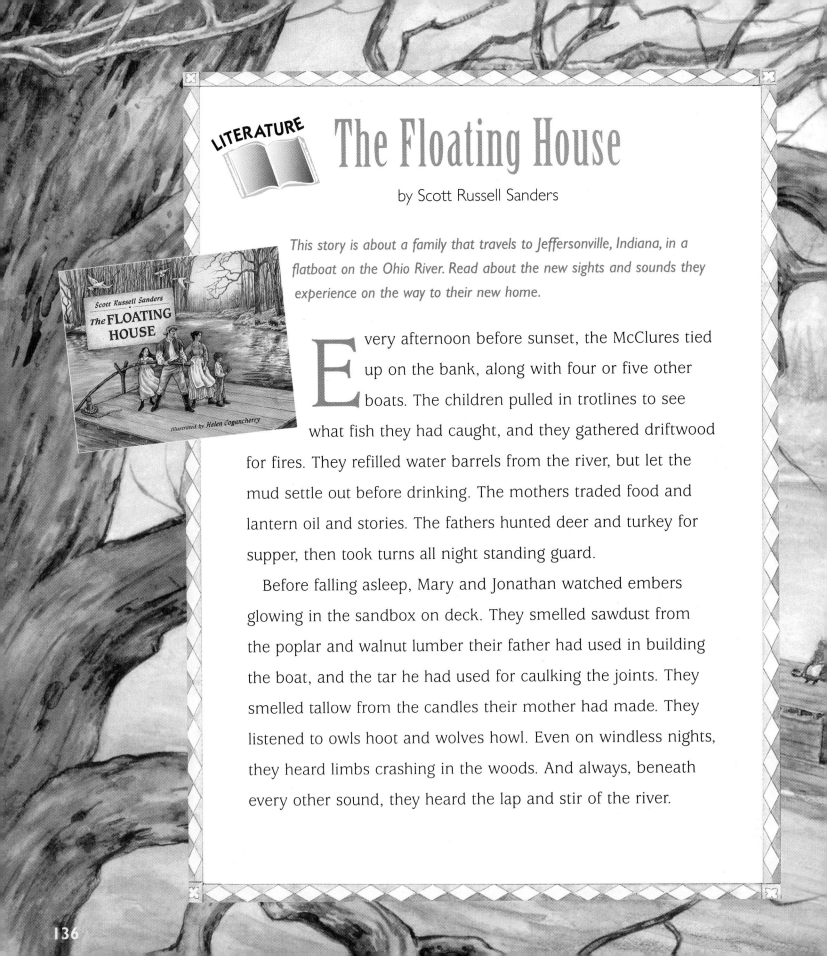

The Floating House

by Scott Russell Sanders

This story is about a family that travels to Jeffersonville, Indiana, in a flatboat on the Ohio River. Read about the new sights and sounds they experience on the way to their new home.

Every afternoon before sunset, the McClures tied up on the bank, along with four or five other boats. The children pulled in trotlines to see what fish they had caught, and they gathered driftwood for fires. They refilled water barrels from the river, but let the mud settle out before drinking. The mothers traded food and lantern oil and stories. The fathers hunted deer and turkey for supper, then took turns all night standing guard.

Before falling asleep, Mary and Jonathan watched embers glowing in the sandbox on deck. They smelled sawdust from the poplar and walnut lumber their father had used in building the boat, and the tar he had used for caulking the joints. They smelled tallow from the candles their mother had made. They listened to owls hoot and wolves howl. Even on windless nights, they heard limbs crashing in the woods. And always, beneath every other sound, they heard the lap and stir of the river.

The farther they journeyed, the wilder the land appeared. There were clearings for homesteads, and occasional towns, but mostly the shores were thick with trees, still brown and bare from the hard winter. Grapevines looped from trunk to trunk, and nests clotted the branches. Eagles and hawks circled overhead.

Bears swam across the current, snorting, black eyes gleaming. And once the whole river was blocked by a churning carpet of squirrels.

As the flatboat glided along, people called from shore, "Hello, the boat!"

"Hello, the shore!" the children called back. "What place is this?"

Steubenville, the people might answer, or Wheeling, Marietta, Point Pleasant, Gallipolis, Maysville. So many mysterious names! Jonathan and Mary had never set foot outside Pennsylvania, and here within a month they would see Ohio and western Virginia, Kentucky, and Indiana. Why, Indiana wasn't even a state yet, it was so thinly settled. And that was where they were headed, to a settlement named Jeffersonville, across the river from Louisville, at the falls of the Ohio.

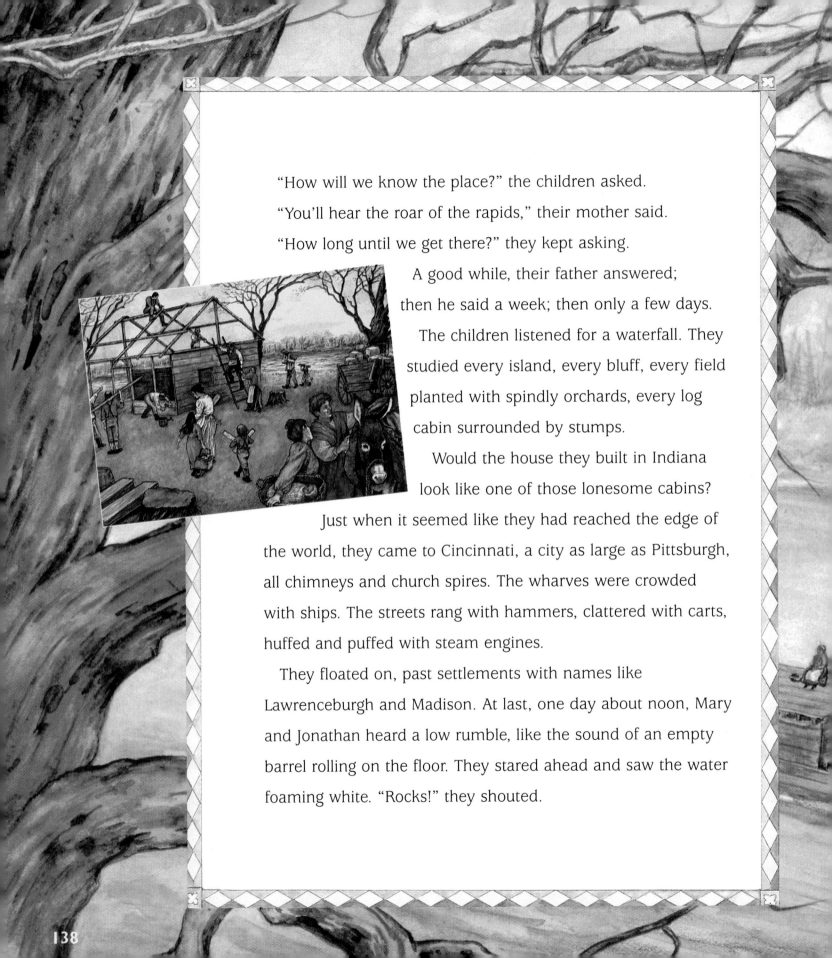

"How will we know the place?" the children asked.

"You'll hear the roar of the rapids," their mother said.

"How long until we get there?" they kept asking.

A good while, their father answered; then he said a week; then only a few days. The children listened for a waterfall. They studied every island, every bluff, every field planted with spindly orchards, every log cabin surrounded by stumps.

Would the house they built in Indiana look like one of those lonesome cabins?

Just when it seemed like they had reached the edge of the world, they came to Cincinnati, a city as large as Pittsburgh, all chimneys and church spires. The wharves were crowded with ships. The streets rang with hammers, clattered with carts, huffed and puffed with steam engines.

They floated on, past settlements with names like Lawrenceburgh and Madison. At last, one day about noon, Mary and Jonathan heard a low rumble, like the sound of an empty barrel rolling on the floor. They stared ahead and saw the water foaming white. "Rocks!" they shouted.

"Those must be the falls," their father said.

"And that must be Louisville," their mother said, pointing to a sizable town on the left bank.

"So that must be Jeffersonville," their father said, steering the boat toward a village on the right bank.

No sooner had the McClures tied up at the dock than dogs came running to sniff them and children came running to meet them and folks of all ages came to help them unload the flatboat.

From the government office, the McClures bought a parcel of land overlooking the falls. Before dark, with more help from these new neighbors, they dismantled the boat, hauled the lumber to their farm, and began building a house with the very same wood.

Back again on dry land, Mary and Jonathan could still hear the river. It poured through their minds, waking and sleeping. Sometimes on windy nights when the rapids were roaring, the children imagined their house might lift from its foundation, slide down the bank, and go riding the river once more, heading downstream to unknown places.

Want to learn more? You can read about the first part of the McClure's adventure by checking the book out of your school or town library.

SHOW WHAT YOU KNOW!

REFOCUS
COMPREHENSION

1. Why did Corydon become the capital of the Indiana Territory?

2. What was the "Constitutional Elm?"

THINK ABOUT IT
CRITICAL THINKING

Was Indiana ready for statehood in 1816? Why or why not?

WRITE ABOUT IT
ACTIVITY

In your Indiana journal, write a diary entry for Mary or Jonathan, telling about her or his experiences on the flatboat.

SUMMING UP

1 DO YOU REMEMBER . . .
COMPREHENSION

1. Why did the new Congress pass land ordinances?

2. What did the Treaty of Greenville require the Miami Confederacy to do?

3. Where was the capital of the Indiana Territory located in 1813?

4. Why did President Washington decide to send General Wayne to fight the Miamis in the Northwest Territory?

5. Why was the capital of the Indiana Territory moved from Vincennes to Corydon?

2 SKILL POWER
UNDERSTANDING CAUSE AND EFFECT

Use what you learned in this chapter to write a cause for each of these events.

1. A huge amount of land was added to the young United States.

2. There were no slaves in the Northwest Territory.

3. Native Americans sent out war parties and raided pioneer settlements.

4. By 1800 the Northwest Territory was cut into smaller parts.

5. The Miamis lost their land in southeastern Indiana.

3 WHAT DO YOU THINK?
CRITICAL THINKING

1. What two different points of view about land ownership led to conflict between Native Americans and settlers?

2. Why do you think Congress wanted to divide the Northwest Territory into several states instead of making it one big state?

3. In what way did Tecumseh support his brother Tenskwatawa's message to Native Americans?

4. How did Harrison's victory at the Battle of Tippecanoe help him to later become President?

5. Why were many Hoosiers in favor of Indiana becoming a state?

4 SAY IT, WRITE IT, USE IT
VOCABULARY

Suppose that you were a member of Congress in 1787. Write a speech to present in Congress describing the terms of the Northwest Ordinance. Include as many vocabulary terms as you can.

civil rights	legislature
confederacy	ordinance
constitution	resist
grant	territory

5 GEOGRAPHY AND YOU
MAP STUDY

1. Name the states that bordered the Northwest Territory on the east.

2. What rivers formed the southern and western borders of the Northwest Territory?

3. In which direction would you travel from Virginia to Lake Michigan?

4. How did the addition of the Northwest Territory change the United States?

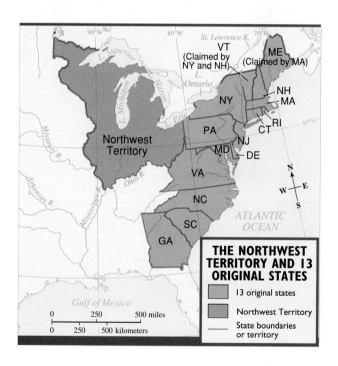

THE NORTHWEST TERRITORY AND 13 ORIGINAL STATES

■ 13 original states

■ Northwest Territory

— State boundaries or territory

0   250   500 miles
0   250   500 kilometers

6 TAKE ACTION
CITIZENSHIP

You read that Jonathan Jennings represented the people of Indiana. With a group of classmates, discuss an issue that you would like to bring to the attention of your state senator. It might involve saving an endangered animal, protecting a local river or shoreline, or preserving a historic building. Write a letter to your senator in which you describe your concern. You can find the name and address in a current almanac.

7 GET CREATIVE
MATH CONNECTION

The population of Indiana has continued to grow since 1816 when it became a state. Use an encyclopedia, almanac, or history of Indiana to find out what the state's population was in 1820, 1870, 1920, 1970, and the current year. Determine how much the population grew between each of those dates. When was population growth the greatest?

LOOKING AHEAD

In the next chapter, learn about the hard-working pioneers who settled in Indiana.

PIONEER LIFE

In the early 1800s, brave men, women, and children journeyed westward to Indiana. With hard work and determination, they were able to make a new life in the young state.

▼ Find out on page 154 why pioneers brought this object to Indiana.

CONTENTS

IN INDIANA

These books tell about some people, places, and events of interest during the time of the early pioneers in Indiana. Read one that interests you and fill out a book review form.

READ AND RESEARCH

...If You Grew Up With Abraham Lincoln
by Ann McGovern (Scholastic, 1992)
Find out what young Abraham Lincoln's house looked like, what children of his time studied in school, and what they did for fun. *(nonfiction)*
• *You can read a selection from this book on pages 158–159.*

The Glorious Fourth at Prairietown by Joan Anderson
(William Morrow, 1986)
The Carpenter family from Pennsylvania stops in Prairietown, Indiana. Read about the Fourth of July festivities they enjoy with their new friends. *(fiction)*

A Pioneer Sampler by Barbara Greenwood, illustrated by
Heather Collins (Ticknor and Fields, 1995)
Follow the Robertson family as they make maple syrup, greet the peddler, and pack for moving to a new house. *(nonfiction)*

Frontier Home by Raymond Bial
(Houghton Mifflin, 1993)
Illustrated with photographs of houses and tools, this book describes the daily life of settlers in the Midwest. *(nonfiction)*

SKILL POWER   Using Scale

Knowing how to use scale will help you understand how to figure distance on maps of different sizes.

UNDERSTAND IT

Maps show where places are located. But maps cannot show distances between places in their true size. To show true size, maps are drawn to scale. This means that the distances shown on maps are smaller than their real size.

When maps are drawn to scale, a certain number of inches on a map stands for a certain number of miles. The map scale tells the real size or distance from one place to another.

Scale is also used to make copies of things in a smaller size. Many model airplanes are built to a scale of 50 to 1. If you build a 1-foot-long model of an airplane, the length of the real airplane is 50 times 1 foot, or 50 feet.

EXPLORE IT

Place a ruler under the scale of Map A on page 145. On this scale, 1 inch equals 75 miles. Then place your ruler in a straight line between Indianapolis and Gary. How many inches are there between the two cities? (If you measured about 2 inches, you are correct.) To find the mileage from Indianapolis to Gary, multiply 2 x 75 Indianapolis is about 150 miles from Gary.

Now measure the distance from Gary to Indianapolis on Map B. The number of inches to miles has changed. But when you use the scale to figure miles, the distance from Gary to Indianapolis remains the same.

This model airplane was made to scale.

MAP A

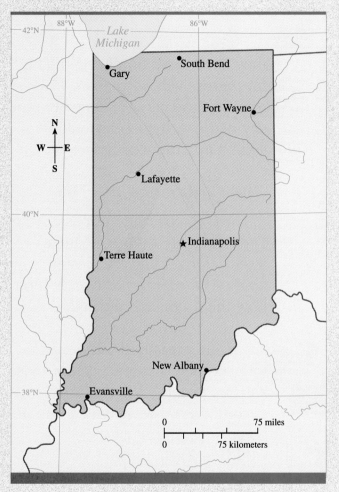

MAP A

42°N 88°W   86°W

Lake Michigan

Gary •South Bend

Fort Wayne •

N
W   E
S

• Lafayette

40°N

★ Indianapolis

• Terre Haute

New Albany •

38°N

• Evansville

0   75 miles
0   75 kilometers

TRY IT

Place your ruler on each map to find out how many inches and then how many miles it is between Terre Haute and Indianapolis. Then choose two cities of your own to measure.

Write your answers on a sheet of paper. Compare your answers with those of a partner.

MAP B

88°W *Lake Michigan* 86°W

Gary • South Bend
Fort Wayne •

N
W   E
S

• Lafayette

40°N

★ Indianapolis

Terre Haute •

New Albany •
Evansville •

38°N

0   75   150 miles
0   75   150 kilometers

SKILL POWER SEARCH

Look at the map scales in this chapter and in other chapters you have read. How do scales help you measure distance?

145

1

Setting the Scene

KEY TERMS
squatter
township
flatboat
gristmill

PIONEER SETTLEMENT

FOCUS *After Indiana was organized for settlement, new settlers poured into the region. They brought few possessions but a great deal of courage.*

A Growing Country

After the American Revolution, the new country grew rapidly. Large numbers of people began to settle in the wilderness west of the Appalachian Mountains.

These pioneers were brave and determined. They were willing to face unknown dangers and hardships so that they might create a better life for themselves and for their families.

At first many settlers were **squatters**. When they found land they liked, they simply claimed it for themselves. By the late 1700s, however, the new U.S. government decided that the land should be settled in a more orderly way.

The Ordinance of 1785

The U.S. government passed the Ordinance of 1785 to create a system for settling the western lands. The chart on this page shows how the ordinance worked.

According to the ordinance, surveyors measured off the land into six-mile squares. Each of these squares became a **township**. Then each township was divided into 36 equal sections.

Finally, each of these 36 sections was divided into smaller lots. These lots were sold for one dollar an acre. The result was a kind of patchwork quilt of neat squares and rectangles. The effects of this land division can still be seen from the air today.

THE LAND ORDINANCE SYSTEM

6 MILES
1 2 3 4 5 6
12 11 10 9 8 7
13 14 15 16 17 18
24 23 22 21 20 19
25 26 27 28 29 30
36 35 34 33 32 31

1 MILE

160 acres

320 acres

80 acres

40 acres

40 acres

INDIANA
The state was divided into many square townships.

TOWNSHIP
Each township was divided into 36 sections.

SECTION
Each section was divided into smaller lots and sold.

squatter A person who settles on land he or she does not own
township Division of land six-miles square

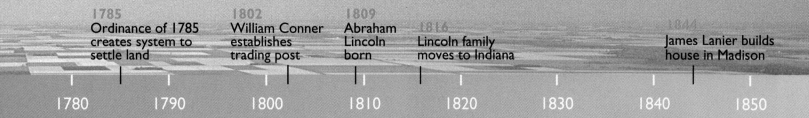

1785	1802	1809	1816	1844
Ordinance of 1785 creates system to settle land	William Conner establishes trading post	Abraham Lincoln born	Lincoln family moves to Indiana	James Lanier builds house in Madison

1780   1790   1800   1810   1820   1830   1840   1850

Indiana Grows from South to North

The French settled parts of northern Indiana during the early 1700s. But after the French and Indian War, only a few groups of French people stayed on near their forts and trading posts in Indiana.

During the early 1800s, most new settlers were farming families looking for new land. They reached Indiana by traveling on the Ohio River. Many came from the nearby southern states of Kentucky, Virginia, North Carolina, and Tennessee. Most settled in southern Indiana near the Ohio River and other nearby rivers.

Settlers gradually followed river valleys into central regions of the state. The north was the last region to be thickly settled as pioneers joined the French who had made their homes there earlier.

The maps on this page show where Indiana's pioneers settled from 1810 to 1830. Notice how a greater area was settled in 1820 than in 1810. What areas were settled by 1830?

The Lincoln Family Joins Indiana's Pioneers

Like many pioneers, Abraham Lincoln's family was able to buy land because of the Ordinance of 1785. In 1816 the Lincolns left their Kentucky farm. They loaded all their belongings onto the backs of their two horses. Sometimes they rode the horses, but mostly they walked. A ferry took them across the Ohio River.

The Lincolns traveled over a hundred miles in the icy December cold. They finally settled in Little Pigeon Creek, Indiana.

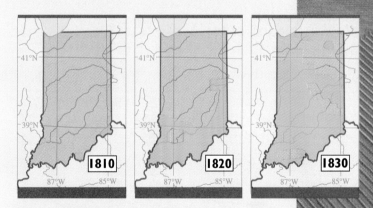

PIONEER SETTLEMENT IN INDIANA

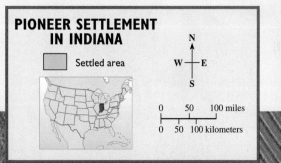

Settled area

N
W—E
S

0   50   100 miles

0   50   100 kilometers

147

Flatboats carried pioneers to Indiana.

Pioneer Travel

How did pioneer families reach Indiana? Many of those who came down the Ohio River floated on flat-bottomed rafts called **flatboats**. Flatboats were steered with long poles, called "sweeps," attached at the top of the boat.

Everything a family needed to start their new life was loaded onto the flatboat. Sometimes the boats would turn over. People could swim ashore. But tools, furniture, food, and clothing were often lost.

Settlers also came to Indiana on horseback or on foot. Some brought Conestoga (Kah nes TOH guh) wagons. These heavy covered wagons were drawn by teams of six oxen or strong horses. The wagon was used only for carrying furniture and other goods. People had to walk alongside.

Big, awkward wagons made slow progress as they creaked along through the wilderness. They often got stuck in the mud. Then the whole family had to help unload the wagon and push it free. Many families had to leave some of their furniture and food on the trail to help make the wagon lighter.

There were few roads in the wilderness, only crooked, narrow paths. Sometimes there was no trail at all. Then settlers had to cut their own trail through the dense forest with axes.

Pioneers loaded their belongings in wagons.

flatboat   A flat-bottomed boat

148

Children brought dolls like this to Indiana.

Many families also brought a cow, a horse or an ox, and a few pigs or sheep. If they did not bring these animals, they bought a few animals after they arrived. Then they could have milk, butter, cheese, meat, and wool.

Most importantly, pioneers brought their determination, courage, and ability to work hard. They knew that they would have to rely on these qualities in order to survive in the harsh Indiana wilderness.

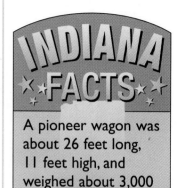

INDIANA FACTS

A pioneer wagon was about 26 feet long, 11 feet high, and weighed about 3,000 pounds.

Hardships of Pioneer Life

When families arrived in Indiana, trees had to be cleared, crops had to be planted, and a rough cabin built. Everyone in the family had to help with these chores.

Pioneer life was difficult and demanding. Men and women married young, worked hard, raised large families, and died young. If you look at the dates on the headstones in a pioneer cemetery today, you will see that many pioneers lived short lives.

Pioneer Possessions

Pioneers brought with them only what would fit in their wagons or on their flatboats. Most families brought a chest of drawers, kitchen tools, bedding, a spinning wheel, and a clock. They also packed seeds for planting crops during the first year. To save space, they brought only the metal parts for knives and tools. They could make new wooden handles in Indiana.

Pioneers brought metal pots with them.

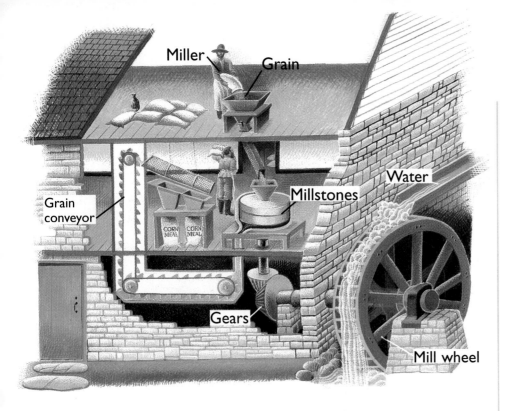

Miller
Grain
Water
Millstones
Grain conveyor
Gears
Mill wheel

power to move the mill's heavy millstones. In other mills, a horse pulled a pole that turned the millstones. Gristmills could grind wheat into flour or corn into cornmeal in a fraction of the time it took a settler to grind the grain himself.

Spring Mill Village, in southern Indiana, grew up around a gristmill in the early 1800s. Today visitors can still see the mill's heavy stones grind local corn into cornmeal.

Other Village Buildings

Another important building in a pioneer village was the general store. There villagers bought the supplies they couldn't make or grow themselves. People also

Villages Begin to Grow

As more settlers moved to a region, small villages began to grow. One of the first people a village needed was a miller who could grind grain.

Most settlers were able to grow their own food and trade with neighbors for supplies. But without a miller, they had to grind grain by hand. It could take hours to grind flour to make a loaf of bread.

As soon as a miller moved nearby, everyone in the area helped build a **gristmill**. Many mills were built on rivers or streams. Then they could take advantage of water

Pioneer villages were built near a river, stream, or creek.

Covered bridge

gristmill A building with machinery used for grinding grain into flour

gathered at the general store to discuss the news of the day.

As a village grew, settlers gathered together to build a church and a schoolhouse. Most villages also had an inn where travelers could spend the night. In 1819 innkeepers charged about 12 cents a night to stay at an inn.

Outside a village were vegetable gardens and fruit trees. A covered bridge often stood across a nearby river or stream. Find these buildings and places in the illustration below.

From Villages to Towns

A village often had a sawmill for cutting logs into boards. The blacksmith made and repaired metal tools for villagers. The cooper made barrels and buckets. The wainwright (WAYN ryt) made wagons. The wheelwright made wagon wheels.

As more people moved into the village, more services were offered. More people came to the village who could grind grain, saw logs, and make furniture. Soon the village grew into a town.

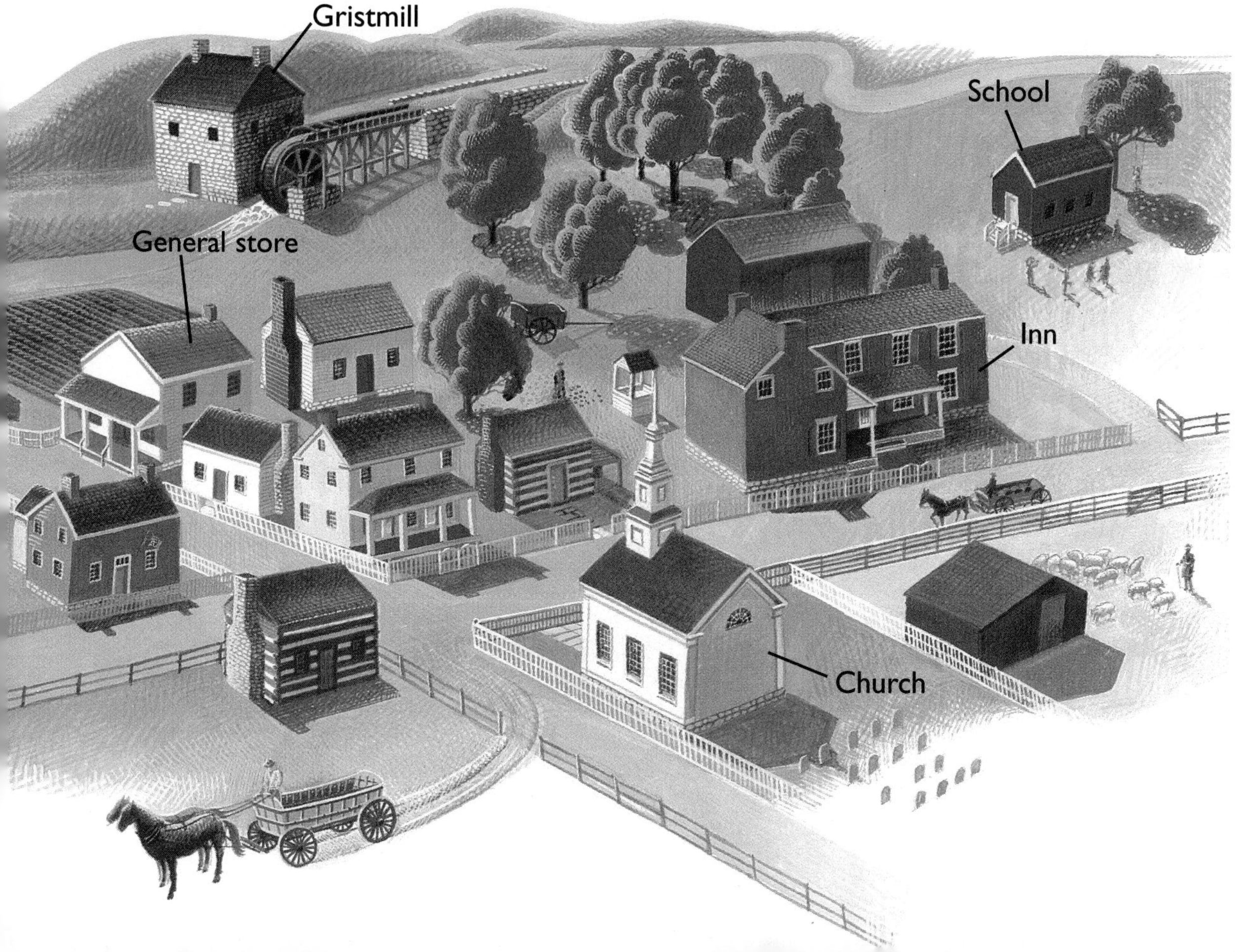

SHOW WHAT YOU KNOW!

REFOCUS
COMPREHENSION

1. What was the Ordinance of 1785?

2. Why did villages grow up near gristmills?

THINK ABOUT IT
CRITICAL THINKING

Give reasons why you would or would not have liked your family to move to Indiana in the early 1800s.

WRITE ABOUT IT
ACTIVITY

In your Indiana journal, write a letter to a friend describing your journey by wagon or flatboat to pioneer Indiana.

Gristmill

General store

School

Inn

Church

KEY TERMS

lean-to
homespun

PIONEER LIFE

FOCUS *Pioneers were independent people who survived in many different ways. They found ways to live off the land, rivers, and forests.*

Clearing the Land

One early settler described pioneer Indiana as nothing but "woods, woods, woods, as far as the world extends!" Trees provided logs for cabins and rails for fences. They also provided fruits, nuts, and maple sap. Wood-fueled fires were used for light, heat, and cooking. But trees also stopped settlers from growing their crops. Before they could grow crops, settlers had to get rid of the trees.

Saplings could be cut down with axes. But what could be done with huge trees that measured up to six feet across? The pioneers circled, or girdled, these giants by cutting a deep ring around each trunk. Then sap could not feed the leaves. The trees died and allowed sunlight to reach the settlers' crops. Later, the tree trunks were burned and the tough roots dug up.

An axe was an important pioneer tool.

 This log cabin is at the Lincoln Boyhood National Memorial.

Building a Log Cabin

The first home for a pioneer family was usually a **lean-to**, or three-sided shelter made of bent saplings. The saplings were covered with branches to make a roof.

After crops were planted, the family could think about building a real cabin. The cabin was built as a single room about 20 feet square. First the family laid four cornerstones

lean-to   A shelter with a sloping roof

152

in a clearing. With the help of neighbors, they cut logs to the proper length, skinned off the bark, and rolled them into place. The ends of the logs were notched to fit snugly at the corners. A chimney was built at one end.

Chimneys and cracks between logs were "chinked," or filled with mud mixed with rocks and grass. Doors and windows were cut. Logs were split for the roof, doors, and window shutters. Floors were made of sand and packed dirt.

After ox-drawn plows loosened the soil, women and children planted seeds.

A log cabin was built to change. As the family grew, a sleeping loft for the children could be added under the roof. It was reached by a ladder of pegs in the wall. There children usually slept on a mattress of animal skins thrown over dried leaves or corn husks.

Feeding the Family

Most pioneer foods came from woods, streams, gardens, and fields. Corn was on the table three times a day, almost every day of the year. There was cornmeal mush, corn soup, corn pone, johnnycake, and hoecake—each made in a different way. Pioneers also planted potatoes, pumpkins, and squash. Men and older boys hunted deer, bear, wild turkeys, quail, and rabbits. They fished and trapped. As wild game became harder to find, settlers planted more corn and raised hogs.

Life for Women

Pioneer women had special chores in addition to everyday cooking and cleaning. They preserved foods by drying, salting, or storing them in underground root cellars. They baked breads, cookies, and cakes in bake ovens built in the fireplace or outside the cabin.

Women made candles by dipping strings again and again into melted animal fat or beeswax. Cleaning was always a major chore. Soap was made from lye, a strong cleaner made from ashes, and animal fat. Water was carried from a spring or well and heated for baths or for washing dishes and clothes. Women made brooms from reeds and straw.

Many pioneer women made clothes by spinning yarn, weaving cloth, and sewing by hand. Cloth made at home was called **homespun**.

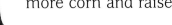

▲ Pioneer women wore clothing that they sewed themselves.

★ *homespun* Cloth made at home by spinning and weaving

Life for Children

Pioneer children gathered nuts, berries, and wild plants. Their few, simple toys were homemade. A dried gourd with the seeds inside, for example, made a good rattle for a baby.

In summer children gathered for swimming and games. They frightened birds away from eating the corn by blowing loud whistles and beating pots. In winter they gathered to sled and skate. They looked forward to collecting maple sap. After boiling, the syrup was poured on snow to make candy.

▼ Women used spinning wheels to make yarn.

Quilting bees let settlers visit each other while they worked.

Working Together

Pioneers worked together when big jobs had to be done. Everyone joined to help build houses and barns. They cleared land and harvested crops together. These work sessions were called *bees*.

Husking bees were always popular. In the fall, stalks of corn were piled beside one settler's barn. Then neighbors gathered to husk, or peel, the corn. When the work was finished, they ate, talked, and danced until late at night.

Settlers also gathered for quilting bees to share the work of making quilts. At apple bees, they cored and pared apples. Then the apples were made into applesauce or cider for the winter.

Pioneers shared work and happy times with food, games, and music. They also shared sad times. When a cabin burned, the community helped to rebuild it. If a family lost a loved one, people took care of the family's chores and brought food.

Pioneer life was difficult. Settlers needed to help each other with many tasks. They also needed one another's company to help ease the loneliness of living on the frontier.

SHOW WHAT YOU KNOW!

REFOCUS
COMPREHENSION

1. Explain how early settlers cleared the land.

2. Describe three chores that pioneers did.

THINK ABOUT IT
CRITICAL THINKING

Why did pioneer families plant crops before they built their houses?

WRITE ABOUT IT
ACTIVITY

Write a paragraph describing how you might have felt as a pioneer first arriving in Indiana.

Citizenship

KEY TERMS

blab school
slave

LITERATURE

... If You Grew Up
With Abraham
Lincoln

ABE LINCOLN IN INDIANA

FOCUS *Like other pioneer families, Abe Lincoln's family faced the challenges of pioneer life. Later Abe became one of our country's greatest Presidents.*

The Lincolns in Indiana

Indiana was part of the frontier in 1816 when the Lincolns moved there. The family's first winter was as difficult for the Lincolns as it was for other pioneers. Abe's father, Tom, built a rough shelter for Abe, his sister Sarah, and their mother, Nancy Hanks Lincoln. Tom hunted wild animals for food.

Abe was tall and strong. Although he was barely eight years old, he learned to use an axe to cut wood. He also learned to split logs to make fences.

In October 1818, "milk sickness" killed Abe's mother. This disease was caused when cows ate the poisonous snake-root plant and people drank the milk. Sad times followed for the Lincolns.

In 1819 Tom married Sarah Bush Johnston, who was called Sally. Her strength and love became a strong influence throughout Abe's life.

In the mid-1800s Abe wrote about life in Indiana:

When first my father settled here, 'Twas then the frontier line: The panther's scream filled night with fear And bears preyed on the swine.

▲ This photograph of Sally Lincoln was taken in the 1860s.

Books and Schooling

Sally Lincoln made sure that Abe went to school. In Abe's school, students recited, or "blabbed," their lessons aloud to the schoolmaster. For this reason, his school was called a **blab school**.

With time spent on chores, Abe had only about one full year of school. Yet he loved reading. When he plowed a field, he took a book along to read at the end of each

---

 blab school   A school where students recite their lessons aloud

row while the horse rested. Books were hard to come by in the wilderness. Abe sometimes had to walk many miles to borrow books, but he always took care to return them to their owners.

Abe copied sums into his notebook to learn arithmetic.

Abe as a Young Man

River boats often stopped on the Ohio River some miles from the Lincoln farm. Watching the boats made Abe want to see more of the world.

Soon Abe got his chance. He and his friend Allen Gentry built a flatboat and loaded it with pork, chickens, and corn meal. Then they floated south down the Ohio and Mississippi rivers to New Orleans. There the boys sold their cargo and came home by steamboat.

While he was in New Orleans, Abe saw African Americans being sold as slaves. He remembered this terrible sight for the rest of his life.

In 1830 Tom Lincoln moved his family to Illinois. Abe, now 21, soon struck out on his own. He settled in New Salem, Illinois, and worked in

a general store. Here he developed a reputation for honesty that stayed with him his whole life. Once, a woman paid too much for her order. Abe walked six miles to return her money to her.

Abe Becomes President

In Illinois, Abe kept reading and improving himself. He joined a debating group to practice speaking in public. Borrowing books, he studied hard to become a lawyer.

In 1832 Lincoln ran for state office—and lost. But it was the beginning of his career in politics. Lincoln was later elected to the Illinois legislature, then to the United States Congress. In 1860 he became the sixteenth President of the United States.

The boy from Indiana had grown up to become one of our nation's greatest citizens. Today he is remembered as one of our greatest presidents.

This statue shows Abe holding a book and an axe.

 slave A person owned by another person

157

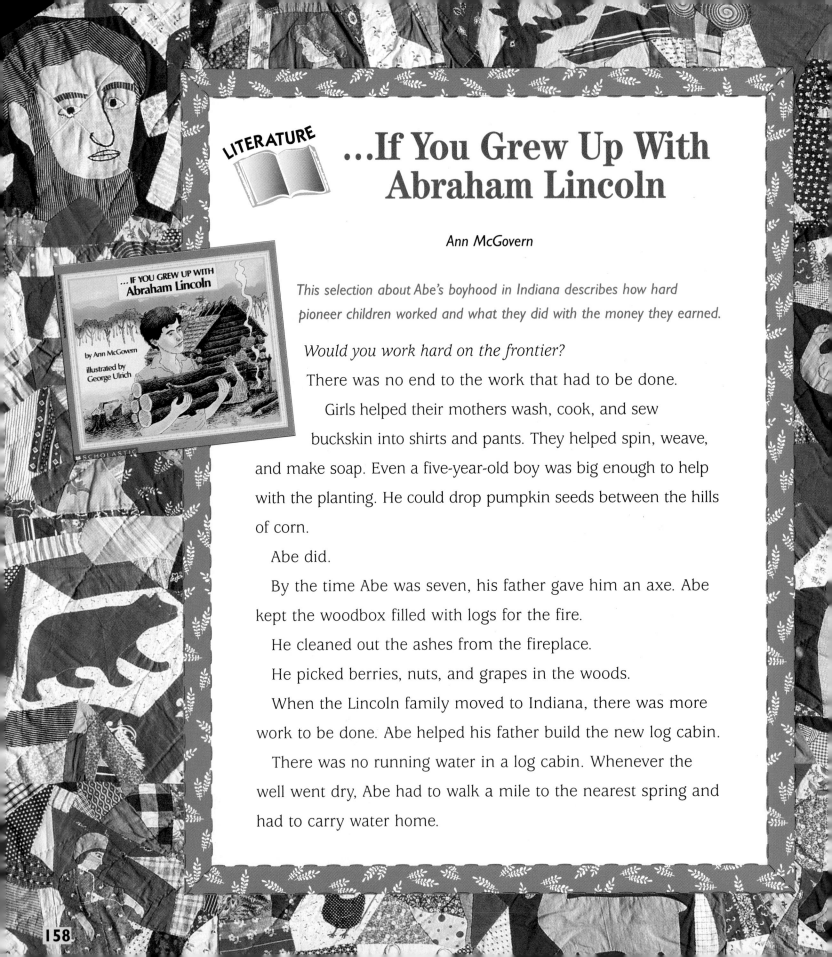

...If You Grew Up With Abraham Lincoln

Ann McGovern

This selection about Abe's boyhood in Indiana describes how hard pioneer children worked and what they did with the money they earned.

Would you work hard on the frontier?

There was no end to the work that had to be done.

Girls helped their mothers wash, cook, and sew buckskin into shirts and pants. They helped spin, weave, and make soap. Even a five-year-old boy was big enough to help with the planting. He could drop pumpkin seeds between the hills of corn.

Abe did.

By the time Abe was seven, his father gave him an axe. Abe kept the woodbox filled with logs for the fire.

He cleaned out the ashes from the fireplace.

He picked berries, nuts, and grapes in the woods.

When the Lincoln family moved to Indiana, there was more work to be done. Abe helped his father build the new log cabin.

There was no running water in a log cabin. Whenever the well went dry, Abe had to walk a mile to the nearest spring and had to carry water home.

... IF YOU GREW UP WITH Abraham Lincoln

by Ann McGovern
illustrated by George Ulrich

SCHOLASTIC

He helped his father farm. He plowed. He planted. He weeded.

He chopped down trees. He split logs into rails for fences.

People on the frontier said that a rail fence should be horse-high, bull-strong, and pig-tight. That meant it should be high enough so a horse could not jump over it. It should be strong enough so a bull could not push it over. And it should be tight enough so a pig could not squeeze through it.

Abe made many rail fences that were horse-high, bull-strong, and pig-tight.

If a man didn't need his son to help him on the farm, he sent him to work for neighbors.

What would you do with the money you earned?

The money you earned, you were supposed to give to your father. That was the law.

When a boy became twenty-one years old, he could keep the money he earned.

Boys on the frontier did not get paid much for their work. Abe was hired out to farmers for twenty-five cents a day.

You can find out about more Abe Lincoln's life in Indiana by checking the book out of your school or public library.

SHOW WHAT YOU KNOW!

REFOCUS
COMPREHENSION

1. How did Abe acquire the books he read?

2. What is a blab school?

THINK ABOUT IT
CRITICAL THINKING

Describe the qualities that made Abe Lincoln a good citizen.

WRITE ABOUT IT
ACTIVITY

Write an entry in your Indiana journal describing the chores that Abe Lincoln did.

MADISON AND CONNER PRAIRIE

FOCUS *Life was very different in a pioneer village in central Indiana than in a river town in southern Indiana. Some of these differences can still be seen today.*

Two Different Ways of Life

Indiana's early settlers used rivers as their highways. They also settled along rivers. They could use rivers for transportation, trade, and power to run their mills.

Madison, in southern Indiana, was founded by Indiana's pioneers. Located on the Ohio River, it was settled in the early 1800s and grew quickly. Residents lived a bustling town life. Because of its location, goods from the East Coast were easy to obtain. Wealthy citizens built grand houses filled with fine furniture and china.

Further north, life was more rugged. Goods had to be hauled through the wilderness by wagon. People had few luxuries. They built simpler buildings than the buildings in Indiana's cities. Today Conner Prairie, located just north of Indianapolis, recreates an Indiana pioneer town as it would have appeared in 1836.

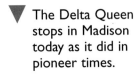

The Delta Queen stops in Madison today as it did in pioneer times.

Life in a Port Town

In the 1800s Madison was a major port for shipping hogs and wheat from central Indiana to the rest of the country. It was also a gateway for immigrants coming to find work. Madison's citizens built houses, stores, churches, and the state's first railroad.

Suppose you are visiting Madison in the early 1800s. These are some of the sights and sounds you would see and hear:

You follow snorting pigs through muddy streets. You listen to German workers as they butcher, cure, and load pork on boats docked along the riverfront. You watch black smoke rising from the chimneys of iron factories. You see the strained faces of Irish workers as they cut through stone cliffs to lay the new state's first railroad ties.

Lanier House has marble columns, a spiral staircase, and beautiful rooms.

Lanier House

Today visitors can go inside some of the **mansions** built in the 1800s by Madison's most wealthy citizens. One of these is Lanier (luh NEER) House. It was built by James Lanier, one of Indiana's best-known citizens.

Lanier was a lawyer and a banker. He is honored for lending the state a million dollars during the Civil War.

In 1844 Lanier built his grand house near the Ohio River. He modeled it to look like an ancient Greek building. Buildings in this style had a large porch supported by large columns.

Because he lived in a river town, Lanier could have luxury goods shipped to him from the East Coast. He decorated his mansion with wallpaper painted with real gold, fine furniture, and beautiful carpets. His house resembled the homes of wealthy citizens of large

 mansion A large house

East Coast cities like Philadelphia and Boston.

In 1816, when Indiana became a state, the busy port of Madison was the new state's largest city. Central regions of the state, however, were still largely unsettled and wild.

Conner Prairie

William Conner lived on the **prairie** of central Indiana. Like other pioneers, he and his family lived in a one-room cabin. Conner ran a small trading post for pioneers on nearby farms.

As the new state grew during the 1820s and 1830s, central Indiana became more settled. The Conners opened a store and built a two-story house. It was not as grand as Lanier House, but it was a fine, large house for the prairie.

By the 1900s, however, the Conner House had fallen into ruins. An Indiana businessman, Eli Lilly, bought the house in 1934. He **restored** Conner House so that visitors could learn about the region's first settlers.

Lilly's restoration was the beginning of Conner Prairie. Conner Prairie is a pioneer village that has been frozen in time during the year 1836. Some of its buildings are located on their original site. Many were moved from other places in Indiana.

Guides at Conner Prairie recreate the life and times of early settlers in Indiana. They dress and speak like real people who might have lived in 1836. They also do the work, such as farming and cooking, that Indiana pioneers might have done. In this way, they give visitors a picture of life in a pioneer village in central Indiana.

▲ The Conner House (left), a pioneer dinner (center), and the schoolhouse (right) look as they did in 1836.

★ *prairie*   A region of flat, grassy land

★ *restore*   To make like new

A costumed guide works at the Conner Prairie store.

The Blacksmith Shop

It is not hard to find the blacksmith shop in Conner Prairie. You only have to listen for the clang of the blacksmith's hammer.

In the 1830s blacksmiths shaped shoes to protect horses' hooves. They also made nails for attaching the shoes and for building houses. The blacksmith was one of the most important craftspeople in a pioneer village.

A Pioneer Store

If you visited Conner Prairie, you would probably see the general store. A general store contains a little bit of everything. The store's shelves would be lined with cloth, teas, and spices, as well as kitchen and farm tools.

Few customers in the 1830s had money to pay for their purchases. Instead, the shopkeepers traded their goods for items made by the villagers or for farm products grown by them. Sometimes villagers exchanged their furs and farm products for fine cloth and china from the East Coast and Europe.

The blacksmith used tools like these to make things from metal.

SHOW WHAT YOU KNOW!

REFOCUS
COMPREHENSION

1. Describe what you might see if you visited Lanier House.

2. How did villagers in central Indiana pay for goods?

THINK ABOUT IT
CRITICAL THINKING

Why did river towns in Indiana grow quickly?

WRITE ABOUT IT
ACTIVITY

Suppose you have moved from central Indiana to Madison during the 1830s. Write an entry in your Indiana journal explaining how your life has changed.

SUMMING UP

1 DO YOU REMEMBER . . .
COMPREHENSION

1. Where did most farming families settle in Indiana?

2. By what means of transportation did pioneers travel to Indiana?

3. Give three examples of ways in which pioneers worked together.

4. Describe the different jobs and careers at which Abe Lincoln worked.

5. What is Conner Prairie? What can you see there?

2 SKILL POWER
USING SCALE

Working with a partner, find maps of Indiana in encyclopedias and atlases. Notice the scales on those maps. How are the scales different from the ones in this chapter? Select two maps of Indiana from different resource books. Measure the distance between two cities on both maps. Are the distances the same?

3 WHAT DO YOU THINK?
CRITICAL THINKING

1. Of all the possessions that pioneers brought to Indiana, which do you think was the most important? Why?

2. What might have happened if Congress had allowed squatters to continue living on land in the West?

3. Compare the things that pioneer children did for fun with the things children do today.

4. What did you read in Lesson 3 that let you know that Abe Lincoln thought education was important?

5. Why is it important to preserve pioneer villages like Conner Prairie today?

4 SAY IT, WRITE IT, USE IT
VOCABULARY

Write a story about a pioneer family who moves first to a town along the Ohio River and then into central Indiana. Use as many vocabulary terms as possible in your story.

blab school	prairie
flatboat	restore
gristmill	slave
homespun	squatter
lean-to	township
mansion	

5 GEOGRAPHY AND YOU
MAP STUDY

1. About how much of Indiana had been settled by 1820?

2. What part of the state was settled last?

3. According to these maps, was the area in which you live settled by 1830?

4. Write two sentences explaining what these maps show about where pioneers settled in Indiana.

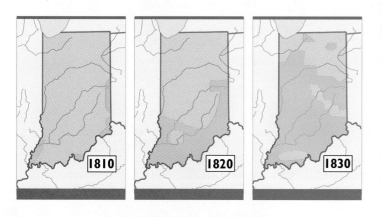

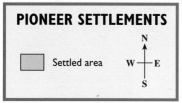

PIONEER SETTLEMENTS

☐ Settled area

N
W—E
S

6 TAKE ACTION
CITIZENSHIP

Protecting Our Rivers
Sarah Carroll
Grade 4

In Chapter 7 you read that the early settlers in Indiana settled along rivers and used rivers as their highways. Today we recognize the importance of protecting rivers. Think of ways to help keep rivers such as the Ohio River clean and safe. With a partner make a booklet in which you explain how people can help protect a body of water or waterway in your community or state.

7 GET CREATIVE
LANGUAGE ARTS CONNECTION

You learned that the pioneers in Indiana ate corn at every meal. Today Indiana is one of the leading corn-growing states. What is your favorite way to eat corn? It might be corn on the cob, cornbread, tortillas, or popcorn. Find a recipe for a healthy corn dish, illustrate it, and share it with the class. Make a class cookbook by copying all the recipes.

LOOKING AHEAD In the next chapter, find out about the many changes that took place in Indiana after it became a state.

Change AND Challenge

How Did the State of Indiana Grow?

Explore the many changes that took place in Indiana after it became a state. Journey alongside Hoosiers as they face the challenges of the Civil War, two world wars, the rise of industry, and the growth of their cities.

A GROWING STATE

As pioneers streamed westward, Indiana grew and changed. New towns and businesses sprang up. Roads, canals, and railroads crisscrossed the new state and connected Indiana with the growing nation.

CONTENTS

▼ Study page 181 to find out why shovels were important to Indiana's growth.

IN A GROWING NATION

These books tell about some of the people, places, and events of interest during the early years of Indiana statehood. Read one that interests you and fill out a book-review form.

READ AND RESEARCH

A Clearing in the Forest: A Story About a Real Settler Boy by Joanne Landers Henry and illustrated by Charles Robinson (Four Winds Press, 1992)
Follow the adventures of Elijah Fletcher in 1830 as he attends the county fair, switches schools, and watches steamboats on the Ohio River. *(fiction)*
• *You can read a selection from this book on page 186.*

The Amazing Impossible Erie Canal by Cheryl Harness (Macmillan, 1995)
Canal fever spread to Indiana following the success of the Erie Canal. Discover what it takes to build a canal and how the locks of a canal operate. *(nonfiction)*

Early City Life by Bobbie Kalman (Crabtree Publishing Company, 1991)
Find out about the houses people built in early American cities and the jobs they worked at. Learn about their newspapers, stores, roads, and more! *(nonfiction)*

SKILL POWER: Finding Information

Knowing how to find information can help you get facts quickly and easily.

UNDERSTAND IT

The library is one of the best places to find information. The facts you need are right there in the library's books, videocassettes, and computer disks.

Libraries have many books that contain facts on special topics. There are books about the geography of your state. There are stories about people's lives, called biographies.

Libraries also have reference books. They contain information on different subjects. Encyclopedias have articles about people, places, and things. If you want to know the meaning of a word, you would use a dictionary. For a map of your state, you would use a book of maps, called an atlas. An almanac, published yearly, is a book of facts on many subjects.

EXPLORE IT

Suppose you want to learn about different kinds of transportation. Where would you look? One of the best places to look is in a card catalog. This is a file—or drawer—with a list of all the books and materials in the library. The books are listed on cards in alphabetical order. The cards are set up in three ways—by subject, by title, and by the author's last name. Many libraries have this same kind of information on a computer.

```
         Transportation
629.04   Stacy, Tom
STACY      Wings, Wheels and Sails. Random
           House, c1991.
           64 p. Includes index.


           1. Transportation
```

```
629.04   Stacy, Tom
STACY      Wings, Wheels and Sails. Random
           House, c1991.
           64 p. Includes index.

           Summary: Questions and answers
           address the many ways in which
           humans move from place to place,
           examining airplanes, cars, trains,
           bicycles, and other forms of
           transportation.

           1. Transportation
```

These card-catalog cards give information by subject and author.

Library computers have lists of the library's books and materials.

TRY IT

Select a place in the Southern Hills and Lowlands region to learn more about. For example, you might choose the limestone caves. Or perhaps you want to learn more about the exhibits at the Falls of the Ohio State Park. Use the library's reference books to find some interesting facts about the place you choose. Investigate what your library's computer has to offer.

Work with a group of classmates to prepare a travel brochure featuring the Southern Hills and Lowlands region. Use the information about places in the region that you each gathered during your library search.

▲ Indiana's highways and lakes offer many report topics of interest.

SKILL POWER SEARCH *Select five facts from this chapter. Use materials in the library to look up and check each fact.*

Setting the Scene

KEY TERMS

textile
canal

THE NEW STATE GROWS

FOCUS *Once Indiana became a state, many changes took place in population, transportation, and business.*

A New State Capital

In 1818, Indiana took over huge pieces of land below the Wabash River from the Miamis, the Kickapoos, and other Native Americans. When this happened, it made sense to move Indiana's capital from Corydon to a more central location. Indiana's legislature, the General Assembly, chose a site where Fall Creek drained into the White River.

The name chosen for the new capital was Indianapolis. This name combines *Indiana* with the ancient Greek word *polis,* meaning "city." Alexander Ralston was the surveyor in charge of creating a design for this new city. Ralston's mile-square plan for Indianapolis resembled the design of Washington, D.C., the national capital. You can see Ralston's plan for Indianapolis on this page. It called for 11 streets running north and south—and 11 running east and west. From each corner, a street would run to the city's center. Important government buildings were planned near the center of town.

Moving the Capital

In October 1824, state records were moved from the old capital at Corydon to Indianapolis. Horse-drawn wagons carried government papers over bumpy roads.

A woman who was a child at the time later recalled arriving in the new capital "with fine, large, strong horses strung with bells, all ringing." The move, not much more than 100 miles, took ten days.

People moved to the new capital to open stores and businesses. Indianapolis grew quickly. In 1825, the city had about 50 buildings, including 9 houses and 2 log cabins. By 1827, 1,000 people lived in Indianapolis, and there were more than 160 houses. Within a few years, the National Road also

▼ Ralston's 1821 plan for Indianapolis

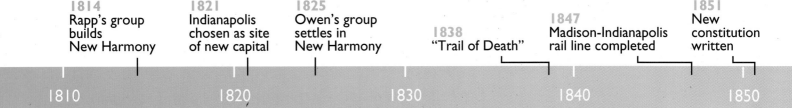

1814 Rapp's group builds New Harmony

1821 Indianapolis chosen as site of new capital

1825 Owen's group settles in New Harmony

1838 "Trail of Death"

1847 Madison-Indianapolis rail line completed

1851 New constitution written

1810   1820   1830   1840   1850

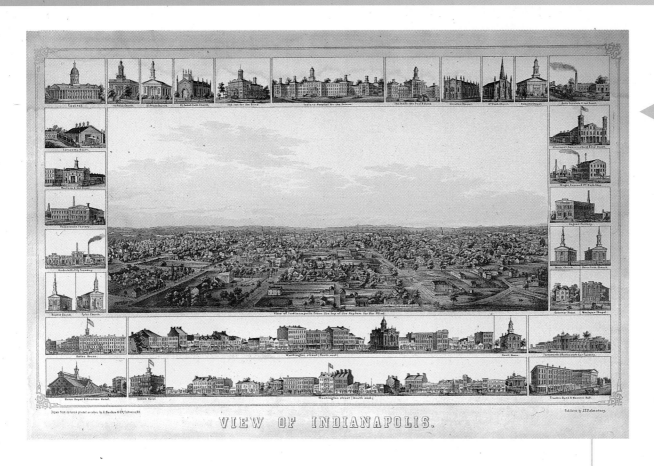

VIEW OF INDIANAPOLIS.

By 1854, Indianapolis had become a city with many large buildings.

reached the capital. This road is now U.S. Highway 40. It is called Washington Street when it passes through Indianapolis.

Farms and Towns: Hand in Hand

Early Indiana was farming country. Along with farms, many towns sprang up.

Planners and business people developed many of the towns. They chose each site carefully to best serve farmers with stores and services and to make money by selling land. For example, a spot near a river was desirable. They also wanted to be close to where a road was soon to be built. Their goal was to attract many settlers.

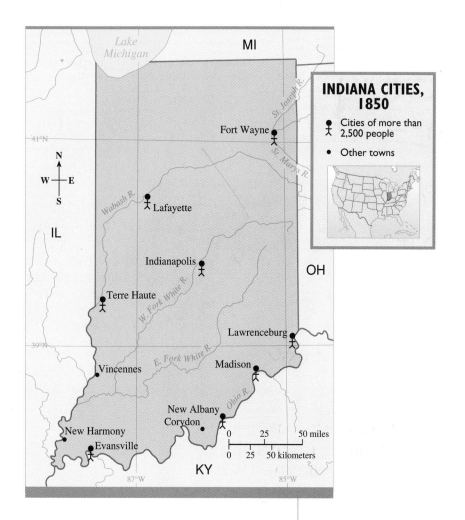

INDIANA CITIES, 1850

- Cities of more than 2,500 people
- Other towns

advantage. In 1850, New Albany was Indiana's largest city, followed by Indianapolis and Madison. Locate these cities on the map.

Factories and Industry

Like the first cities, early industry revolved around farming. By 1850, Indiana was the fourth-largest producer of corn and the third-largest producer of hogs in the nation. People built gristmills to grind farmers' corn and wheat into flour and meal. Pork-packing became an important industry, too.

Merchants and storekeepers supplied farmers with groceries, cloth, and other things they needed. Blacksmiths, tanners, and toolmakers also set up businesses to serve farmers.

Cities Grow and Prosper

In 1850, Indiana had many small towns and villages, but most people still lived in rural areas. Indiana's population was growing rapidly as you can see from the chart on the right. A few towns were becoming cities. These towns were mainly centers for buying and selling corn, hogs, and other produce from nearby farms.

At first, the largest cities were those on the Ohio River. Their location gave them a trading

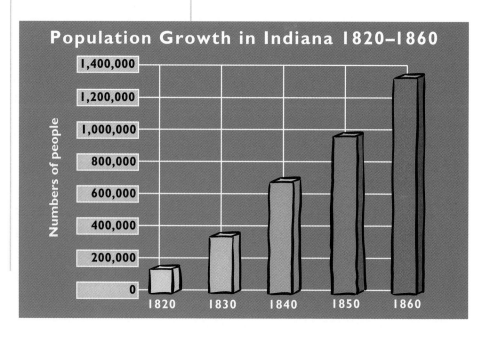

Population Growth in Indiana 1820–1860

In 1852, Henry and Clement Studebaker opened a blacksmith and wagon shop in South Bend. The Studebaker Wagon Works grew quickly, supplying wagons to farmers and to the army. Later, Indiana became a major producer of farm machinery.

This fancy Studebaker wagon was built in South Bend, Indiana.

Mississippi riverboats brought raw cotton from southern states to Indiana mills that made **textiles**. In 1850, Indiana's largest factory was the Indiana Cotton Mills at Cannelton on the Ohio River.

Moving People and Goods

To grow and prosper, farms and industries needed markets for their goods. To reach these markets, they had to have transportation. Indiana, like the other frontier states, also needed roads and waterways to bring settlers west. In the early 1800s, these methods of transportation were slow and not dependable. The state and national governments responded.

First they built better roads; then they invested in **canals**. Soon, both roads and canals snaked west from the East to Indiana and beyond. Then in the 1830s, "railroad fever" swept America. In a short time, iron rails also crisscrossed the land.

A New Constitution

From 1850 to 1851, delegates met to write a new constitution for Indiana. They believed that the General Assembly had made mistakes. Indiana's legislature, they said, had spent too much money on canals and railroads. This time, the new constitution put strict limits on how much the General Assembly could spend.

INDIANA FACTS

In Indiana, 472 miles of canals were built at a cost of about $10 million. Today, 15 miles have been restored near Metamora.

 textile A fabric made by weaving

 canal A waterway that is made by artificial means, as by digging

New Harmony

During this time of growth and new ideas, some people dreamed of a different kind of community. They hoped to build perfect societies. In Indiana, several groups started such communities.

The most important of these settlements were located in New Harmony, in southwest Indiana. In other parts of the state, the Amish, a religious group, also started their own communities. These groups became an important part of Indiana's pioneer heritage.

The Harmony Society was a small religious group from Germany. First they immigrated to Pennsylvania. Then in 1814, they followed their leader, George Rapp, to Indiana. On 25,000 acres near the Wabash River, they built a successful farming community. In 1825, the Harmony Society sold its

George Rapp (left) and Robert Owen (right)

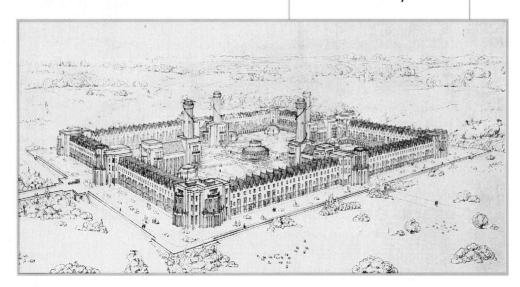

Robert Owen's proposed plan for New Harmony

land and left Indiana. The new owner was Robert Owen, a rich mill owner from Scotland.

Robert Owen's Dream

Owen had a plan for improving society. He dreamed of setting up villages of 500 to 2,500 people. Villagers would farm, make goods, and run businesses. They would share cooking and other chores— as well as profits from their work.

Sadly, New Harmony never lived up to Robert Owen's dreams. People disagreed about religion and government. Some refused to work or to contribute to the community.

Owen's plan for New Harmony failed. But the community's successes in art, science, and learning lived on.

Artist George Winter painted this scene of Potawatomis at Logansport.

The Removal of Native Americans

As new communities continued to spring up in Indiana, Native Americans feared that they would lose their lands. They had reasons for their fears. Settlers were eager to take over Native American territory in Indiana.

In 1830, the federal government passed the Indian Removal Act. The purpose of this law was to move Native Americans from their homelands onto unfamiliar lands west of the Mississippi River.

In Indiana, many Native Americans made treaties and left the state. Others were forced to leave.

In 1832, Native Americans in Illinois clashed with settlers. Soldiers put down this rebellion. The Illinois rebellion alarmed settlers in Indiana. They increased their pressure on the Native Americans who remained in Indiana.

In 1838, the Potawatomi chief Menominee refused to leave his village near Logansport. He claimed he had never signed a treaty or sold his land. Soldiers arrived. They forced more than 800 Potawatomi men, women, and children to leave. During their 62-day march to Kansas, many Native Americans died. This sad event is remembered today as the "Trail of Death."

SHOW WHAT YOU KNOW!

REFOCUS
COMPREHENSION

1. What were Indiana's two most important farm products in 1850?

2. What was the "Trail of Death"?

THINK ABOUT IT
CRITICAL THINKING

Explain the following statement: "Indiana's first cities and industries were built around farming."

WRITE ABOUT IT
ACTIVITY

In your Indiana journal, write an advertisement encouraging settlers to come to the Hoosier state in 1850.

INDIANA SPEEDS AHEAD

FOCUS *Like the rest of the country, Indiana wanted new kinds of transportation: roads, canals, railroads. These new ways of traveling changed the state.*

Flatboats and Keelboats

Most of Indiana's early settlers came west on the Ohio River by flatboat. These rectangular boats moved only in one direction—downstream with the river's current. At the end of a trip, settlers often broke up their flatboats and used them for lumber.

Indiana farmers loaded flatboats with corn, pork, and other goods. Flatboats floated their products down the Ohio to the Mississippi River and on to New Orleans. Until the 1850s, flatboats remained Indiana's most important means of transporting goods.

Keelboats were also popular for river travel. Unlike flatboats, these pointed boats could go upstream or downstream. Moving a keelboat upstream against the river's current was hard work. The boats averaged about six miles a day. Boatmen used poles, sails, or paddles to do this tough job. Sometimes they stood on the river shore and pulled the boat upstream with ropes.

Traveling the Ohio River was dangerous. Sandbanks, swirling currents, waterfalls, and fallen trees, called "snags," could slow a trip or end it.

Steamboats

In 1811, the *New Orleans* became the first steamboat to chug down the Ohio River. Powered by steam engines, steamboats were much

▼ The living area inside a flatboat often included a fireplace.

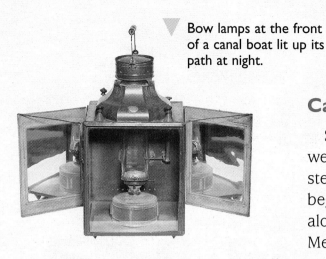

Bow lamps at the front of a canal boat lit up its path at night.

faster than flatboats or keelboats. What's more, they could travel easily against the current. Upriver trips that once took four weeks now took eight days.

Special steamboats were designed for travel on the Ohio and Mississippi. Their bottoms were broad and flat for the shallow waters of these rivers. By the 1830s, a steamboat trip from New Orleans to Indiana took only eight days. Steamboats became a common sight on the Ohio River. Towns along the river grew rapidly.

Steamboats traveled up the Wabash and on the Great Lakes, too. Cities on Lake Michigan, such as Michigan City, soon became important shipping ports for farm products from northern Indiana.

Canals in Indiana

Some Indiana rivers were too shallow for steamboats. Hoosiers began building canals along such rivers. Merchants and farmers wanted to connect many towns with deeper rivers. They also wanted to send and receive goods quickly and cheaply.

Indiana's first large canal was the Wabash and Erie Canal. Work started in 1832 and was finished three years later. The canal connected Fort Wayne and Huntington. Along the canal, locks raised and lowered ships from one level to another. The locks kept the boats on an even level as they passed over hills and through valleys.

How a Lock Works

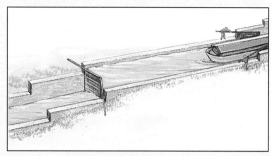

Step 1: A boat enters through the gate.

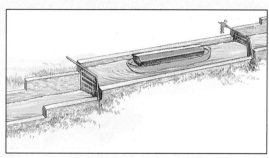

Step 2: The gate closes behind the boat.

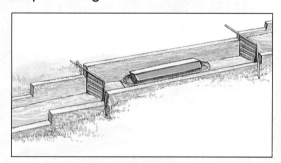

Step 3: Water is let out through the front gate until the water level is the same on each side of the front gate.

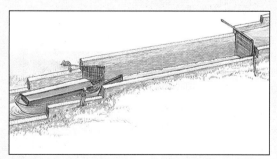

Step 4: The front gate opens and the boat passes through.

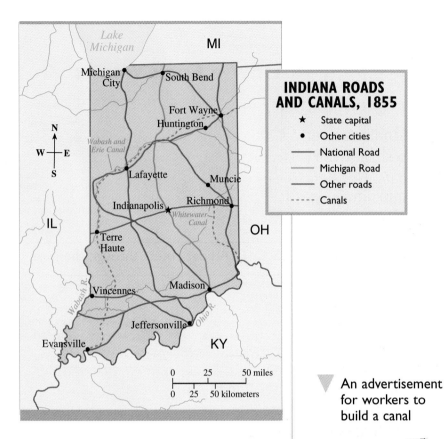

INDIANA ROADS AND CANALS, 1855
- ★ State capital
- • Other cities
- — National Road
- — Michigan Road
- — Other roads
- ---- Canals

It was the country's longest canal. During the 1840s and 1850s, many ships traveled this waterway. Locate Indiana's canal projects on the map.

Hoosier Roads

The first settlers who moved northward, away from the rivers, had no real roads. They used Native American trails. Most of these trails followed buffalo or deer **traces**—natural paths that had been widened and deepened by animals' hooves over many years.

The most famous trail was the Old Buffalo Trace that ran northwest from the Falls of the Ohio to Vincennes. In some places, this trail was 20 feet wide. Two wagons could travel it side by side.

Most trails, however, were narrow. Settlers cut down trees and underbrush along the trails to widen them. Stumps, roots, rocks, and ruts made for uncomfortable travel.

During rainy seasons, the roads became filled with mud. Wagons,

In 1836, the General Assembly passed laws that called for building three major canals. Work started with great fanfare—and then ended suddenly. Difficult economic times had hit Indiana. The state had no more money to give to canal projects.

There were also problems with the canals. Canal banks crumbled. The locks rotted, and in the winter they froze. None of the three projects was ever finished.

However, a planned extension of the Wabash and Erie Canal did reach Evansville. In all, the Wabash and Erie ran 468 miles.

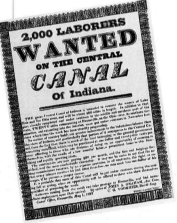

▼ An advertisement for workers to build a canal

2,000 LABORERS
WANTED
ON THE CENTRAL
CANAL
Of Indiana.

trace A natural trail created by animal hooves over time

corduroy road

oxen, and horses got stuck in the soft earth. To give their livestock and wagons something solid to pass over, pioneers put logs across the muddy spots. Settlers called these roads "corduroy roads." Later, they laid flat planks to improve the roads. These "plank roads" were expensive, however, and wore out quickly. Horses slipped on the wet planks. In time, settlers replaced the planks on the roads with gravel.

Covered Bridges

The first bridges were built of logs or boards. Builders soon found they could use stones to make a bridge's base stronger. They put a roof over the bridge to keep it from rotting. Soon covered bridges appeared all over Indiana.

Indiana still has many covered bridges. In Parke County, "the covered bridge capital of America," there are 34 covered bridges.

interstate Between states

Two Major Roads

In the early 1820s, the Indiana General Assembly planned a network of roads. Eventually, it was decided that one major road, the Michigan Road, would be built.

Construction on the Michigan Road started in 1828, and was finished in 1836. Today, it is Highway 421.

At about the same time, the national government built the Indiana part of the National Road. The purpose of the National Road was to link the eastern part of the United States with the West. This interstate road began in Cumberland, Maryland.

▲ A shovel and pickaxe were basic tools for canal, road, and railroad builders.

▼ Melcher Covered Bridge in Parke County, Indiana

plank road

181

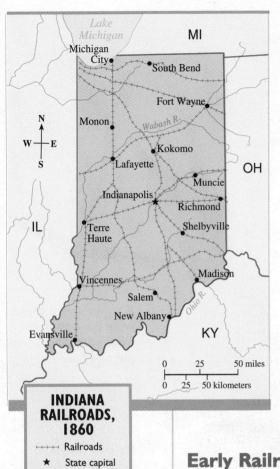

INDIANA RAILROADS, 1860

├┼┼┼┤ Railroads
★ State capital
● Other towns

The Indiana section ran west from Richmond through Indianapolis to Terre Haute on the western side of the state. Today Highway 40 and Interstate 70 follow the old route.

The National Road and Michigan Road were better than many of the early roads in Indiana. However, they were still bumpy and, in wet weather, muddy.

Early Railroads

The first railroads were built to connect steamboat lines or to bring passengers to them. The early trains were slower than steamboats. They couldn't carry as much, either. But trains improved quickly. What's more, building railroads was cheaper than building canals. In a short time, railroads became much more important to Indiana than canals.

In the 1830s, workers in Indiana, like workers in the rest of the nation, were busy laying tracks. Indiana's first track was built near Shelbyville in 1834. It was just over a mile long.

One year later, work started on a railroad from Madison to Indianapolis. Hoosiers celebrated when it reached the capital city in 1847. Steam locomotives sped along the line at ten miles an hour. Locate this railroad on the map.

Another pioneer railroad ran from New Albany on the Ohio River to Michigan City on Lake Michigan. By 1869, tracks connected most of Indiana's cities.

Railroad companies issued their own money.

Labor crews worked on road, canal, and railroad projects throughout Indiana.

Railroads Change Indiana

Railroads brought many changes to Indiana, including new residents. Many workers from Europe, especially from Ireland and Germany, came to Indiana to build the rail lines. After their work ended, many laborers decided to make the Hoosier state their home. Other newcomers came to Indiana by train.

With the railroads, passengers and goods now moved faster and more cheaply. Towns along the rail lines prospered. Hoosier farmers and townspeople living far from rivers no longer had to depend on boats to bring them goods. Now trains could bring them products from other parts of the nation.

Other Links and Changes

Indiana's goods had a much wider market, too. Cities on the East Coast, growing towns in the West, and places in between could enjoy Hoosier corn and pork.

New markets for Indiana goods led to many other changes. Towns became cities. Industry grew. Hoosiers produced more goods—and more kinds of goods. Thanks to the railroads, Indiana was no longer an isolated state on the frontier. Rail lines now linked Indiana's cities with the rest of the nation.

SHOW WHAT YOU KNOW!

REFOCUS
COMPREHENSION

1. Name three kinds of boats that traveled the Ohio River in the early 1800s.

2. Why did Hoosiers build canals?

THINK ABOUT IT
CRITICAL THINKING

In 1845, what type of transportation would you have chosen for moving each of the following: settlers, lumber, corn, hogs? Why?

WRITE ABOUT IT
ACTIVITY

In your Indiana journal, write a diary entry telling how your town changed with the coming of a new railroad line in the mid-1800s.

Map Adventure

INDIANAPOLIS YESTERDAY AND TODAY

FOCUS *Over 175 years have passed since Indianapolis was built as Indiana's state capital. The center of downtown Indianapolis today still resembles the town it once was.*

Indianapolis in 1825

Indianapolis Today

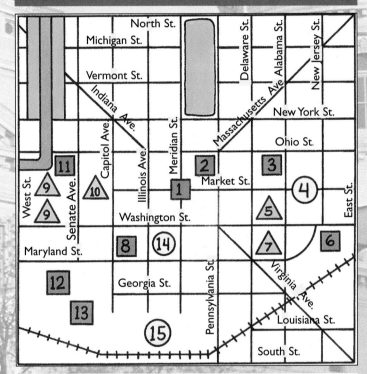

1. Market House	9. Jail
2. Church	10. Indianapolis Hotel
3. Pottery shop	11. Cabinetmaker
4. Blacksmith shop	12. Indianapolis Gazette
5. Hat shop	13. State Treasurer
6. Emigrant's Office	14. Tinker's shop
7. General store	15. Log schoolhouse
8. Courthouse	16. Church

1. Soldiers and Sailors Monument	8. Theater
	9. Government Center
2. Church	10. State House
3. City Market	11. Indiana State Library
4. Market Square Arena	12. Convention Center
5. City-County Building	13. RCA Dome
6. Downtown Heliport	14. Circle Center Mall
7. Marion County Jail	15. Union Station

Capital City Adventure

The people who designed Indianapolis planned for a city built inside a square, one mile on each side. This plan met the needs for the capital in 1825. Today the "old city" is only a small part of Indianapolis. The metropolitan area has spread out in all directions, and there are many more buildings within the original square mile.

Map Key

 government building

 business building

 other building

 park

 forest

MAP IT

1. As a tour guide at the Indianapolis Sightseeing Company, you are giving the daily tour of downtown Indianapolis. Begin the tour in the center of town. What do you see there? What do you tell the tourists about this site in 1825?

2. Continue south to the corner of Meridian and Washington streets. What do you see when you turn west onto Washington Street? What stood near that location on Washington Street in 1825?

3. Continue to walk west along Washington Street heading toward the State House. What is the next street you come to after Illinois Street? What was the name of that street in 1825?

4. Find the Convention Center and the RCA Dome. What would you have seen in their location in 1825?

EXPLORE IT

Plan a historical tour of Indianapolis for a fourth-grade class visiting the capital city for the first time. Choose the sights that you think would be the most interesting. Use the street maps of Indianapolis to plan your tour.

A Clearing in the Forest

by Joanne Landers Henry

In 1833, Elijah Fletcher—or El as everyone calls him—lives in Indianapolis with his family. Read the following selection and see a bit of the town through his eyes, as he races after his big brother Cooley.

El hurried on. Impatiently he dodged around a fast-moving buggy, several riders on horseback, and a heavy Conestoga freight wagon pulled by three teams of horses. Drivers and riders would not take kindly to a boy getting in their way or frightening their horses.

He could remember Father's stern voice warning him to pay heed to the traffic. Just last week a runaway horse had dragged a buggy onto the wood-plank walk in front of the *Indiana Journal* newspaper office. The driver had been badly hurt, almost killed.

Ahead El could still see Cooley. He was well past the brick building where Father's law office was. Nearby was the frame two-story Washington Hall Hotel, which dwarfed the small bank building nearby.

Suddenly Cooley ducked behind a bright blue freight wagon and disappeared from sight.

Sighing, El slowed to a walk. It seemed as if he was always trying to keep up with Cooley, even with Cooley's dreams of adventure.

Cooley said that when he grew up, he was going to leave Indianapolis. After all, he said, it was just an ordinary small town in a clearing in the forest. Some folks called it a hog hole. Cooley dreamed of going back East or maybe even to some foreign country. He might become a famous artist someday, he bragged.

Father, who was a lawyer, didn't put much store in Cooley's boasts. He said being an artist was no way to earn a living. He didn't put much store in what the naysayers had to say about Indianapolis, either. He said one day it would be a fine town, maybe even as important as Cincinnati. It was the state capital. Already it had a few factories, and mills for paper, flour, and wool. There were churches, a variety of shops, and a post office.

"It will grow fast, just like you boys," he told his sons. "Mark my words! Mark my words!"

Want to read more about El Fletcher's adventures? You can find out what happened to him by checking the book out of your school or town library.

SHOW WHAT YOU KNOW!

REFOCUS
COMPREHENSION

1. Name four government buildings in Indianapolis today and in 1825.

2. Identify two Indianapolis street names that are different today from what they were in 1825.

THINK ABOUT IT
CRITICAL THINKING
What are some things that Indianapolis today has in common with Indianapolis in 1825?

WRITE ABOUT IT
ACTIVITY

Write a letter from El to a cousin in Vermont, telling about Indianapolis.

THE SPIRIT OF COMMUNITY

FOCUS *Several different groups, including the Rappites, the Owenites, and the Amish, settled in Indiana and followed their own ways. These groups remind us of the great hopes, dreams, and ideas that inspired settlers and helped shape our state.*

The First New Harmony

When George Rapp and his followers decided to leave Pennsylvania, they needed to look carefully for a new home. They were a religious group that chose to live apart from other pioneer settlements. They wanted enough land to support their community, a location near a river, and a good climate for growing grapes. In 1814, they settled on land in Indiana along the Wabash River. There they built the town of New Harmony.

The word *harmony* means "agreement." The Rappites, as the followers of George Rapp were called, tried to live in agreement. Every person shared equally in the community's work and its wealth. This is called **cooperative** living.

★ **cooperative** Style of living in which members of a community share work, goods, and profits

▼ Swiss artist Karl Bodmer painted this view of New Harmony during a visit in 1832.

The Rappites agreed on the importance of planning, order, and cleanliness. New Harmony was one of America's first pre-planned towns. The Rappites laid out their streets on a rectangle with a large church near the center of town.

They also planned their economy. Some members farmed and raised cattle. Others worked in mills and factories. They made wagons, cloth, rope, leather products, and hats.

The Rappites were very successful. Their community grew so wealthy that it was able to loan money to the state of Indiana.

The Second New Harmony

Robert Owen bought the community of New Harmony from the Rappites in 1825. He had many new ideas about cooperative living. Famous scientists, artists, and teachers who liked his ideas joined Owen in New Harmony, hoping to build a perfect society.

Education was an important goal of the Owenites, as the followers of Owen were called. They set up the first kindergarten, the first free public schools, and the first free public library in the United States.

The Atheneum, overlooking the Wabash River, houses a museum and library.

There was a school for teaching work skills. New Harmony also had the nation's first women's club.

From the beginning, however, Owen's New Harmony was troubled by disagreements and quarrels. There were too few farmers to support the community, and too many people who did not work hard. Robert Owen left New Harmony in 1827.

New Harmony Today

Today, some of the old buildings in New Harmony have been restored and rebuilt. Others, such as a roofless church and the modern Atheneum (ath uh NEE um) have been added. Every year many visitors come to New Harmony to see where the Rappites and Owenites dreamed of living in harmony.

The Amish Come to Indiana

Another group of German-speaking immigrants came to Indiana from Pennsylvania in the early 1840s. They were the Amish.

The Amish and the Rappites were similar in several ways. Both groups started farming communities. Both were very religious. Both chose to live apart from the rest of the world.

The Amish also believed in working together for the good of the community. They solved their problems together—by sharing. For example, if one family's crops failed, the Amish community would help them by sharing food. If an Amish family's barn burned down, everyone would rebuild the barn.

A Close Community

The Amish, unlike the Rappites, stayed in Indiana. They put down roots in Adams, Allen, and Daviess counties. Over time, their communities grew and spread. Today, there are large Amish communities in Elkhart and Lagrange counties, too.

Along Amish roads, you see neat farms, huge barns, and plain white houses. Amish families are often large and extended. Grandparents,

Sometimes the Amish get together to help paint a neighbor's barn.

These Amish girls wear homemade dresses.

The Amish have not taken on modern ways. Most Amish do not use modern farm equipment. They do not use electricity. Windmills pump their water. They cook on wood-burning stoves.

Most Amish families do not own cars or trucks, either. They travel in black horse-drawn buggies. The bright orange and red triangles on the backs of their buggies are the only clue that these are modern times. These triangles allow other drivers to see the buggies at night.

parents, and children live together in one home made up of several attached houses.

Traditional Ways

The Amish still hold three main beliefs. They believe in simple living and worship. They believe in close families and communities. They deeply respect nature.

Today the Amish still live much as the first Amish in Indiana did. They are farmers, and with hard work they have made their farms successful.

Amish Children

Except for their shoes, Amish children today look like children of the past. Girls wear long, plain, homemade dresses of many colors, white aprons, and caps. Boys dress in trousers, shirts, and wide-brimmed hats.

Many Amish children go to public schools. Others go to Amish schools, but only to eighth grade. Many Amish parents believe this is all the formal education their children need.

For fun Amish children play many games and sports, including soccer and basketball. Every child who wants to play is included.

SHOW WHAT YOU KNOW!

REFOCUS
COMPREHENSION

1. Who were the Rappites and the Owenites?

2. Why didn't the two New Harmony communities last?

THINK ABOUT IT
CRITICAL THINKING

Why is it important that groups like the Amish are able to live as they choose as long as they obey the nation's laws?

WRITE ABOUT IT
ACTIVITY

Write a list of five things you believe are important in a society.

SUMMING UP

1 DO YOU REMEMBER . . .
COMPREHENSION

1. What are two of the things planners looked for when choosing a site for a town?

2. How did the settlement of Indiana affect the Native Americans living there?

3. In what important way did the steamboat improve river travel?

4. Where did the railroad companies find workers?

5. What strong beliefs affect Amish life?

2 SKILL POWER
FINDING INFORMATION

Here is a list of topics from the chapter. Choose one of the topics and go to the library to find information about it. Make a list of the books available for each topic. Include the type of book each is—fiction, biography, or reference. Share your list with your classmates.

Indianapolis
Steamboats
New Harmony
Robert Owen
Canals

3 WHAT DO YOU THINK?
CRITICAL THINKING

1. What industry in Indiana depended on a crop grown in the South? Why?

2. How did Native Americans make travel easier for pioneers moving north in Indiana?

3. How did the building of the National Road show that the United States was expanding?

4. In what ways was travel by steamboat and canal limited?

5. Why do you think the second New Harmony failed?

4 SAY IT, WRITE IT, USE IT
VOCABULARY

As a reporter for the *Indianapolis Gazette* in 1850, your assignment is to write an article about the progress that has been made in the state of Indiana in the past 25 years. Use as many of the vocabulary terms as possible in your article.

cooperative   textile
interstate   trace
metropolitan

OUR COMMUNIT
PLANNING OUR FUTUR

CHALLENGE	SOLUTION
We'll need more space to dump garbage.	We can build more recycling center

5 GEOGRAPHY AND YOU

MAP STUDY

1. Name the canals shown on the map.

2. Which three Indiana cities on the map did the Michigan Road connect?

3. How might settlers or goods travel from Fort Wayne to Lafayette?

4. Which roads passed through Indianapolis?

INDIANA ROADS AND CANALS, 1855

★ State capital
● Other cities
— National Road
— Michigan Road
— Other roads
----- Canals

0   25   50 miles
0   25   50 kilometers

6 TAKE ACTION

CITIZENSHIP

You learned about how Indianapolis ha changed since 1825. Every community to face challenges that exist today and for those in the future. For example, wi be enough housing or schools for future citizens? Together with your classmates, a chart listing some of the present-day challenges faced by your community and possible future challenges. Then beside ea challenge, write a possible solution.

7 GET CREATIVE

LANGUAGE ARTS CONNECTION

Suppose that someone has suggested moving the capital of Indiana again. Would you support the suggestion? Write a paragraph in which you express your opinion. Explain why you think the capital should remain in Indianapolis or be moved to a new location. Discuss your opinion with your classmates.

LOOKING AHEAD

In the next chapter, read about the effects of the Civil War on Indiana and the nation.

A DIVIDED

During the Civil War, Hoosiers took up arms to preserve the Union. The bloody Civil War brought many changes to Indiana and the nation.

CONTENTS

▲ Read on
page 207
about the
lives of
soldiers who
wore caps
like these.

NATION

These books tell about some people, places, and events from the time of the Civil War. Read one that interests you and fill out a book-review form.

READ AND RESEARCH

Allen Jay and the Underground Railroad by **Marlene Targ Brill, illustrated by Janice Lee Porter** (Carolrhoda Books, 1993)
When a young Quaker boy decides to help a runaway slave, they both face great danger. Will the slave hunters catch them? *(fiction)*
● *You can read a selection from this book on page 212.*

How Sweet the Sound: African-American Songs for Children **Selected by Wade and Cheryl Hudson, illustrated by Floyd Cooper** (Scholastic, 1995)
This collection of songs celebrates the lives of African Americans yesterday and today. *(poetry)*

Next Stop Freedom: The Story of a Slave Girl by **Dorothy and Thomas Hoobler, illustrated by Cheryl Hanna** (Silver Burdett Press, 1991)
A young slave on a Southern plantation dreams of escaping to freedom. Will her dreams come true? *(fiction)*

Thunder at Gettysburg by **Patricia Lee Gauch, illustrated by Stephen Gammell** (G.P. Putnam's Sons, 1975)
Getting caught in the middle of the Battle of Gettysburg changes a 14-year-old's ideas about war. *(historical fiction)*

Skill POWER Predicting Outcomes

Knowing how to predict outcomes can help you better understand what you read.

UNDERSTAND IT

You probably predict outcomes, or guess what will happen in the future, every day. You predict an outcome when you guess who is going to win a sporting event. For example, you are at a basketball game, and these are the teams' records.

Cougars—6 wins, 2 losses

Bears—1 win, 5 losses

You might predict that, since the Cougars seem to be the better team, they will win the game. At the end of the third quarter, the score is Bears 33, Cougars 21. Now you might want to change your prediction. Only when the game is over and you know its outcome can you verify, or check, your prediction.

EXPLORE IT

You can better understand what you've read by thinking about what you already know and predicting what will happen next.

• First, read some of the story below. Think about what is happening.

• Next, predict what will happen in the story. Look for clues in what you read.

Lizzie rushed through her chores because her family was going to town. They wanted to get the latest news about the Civil War. Lizzie's brother Jeb was a soldier in the Union army. He used to write home every week. But in the last three months, her parents hadn't received one letter. Lizzie prayed that Jeb hadn't been hurt or captured. She wouldn't even let herself imagine anything worse.

• Stop reading and predict what will happen next.

• Continue reading to verify, or check, your prediction.

When Lizzie and her parents reached town, they hurried to the general store. Pages from the latest newspaper were posted on the wall. Lizzie read through the long lists of dead and wounded. Her brother's name wasn't on either list. Lizzie hugged her parents.

• Finally, verify your prediction. Was it correct?

TRY IT

Work with a group of your classmates. Each of you should find a story or an article that interests you. When it's your turn, tell about what happened in the first part of your story. Then let the other group members predict what will happen next in your story. Tell a little more and then ask if anyone wants to change his or her prediction. Then to check classmates' predictions, tell how your story or article ended.

You can predict the outcome of a story as you read.

SKILL POWER SEARCH *As you read this chapter, use predictions to help you understand more about what you read.*

Setting the Scene

KEY TERMS

secede
reaper
threshing machine
reform

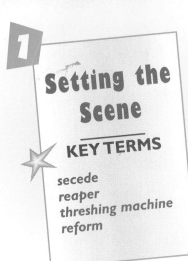

INDIANA AT WAR AND PEACE

FOCUS *Learn about Hoosier contributions to the Union during the Civil War and the effects of the war on Indiana.*

Indiana: A Free State

From its start, Indiana was a free state. Both the Northwest Ordinance and the Indiana constitutions of 1816 and 1851 outlawed slavery. Most Hoosiers, like other people in the North, believed that slavery was wrong.

But many Southern people owned slaves. Southern crops, such as cotton, required many workers. Slaves did the back-breaking jobs of hoeing fields, planting seeds, and picking the crops by hand. So, most Southerners felt strongly that slavery should continue.

The question of slavery had divided the United States for many years. By the mid-1800s, the nation was close to war.

Lincoln's Election

In 1860 most Hoosiers voted Republican. The Republicans opposed the spread of slavery. Indiana's votes helped to elect Republican candidate Abraham Lincoln. Lincoln, who grew up in the Hoosier state, became the nation's sixteenth President.

Lincoln's election made many Southern people angry. They felt that Lincoln would represent the interests of the Northern states, which were against slavery. They believed that his election would mean the end of slavery. This was one reason many Southern states **seceded** from the Union soon after Lincoln's election. This action by the Southern states led quickly to war.

Abraham Lincoln (middle) with two aides, John Hay (left), a Hoosier, and John Nicolay (right)

secede   Break away from an organization or nation

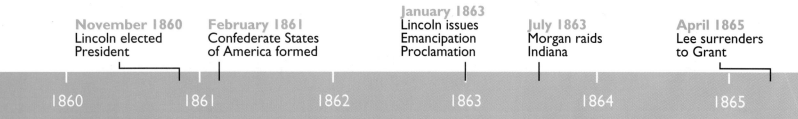

November 1860	February 1861	January 1863	July 1863	April 1865
Lincoln elected President	Confederate States of America formed	Lincoln issues Emancipation Proclamation	Morgan raids Indiana	Lee surrenders to Grant

1860   1861   1862   1863   1864   1865

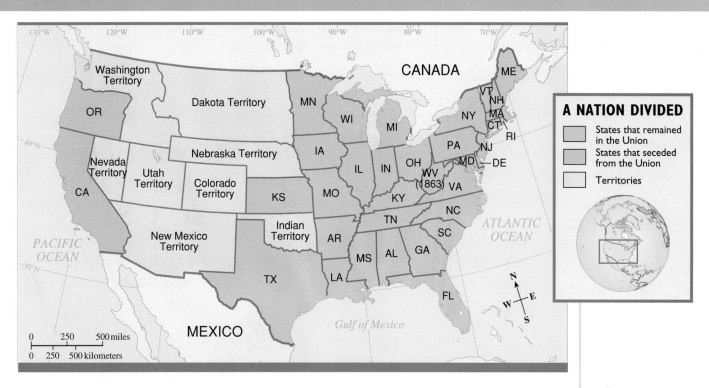

A NATION DIVIDED

- States that remained in the Union
- States that seceded from the Union
- Territories

A Nation Divided

The map above shows how the nation was divided between the free states of the North and the slave states of the South. In February 1861, eleven Southern states formed the Confederate States of America, also called the Confederacy. They elected Jefferson Davis of Kentucky as president.

The Civil War started on April 12, 1861. It was a war between the Confederacy and the Union states.

Hoosiers and the Union

Hoosiers had ties to both the South and to the North. Many Hoosiers had come to Indiana from Southern states and had family ties there. The rivers of the state also served as links to the South.

On the other hand, the new roads and railroads of the mid-1800s linked Indiana to the North. Another important tie to the North was Indiana's opposition to the spread of slavery.

▲ Oliver P. Morton became governor of Indiana in 1861.

Many Hoosiers were against slavery. Indiana was a state of small farms and small businesses. Unlike states with large cotton and tobacco fields, Indiana had little use for slaves. In addition, most Hoosiers came to think that slavery was wrong.

Hoosiers did not want slavery to spread to the new territories opening in the West. They wanted free farmers to settle those lands.

Governor Oliver P. Morton

One of the strongest governors in Indiana's history was Oliver P. Morton. He strongly supported the Union and President Lincoln.

Like President Lincoln, Morton was determined to win the war. This meant signing up men to fight for the Union. It also meant paying huge sums of money to help the Union war effort.

Morton borrowed money to train, clothe, and feed Hoosier soldiers and nurses. He also asked private citizens to give money to support the war.

Hoosier War Contributions

As the chart on the right shows, Indiana played an important part in the Union war effort. Almost three out of four Hoosier men of military age joined the Union army. About one of every eight Indiana soldiers died. They died from cold, wounds, accidents, infections, lack of food, and, above all, diseases. Germs spread quickly in camps and hospitals.

The elderly, women, and children also supported the Union. They took over the work of men at war.

HOOSIERS HELP SAVE THE UNION

Number of Hoosiers who fought in the Civil War: **196,363**

Number of Hoosiers who died in the Civil War: **25,028**

Number of battles in which Hoosier soldiers fought: **308**

Number of Hoosiers who became generals: **39**

They grew extra food, raised money, and made blankets, clothing, and bandages. Women also wrote letters to troops, cleaned camps, and nursed the sick and wounded.

Morgan's Raids

John Hunt Morgan brought the war into Indiana. Morgan was a Confederate general. In July 1863, Morgan decided on his own—and against orders— to raid Indiana and Ohio from Kentucky.

Morgan and about 2,400 raiders robbed banks and stores. They stole money, food, horses, and even ice skates and a bird cage. They burned buildings, bridges, trains, and railroads. They took part in the Battle of Corydon— the only Civil War action on Indiana soil.

Morgan's raids boosted the spirit of the Confederacy. But Morgan and his raiders terrified the people of Indiana

Women carried food and supplies to troops and nursed the wounded.

and Ohio. Southerners called Morgan a bold and brave man. Northerners said he was a robber.

Morgan was chased by volunteers and over 60,000 troops. In Ohio, near the Pennsylvania border, Morgan finally was captured. Later he escaped and returned to Tennessee, where he was killed in battle.

The War Ends

After four years of bloodshed, the Union finally beat the Confederacy. Its victory meant that the United States would remain one nation.

Morgan's Raiders burned and looted Salem, Indiana, on July 10, 1863.

It also meant an end to slavery in the South.

The Civil War brought many other changes. Women worked in factories during the war, and many stayed on. Children also worked, and many never returned to school.

Results of the Civil War

On farms, machinery such as the reaper, the threshing machine, and a new kind of plow helped to do the work of men at war. Other machines increased production in factories. Farm life and factory work were never the same again.

During the war, the Northern railroads grew in order to carry

reaper   Machine that cuts crops for harvesting
threshing machine   Machine that cuts and separates grain

The Tyree family gathers on their front porch in Indianapolis in 1895.

In 1870, Indiana was fourth in the nation in wheat production and fifth in corn production.

soldiers and supplies. After the war, railroads continued to grow. Now trains carried passengers and goods across the continent.

The war also changed where people settled. Many Hoosiers moved from rural areas to cities. They also moved from the southern to the northern part of the state.

During and after the Civil War, African Americans moved to Indiana. Many settled in border cities along the Ohio River. Large groups moved to Indianapolis. By 1900, almost one out of ten people in the capital city was African American. Most black Hoosiers lived in separate communities with their own churches, schools, and businesses.

Ku Klux Klan

In 1866, the first Ku Klux Klan, also known as the KKK, met in the South. The purpose of the Klan was to preserve the power of white people. Klan members wanted to keep African Americans from getting ahead. The Klan also did not want them to vote.

Klan members dressed in white robes with hoods. They beat and sometimes murdered innocent black people. The Klan burned barns and houses.

In the 1920s, the Klan became very strong in Indiana. Klan members opposed immigrants, especially Catholics and Jews. The Klan lost most of its power in Indiana before the 1940s. But it has had some members in Indiana in recent years.

The Reform Spirit

With the end of the Civil War, slavery was abolished in the United States. Many people now turned their energies to reforms.

Many soldiers' families needed help after the war. So did newly freed slaves, who often had no education and no jobs. Reformers set up public schools and libraries. They built orphanages for children who had lost their parents.

Some reformers worked to improve prisons. Others helped the deaf and the blind. Some worked for women's voting rights.

Benjamin Harrison

Between 1869 and 1921, four Vice Presidents came from Indiana. For that reason, the Hoosier state became known as "the Mother of Vice Presidents."

Hoosiers celebrated Benjamin Harrison's election.

A Hoosier from Indianapolis became President during this time, too. In 1888, Benjamin Harrison, the grandson of William Henry Harrison, was elected the twenty-third President of the United States.

 reform Correction of faults or evils

REFOCUS
COMPREHENSION

1. In what ways did Indiana help the Union war effort?

2. Why did most Hoosiers want to remain a part of the Union?

THINK ABOUT IT
CRITICAL THINKING

Compare Indiana before the Civil War with Indiana after the war.

WRITE ABOUT IT
ACTIVITY

In your Indiana journal, write a letter from President Lincoln to Governor Morton thanking Indiana for its help during the war.

MORGAN'S RAID

FOCUS When Confederate soldier John Hunt Morgan and his raiders invaded Indiana, they robbed, burned, and terrorized townspeople for five days.

N
W E
S

OHIO

Whitewater River 6

5

4

Dupont Bryantsburg

Paris

Muscatatuck River

Lexington

3

INDIANA

KENTUCKY

Palmyra

2

Louisville

Ohio River

Mauckport

1

MORGAN'S RAID

MI

IL IN OH

KY

25 MILES

25 KILOMETERS

Follow Morgan's Raiders

Morgan's Raiders rode into Indiana on horseback and were heavily armed with **artillery**. Union soldiers and Indiana volunteers chased the raiders for five days. You have volunteered to help stop the terror.

Map Key

1 Brandenburg, KY Morgan stole two steamboats and crossed the Ohio River. Soldiers in Indiana fired at them. Morgan's Raiders forced the soldiers to retreat.

2 Corydon Local soldiers blocked the city of Corydon when they heard about Morgan's approach. They were quickly defeated in the only Civil War battle fought in Indiana.

3 Salem Morgan captured Salem, causing more damage there than anywhere else. The raiders burned the railroad station, tore up the railroad track, and burned bridges.

4 Vernon Local soldiers protected Vernon, an important railroad center, from attack by the raiders. Morgan decided to avoid the city.

5 Versailles Morgan's last raid in Indiana took place in Versailles, where he stole money from the county treasury.

6 Harrison, OH After leaving Indiana, Morgan's Raiders crossed the Whitewater River and entered Harrison. They burned the bridge behind them.

☆ *artillery* Large guns, such as cannons, that are too heavy to carry

MAP IT

1. On July 8, 1863, Morgan's Raiders arrive in Brandenburg. After crossing the Ohio River, what Indiana city do they enter?

2. The raiders head toward Corydon. In which direction do they travel?

3. The raiders travel north to Salem. Which direction do they follow as they ride from Salem to Lexington?

4. From Lexington the raiders head north again. What city is their destination?

5. After avoiding Vernon, Morgan raids Versailles. What cities does he travel through to get there?

EXPLORE IT

You have been asked to describe your experience as an Indiana volunteer during Morgan's raid. Tell about the events and include some of your reactions.

HOOSIERS BATTLE FOR THE UNION

FOCUS *Find out how Indiana's soldiers contributed to the war effort.*

The Call to Arms

In Indiana, volunteers rushed to join the Union army as soon as the Civil War began. Patriotism was in the air. During the first week of the war, over 12,000 Hoosiers enlisted. Soon 6 **regiments** from Indiana were formed. During the four-year war, 129 regiments of foot soldiers from Indiana fought for the Union.

Under Governor Morton, Indiana not only raised troops, it also helped to supply them. The state provided food, clothing, equipment, and, most important, arms.

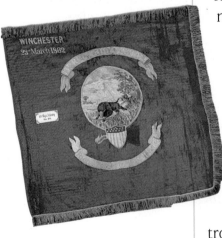

▼ The flag of Indiana's Thirteenth Regiment

▲ Indiana's Fourteenth Regiment

African Americans Fight

African Americans were eager to serve in the Union army. But a 1792 law prevented them from joining the army. The United States government **repealed** this law so black troops could fight.

Some black Hoosiers joined the Massachusetts Fifty-Fourth. This regiment included men from every state, as well as Canada.

In November 1863, Governor Morton was asked to raise a regiment of black soldiers from Indiana. The Twenty-Eighth Regiment, United States Colored Troops, was formed as a result of Morton's call for black soldiers.

 regiment A unit of soldiers made up of ten companies of about 100 soldiers each

 repeal Put an end to, withdraw

▲ These are some items that soldiers carried or wore during the Civil War.

The Twenty-Eighth was the only African American regiment from Indiana. It numbered about 1,500 men.

Army Life

Army life was tough. Troops lived in small tents, called "pup" tents because of their size. Army food included dried milk and vegetables and dried salted meat. Hardtack was another part of the basic army diet. The troops called these hard crackers "sheet-iron crackers," "teeth dullers," and "worm castles."

For recruits, the first order of the day was getting ready for battle. New troops had to learn to use their weapons and other equipment. They had to be able to follow orders from their leaders without hesitation. Long days were spent drilling and drilling.

Recruits also faced boredom, homesickness, and fear. To keep themselves busy, they sang songs, played cards and dice, and wrote letters and journals.

Hoosier Soldiers

Soldiers from Indiana took part in every major Civil War battle. They fought in Virginia at the start of the war—and at the end. By some accounts, an Indiana soldier was the last man killed in action.

In every battle, thousands and thousands of bullets ripped through the air. At times so many men died they were buried in mass graves.

Indiana's regiments fought bravely. Their contribution helped to keep the nation together.

SHOW WHAT YOU KNOW!

REFOCUS
COMPREHENSION

1. What was the Twenty-Eighth Regiment?

2. Describe army life during the Civil War.

THINK ABOUT IT
CRITICAL THINKING

Why was Indiana important to the Union cause?

WRITE ABOUT IT
ACTIVITY

In your Indiana journal, write a new soldier's diary entry that describes getting ready for a battle.

Citizenship

KEY TERMS

abolitionist
discrimination
temperance

LITERATURE

Allen Jay and
the Underground
Railroad

HOOSIERS AND REFORM

FOCUS *Explore how and why Hoosiers supported reforms that they thought would lead to a better state.*

The Abolitionists

Many Northerners opposed slavery. They wanted to keep it out of the new territories in the West. Some, however, were willing to let slavery continue in the South.

Abolitionists wanted an end to slavery immediately. They believed that slavery was evil.

In Indiana and other free states, abolitionists gave antislavery lectures. They wrote books that described the horrors of slavery. They also started newspapers, such as the *Free Labor Advocate* and *Anti-Slavery Chronicle* of Newport, Indiana. The abolitionist movement helped to educate people about slavery and to influence politicians.

The Underground Railroad

Many abolitionists took part in the Underground Railroad. This railroad was not a train track. It was a network of secret routes. Along these routes, slaves could make their way to freedom in the Northern states or Canada. Many free black people were involved in the Underground Railroad.

Indiana was located between the Southern slave states and Canada, so it was an important link in the network. As you can see from the map on this page, three major routes passed through Indiana. There were more than 30 cities along these routes.

THE UNDERGROUND RAILROAD IN INDIANA

- ○ Depots
- — Underground Railroad routes
- ㉗ Present-day U.S. Highway 27
- ★ State capital

Lake Michigan
Michigan
South Bend
St. Joseph R.
㉗
St. Joseph R.
Plymouth
Auburn
Maumee R.
Fort Wayne
St. Marys R.
Rensselaer
Logansport
Decatur
Wabash R.
Portland
Russiaville
㉗
Lafayette
Winchester
Ohio
Darlington
Westfield
Crawfordsville
Fountain City
Bloomingdale
Richmond
Brazil
Indianapolis
Terre Haute
Greensburg
Columbus
W. Fork White R.
Bloomington
Lawrenceburg
E. Fork White R.
Brownstown
Madison
Wabash R.
Salem
Vincennes
Ohio R.
Leavenworth
New Albany
Kentucky
Evansville
Illinois

0   25   50 miles
0   25   50 kilometers

42°N, 41°N, 40°N, 39°N, 38°N
88°W, 87°W, 86°W, 85°W

★ **abolitionist** A person who wanted to put an end to slavery

Katie and Levi Coffin

Escape to the North

Many runaway slaves had to find their way North without maps or help. Some of their songs, such as "Follow the Drinking Gourd," contained hidden directions to help guide fleeing slaves to the North. The Drinking Gourd is the group of stars that is also called the Big Dipper. The North Star is part of the Drinking Gourd.

Homes, barns, and churches with secret hiding places served as "depots" or "stations" along the railroad. At each hiding place, "station masters"—both black and white—fed and nursed fleeing slaves. "Conductors" helped the slaves to reach the next depot.

This painting shows the Coffins helping runaway slaves.

Follow the Drinking Gourd

Follow the drinking gourd!
Follow the drinking gourd.
For the old man is awaiting
for to carry you to freedom
If you follow the drinking gourd.

When the sun comes back
and the first quail calls,
Follow the drinking gourd,
For the old man is awaiting
for to carry you to freedom
If you follow the drinking gourd.

Escaped slaves were always in danger. Station masters also faced huge risks.

The Coffins of Indiana

Katie and Levi Coffin were Quakers from eastern Indiana. The Quakers, or Friends, are a religious group that opposed slavery. The Coffin home was an important station on the Underground Railroad. Between 1827 and 1847, the Coffins sheltered at least 2,000 escaped slaves.

Today, Levi Coffin is remembered as the "President" of the Underground Railroad. The Coffins' Fountain City home, with its hiding places, is open to visitors.

After the Civil War, Indiana Quakers continued to help former slaves. They provided transportation, set up relief camps, and gave out food, clothing, and other supplies.

In 1888 these orphans came to Goshen, Indiana, from New England.

Helping Freed Slaves

With the end of the Civil War, many freed slaves moved to Indiana from the South. The majority were uneducated and poor. In many areas, white people were unfriendly to them. Most efforts to help the newcomers were carried out by other black people.

During this time, black Hoosiers banded together to demand political rights. They fought **discrimination** in public places, such as restaurants, hotels, and train stations. Like Booker T. Washington, a national leader, they also pushed for better education.

In much of the South, teaching a slave to read or write had been against the law.

Booker T. Washington encouraged black people to learn trades.

African American churches started black schools in Indiana. They got some help from white churches and Quaker groups. Finally, Indiana passed a state law to fund separate schools for black children. But these schools did not receive as much money as white schools.

Other Reform Causes

The Civil War created hardships for many people. Soldiers' Aid Societies collected food, fuel, and clothing for soldiers' families.

After the war, private aid groups continued to grow and help those in need. Among the needy were widows and war orphans. Aid societies opened orphanages in many cities.

 discrimination Unfair treatment of a particular person or group

210

Helen Gougar

State and local governments also took on more social responsibilities after the Civil War. A number of hospitals were opened, such as Indianapolis City Hospital, now called Wishard Memorial.

Efforts were made to stop the spread of diseases. "Reform schools" were built to give young offenders a chance to change, instead of sending them to jail.

Women's Rights

By 1850, some Indiana women and men had asked the state legislature to allow women to own property and to vote. But the General Assembly had refused.

After the Civil War, the fight for women's rights continued. Women's groups pushed the state legislature to give women the vote. Two of the most important leaders in Indiana at that time were Alice Hamilton and Helen Gougar.

Temperance

Women were leaders of the temperance movement, too. Churches also worked to stop the manufacture and sale of alcohol. Temperance groups believed that alcohol was the cause of many social problems, such as poverty. Laws were passed to make Indiana "dry"—or alcohol free.

At first, the Indiana Supreme Court declared these laws illegal. Finally, in 1919, the Eighteenth Amendment to the Constitution made the whole nation dry. People continued to make and sell alcohol illegally, however, until the amendment was repealed in 1933.

Temperance poster

★ **temperance** Drinking little or no alcohol

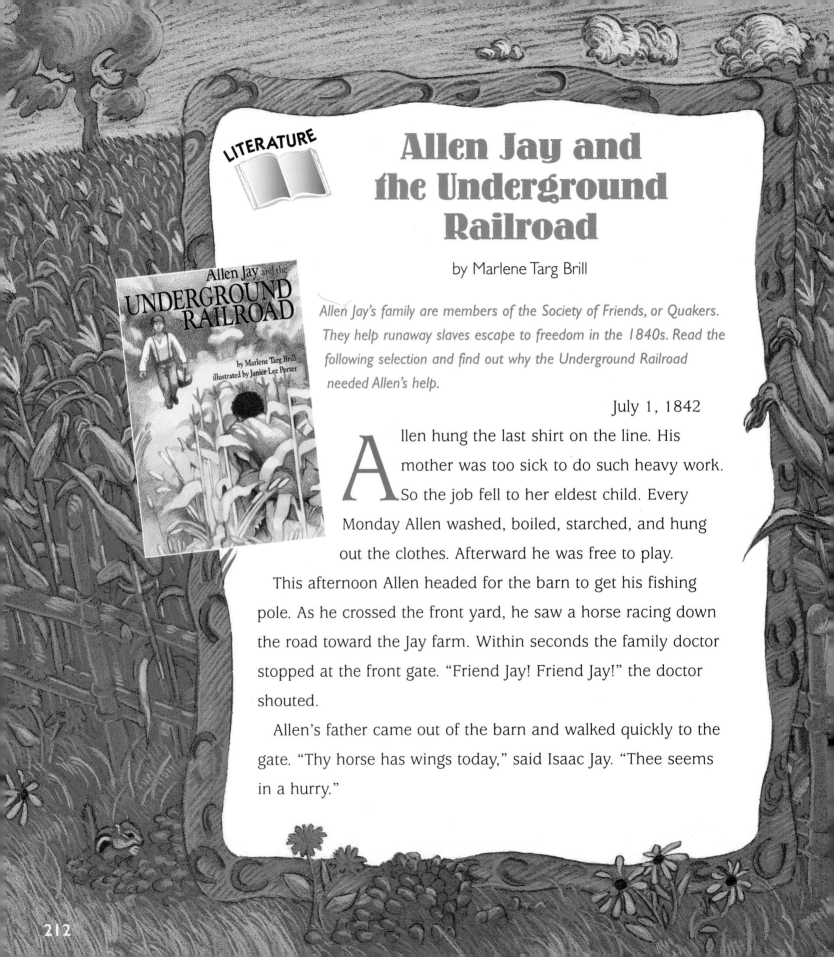

Allen Jay and the Underground Railroad

by Marlene Targ Brill

Allen Jay's family are members of the Society of Friends, or Quakers. They help runaway slaves escape to freedom in the 1840s. Read the following selection and find out why the Underground Railroad needed Allen's help.

July 1, 1842

Allen hung the last shirt on the line. His mother was too sick to do such heavy work. So the job fell to her eldest child. Every Monday Allen washed, boiled, starched, and hung out the clothes. Afterward he was free to play.

This afternoon Allen headed for the barn to get his fishing pole. As he crossed the front yard, he saw a horse racing down the road toward the Jay farm. Within seconds the family doctor stopped at the front gate. "Friend Jay! Friend Jay!" the doctor shouted.

Allen's father came out of the barn and walked quickly to the gate. "Thy horse has wings today," said Isaac Jay. "Thee seems in a hurry."

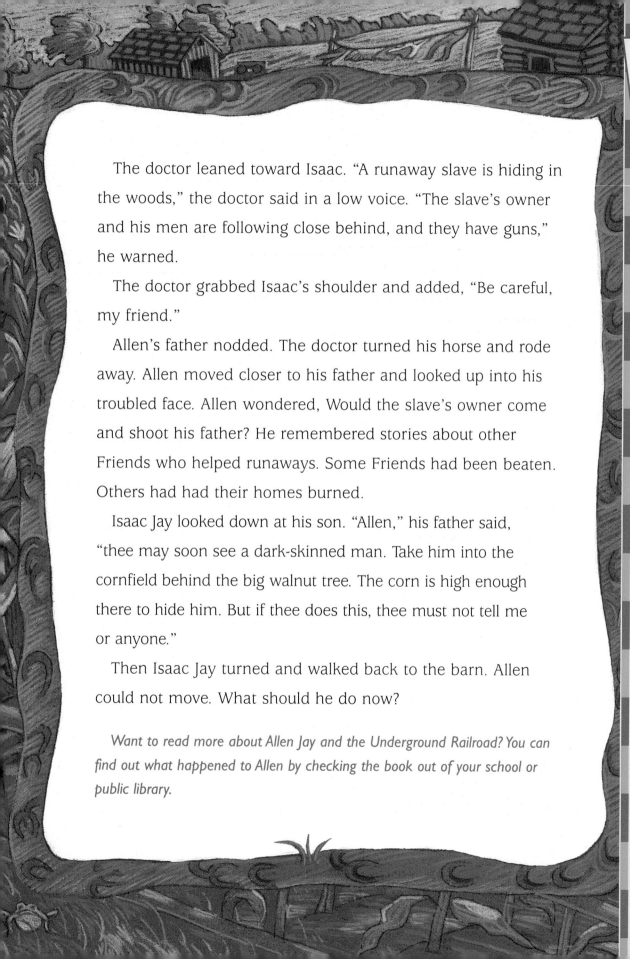

The doctor leaned toward Isaac. "A runaway slave is hiding in the woods," the doctor said in a low voice. "The slave's owner and his men are following close behind, and they have guns," he warned.

The doctor grabbed Isaac's shoulder and added, "Be careful, my friend."

Allen's father nodded. The doctor turned his horse and rode away. Allen moved closer to his father and looked up into his troubled face. Allen wondered, Would the slave's owner come and shoot his father? He remembered stories about other Friends who helped runaways. Some Friends had been beaten. Others had had their homes burned.

Isaac Jay looked down at his son. "Allen," his father said, "thee may soon see a dark-skinned man. Take him into the cornfield behind the big walnut tree. The corn is high enough there to hide him. But if thee does this, thee must not tell me or anyone."

Then Isaac Jay turned and walked back to the barn. Allen could not move. What should he do now?

Want to read more about Allen Jay and the Underground Railroad? You can find out what happened to Allen by checking the book out of your school or public library.

SHOW WHAT YOU KNOW!

REFOCUS
COMPREHENSION

1. Name five areas in which reformers worked for changes after the Civil War.

2. What was the Underground Railroad?

THINK ABOUT IT
CRITICAL THINKING

Why did many people turn their energies to reform after the Civil War?

WRITE ABOUT IT
ACTIVITY

In your Indiana journal, tell what Allen decided to do about the runaway slave, and why.

WORDS OF FREEDOM

FOCUS *Read about some famous documents that were an important part of the Civil War period.*

UNCLE TOM'S CABIN

In March 1852, *Uncle Tom's Cabin* was published. This novel, by Harriet Beecher Stowe, shows the evils of slavery. In Indiana and other free states, it was very popular. It sold over 300,000 copies in its first year in print.

The characters were extremes of good and evil. There was Simon Legree, a brutal slave holder; Eliza, a mistreated slave determined to escape; and Tom, a kind and brave slave. The story set off a strong wave of antislavery feelings.

EMANCIPATION PROCLAMATION

On January 1, 1863, in the middle of the Civil War, President Lincoln issued the Emancipation Proclamation. It declared that enslaved people in rebelling states were free.

The Confederacy had depended on slaves to raise crops and produce clothing and weapons. What's more, slaves had worked for the Confederate army. After the Emancipation Proclamation, 190,000 freed slaves joined the Union army and navy. They helped the Union to win the war.

GETTYSBURG ADDRESS

On November 19, 1863, President Lincoln delivered a speech in Gettysburg, Pennsylvania. It honored the thousands of soldiers who had died in a battle there.

Lincoln's speech was short but powerful. It reminded Americans that their nation was founded on the idea that "all men are created equal."

Today, people around the world remember Lincoln's famous words. School children recite his Gettysburg Address as one of the world's greatest lessons on democracy.

1852
Uncle Tom's Cabin published

January 1, 1863
Lincoln issues Emancipation Proclamation

November 19, 1863
Lincoln gives Gettysburg Address

April 1, 1865
Lee signs Articles of Surrender at Appomattox

December 18, 1865
Thirteenth Amendment becomes law

1852 1862 1863 1864 1865 1866

SHOW WHAT YOU KNOW!

REFOCUS
COMPREHENSION

1. Who signed the Articles of Surrender at Appomattox, Virginia?

2. What was the Emancipation Proclamation?

THINK ABOUT IT
CRITICAL THINKING

Why was *Uncle Tom's Cabin* important in the Civil War period?

WRITE ABOUT IT
ACTIVITY

Write headlines for the front page of your local newspaper on the day each of the three new amendments became law.

THE ARTICLES OF SURRENDER

On April 9, 1865, two generals met at Appomattox, Virginia, to formally end the Civil War. General Robert E. Lee, leader of the Confederate army, and Ulysses S. Grant, leader of the Union army, agreed on the terms of the South's surrender.

According to the agreement, Confederate soldiers would be treated fairly. They would not be punished as traitors. Those who owned horses or mules could keep them. With the end of the Civil War, Hoosier soldiers could also return to their families, fields, and factories.

THE WAR AMENDMENTS

After the Civil War, the United States government added three amendments—or changes—to the Constitution. They became known as the War Amendments. They guaranteed the same rights to citizens of all races.

On December 18, 1865, the Thirteenth Amendment became law. It outlawed slavery. In 1868, the Fourteenth Amendment gave citizenship to 4 million former slaves. Finally, in 1870, the Fifteenth Amendment gave African American men the right to vote and hold office.

Indiana's constitution was changed to include the terms of the three War Amendments.

215

SUMMING UP

1 DO YOU REMEMBER . . .
COMPREHENSION

1. Why did most Hoosiers oppose slavery?

2. Where did the one Civil War battle in Indiana take place?

3. How did Governor Morton contribute to the war effort in Indiana?

4. What was the goal of the abolitionists?

5. How were Confederate soldiers to be treated after the Civil War ended?

2 SKILL POWER
PREDICTING OUTCOMES

Read the paragraph below. Use clues to help you predict what will happen next.

Early in 1861 your cousin from Georgia visits you and your family in Indianapolis. Over dinner, a discussion about slavery begins. You and your father are against the idea of slavery, but your cousin insists that it is a necessary system. Suddenly, your neighbor bursts in. "Georgia has left the Union!" he cries. "Civil war is almost certain!"

1. What do you think the cousin will do next?

2. Write another paragraph of the story in which your father reacts to your cousin's decision.

3 WHAT DO YOU THINK?
CRITICAL THINKING

1. How did Abraham Lincoln's election as President help lead to the Civil War?

2. Was John Hunt Morgan a hero or a bandit? Explain your answer.

3. Why were African Americans eager to join the Union army?

4. Why do you think Quakers and others risked their lives by working for the Underground Railroad?

5. Of the famous documents described in Lesson 5, which do you think had the biggest effect on our nation? Why?

4 SAY IT, WRITE IT, USE IT
VOCABULARY

Suppose that you are a Union general during the Civil War. Write a speech to boost the spirits of your troops. Use as many vocabulary terms as possible in your speech.

abolitionist	regiment
artillery	repeal
discrimination	secede
reaper	temperance
reform	threshing machine

5 GEOGRAPHY AND YOU
MAP STUDY

1. Did more states belong to the Union or to the Confederacy?

2. Name the Confederate states.

3. What Confederate state is the farthest west?

4. What Union states are the farthest west?

A NATION DIVIDED

- States that remained in the Union
- States that seceded from the Union
- Territories

6 TAKE ACTION
CITIZENSHIP

You have read about how the people of Indiana worked together to help in the war effort during the Civil War. People grew extra food and made blankets, clothing, and bandages. With a group of classmates, discuss situations when people today might be in need of help. For example, their homes and possessions might have been burned in a fire or destroyed in a flood or a tornado. Think of ways in which others can help those in need. Create a list of your ideas and share it with your class.

7 GET CREATIVE
LANGUAGE ARTS CONNECTION

Suppose that it is July 1863. Morgan's Raiders have just swept through Indiana. Television has not yet been invented, but if it had, the nightly news would have been sure to cover this dramatic story. Write a news broadcast from the viewpoint of someone living in Indiana. Deliver the broadcast to your classmates.

LOOKING AHEAD
In the next chapter, find out about the age of inventions, industries, and new ideas in Indiana.

LEARN HOW

CHAPTER 10

INDIANA ENTERS

After the Civil War, many changes came to Indiana. Cities grew, the steel industry boomed, and new inventions made daily life easier. Hoosier writers and artists became famous throughout the nation.

See page 226 to find out when bicycling first became popular.

CONTENTS

A NEW CENTURY

These books tell about some people, places, and events of interest from Indiana's Golden Age. Read one that interests you and fill out a book-review form.

READ AND RESEARCH

Kids at Work: Lewis Hine and the Crusade Against Child Labor by Russell Freedman with photographs by Lewis Hine (Clarion Books, 1994)
Lewis Hine took photos of children at work in factories, mills, and mines. Look at his photos to learn about the lives of these child workers. *(nonfiction)*

Bicycle Rider by Mary Scioscia, illustrations by Ed Young (HarperTrophy, 1983)
Marshall Taylor's love of bicycles earned him a job at a bike shop. When his boss enters Marshall in a big race in Indianapolis, he learns how deep his love of bicycle racing really is. *(historical fiction)*

Steel by Andrew Langley (Thomson Learning, 1993)
Follow the steel-making process from start to finish as you look inside a steel mill to find out how steel is made. *(nonfiction)*

Madam C. J. Walker: Building a Business Empire by Penny Colman (The Millbrook Press, 1994)
Sarah Breedlove Walker started her life picking cotton and doing laundry. Follow her as she develops a successful business and works to improve the lives of others. *(biography)*

SKILL POWER

Identifying the Main Idea

Identifying the main idea of a paragraph helps you understand the most important idea that the writer is telling you.

UNDERSTAND IT

What do you think the phrase "get to the point" means? People use this phrase when they want to know exactly what someone else is talking about. "Getting to the point" means finding the main idea of what someone is trying to tell you.

When you read something, you want to find the main idea. To understand the focus of a particular paragraph, you need to know how to find the main idea. In a paragraph, the main idea is usually stated in a single sentence. This is called a topic sentence. Other sentences in the paragraph support the main idea with details.

Look at the diagram on this page to see how a main idea and details are related. Then read the following paragraph.

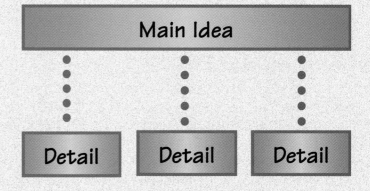

Main Idea

| Detail | Detail | Detail |

Main Idea   Johnny Gruelle created the Raggedy Ann stories.

Details   He found an old rag doll in the attic. He told his daughter stories about the doll. These stories became the famous Raggedy Ann stories.

EXPLORE IT

In the paragraph on page 220, the main idea is stated in the first sentence. The details tell more about the main idea. Sometimes the main idea appears at the end of a paragraph. How do you find the main idea? Use these steps.

1. Decide what the paragraph is about. Ask yourself, "What is the topic or main idea?"

2. Read the entire paragraph to see what the sentences tell about the topic.

3. Look for the topic sentence. It may be at the beginning or at the end of the paragraph.

TRY IT

Read the paragraph below. Use the steps listed on this page to help you find the main idea. Write the main idea on a separate sheet of paper. Check with your classmates. Do you all agree?

Johnny Gruelle was born in 1880 and started his career as a cartoonist. Later he began writing fairy tales and illustrating them himself. In 1918 he published a book of stories about a character named Raggedy Ann. Soon his Raggedy Ann dolls became world famous. By the 1920s, Gruelle was well known as the writer and illustrator of books about Raggedy Ann.

Johnny Gruelle wrote stories about Raggedy Ann.

SKILL POWER SEARCH As you read this chapter, identify at least five main ideas. List them on a separate sheet of paper.

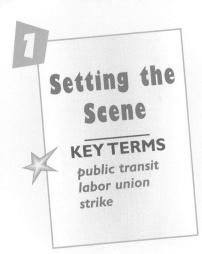

INDIANA'S GOLDEN AGE

FOCUS *As the 1800s ended, Indiana's industries grew and its cities became more modern. Artists and writers helped create a Golden Age in the state.*

Changes After the War

After the Civil War, more Hoosiers moved from farms to cities. Newcomers came from the southern states and Europe.

For many Hoosiers, this period was a Golden Age. This means that it was a time of peace, hope, and a flowering of the arts.

New Inventions and New Ways of Life

Brilliant inventions also changed the way Hoosiers lived. The telephone was invented in 1876. It let Hoosiers communicate more rapidly than ever before. Thomas Edison invented the first inexpensive electric light bulb in 1879. Electric lights began to replace gas and oil lamps throughout Indiana.

Farm life also changed. Better roads let farm families see each other more often than in the past. Families began to meet at Indiana state and county fairs to share ideas and to compete for prizes for the best crops and livestock.

Cities Grow and Change

All over the United States, cities grew during the late 1800s and early 1900s. Indiana cities like Indianapolis, Fort Wayne,

▲ Electric lights replaced gas and oil lamps during the late 1800s.

◀ This 1885 poster advertises the Indiana State Fair.

1894
Elwood Haynes builds early automobile

1907
Theodore C. Steele settles in Brown County

1910
Madame Walker moves business to Indianapolis

1916
Indiana centennial

1918
World War I ends

1890   1895   1900   1905   1910   1915   1920

and Muncie began to spread out for miles beyond their downtowns.

Public transit systems transported suburban workers to and from their downtown jobs. Rail lines between cities also grew quickly from the 1890s on. They spread out from Indianapolis like a spider web, linking nearby cities and towns.

City life brought issues of health and safety. Wooden city buildings could burn rapidly. While most towns depended on volunteer fire fighters, some cities set up paid fire departments. Cities also began to pave streets and supply clean drinking water.

Early Industry

Indiana's first industries were small companies using local products. Many companies packed meat or made wooden furniture from Indiana lumber.

After the Civil War, natural gas was found in east central Indiana.

★ *public transit* Transportation available to everyone

This new energy source brought an industrial boom to the state.

Glassmaking and canning became Indiana's most important industries. By 1900, Ball Brothers in Muncie was the largest maker of glass jars in the country.

Indiana also played an important role in early auto manufacturing. During the early 1900s, Indiana was the leading auto manufacturing state in the country. But the auto business in Indiana did well for only a short time.

▼ Steam fire engines were used in Indiana in the early 1900s.

By 1920, the center of the car industry had moved from Indiana to Detroit, Michigan, where cars were made more cheaply. People began to buy the cheaper Detroit cars rather than the more expensive cars made in Indiana.

Making glass jars was an important Hoosier industry in the early 1900s.

Iron and Steel

In the early 1900s, Indiana's gas supply began to run low. A new industry—the making of steel—began to replace glassmaking and canning as Indiana's most important industry.

Indiana's northwest corner—called the Region—is a perfect location for steelmaking. Iron ore, coal, and limestone are the main resources needed to make steel. The Region is near these resources.

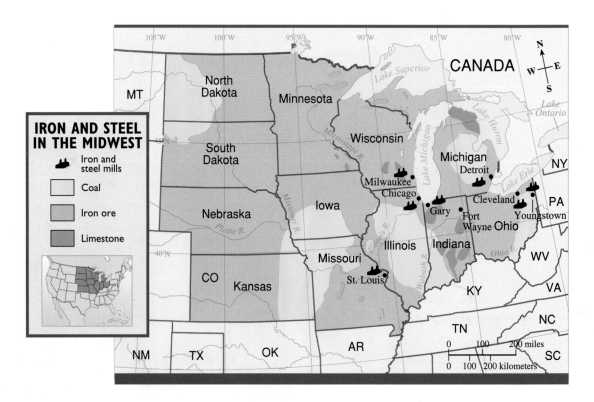

IRON AND STEEL IN THE MIDWEST

- Iron and steel mills
- Coal
- Iron ore
- Limestone

This boy worked at a glassmaking factory in Indiana.

Huge lake ships brought iron ore to the Region from Wisconsin and Minnesota. Trains brought coal and limestone from southern Indiana and Illinois. Then ships and trains transported iron and steel products to markets throughout the country.

Factory Work

Following the Civil War, Indiana's new industries needed many workers. People flocked to factories in search of work. But the life of a factory worker was hard and grim.

Most factory workers worked six days a week, for ten or twelve hours a day. For all their hard work, factory workers earned little money.

Even Hoosier children worked. They held jobs in coal mines, textile mills, and laundries. Laws tried to protect children from overwork. Still, many young boys and girls worked long hours for little pay in some industries.

Workers Organize

By the late 1860s, some workers decided they had to change their working conditions. Long hours and low pay were not the only problems. Factory work was dangerous. Workers were often hurt by unsafe machines that caught their fingers and hair.

One worker alone had no power to deal with factory owners. So groups of workers formed organizations called **labor unions**. Labor unions worked for goals such as higher pay, an eight-hour workday, and more limits on child labor.

If business owners did not agree to their demands, labor unions could tell their members to **strike**, or refuse to work. During the 1870s, Indiana coal miners and railroad workers went on strike.

labor union A group of workers joined together to work for higher pay and better working conditions
strike To refuse to work until certain demands, such as higher pay, are met

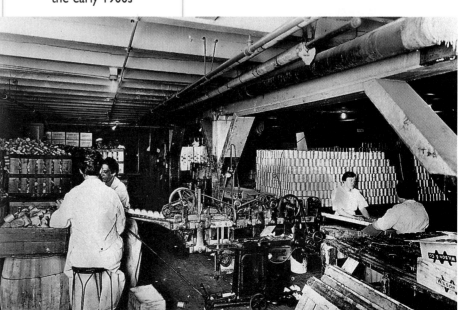

Workers at a canning factory in the early 1900s

Bicycling was one of the most popular activities in Indiana in the early 1900s.

Conditions gradually improved for many factory workers. Many workers were able to work fewer hours for better pay.

Spending Free Time

By the late 1800s, for almost the first time in history, most Hoosiers had leisure, or free, time. Labor reforms had resulted in at least a half day of free time each week for most people. New inventions such as washing and sewing machines also allowed people to have more free time.

Hoosiers flocked to amusement parks and circuses. Families went on picnics or played croquet. People spent time outdoors, camping and fishing. Cycling became the newest popular sport.

Team sports also became popular. Young men played on town baseball teams. College students became excited about the new sport of football. The first Indiana University football team was organized in 1886. Basketball was invented in 1891. It soon became one of the most popular sports in Indiana.

Changes in Education

Education in Indiana improved for many students after the Civil War. Brick buildings replaced log schoolhouses. The length of the school term increased and more children went to school.

Universities grew during the late 1800s and early 1900s. Indiana State Teacher's College and Ball State University were founded

This cartoon shows a whole family of Hoosier writers.

during this time to train teachers. Purdue University was founded to teach the latest farming methods.

Indiana Writers and Artists

Since the days of the pioneers, Hoosiers had written about Indiana. By the 1900s, nearly everyone seemed to be a writer.

Painters also moved to Indiana during this time. They formed artists' "colonies," or small communities. The most famous artists' colony was in Brown County.

World War I

In 1914, war broke out in Europe. So many countries were drawn into the war that it was called a "world war." In 1917, Americans went to war on the side of the Allies—England, France, and their supporters. These countries fought against Germany and its supporters. More than 130,000 Hoosiers fought in World War I.

At home, farmers grew more crops to help feed the soldiers. Indiana workers made iron and steel for guns, planes, and tanks.

Many African Americans came north during the war to work in Indiana industries. Women took jobs in stores and factories to replace the men in the army.

The war ended in 1918 with an Allied victory. The war confirmed America's position as one of the world's strongest nations.

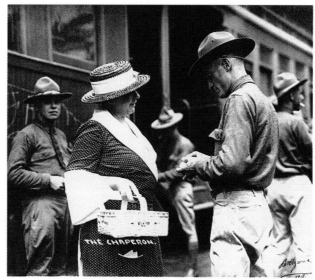

An Indiana woman greets a World War I soldier.

SHOW WHAT YOU KNOW!

REFOCUS
COMPREHENSION

1. Describe how cities changed after the Civil War.

2. What were the goals of labor unions in the late 1800s?

THINK ABOUT IT
CRITICAL THINKING

Describe how people spent their leisure time before World War I. How were their activities similar to those of people today?

WRITE ABOUT IT
ACTIVITY

In your Indiana journal, describe a new invention that would make daily life easier for people today.

INDIANA MILESTONES

FOCUS *As the twentieth century began, Hoosiers saw many changes take place in their state and in the rest of the world.*

PURDUE UNIVERSITY OPENS

About the time of the Civil War, people realized that education could make good American farmers even better. In 1862, the U.S. government gave states public land to sell to raise money to build colleges that taught farming skills. They were called "land grant" colleges.

The state of Indiana used a land grant to found an agricultural college. John Purdue, a merchant and a newspaper publisher, donated much of the money to build the college. The new school, named Purdue University, opened in 1874.

MAJOR TAYLOR BECOMES BICYCLE CHAMPION

People in the 1890s were crazy about bicycle racing! Indiana produced a bicycle racing champion in Hoosier racer Marshall Taylor.

When he was still a boy, Taylor became a trick rider for an Indianapolis bike shop. He was called "Major" because of the military-style uniform he wore.

Major Taylor soon won several bicycle races in Indiana. He went on to set many racing records. He was American champion in 1898 and a world champion in 1899.

CITY OF GARY IS FOUNDED

In 1906 the U.S. Steel Company began to build a huge steel mill beside Lake Michigan. Nearby, the company planned a new town where workers' families would live. It was named after Judge Elbert H. Gary, a company leader.

Builders flattened sand dunes, planted grass, and designed a street plan for Gary. Soon thousands of people from other parts of the United States and from Europe flocked to live and work in Gary.

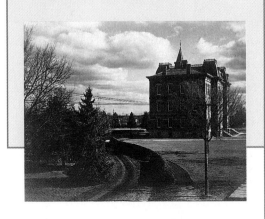

1874
Purdue University opens

1899
Major Taylor becomes world bicycle champion

1906
Gary is founded

1916
Indiana centennial

1918
World War I ends

1870   1900   1905   1910   1915   1920

INDIANA CELEBRATES ITS FIRST 100 YEARS

In 1916, Indiana celebrated 100 years of statehood. All over the state, people celebrated Indiana's hundredth birthday, or centennial (sen TEN ee ul).

Some Hoosier towns put on plays about local history. Other towns held parades, baseball games, and fireworks. Bands played and choruses of schoolchildren sang. Connersville served an Indiana Products Day meal, using only foods grown in the state.

WORLD WAR I IS OVER!

Indiana and the world celebrated in 1918. It was the end of World War I, a bitter and destructive war. People shouted with joy!

The agreement to end the fighting was signed on November 11, 1918. November 11 was later named Veterans Day to honor those who have served in the armed forces.

More than 3,000 Hoosiers lost their lives in the war. To honor these men and women, the Indiana War Memorial was built in Indianapolis during the 1920s. Today the memorial honors those who died in later wars as well.

SHOW WHAT YOU KNOW!

REFOCUS
COMPREHENSION

1. What is a "land grant" college?

2. What group do we honor on Veterans Day?

THINK ABOUT IT
CRITICAL THINKING

What activities would you choose to celebrate on Indiana's two-hundredth birthday?

WRITE ABOUT IT
ACTIVITY

Suppose you are living in 1906. Write an advertisement encouraging people to move to the new city of Gary.

229

THE STEEL INDUSTRY

FOCUS *During the 1860s, steelmaking became one of the country's most important industries. Today Indiana produces more steel than any state in the nation.*

Making Iron and Steel

Much of our world today depends on steel. It is used to make many things, from tiny needles to the frameworks of skyscrapers. Planes, trains, and automobiles all have steel frames. Even "tin" cans are usually made of steel. Many of these products are made of steel from Indiana.

Steel is made from iron ore. Iron ore is a rock or mineral that contains iron. Iron ore was created millions of years ago when the earth's crust was formed.

Miners dig iron ore out of the ground. After the iron ore is mined, it is sent by truck, train, or ship to a steel mill. At the steel mill, the iron is mixed with limestone and a fuel

▼ The steelmaking process

This drawing shows an inside view of a blast furnace. Iron ore, limestone, and coke are put into the furnace. The iron is smelted out of the iron ore.

The liquid iron is poured into an oxygen furnace.

Oxygen is blown into the furnace. The heat in the furnace removes waste substances, including carbon, from the iron.

As the carbon is removed, the iron turns into steel. The furnace is tipped over to pour out the liquid steel.

made from coal called coke. These materials are placed inside a **blast furnace**, where the iron is melted out of the rock. This process is called **smelting**.

When iron is heated to a high temperature, waste substances are given off. What remains is steel.

Iron is a strong, useful metal. Steel is even more useful because it is stronger and less likely to crack than iron.

blast furnace Enclosed place where heat is produced to melt iron out of iron ore
smelt To melt in order to separate the pure metal from the waste substances

The History of Steelmaking

Steel used to be made by heating iron again and again to take out waste substances. This process was time-consuming and expensive.

Then in the 1850s, inventors found a quicker, cheaper way to make steel. It is called the Bessemer (BES uh mur) process, after a British manufacturer.

The Bessemer process uses a sudden blast of air on red-hot iron. This method quickly separates the waste substances from the iron. Modern steelmaking methods still use this basic idea.

Liquid steel is shaped into long bars and cooled. These bars can be made into many different shapes and sizes.

Steel is made into many useful objects, including cars, bridges, trains, tools, and kitchen appliances.

The Steel Industry

Using the Bessemer process, factories could produce many tons of steel. Suddenly, the modern steel industry began to grow. By the early 1900s, huge steel mills were springing up in northwest Indiana.

This region became the heart of the steel industry in the United States. From there, Indiana steel was shipped throughout the country and the world.

Steelmaking Today

Indiana's steelmaking industry has faced challenges in recent years. Equipment has become outdated at some steel mills. Also, mills have had to install costly new equipment to control pollution.

Other countries used to buy all their steel from the United States and Europe. Today, however, many have their own steel mills.

Japan, China, Mexico, Brazil, South Korea, and Venezuela all produce large amounts of steel. Steel mills in these countries are competing for business with Indiana steel.

Despite competition, the United States remains a world leader in steel production. Indiana is still the nation's leading steel-producing state.

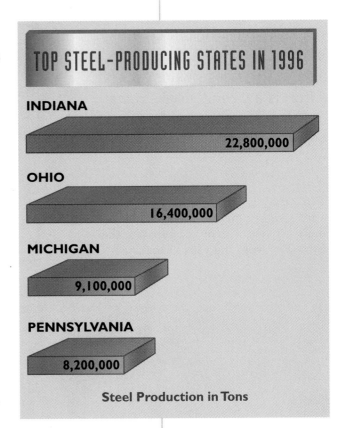

TOP STEEL-PRODUCING STATES IN 1996

INDIANA 22,800,000

OHIO 16,400,000

MICHIGAN 9,100,000

PENNSYLVANIA 8,200,000

Steel Production in Tons

SHOW WHAT YOU KNOW!

REFOCUS
COMPREHENSION

1. How did the Bessemer process change steelmaking?

2. What are two challenges facing the steel industry today?

THINK ABOUT IT
CRITICAL THINKING

How would your life be different without objects made from steel?

WRITE ABOUT IT
ACTIVITY

Create a poster that illustrates the title "Indiana: First in Steel."

Citizenship
KEY TERM
tribute

MADAME C. J. WALKER

FOCUS *Madame C. J. Walker was one of America's first successful women in business. She gave freely of her time and money to help others.*

Millionaire and Good Citizen

Madame C. J. Walker was no ordinary business-woman. She was the first American woman to become a millionaire.

Madame Walker made her money by starting her own business in the early 1900s. The Madame C. J. Walker Company made hair and skin care products.

But Madame Walker did more than make money. She helped other people by giving freely of her time and money. She particularly helped other African Americans gain equal rights.

Born Into Poverty

Madame Walker was not always wealthy. She was born Sarah Breedlove in Delta, Louisiana, in 1867. For most of her childhood,

▲ Madame Walker started a business making hair and skin care products.

she lived in a one-room cabin. Her family worked long hours planting and picking cotton. Sarah's parents were former slaves who had long dreamed of freedom. They soon realized, however, that freedom brought little change to their lives. Laws had been passed giving African Americans new rights. But many people did not obey these laws.

Making a Better Life

Sarah's parents had hoped for a better life for their children. But they both died in 1874, leaving Sarah an orphan.

Sarah was married when she was very young. By the time she was 20, her husband had died. Sarah was left to raise her young daughter, Lelia, by herself.

This plaque honors
Madame Walker's generosity.

By the late 1880s, African Americans had gained some rights. But life was still difficult for black Americans, especially in the South.

Sarah realized that she would have to move north in order to improve her life. She and Lelia moved to Missouri and later to Colorado. Sarah did people's laundry and worked as a cook to earn a living.

Creating a Business

Sarah worked hard. She never gave up hope for a better life. But opportunity came unexpectedly.

One day, after experimenting in her kitchen, Sarah discovered a mixture that would make her hair thick and soft. Soon neighbors began asking her how she got such beautiful hair. They asked if they could buy her product. Sarah developed more hair care products and began to sell them.

In 1906 Sarah married C. J. Walker, a journalist. From then on, she always called herself "Madame C. J. Walker." Her business boomed.

Helping Black Americans

In 1910 Madame Walker moved her business to Indianapolis. At its peak, her company employed more than 20,000 people throughout the United States.

Madame Walker's business was good for the black community, especially for black women. Most stores and offices in the early 1900s did not hire African

Madame Walker stands with other community leaders at a YMCA in Indianapolis.

▽ The Walker Center hosts meetings and concerts.

Americans. But Madame Walker did. A woman who worked for Madame Walker had a chance to be successful and independent.

Madame Walker also used her wealth to help people. She made large donations to schools and organizations that helped African Americans both in Indianapolis and in the South.

During the early 1900s, Madame Walker traveled and made speeches in support of equal rights for black Americans. She continued to fight for African American equality until her death in 1919.

The Madame Walker Urban Life Center

After Madame Walker's death, her daughter, Lelia, donated money to build the Walker Building. The building was a **tribute** to Madame

Walker's generosity toward Indiana's black community. It contained offices for the Walker Company and a theater.

In 1979 the Walker Building was rebuilt as a cultural center for black Americans. It was renamed the Madame Walker Urban Life Center.

Today, audiences at the Walker Center enjoy music, dance, and films. The center's Youth in Arts program introduces young people to music, dance, drama, and art. Special programs also give young people an opportunity to attend the Walker Theater. There they learn more about black culture.

 tribute Something given or done to show thanks or respect

SHOW WHAT YOU KNOW!

REFOCUS
COMPREHENSION

1. Describe Madame Walker's childhood.

2. How did Madame Walker's business help African Americans?

THINK ABOUT IT
CRITICAL THINKING

Explain why Madame Walker was a good citizen.

WRITE ABOUT IT
ACTIVITY

In your Indiana journal, write a poem describing how Madame Walker made a better life for herself and her daughter.

INDIANA'S WRITERS AND ARTISTS

FOCUS *During the late 1800s and early 1900s, Indiana was home to many well-known writers and artists.*

A Golden Age of Culture

During the late 1800s and early 1900s, many Hoosier writers wrote about Indiana and its people. Artists painted Indiana's beautiful scenery. These writers and artists created a Golden Age of literature and painting in Indiana.

Many Hoosier writers became famous throughout the country during this time. George Ade, for example, was known for his humorous stories. He also wrote for the movie industry.

Lew Wallace, a hero of the Civil War, was a well-known writer. His exciting book *Ben Hur,* about life in Roman times, was made into a popular Hollywood movie. Theodore Dreiser (DRYE sur) wrote the novels *Sister Carrie* and *An American Tragedy.* He also wrote poetry and plays.

▲ Indiana poet James Whitcomb Riley talks to children.

Indiana's Favorite Poet

The most popular Hoosier writer was the poet James Whitcomb Riley (1849–1916). During the 1870s, Riley traveled around Indiana working as a sign painter. He came to know Indiana's farms and small towns and began to write about them.

Soon people were memorizing and reciting Riley's poems. Within a few years, Riley was famous as "the Hoosier poet."

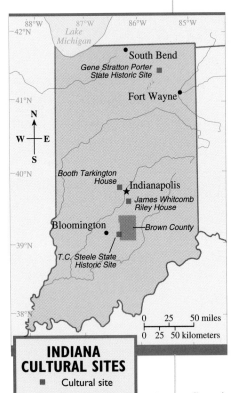

INDIANA CULTURAL SITES
- ■ Cultural site
- ★ State capital
- • Other cities

By 1900, almost everyone could quote lines from Riley's poetry. The following lines describe autumn in Indiana. *Fodder* is grain for cows and horses. A *shock* is a bundle of grain:

O, it sets my hart a-clickin'
like the tickin' of a clock,
When the frost is on the punkin
and the fodder's in the shock!

Riley's poems remind readers of long-ago times in Indiana. Many are written in **dialect**. This means that Riley's poems sound the way rural people used to talk.

Riley's poems tell about people such as an old farmhand in "The Raggedy Man." "Little Orphant Annie" tells of a girl who works for a farm family.

Gene Stratton-Porter

Writer Gene Stratton-Porter (1863–1924) grew up on a farm in Wabash County. Throughout her life, she loved the Indiana countryside and wrote about it in her novels.

As a child, Porter roamed the woods by herself. She chased butterflies and learned about birds and plants. As an adult, Porter wrote books that combined stories about life in Indiana with her love

Gene Stratton-Porter

of nature. Her most famous books include *Freckles, Laddie: A True Blue Story,* and *The Harvester*.

A Girl of the Limberlost, like many of Porter's other books, takes place in the marshy Limberlost region of northeastern Indiana. Porter loved this part of the state. She and her husband lived there for 17 years. Their cabin is now part of a state historic site.

Limberlost swamp was destroyed in 1913. Porter moved farther north, to a home near Rome City, Indiana. An area there, called Wildflower Woods, has been set aside as a memorial to this well-loved Indiana writer.

THE STRIKE AT SHANE'S.

GOLD MINE SERIES No. 2,
Sequel to "BLACK BEAUTY."

A PRIZE STORY OF INDIANA.

A. FLANAGAN COMPANY,
CHICAGO.   NEW YORK.

Porter wrote many books about nature and Indiana.

dialect Language used only in a certain place or by a certain group of people

▲ A scene from the movie *Alice Adams*

Booth Tarkington

One of America's most popular writers in the early 1900s was Hoosier Booth Tarkington (1869–1946). He wrote novels, plays, short stories, and essays. Many of his books poked gentle fun at people and society in Indiana.

Tarkington's first book, *The Gentleman from Indiana*, was about a small-town newspaper man. *Penrod* and *Penrod and Sam* are two famous collections of stories about the joys of being a young boy. Two of Tarkington's books, *The Magnificent Ambersons* and *Alice Adams*, were made into movies.

Tarkington was interested in everything that had to do with Indiana. He even served a term in the Indiana government.

The Brown County Painters

About 1900, a group of painters discovered the beautiful scenery of Brown County in southern Indiana. This region has hills, valleys, forests, and creeks. The air is often hazy, and colorful wildflowers grow everywhere.

As one artist said when she first saw Brown County, "A sense of peace and loveliness came over me and I felt that I had found the ideal sketching ground."

Many artists who came to Brown County painted outdoor scenes, or

◀ Ada Walter Shulz, a Brown County artist, painted *Pet Duck* in 1928.

Theodore C. Steele painted *Selma in the Garden* in 1910.

landscapes. By the 1920s, people throughout the country knew the work of these artists.

Theodore C. Steele

Many of the artists who visited Brown County were men and women from Chicago, Illinois. They spent long hours traveling in trains or wagons to reach southern Indiana each summer.

One midwestern painter, Theodore C. Steele, loved Brown County so much that he decided to settle there. In 1907, Steele built a hilltop home known as "The House of the Singing Winds."

Steele was the leader of the men and women who made up the Brown County art colony. Steele and his artist friends hiked across hills and through woods looking for scenes to paint.

Other artists soon learned about this wonderful place. Like Steele, a number of artists decided to settle in Brown County. They spent their days painting pictures of the beautiful Indiana landscape.

⭐ **landscape** A picture of an outdoor scene

▼ These paints and this brush were used by Brown County artists.

SHOW WHAT YOU KNOW!

REFOCUS
COMPREHENSION

1. Who were the Brown County painters?

2. Why do Riley's poems remind people of life in the past?

THINK ABOUT IT
CRITICAL THINKING

How did Indiana's writers and artists use life in Indiana in their work?

WRITE ABOUT IT
ACTIVITY

In your Indiana journal, write a poem or a short story that takes place in Indiana.

239

SUMMING UP

DO YOU REMEMBER . . .
COMPREHENSION

1. Describe how education changed in Indiana after the Civil War.

2. What company planned the new city of Gary?

3. How is steel more useful than iron?

4. What products did Madame C. J. Walker's company make?

5. Why did many writers and artists choose Indiana as the subject of their work?

2
SKILL POWER
IDENTIFYING THE MAIN IDEA

With a partner, choose a paragraph from Lesson 4 of this chapter. Separately, write down the sentence that tells the main idea. Exchange papers with your partner. Did you both choose the same sentence?

3
WHAT DO YOU THINK?
CRITICAL THINKING

1. Why was Indiana's location on Lake Michigan important to its steel industry?

2. How was the opening of Purdue University an example of the changes in education happening across the nation?

3. Identify at least three jobs created by steel-making.

4. Explain three ways that Madame C. J. Walker worked to improve her life.

5. How did Gene Stratton-Porter's childhood influence her writing?

4
SAY IT, WRITE IT, USE IT
VOCABULARY

Write and illustrate a comic book about a cartoon character named "Travelin' Hoosier," who travels through Indiana in the late 1800s and early 1900s. Use as many vocabulary terms as possible in your comic book.

blast furnace	public transit
dialect	smelt
labor union	strike
landscape	tribute

5 GEOGRAPHY AND YOU

MAP STUDY

1. Which two main resources needed to make steel are found in Indiana?

2. Which resource needed to make steel must come from another state?

3. What would be the best way to transport iron ore from Minnesota to Gary, Indiana?

4. In which state, west of Indiana and east of the Mississippi River, is a large coal deposit located?

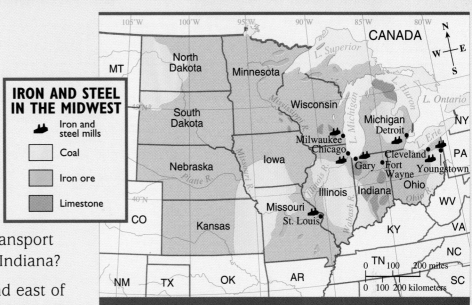

IRON AND STEEL IN THE MIDWEST

- Iron and steel mills
- Coal
- Iron ore
- Limestone

6 TAKE ACTION

CITIZENSHIP

You have read how important steel is in today's world. Yet the production of steel has created problems for the environment. For example, soot and smoke from steel mills have polluted the air. Steel mill owners are working to limit the pollution coming from the mills. With a partner create a poster that illustrates an environmental problem caused by the steel industry. Create another poster that shows a positive result of the steel industry.

7 GET CREATIVE

SCIENCE CONNECTION

Phonograph

Car

In the late 1800s, inventions such as the electric light bulb changed the way people lived. Learn about some of the other important inventions from that time. Use an encyclopedia or books about inventions from the library. Draw an illustration or diagram of an invention. Label your drawing with the name of the invention, the inventor, and a description of how the invention changed the way people lived.

LOOKING AHEAD In the next chapter, learn about the changes in Indiana and the nation in the twentieth century.

EXPERIENCE

CHAPTER 11

INDIANA MOVES

Hoosiers saw enormous changes following World War I. These changes included hard economic times during the 1930s, another world war, struggles for equality for women and for African Americans, and many changes in daily life.

▼ See page 259 to learn about the history of Indiana's state parks.

CONTENTS

FORWARD

These books tell about some people, places, and events of interest during the twentieth century. Read one that interests you and fill out a book-review form.

READ AND RESEARCH

A Long Way to Go **by Zibby Oneal, illustrated by Michael Dooling** (Viking, 1990)
Lila learns from her grandmother what it means for women to gain the right to vote. *(historical fiction)*

Great Inventions **edited by Richard Wood** (Time-Life Books, 1995)
A time line and photographs show you some great inventions such as the telephone and the radio. Learn how these and other inventions have changed our lives. *(nonfiction)*

The Great Depression **by R. Conrad Stein** (Children's Press, 1993)
Learn how Americans tried to cope with the hardships of the Great Depression. Meet some of the nation's leaders during this bitter time. *(nonfiction)*

When I Was Young in Indiana: A Country Life **by Dorothy Strattan Hinshaw, illustrated by Jenny E. Hinshaw** (Guild Press of Indiana, 1993)
Meet the Strattan family of Knightstown, Indiana, and follow their lives on the farm and at school. *(biography)*

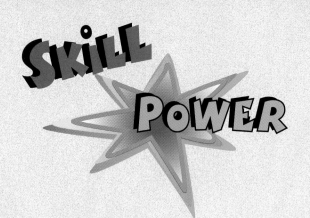

Writing an Outline

Knowing how to write an outline helps you organize information and see how main ideas and supporting details are related.

Title

Roman numeral for main idea

Capital letter for supporting idea

THE STATE PARKS OF INDIANA

I. Outdoor activities
   A. Hiking, backpacking, picnicking
   B. Bicycling, horseback riding
   C. Swimming, water-skiing
   D. Fishing, boating
   E. Skiing, skating, sledding

II. Fish and wildlife
   A. Bass, bluegill, catfish, northern pike, trout
   B. Pheasants, quails, ducks, turkeys
   C. Deer, foxes, raccoons, rabbits

III. Other attractions
   A. Ponds, lakes, rivers, waterfalls, marshes
   B. Fields, woods, sand dunes
   C. Native American mounds
   D. Historic sites
   E. Canals

UNDERSTAND IT

An outline is a written plan for organizing information. You can use an outline to organize information that you have read or as a plan for writing a research report.

In an outline, the main ideas are listed in a certain order. Supporting ideas, or details, are listed under the main ideas and help to explain them.

Every outline has a title. Main ideas are identified by Roman numerals. Details are identified by capital letters.

This student is planning an outline for an article she read in a magazine. ▶

SKILL POWER SEARCH *As you read through the chapter, notice how sections are organized by looking at headings and at the main ideas of paragraphs.*

1 Setting the Scene

KEY TERMS

migration
depression
dictator
ration
front

INDIANA IN THE TWENTIETH CENTURY

FOCUS *After the 1920s, Hoosiers met many challenges, including hard economic times, another world war, and the struggle for equality.*

The Roaring Twenties

The 1920s were years of good times, hope, and freedom for many Americans. The times were so lively, in fact, that historians call those years the "Roaring Twenties."

The American economy grew rapidly during the 1920s. In Indiana, steel and auto parts became the state's major products.

Migration to the industrial cities of northern Indiana continued to increase. Among the newcomers were many African Americans and Mexicans.

Many Hoosiers bought their first automobiles during the 1920s. Indiana built a system of state highways during this time.

With more cars and more free time, Hoosiers enjoyed driving around the countryside and visiting the outdoors. Indiana's state park system, created in 1916, grew during the 1920s to include many new parks.

Women gained new freedoms during these years. New appliances made housework easier. Some women cut their hair short and shortened their skirts. Women wore pants and drove automobiles for the first time.

The Nineteenth Amendment became law in 1920. This law guaranteed women the right to vote in every state of the union.

The Great Depression

With the economy booming, American workers were soon making more goods than people could buy. So businesses cut back on production.

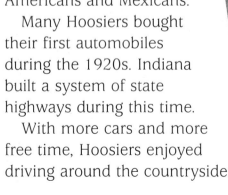

People enjoyed a dance called the Charleston during the 1920s.

---

migration Movement of people from one region to another

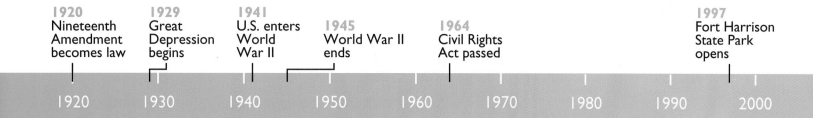

| 1920 Nineteenth Amendment becomes law | 1929 Great Depression begins | 1941 U.S. enters World War II | 1945 World War II ends | 1964 Civil Rights Act passed | | 1997 Fort Harrison State Park opens |

1920   1930   1940   1950   1960   1970   1980   1990   2000

Workers therefore lost their jobs. Industry began losing money.

In October 1929, the American economy fell into a rapid decline, or **depression**. Small depressions are common. But this decline was so serious and wide-reaching that it is known as the Great Depression.

Hoosiers were hit hard by the Great Depression. Indiana's mining and quarrying industries failed. Many banks closed.

Indiana's industrial cities were hit especially hard. In Gary, more than 90,000 workers lost their jobs at United States Steel. By 1932 one quarter of all people of working age in Indiana were without jobs.

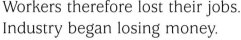
★ *depression*   A time when businesses suffer and people lose their jobs

The New Deal

In 1933 newly elected President Franklin D. Roosevelt started his plan to fight the Great Depression. This New Deal, as the plan was called, created many new programs. Two programs with lasting effects in Indiana were the Works Progress Administration (WPA) and the Civilian Conservation Corps (CCC).

WPA workers built roads, fire stations, school buildings, city halls, and airfields throughout Indiana. They also painted murals in the State Capitol and in post offices around the state.

▼ This mural was painted in the Gas City post office in 1938.

247

President Roosevelt visited an Evansville airplane factory in 1943.

The CCC hired young men to improve Indiana's state parks. These included Spring Mill, Clifty Falls, Brown County, Dunes, Pokagon, and McCormick's Creek.

CCC workers lived at state parks. They built cabins, camping areas, and trails. They also planted trees. Most of the money they made for their work was mailed home to their families.

World War II

In the 1930s, dictators came to power in Germany, Italy, and Japan. These countries were called the Axis powers. They expanded their territory by attacking other countries. These attacks led to World War II.

The United States entered the war when Japan bombed Pearl Harbor, Hawaii, on December 7, 1941. American troops fought on the side of the Allies. The Allies included Great Britain, France, and the Soviet Union.

For four long years, American troops fought in Europe, in North Africa, and on islands in the Pacific Ocean. In August 1945, the Allies finally defeated the Axis powers. World War II was over!

Effects of the War in Indiana

As they had during World War I, Indiana factories played an important role in the war effort. Hoosier automobile plants made airplane engines. Steel mills

Walkie-talkie, helmet, and canteen from World War II

made armor to protect tanks. Some factories were open 24 hours a day, 7 days a week, to meet the huge demand for war materials.

The war made some products, such as gasoline and sugar, difficult to get. Some goods were **rationed**. Hoosiers could buy only a certain amount of these goods. Everyone knew the motto, "Use it up, wear it out. Make do, or do without."

The war brought other changes to Indiana. Over 300,000 Hoosiers joined the armed forces. The new soldiers left Indiana for duty in Europe or the Pacific.

News of the war reached Indiana through stories like those written by Hoosier Ernie Pyle. Pyle wrote about the daily lives of soldiers at the **front**. He was killed by enemy gunfire just before the war ended.

ration To limit the amount of something that a person can get
front The place where two opposing armies meet

Ernie Pyle with children in the Pacific ▲

Women and the War

War meant many changes for women in Indiana. Some women joined the armed forces. They drove trucks, trained men for combat, and piloted planes that flew people and cargo to the front.

▼ The USS *Indianapolis* was sunk in the Pacific during World War II.

Women took jobs in factories to help the war effort.

Life was not easy for everyone, however. Many women lost their wartime jobs to soldiers returning home. African Americans began to protest against unequal treatment in schools, housing, and jobs.

Growth of the Suburbs

During the war, people had put off getting married. With the war's end, many Hoosiers married and raised families.

As a result, Indiana's population, like that of the rest of the nation, grew rapidly. So many babies were born that people spoke of a baby boom during the years from 1945 to 1960.

In Indiana, industry needed workers badly. Some factories hired women for jobs previously not open to them. These included jobs in the steel, auto parts, and construction industries.

Changes Sweep Indiana

Peace brought change to Americans once again. Hoosier factories returned to making new products, such as cars and appliances, instead of making war materials. People in Indiana, as well as in other states, eagerly bought these new goods.

Television ownership increased after World War II. Television quickly became a popular source of entertainment for many families. A new kind of music, called rock 'n' roll, blasted from American radios.

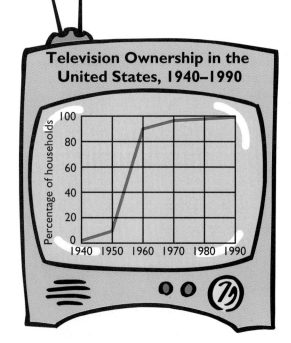

Television Ownership in the United States, 1940–1990

250

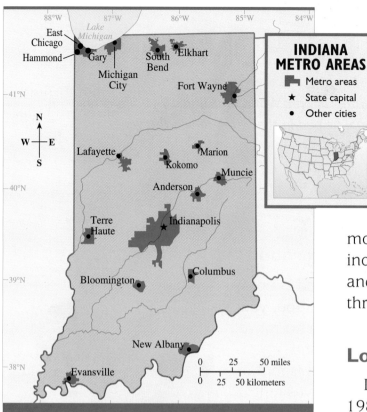

INDIANA
METRO AREAS

Metro areas
★ State capital
• Other cities

Schools, stores, and businesses were often far from people's homes in the suburbs. To get to these places, travel by car became more and more necessary. Car sales increased to meet demand and more roads were built throughout the state.

Looking Ahead

During the 1970s and 1980s, Indiana's population growth slowed. Some Hoosiers migrated to warmer climates in southern and western parts of the country.

Some businesses also moved out of Indiana. In addition, fewer companies worldwide were buying Indiana steel. Thousands of Hoosiers lost their jobs when several steel mills in Indiana closed during the 1970s and 1980s.

Today, new high-technology and service industries are moving to Indiana. These industries are creating many new jobs throughout the state. Hoosiers are looking forward to a new period of economic growth as Indiana enters the twenty-first century.

In rural areas of Indiana, new machines and farming methods continued to be introduced. Therefore, fewer farmers were needed on Hoosier farms. Many farmers sold their land and moved to Hoosier cities.

At the same time, many Hoosiers who had lived in cities moved out to the suburbs. Houses sprang up in areas that had once been farmland. New stores, movie theaters, and restaurants moved out to the suburbs as well.

Hoosier cities expanded to include nearby suburbs. Cities and their suburbs are called metropolitan—or metro— areas.

THE INDIANA HOME FRONT

FOCUS *When the United States entered World War II in 1941, life changed in Indiana. Everyone—even children—helped in the effort to win the war.*

Helping to Win the War

Grandpa says, "We all have to help win the war!" So you and your sister pull your wagon around the neighborhood to collect materials to recycle. You knock on doors and ask people for scrap paper, metal, and rubber.

The neighbors bring out old pots, cans, hoses with holes in them, and rubber bands. This scrap will be used to make airplanes, trucks, and tires to fight the war. You are helping to win the war on the home front—at home in Indiana.

A New Neighborhood

The neighborhood is not very familiar to you yet. You, your sister, and your mother have moved in with Grandma and Grandpa while Dad is in the Army. This plan saves rent and helps keep everyone from being lonely with Dad away in Europe.

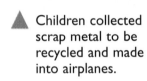

▲ Children collected scrap metal to be recycled and made into airplanes.

Buy YOUR share in the NEW VINCENNES NOW!

Your EXTRA WAR BOND says... They can't sink an INDIANA FIGHTING SHIP

you buy the stamps with is used by the government to help pay for the war. By saving only a dime a week, in a few years you can buy a twenty-five-dollar war bond. This seems like a lot of money!

Even shoes are rationed. The grown-ups can get new soles put on their old shoes. But your feet do not stop growing just because there is a war on! Luckily, your cousin Jonathan's feet are a size bigger than yours. You get to wear his hand-me-downs.

Besides, houses are needed for all the people coming to work in the steel mills near Gary, where you are staying with Grandma and Grandpa. Your mother will be starting a job in one of the steel mills soon.

The house is small for so many people. You and your sister sleep on bunk beds in a tiny spare bedroom near the kitchen.

How Much Can We Buy?

Every week the grown-ups sit down in the kitchen and write out a shopping list. Many things are rationed. Your family can purchase only small amounts of meat, sugar, butter, coffee, and gasoline. Everyone has a ration book with coupons that they can trade in for goods.

Since you cannot spend your allowance on candy, you buy special savings stamps to put in your **war bond** book. The money

Tending the Victory Garden

Grandma and Grandpa's back yard used to be a great place for playing catch, croquet, and badminton. Now it is full of vegetables. Grandma calls it her victory garden.

Victory gardens helped the war effort.

THIS IS A VICTORY GARDEN
Pests... Keep Out!

⭐ **war bond** A certificate sold by the government to raise money

You enjoy eating raw peas from the garden. And you feel proud that your family is growing its own food. That way, more food can be sent to the troops overseas. But weeding the garden has never been your favorite chore!

Sending a Package

It's fun to send a package overseas. Your mother makes cookies to send to Dad. You and your sister contribute your sugar rations for the cookies.

Grandma knits gloves to send to Dad. When she runs out of yarn, she pulls apart an old sweater. Then she reuses the yarn to finish making the gloves.

In school, your teacher asks everyone in the class to write a letter to a soldier. It's hard to think of what to say to a stranger. So you thank him for fighting for freedom.

A Dutch Friend

One day your mom says you will be moving into the living room to sleep on the sofa. A visitor named Miep is coming from Holland. Her parents are sending her to the United States so she can get away from the war in Europe.

Luckily, Miep speaks English and is very friendly. She attends school with you. Your classes are already overcrowded with children whose parents have moved to Gary to work in the steel mills.

It's hard not to worry about the war. Every day you wonder where your dad is. You wonder how Miep's parents are doing.

Indiana families sent letters and packages to soldiers overseas.

You think how brave Miep is to come to a strange country without her parents. But you know that she will be safe living in Indiana.

Following War News

One day Grandpa puts a map of the world up on a wall in the kitchen. He puts colored thumbtacks on the map to show where the fighting is.

Each evening after supper, everyone gathers in the living room. Grandpa reads the newspaper headlines out loud to the family. Then everyone listens to the news from Europe and the Pacific on the radio.

News of the war seems to be everywhere. Even the comics have stories about war heroes. When you go to the movies, a newsreel—a short movie about current events—is shown before the main feature. Newsreels help people learn more about the war.

The newsreels usually show fighting and long lines of **refugees** fleeing from their homes. They carry heavy suitcases and boxes tied with rope. You feel very sorry for them and wish you could help.

Today, however, the newsreel is an exciting war story about brave fighter pilots. You feel proud of the American soldiers. But you hope the war will be over soon. Then Dad will be able to come back home to Indiana!

 refugee A person who flees from his or her home or country to seek safety

▲ Hoosiers learned about World War II from maps and even from comics.

SHOW WHAT YOU KNOW!

REFOCUS
COMPREHENSION

1. Why did people plant victory gardens?

2. How did people learn about the events of World War II?

THINK ABOUT IT
CRITICAL THINKING

Suppose you are sending a package to someone in the armed forces today. What are three things you might include?

WRITE ABOUT IT
ACTIVITY

Write an entry in your Indiana journal explaining what children did to help the war effort.

255

THE STRUGGLE FOR EQUALITY

FOCUS *In Indiana and in the nation, women and African Americans have fought hard to gain equal rights.*

Gaining Rights

Throughout Indiana's history, women and African Americans have faced discrimination, or an unfair difference in treatment. Both of these groups have struggled to win their civil rights.

Civil rights are the rights of all people to be treated fairly under the law. Civil rights laws guarantee equality regardless of race, sex, religion, or skin color.

The Right to Vote

As early as the 1850s, women in Indiana began to ask Congress for **suffrage**, or the right to vote. Women's leaders Susan B. Anthony and Elizabeth Cady Stanton traveled throughout the country to address women's suffrage meetings. They spoke in Indianapolis many times during the 1870s and 1880s.

These efforts did not convince Congress to grant women the right to vote. But Indiana suffrage worker and writer Ida Husted Harper did not give up.

Harper wrote magazine and newspaper articles that were read throughout the country. Her articles urged women to keep working to gain the same rights as men, including suffrage.

▲ Ida Husted Harper worked for suffrage in Indiana.

VOTES FOR WOMEN

The Nineteenth Amendment

The right of citizens of the United States to vote shall not be denied or abridged by the United States or by any State on account of sex.

⭐ **suffrage** The right to vote

Today women work in jobs that were once held mainly by men.

Hard work finally paid off. The Nineteenth Amendment to the Constitution became law in 1920. It granted women in every state the right to vote.

Women's Rights Today

As the twentieth century progressed, women became better educated. They began to take jobs that had been open mainly to men. They became doctors, lawyers, and construction workers.

Even today women are still working for equal rights. But they have made great progress.

The Civil Rights Movement

During the 1880s, many states passed segregation laws. These laws separated black people and white people in schools and on trains and buses. Schools and other public buildings for black Americans were not as good as those for white Americans.

After World War II, black Americans began to protest these unfair laws. They organized boycotts and marches.

In 1954 the U.S. Supreme Court declared school segregation illegal. The next year Rosa Parks, a black American from Alabama, refused to give her seat on a bus to a white person, as required by law. This action led to a city bus boycott and the repeal, or end, of the law.

> **segregation** The practice of separating people of different races
> **boycott** To refuse to buy, use, or sell something

People marching in support of civil rights during the 1960s

Protests continued until 1964, when Congress passed the Civil Rights Act. This law made discrimination illegal. Today there is still work to be done. But black Americans have made huge gains in their fight for equal rights.

Civil Rights in Indiana

Many people have worked to end segregation in Indiana. The state's fight against school segregation was led by Henry J. Richardson, Jr. Indiana made school segregation illegal in 1949, five years ahead of the U.S. Supreme Court.

Indiana State Senator Robert L. Brokenburr won the passage of two civil rights laws in 1961 and 1963. These laws prevented many forms of discrimination, including discrimination in hiring for jobs.

The people of Gary were leaders in the civil rights movement. In 1967 they elected Richard Hatcher mayor of Gary. He was one of the first black mayors of a major American city.

Hatcher served for 20 years as mayor of Gary. He improved housing and started job-training programs. Hatcher helped Indiana become a leader in the struggle for civil rights.

▲ Richard Hatcher was elected mayor of Gary in 1967.

SHOW WHAT YOU KNOW!

REFOCUS
COMPREHENSION

1. Why was the Nineteenth Amendment important?

2. Describe the contributions that Hoosiers have made to the struggle for civil rights.

THINK ABOUT IT
CRITICAL THINKING

Do you think that women and African Americans have achieved their goals of equality? Why or why not?

WRITE ABOUT IT
ACTIVITY

Write a letter to the editor of a local newspaper in 1920 explaining why women should have the right to vote.

258

Citizenship

KEY TERMS
committee
canyon
overuse
habitat

FOUNDING INDIANA'S STATE PARKS

FOCUS *Indiana's state park system began with the work of Richard Lieber in 1916. Since that time, the system has grown to include some of the most beautiful land in Indiana.*

The Need for State Parks

As Indiana became more industrialized, land was gobbled up to build factories and houses. Many Hoosiers saw the need to set aside land for recreation and for preserving Indiana's natural beauty.

Persuading people to set aside land for parks was not easy, however. For example, early efforts to make the Indiana dunes a state park failed. Luckily, Hoosiers continued to fight to create parks in their state.

The First State Parks

Indiana businessman Richard Lieber wanted to help save Indiana's open spaces. So did Indianapolis writer Juliet Strauss.

The movement to create Indiana's parks began in 1915 when Strauss wrote a letter to Indiana Governor Samuel Ralston.

She wanted the Turkey Run area in west central Indiana to be saved from logging. The governor agreed.

Governor Ralston set up a state park **committee** to buy land for state parks. He made Richard Lieber its head.

▼ Juliet Strauss helped create Turkey Run State Park.

▲ Richard Lieber stands in Turkey Run State Park.

---

committee   A group of people chosen to study or to do a certain thing

INDIANA DUNES STATE PARK

Lieber had come to Indiana from Germany. He loved his new country and wanted to be a good citizen. He believed that state parks would give Hoosiers a chance to understand their American heritage.

Lieber's committee purchased the rugged area of McCormick's Creek in 1916. McCormick's Creek became Indiana's first state park. Turkey Run soon became the state's second park.

For 16 years, Lieber worked to expand the park system. He created a number of parks in that time. Lieber later wrote that the years he spent developing the state park system were the happiest of his life.

State Parks Today

Today, Indiana's state parks offer visitors many choices of scenery and recreation. In Indiana Dunes State Park, visitors can swim in summer and cross-country ski in winter. Clifty Falls has Indiana's highest waterfall—over 70 feet high.

The largest Indiana state park is Brown County State Park. It is known for its wildlife, forests, and beautiful fall colors.

BROWN COUNTY STATE PARK

Turkey Run is famous for its **canyons** and beaches. Many visitors to Turkey Run enjoy canoeing past the tall sandstone cliffs that border Sugar Creek.

 canyon A long, narrow valley with high cliffs on each side

CLIFTY FALLS STATE PARK

TURKEY RUN STATE PARK

State park pass

Historic Sites

Richard Lieber had hoped to educate people about their state's heritage. So historic sites are included in the state park system.

Historic sites include Lincoln State Park, Spring Mill State Park, and Mounds State Park. Fort Benjamin Harrison, built in 1903 as an army post, is one of Indiana's newest state parks. It opened in 1997.

Preserving State Parks

Indiana's state parks are becoming more and more popular. This popularity threatens Indiana's parks with overuse.

Hikers crowd trails. Water skiers crowd lakes. Wildlife habitats are destroyed by people who do not stay on trails.

Indiana's parks depend on responsible citizens. Concerned

Hoosiers take care of their parks by staying on trails. They follow the motto, "Take nothing but pictures; leave nothing but footprints."

By taking care of their parks, Hoosiers are carrying on the work of Richard Lieber and Juliet Strauss. They are making Indiana's natural beauty available to everyone.

overuse   Too much or too frequent use
habitat   Native home of a plant or animal

INDIANA'S STATE PARKS

- 🌲 State parks
- ★ State capital
- ● Other cities

Map labels: Lake Michigan, Gary, Indiana Dunes State Park, South Bend, Potato Creek State Park, Pokagon State Park, Bass Lake Beach State Park, Chain O'Lakes State Park, Fort Wayne, Tippecanoe River State Park, Ouabache State Park, Fort Benjamin Harrison State Park, Shades State Park, Mounds State Park, Summit Lake State Park, Turkey Run State Park, Indianapolis, Shakamak State Park, McCormick's Creek State Park, Whitewater Memorial State Park, Versailles State Park, Brown County State Park, Clifty Falls State Park, Spring Mill State Park, Charlestown State Park, Falls of the Ohio State Park, Harmonie State Park, Lincoln State Park, Evansville

0   25   50 miles
0   25   50 kilometers

SHOW WHAT YOU KNOW!

REFOCUS
COMPREHENSION

1. Why did Hoosiers first see a need for state parks?

2. Describe the work of Richard Lieber and of Juliet Strauss.

THINK ABOUT IT
CRITICAL THINKING

More and more people are visiting Indiana's state parks. How can Hoosiers avoid the problems caused by overuse?

WRITE ABOUT IT
ACTIVITY

Make a poster that shows some of the activities you enjoy at state parks or other outdoor areas.

March of Time

1921
TO
1994

CHANGES COME TO INDIANA

FOCUS *New inventions created many changes in the lives of Hoosiers from the 1920s through the present.*

FIRST RADIO STATION IN INDIANA

The first radio station in Indiana was located in a garage in Indianapolis. A Purdue University graduate, Francis Hamilton, built a transmitter to send out radio signals.

Hamilton invited Mayor Lewis Shank to speak over his transmitter on New Year's Eve, 1921. The broadcast was picked up by only a few nearby radios.

Radio soon grew in popularity. Radio broadcasts brought news, music, sports, and comedies to living rooms across Indiana.

ELECTRICITY COMES TO RURAL INDIANA

Cities began using electricity for public lighting in the 1880s. One of the first cities in the country to use electricity was Wabash, Indiana. It used electric lamps to light up the dome of its courthouse in 1880. But farmers in rural areas of Indiana had to wait until 1935 for electricity to reach their homes.

Electricity let farmers use labor-saving appliances. Farmers could also enjoy more hours of light in the evenings. Hoosiers in rural areas could have many of the comforts enjoyed by people in the cities.

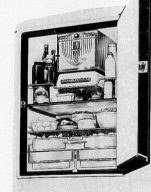

FIRST TELEVISION STATION IN INDIANA

In 1949, WFBM-TV, Channel 6 in Indianapolis, became the first television station in Indiana. One of its first broadcasts was that year's Indy 500. At the time, there were about 7,200 television sets in Indianapolis.

As television became more popular, it had a huge effect on people's lives. Television has influenced everything from presidential elections to what people eat each day.

1921
Indiana's first radio station

1935
Electricity comes to rural Indiana

1949
First commercial TV station in Indiana

1984
First compact disc in U.S. made in Terre Haute

1994
Access Indiana goes on-line

1920　1930　1940　1950　1960　1970　1980　1990　2000

THE FIRST COMPACT DISC

The first compact disc (or CD) in the United States was made in September 1984 in Terre Haute. The new technology made it possible to store much more music in much less space than on a record. CDs soon became more popular than records or tapes.

The recorded music on a compact disc is read by a laser beam—a very narrow and strong beam of light. CDs are smaller and lighter than records. They are also less easily damaged. CDs allow people to select a particular part of a recording without risk of scratching the CD.

ACCESS INDIANA GOES ON-LINE

The Internet is a computer network that allows people to send information from one computer to other computers. The World Wide Web is part of the Internet. The Web is a huge collection of sites, or files containing text and graphics, that can be linked to other sites on the Web. Schools, businesses, clubs, or individuals can build Web sites.

Access Indiana is a Web site that was started by Governor Evan Bayh in 1994. It lets people across Indiana get information about their state, its services, and its activities.

SHOW WHAT YOU KNOW!

REFOCUS
COMPREHENSION

1. How did electricity change life in rural Indiana?

2. What is a Web site?

THINK ABOUT IT
CRITICAL THINKING

How has the invention of the computer changed the way people communicate?

WRITE ABOUT IT
ACTIVITY

Suppose that you are an inventor. Write an entry in your Indiana journal about a new communication machine you would like to invent.

SUMMING UP

1 DO YOU REMEMBER ...
COMPREHENSION

1. How were Hoosiers affected by the Great Depression?

2. Why did people save scrap metal and rubber during World War II?

3. How did African Americans challenge unfair laws after World War II?

4. Name Indiana's first state parks.

5. What is Access Indiana?

2 SKILL POWER
WRITING AN OUTLINE

In this chapter you learned that writing an outline can help you organize information and see how main ideas and details are related. Choose a section in Lesson 1 of this chapter. Write an outline for the section. Be sure to list the main idea and the details. Share your outline with one of your classmates. See if he or she can understand the information you have outlined.

3 WHAT DO YOU THINK?
CRITICAL THINKING

1. How did Indiana's industries contribute to the prosperity of the "Roaring Twenties"? How did they contribute to the war effort during World War II?

2. Describe how World War II affected the lives of children in Indiana.

3. Why are civil rights important to all people?

4. In what ways has the success of the Indiana state park system caused some new problems?

5. How did the coming of radio and television affect life in Indiana?

4 SAY IT, WRITE IT, USE IT
VOCABULARY

Suppose you are a child from Europe who comes to live in Indiana during World War II. Write a letter to your family and describe life in the United States. Use as many vocabulary terms in your letter as you can.

boycott	migration
canyon	overuse
committee	ration
depression	refugee
dictator	segregation
front	suffrage
habitat	war bond

5 GEOGRAPHY AND YOU
MAP STUDY

1. How many state parks are located fifty miles or less from Indianapolis? Name the parks.

2. Which state park is closest to South Bend?

3. In which direction would you travel from Fort Wayne to Tippecanoe River State Park?

4. Which state park is located on Lake Michigan?

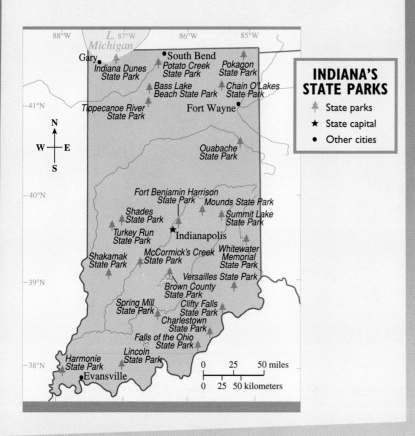

INDIANA'S STATE PARKS
- 🌲 State parks
- ★ State capital
- ● Other cities

6 TAKE ACTION
CITIZENSHIP

In this chapter you learned about how Americans helped one another survive the Great Depression. You also learned how Americans on the home front cooperated to support the war effort. With your classmates, find out about programs in your community designed to help others. Programs might include building a playground at an elementary school, restoring a historic house, or planting flowers and shrubs in a local park. Choose a project in which your class can participate.

7 GET CREATIVE
LANGUAGE ARTS CONNECTION

In this chapter you learned that movies in the World War II era often began with a newsreel. Choose a topic and write the script for a newsreel. Your topic might be the Great Depression, World War II, the struggle for equality, or the age of inventions. Use what you learned in the chapter and what you can find in books from the library. With some of your classmates, perform your newsreel in class.

LOOKING AHEAD
In the next chapter find out about Indiana state and local government.

Indiana Today

How Are Hoosiers Prepared to Meet Future Challenges?

Learn about the important people in Indiana's recent history. Find out how Hoosiers will continue to shape the world of the future through education, agriculture, manufacturing, and technology.

CHAPTER 12

GOVERNMENT

How many representatives does Indiana send to the United States Congress? Who were the five Vice Presidents from Indiana? In this chapter you will find answers to these questions and learn some interesting facts about our national, state, and local governments.

▼ Read on page 288 about how young people can be active citizens.

CONTENTS

IN INDIANA

These books tell about some people, places, and events related to Indiana's government today. Read a book that interests you and fill out a book-review form.

READ AND RESEARCH

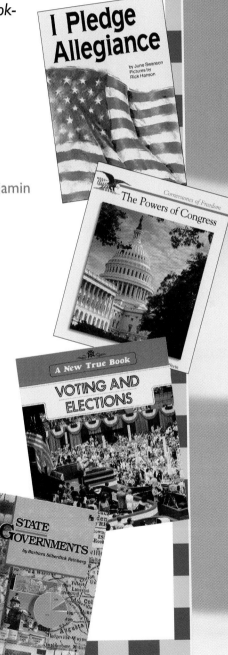

I Pledge Allegiance by June Swanson, illustrated by Rick Hanson (Carolrhoda Books, 1990)
Learn how the Pledge of Allegiance was written and what role Benjamin Harrison played in its history. *(nonfiction)*

The Powers of Congress by R. Conrad Stein
(Children's Press, 1995)
In this fact-filled book, discover what Congress can and cannot do. *(nonfiction)*

Voting and Elections by Dennis B. Fradin
(Children's Press, 1985)
Explore the history of voting in the United States. *(nonfiction)*

State Governments by Barbara Silberdick Feinberg
(Franklin Watts, 1993)
Find out how state governments work and how they differ from one another. *(nonfiction)*

Skill POWER Organizing Information

When you organize information, you put it in a form that makes it easy to understand.

UNDERSTAND IT

To make large amounts of information easy to understand, you can organize facts and figures into graphs and tables. Look at the table below showing Hoosier Vice Presidents of the United States.

Tables have columns and rows. The columns below identify each Hoosier Vice President. The rows give specific information about each one. Columns should be read from top to bottom. Rows should be read from left to right.

Vice President	Schuyler Colfax 1869–1873	Thomas A. Hendricks 1885 (8 months)	Charles W. Fairbanks 1905–1909	Thomas P. Marshall 1913–1921	J. Danforth Quayle 1989–1993
Born/Died	1823–1885	1819–1885	1852–1918	1854–1925	1947–
Arrival in State	1836	1820	1874	born in Ind.	born in Ind.
Hometown	New Carlisle	Shelbyville	Indianapolis	N. Manchester	Huntington
Other Elected National Office	1855–1869 U.S. House	1851–1855 U.S. House 1863–1869 U.S. Senate	1897–1905 U.S. Senate	none	1977–1981 U.S. House 1981–1989 U.S. Senate
President Served Under	Ulysses S. Grant	Grover Cleveland	Theodore Roosevelt	Woodrow Wilson	George Bush

Look at the columns and rows in the table about Hoosier Vice Presidents on page 270. Use the table to answer these questions.

1. How many Vice Presidents are listed?

2. How many were born in Indiana?

3. How many served more than four years as Vice President?

4. How many served in the U.S. Senate?

TRY IT

Think of other information that can be organized in a table. If you collect baseball cards, you could make a table showing each card you have, when you bought it, and how much it cost. If you are working on a school play, you could make a table of the jobs that need to be done and who will do them.

Look at the table on this page showing the rehearsal schedule for a school play. Who plays the part of Katie Coffin? When does rehearsal start for her part? When does it end?

Work by yourself or with a small group of classmates to develop a useful table. Give your table a title. Share your table with the class.

School Play—*Indiana Through the Years*

Name	Part	Rehearsal Time
Sam	Jonathan Jennings	3:15–3:30
Karl	Johnny Appleseed	3:30–3:45
Wanda	Katie Coffin	3:45–4:00
Sean	Little Turtle	4:00–4:15
Hector	Marshall Taylor	4:15–4:30
Marcia	Madame C.J. Walker	4:30–4:45

SKILL POWER SEARCH *Look in this chapter to find at least three ways in which information is organized.*

Setting the Scene

KEY TERMS

naturalized citizen
Bill of Rights
checks and balances
separation of powers
congressional district

UNDERSTANDING OUR GOVERNMENT

FOCUS *There are three levels of government in the United States—national, state, and local. Every level of government has responsibilities to the people it represents. The people also have responsibilities to the government.*

What Is a Citizen?

Every morning in schools across the United States, children start their day with the Pledge of Allegiance. What does it mean to pledge allegiance? It means that you are promising to be loyal to your country and obey its laws.

You make this pledge as an American citizen. A citizen is a person who obeys and is protected by the laws of a particular country.

If you were born in this country, you are an American citizen. If you were born in another country to American parents, you are still an American citizen. If your parents were not American citizens when you were born, you may become a **naturalized citizen** of the United States. A naturalized citizen has the same rights and protections as a person who is a citizen by birth.

Rights and Freedoms

The **Bill of Rights** is a document that lists the rights and freedoms of all U.S. citizens. This document is part of the U.S. Constitution.

naturalized citizen A person who was not born here but became a U.S. citizen
Bill of Rights A list of citizens' basic rights

The Pledge of Allegiance

I pledge allegiance
to the Flag of
the United States
of America and
to the Republic
for which it stands,
one Nation under
God, indivisible,
with liberty and
justice for all.

Every Fourth of July Americans celebrate their nation's independence.

WHAT MAKES a GOOD CITIZEN?

It guarantees freedom of speech, freedom of the press, and freedom of religion. All citizens also have the right to a fair and speedy trial. What's more, the Bill of Rights protects U.S. citizens from unfair treatment, such as unreasonable searches of their homes.

The Indiana Constitution also guarantees our freedoms and rights. This means that our basic rights are protected by two governments—that of the United States and that of Indiana.

Duties and Responsibilities

Duties are also part of citizenship—or of being a citizen. A duty is something you must do. For example, it is your duty to obey laws. Citizens have certain responsibilities, too. These are things you should do.

Citizens who are 18 years old or older have the right and the responsibility to vote. Voting in elections is how citizens choose the people they want for local, state, and national offices.

Citizens also have another responsibility—to vote wisely. That means learning about the people running for office and finding out what they plan to do if elected.

What Is Government?

We follow rules all the time. There are rules at home and at school. As citizens of a state and a nation, we follow rules called laws. Who makes laws and makes sure we follow them? Our government does. In our country, there are three levels of government: national, state, and local.

▼ Immigrants to the United States can become naturalized citizens.

Our Nation's Government

Each country in the world has a government. Our government is a democratic republic. This means that citizens vote for people to represent them and to pass laws. The U.S. Constitution created our national government.

Our national government is based in Washington, D.C. It is the capital of the United States. The federal government does its work in Washington, D.C. The abbreviation *D.C.* stands for District of Columbia.

The national government has many responsibilities to its citizens. One responsibility is to protect its citizens. The government does this by passing laws to protect our food, land, water, and air. It also protects us by keeping up our armed

▲ The Supreme Court, the nation's highest court, has nine justices.

forces—the Army, Navy, Marines, and Air Force. To support these and many other services, we pay taxes.

The Three Branches of Government

Our national government is divided by the U.S. Constitution into three parts, or branches. These branches are the legislative, the executive, and the judicial.

The Constitution provides for a system of checks and balances among the three branches. This means that the powers of the national government are divided among the three branches. It also means that each branch can check, or control, the other two branches.

---

checks and balances   A government system that prevents one branch of government from becoming too powerful

Do You Know...

☆ **The President who served the longest term (12 years, 38 days)?**
   Franklin Delano Roosevelt

☆ **The President, a Hoosier, who served the shortest term (32 days)?**
   William Henry Harrison

☆ **The two Hoosiers who served as Justices of the U.S. Supreme Court?**
   Willis Van Devanter (1911–1937)
   Sherman Minton (1949–1956)

The U.S. Constitution gives each branch separate responsibilities, as well. This is called separation of powers.

The Legislative Branch

The legislative branch of the national government, called the legislature, makes the laws. Congress is the legislative branch. Congress is made up of the Senate and the House of Representatives.

People elected to the Senate are called senators. They serve a six-year term. People elected to the House of Representatives are called representatives. They serve a two-

separation of powers A way of dividing the powers of government among its branches

▼ Presidential seal

year term. However, senators and representatives can be elected for more than one term.

The Executive Branch

The executive branch is in charge of carrying out the laws made by the legislative branch. The chief executive is the President. The Vice President is also a member of the executive branch. Dan Quayle of Indiana was Vice President from 1989 to 1993.

The group of advisors that helps the President make decisions is called the Cabinet. The President's Cabinet is also part of the executive branch of government.

▼ The President of the United States lives in the White House in Washington, D.C.

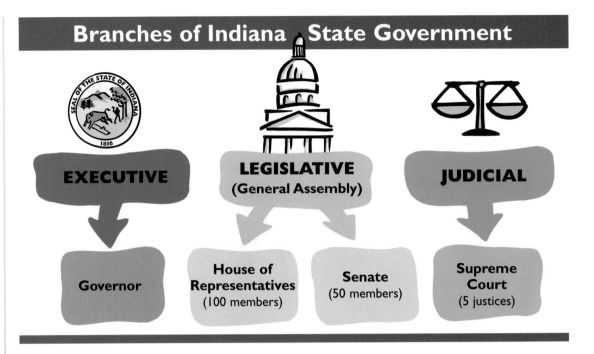

Branches of Indiana State Government

Our state government is organized in the same way as is our national government.

EXECUTIVE

LEGISLATIVE (General Assembly)

JUDICIAL

Governor

House of Representatives (100 members)

Senate (50 members)

Supreme Court (5 justices)

Birch Bayh, Jr., (top) and Richard Lugar (bottom)

The Judicial Branch

The judicial branch of government interprets, or explains, the laws. This branch of government includes a system of courts. A court is a place where arguments about laws are settled.

The Supreme Court is the highest court in the United States. There are nine judges, called justices, who make up the nation's Supreme Court. They make the final decisions on any court cases having to do with questions about the U.S. Constitution.

Indiana and the Nation

Many Hoosiers have played an important role in national government. For example, Birch Bayh, Jr., served Indiana for 18 years in the U.S. Senate. He helped to lower the voting age from 21 to 18 for all elections. Richard Lugar has been a leader in the Senate since 1977.

Indiana has sent other important leaders to serve in Washington, D.C., including the five Vice Presidents you read about on pages 270 to 271. Although Abraham Lincoln was born in Kentucky and later lived in Illinois, he grew up in Indiana.

Many Hoosiers have run for the office of President, including Wendell Willkie, Eugene Debs, and Richard Lugar. Two Hoosiers were elected President—William Henry Harrison in 1840 and his grandson, Benjamin Harrison, in 1888.

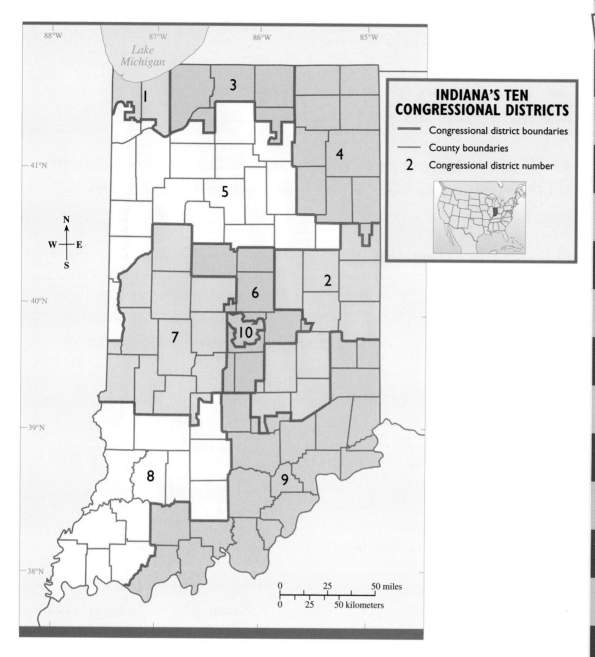

INDIANA'S TEN CONGRESSIONAL DISTRICTS

— Congressional district boundaries
— County boundaries
2 Congressional district number

SHOW WHAT YOU KNOW!

REFOCUS
COMPREHENSION

1. What is the separation of powers? What is its purpose?

2. Why is the Bill of Rights important?

THINK ABOUT IT
CRITICAL THINKING

How might the national government be affected if there were no checks and balances among the three branches?

WRITE ABOUT IT
ACTIVITY

In your Indiana journal, write a paragraph about why it is important to protect civil rights.

Membership in Congress

Representation in the U.S. House is based on population. Indiana sends ten representatives—one person from each **congressional district**—to Washington, D.C. The map above shows Indiana's ten congressional districts. Each district has about the same number of people.

Indiana has two senators, the same number as other states. Each senator represents the entire state.

 congressional district   A special division of a state from which people elect a representative to Congress

Spotlight

★ **KEY TERMS**

popular
   sovereignty
budget
bill
veto
appeal

OUR STATE GOVERNMENT

FOCUS *The plan for our state government was first laid out in the Indiana Constitution of 1851. The Indiana government provides many services to citizens of our state.*

The Indiana Constitution

The Indiana Constitution of 1851 is our basic state law. It lays out the plan of our state government. It replaced an earlier constitution written in 1816.

The interior dome of the Capitol Building in Indianapolis

Some things in the first constitution were kept in the second one. For example, both prohibited slavery, and both required the state to provide free public education.

The Constitution of 1851 also added some things. For example, it divides Indiana's government into three branches—executive, legislative, and judicial. Each branch has the power to check the other's power. The Constitution of 1851 also forbids the state to go into debt.

The Indiana Constitution contains two important ideas. One idea is **popular sovereignty** (SAHV run tee). It means that political power comes from the people. This power is put into action when voters elect people to represent them.

The other idea is limited government. It means that the government is limited in what it is allowed to do.

Indiana's Bill of Rights

The Indiana Constitution has its own Bill of Rights. It guarantees many of the basic rights in the U.S. Constitution, including freedom of speech and religion. It also contains rights not listed in the U.S. Constitution. For example, the Indiana Bill of Rights states that no citizens may have special privileges or titles such as "king" or "queen."

★ ***popular sovereignty*** The idea that all political power comes from the people

IMPORTANT HOOSIER STATE SERVICES

EDUCATION
Money to help pay for teachers' salaries, school transportation, and public colleges

TRANSPORTATION
Building and taking care of highways, bridges, and roads

NATURAL RESOURCES
State forest system and state park system

SAFETY
State prison system and state police

What the State Provides

The state protects its citizens' rights. It also provides many services for its residents. The chart above shows that the state spends money on education, natural resources, transportation, and safety. Most of the money for these services comes from a state sales tax and a state income tax.

Indiana also spends money on running its government, developing its economy, and providing health services. More than one third of the state **budget** goes to education.

Indiana's Government

As the diagram on page 276 shows, Indiana's government is modeled after our national government. That is, there are three branches of government—the legislative branch, the executive branch, and the judicial branch. The government offices in charge of these branches are located in Indianapolis, the state capital of Indiana.

The State Legislature

Indiana's legislative branch is called the General Assembly. It can write **bills** and pass laws about everything from how seat belts are to be used to how local governments can be run.

The General Assembly also sets state taxes and controls the state budget—and, therefore, how state money is spent. Control of the budget makes the General Assembly powerful.

The Indiana General Assembly has two parts, or houses—the House of Representatives and the

The Indiana state government spends more than $4 billion on education each year.

---

 budget A careful plan for spending money

 bill A draft for a possible law

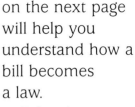

on the next page will help you understand how a bill becomes a law.

Other important officers in the executive branch are the lieutenant governor, the secretary of state, and the attorney general. If anything causes the governor to leave office, the lieutenant governor takes over.

Senate. The Senate has 50 members. Each senator is elected to a four-year term. The House has 100 members. Each representative is elected to a two-year term. Can you name the state representative or the state senator from your area?

The Governor's Job

The leader of the executive branch is the governor. Hoosiers elect their governor for a four-year term. It is the governor's job to appoint judges and to recommend a state budget each year.

The governor also suggests new bills to the General Assembly. The governor cannot pass laws or budgets. However, the governor can **veto**, or stop, a bill that has been passed by the legislators. The chart

Pamela Carter was elected attorney general in 1992. Like other state government officials, she has an office in the Capitol Building.

▼ A judge uses a gavel to call a court to order.

The Judiciary

The third branch of Indiana's government is the judicial branch. This branch includes the court system, just as our national judicial branch does. When someone is accused of breaking a law, the judicial branch makes sure that he or she receives a fair trial.

The highest court in Indiana is the Indiana Supreme Court. The Supreme Court has 5 judges. The next highest court is the Court of Appeals, which has 15 judges. These judges hear **appeals** of criminal cases. Then there are the circuit courts. These courts handle many different types of cases.

 veto To reject a proposed law
appeal A request to have a decision in a law case reviewed by a higher court

How a **Bill** Becomes a **Law**

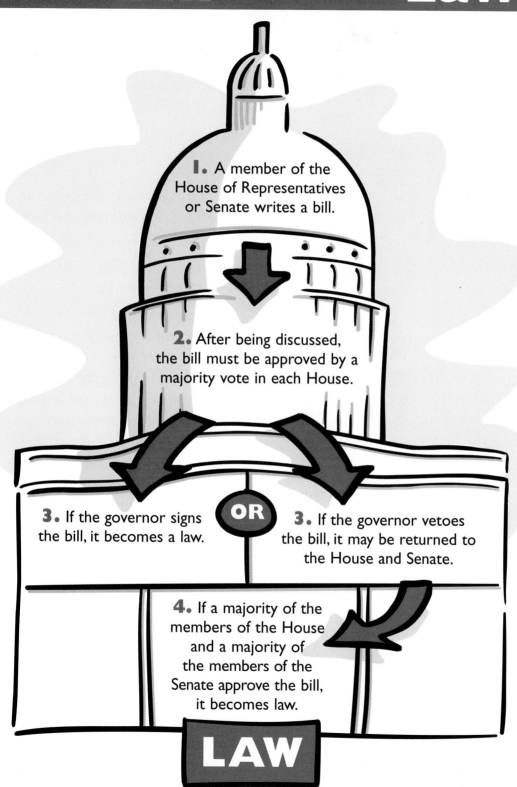

1. A member of the House of Representatives or Senate writes a bill.

2. After being discussed, the bill must be approved by a majority vote in each House.

OR

3. If the governor signs the bill, it becomes a law.

3. If the governor vetoes the bill, it may be returned to the House and Senate.

4. If a majority of the members of the House and a majority of the members of the Senate approve the bill, it becomes law.

LAW

REFOCUS
COMPREHENSION

1. Name three services provided by Indiana's state government.

2. How does a bill become a law in Indiana?

THINK ABOUT IT
CRITICAL THINKING

How does the governor influence which bills become law?

WRITE ABOUT IT
ACTIVITY

In your Indiana journal, explain some ways that state government affects your life.

A DAY WITH A PAGE AT THE LEGISLATURE

FOCUS *Learn about a day in the life of a page working in the Indiana Senate.*

First Day as a Page

Today you will get to see Indiana's state government up close. You are traveling to Indianapolis to be Senator Katie Wolf's page, or messenger.

Now you are climbing the Capitol steps on your way to the Page Room. Here you meet many pages. They are all young volunteers like you, invited to help senators and representatives for a day. As a page, you will deliver messages all over

▲ Pages Alisia Epps from Jeffersonville (left) and Timothy Sledd from Delphi (right)

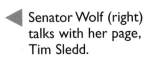

◄ Senator Wolf (right) talks with her page, Tim Sledd.

the Capitol Building, including the Senate Chamber, where the Senate meets.

On to the Senate

At last, you enter the Senate Chamber and are assigned a "standing" post. People are already sitting in a balcony called the Visitor's Gallery. They are waiting to watch the Senate in session.

On the Senate floor, you see Senator Wolf sitting at one of the 50 desks. Your heart jumps as she motions to you. At her desk, she has a laptop computer. She uses her computer to get information to help her vote.

Back at your post, you rise with the senators and other pages. The lieutenant governor calls the session to order with a prayer and the Pledge of Allegiance.

After the roll call, the lieutenant governor, who is president of the Senate, leads senators through bills.

Senator Vi Simpson (left) gets a message from Alisia Epps, a page.

These bills deal with issues such as state parks, school transportation, and snow days for schools. Senators step to the microphone to speak for and against each bill.

Work in the Senate

You deliver many messages to Senator Wolf from the people of Indiana. They are telling the senator how they think she should vote. At one point, she even asks for your opinion on a vote.

When each vote is called, a video board shows senators' names, their votes on a given bill, and the totals for and against each one. Most bills pass with a **majority** of "yes" votes, but some fail.

Between bills, the senators honor retiring coaches, winning teams, and state workers for excellence on the job. They also meet in small groups to rewrite bills.

As you leave the Capitol at the end of the day, you think, "Maybe someday I'll be a senator. Then I'll invite students to be pages to learn how Indiana's government works for us."

Pages meet with representatives.

★ *majority* More than half

SHOW WHAT YOU KNOW!

REFOCUS
COMPREHENSION

1. What do pages do?

2. What does the lieutenant governor do in the Senate?

THINK ABOUT IT
CRITICAL THINKING

Why do people voice their opinions to their senators and representatives?

WRITE ABOUT IT
ACTIVITY

Write an article for your school paper explaining what you might learn if you were a page in the Indiana Senate.

OUR COMMUNITY GOVERNMENTS

FOCUS *Indiana's community governments are important to our everyday lives. They provide many services, such as policing our neighborhoods, fighting fires, and collecting trash. They also run our libraries, parks, and schools.*

Indiana Counties

Indiana counties, cities, and towns have governments, just as our nation and our state do. These governments are called local governments. County governments are the largest units of local government. Taxes support county governments. As you can see from the map on the next page, Indiana is divided into 92 counties.

County boundary lines were determined without regard for population. That is why some counties have many people while others contain few people. Marion County, for example, has about 800,000 people, but Ohio County has fewer than 6,000 people.

Most counties have a board of commissioners. Each board is made up of three elected officials. They can pass county laws called ordinances. They also control such

 Some city and county services

county property as libraries, hospitals, and jails. Another job of the board is to supervise the building of county roads. The board also sets up animal shelters and posts speed limits.

Each county has a **sheriff's** department in charge of protecting people who live and work in the county. What's more, counties keep records of marriages, births, and deaths. They also register voters.

City Government

Another part of Indiana government is city government. There are 115 cities in Indiana. These cities are divided by law into three classes. First-class cities have 250,000 or more people. Only Indianapolis is a first-class city. Second-class cities have 35,000 to 250,000 people. Third-class cities have fewer than 35,000 people.

★ *sheriff* The chief county law officer

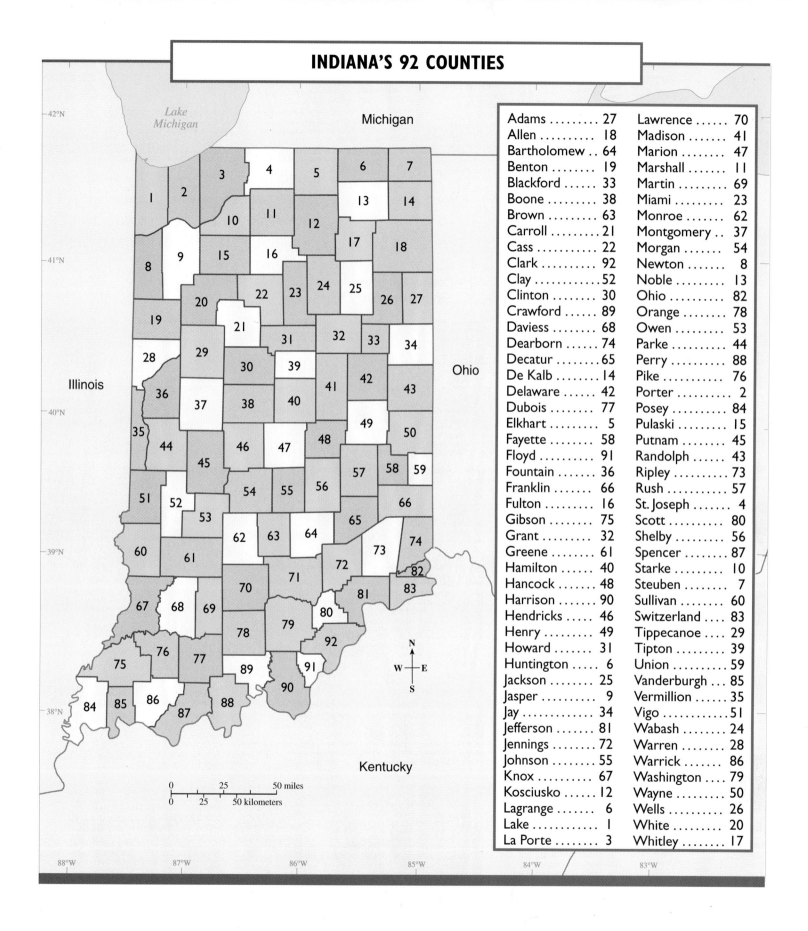

INDIANA'S 92 COUNTIES

Lake Michigan
Michigan
Illinois
Ohio
Kentucky

County	No.	County	No.
Adams	27	Lawrence	70
Allen	18	Madison	41
Bartholomew	64	Marion	47
Benton	19	Marshall	11
Blackford	33	Martin	69
Boone	38	Miami	23
Brown	63	Monroe	62
Carroll	21	Montgomery	37
Cass	22	Morgan	54
Clark	92	Newton	8
Clay	52	Noble	13
Clinton	30	Ohio	82
Crawford	89	Orange	78
Daviess	68	Owen	53
Dearborn	74	Parke	44
Decatur	65	Perry	88
De Kalb	14	Pike	76
Delaware	42	Porter	2
Dubois	77	Posey	84
Elkhart	5	Pulaski	15
Fayette	58	Putnam	45
Floyd	91	Randolph	43
Fountain	36	Ripley	73
Franklin	66	Rush	57
Fulton	16	St. Joseph	4
Gibson	75	Scott	80
Grant	32	Shelby	56
Greene	61	Spencer	87
Hamilton	40	Starke	10
Hancock	48	Steuben	7
Harrison	90	Sullivan	60
Hendricks	46	Switzerland	83
Henry	49	Tippecanoe	29
Howard	31	Tipton	39
Huntington	6	Union	59
Jackson	25	Vanderburgh	85
Jasper	9	Vermillion	35
Jay	34	Vigo	51
Jefferson	81	Wabash	24
Jennings	72	Warren	28
Johnson	55	Warrick	86
Knox	67	Washington	79
Kosciusko	12	Wayne	50
Lagrange	6	Wells	26
Lake	1	White	20
La Porte	3	Whitley	17

N
W — E
S

0   25   50 miles
0   25   50 kilometers

285

UNIGOV—the Consolidated City

In 1970, Indianapolis and Marion County were **consolidated** into one government. This government is called UNIGOV. Now the people of Indianapolis and Marion County receive many services from UNIGOV.

UNIGOV has a mayor elected for a four-year term. The mayor runs the city government. UNIGOV also has a council with 29 elected members. They serve four-year terms as well.

Council members pass laws for UNIGOV. The mayor appoints people to head UNIGOV's departments, such as public safety and transportation. The council must approve the mayor's choices.

Mayors also run second- and third-class cities. Second-class cities have councils with nine members. Councils of third-class cities have five or seven members. City councils pass local laws and make budget decisions. A mayor can veto laws passed by the city council.

City Services

City governments provide many services. Taxes pay for these services. Cities run police and fire departments and repair city streets.

The city government is also in charge of the local water supply as well as city parks, transportation, and buildings. Other city services may include running zoos, collecting trash, and saving historic buildings. Clearly, city governments help us in many ways.

City-County Building in Indianapolis ▼

 consolidate Join together; unite

Workers feed penguins at the Fort Wayne Zoo, which is run by the city.

SHOW WHAT YOU KNOW!

REFOCUS
COMPREHENSION

1. Name three forms of local government.

2. What is UNIGOV?

THINK ABOUT IT
CRITICAL THINKING

Why are community governments important?

WRITE ABOUT IT
ACTIVITY

Make a five-inch quilt square on drawing paper. On the square, write a paragraph describing one special thing about your community. Then decorate the square.

School Districts

Another form of local government is the special district. A special district manages one special service that is not provided by any other unit of government. School districts are an important example.

At one time, cities and towns ran their own public schools. Then, in 1959, Indiana's General Assembly passed a new law. It set guidelines for reorganizing school districts. As a result, Indiana has fewer school districts today, but they are larger than they used to be.

The state of Indiana governs the education of its children. For example, the Indiana Constitution states that public schools should be "equally open to all." This means that all children, regardless of sex, race, ethnic origin, or religion must be treated equally in the schools.

The General Assembly gives local school boards their power. It also decides what subjects must be taught and sets the number of days that schools will be open each year.

Participating in Government

Many Hoosiers take part in local government. Some people are leaders in community government. A leader is someone who is able to express the ideas of the people he or she represents.

Others do volunteer work. Some volunteers help run libraries, fire departments, or rescue squads.

YOUR ROLE AS A CITIZEN

FOCUS *As a citizen of Indiana and of the United States, you have many rights and responsibilities.*

Participating in Government

Until you reach the age of 18, you don't have the right to vote in state or national elections. But you can have some effect on who gets elected to office or how tax dollars are spent. You can do this by working for a candidate or helping groups that support issues you believe in.

Elections are about **politics**—about taking part in government. What makes politics so interesting is that people don't agree on what should be done. That is why we have elections.

Although you can't vote yet, you can take part in politics. You can learn about issues and candidates. You can also play a role in school politics by running for a class or school office. You might attend school board meetings, too.

Participating in school elections teaches students about politics.

The Right to Petition

The right to make a **petition** is guaranteed in the U.S. Constitution. It means that citizens may ask the government to make changes. A petition is a written request. Getting a lot of people to sign a petition shows that a request has support.

For instance, if you and your friends want a new bicycle path, you might start a petition for your town to build one. You would collect as many signatures as possible. Then you could present the petition to the mayor or the city council.

Leaders review petitions, especially those that have strong public support. Sometimes they take action based on petitions.

Solving Problems

As a citizen, you have many rights. But you also have certain responsibilities. One responsibility is helping to solve problems.

⭐ ***politics*** The act of taking part in government affairs

⭐ ***petition*** A written request to someone in authority signed by a number of people

Young people can solve problems with positive action.

Have you ever helped clean up your neighborhood or collected money for a good cause? Taking positive action is your responsibility as a citizen.

Expressing Opinions

Maybe you have opinions about how to solve problems. You can write letters stating your ideas. You can write to the mayor, to the governor, or even to the President.

You might be surprised at how seriously leaders take your ideas. They want to know what citizens are thinking—even young citizens. They understand that it is easier to solve problems with public support.

Staying Informed

All citizens have the important responsibility to stay informed. Staying informed means reading newspapers, magazines, and books about public issues. It means watching TV news shows and attending town meetings. It also means discussing important issues with your parents and teachers. Asking questions is part of staying informed.

If you are well informed when you vote or express your opinion, you will do so intelligently. Everyone has a right to express opinions, but opinions should be based on knowledge and facts.

As a young citizen, you have a responsibility to stay as informed as possible. By staying informed, you will always have a voice in decisions that affect your life.

SHOW WHAT YOU KNOW!

REFOCUS
COMPREHENSION

1. What are some responsibilities of a citizen?

2. Why is staying informed important?

THINK ABOUT IT
CRITICAL THINKING

Why is the right to make a petition important?

WRITE ABOUT IT
ACTIVITY

In your Indiana journal, list three ways you can become a better citizen.

SUMMING UP

1 DO YOU REMEMBER...
COMPREHENSION

1. What is the main responsibility of each of the three branches of the national government?

2. Name three responsibilities of Indiana's governor.

3. What kinds of work do state senators do in addition to voting on bills?

4. What is a special district?

5. Name two ways that you can participate in government and politics.

2 SKILL POWER
ORGANIZING INFORMATION

Read the paragraph below. Then make a table, like the one on page 270, in which you organize the information in the paragraph.

The Indiana General Assembly has two houses: the House of Representatives and the Senate. The Senate has 50 members. Each senator is elected for a four-year term. The House has 100 members. Each representative is elected for a two-year term.

3 WHAT DO YOU THINK?
CRITICAL THINKING

1. Why might a heavily populated state have more power in the House of Representatives than a state with a small population?

2. How can the governor of Indiana use checks and balances?

3. Why is the lieutenant governor's job important?

4. Which of these tasks would be performed by a county government? (a) registering voters; (b) repairing a pothole in a city street; (c) hiring a new sheriff.

5. What responsibility of citizenship do you think is most important? Why?

4 SAY IT, WRITE IT, USE IT
VOCABULARY

You have been asked to create a handbook for new American citizens that outlines how national, state, and Indiana local governments operate. Write this handbook, using as many vocabulary terms as possible.

appeal   naturalized citizen
bill   petition
Bill of Rights   politics
budget   popular sovereignty
checks and balances   separation of powers
congressional district   sheriff
consolidate   veto
majority

CHAPTER 12

5 GEOGRAPHY AND YOU

MAP STUDY

Use the map below and the map on page 285 to answer the following questions.

1. Which congressional districts are on Indiana's northern border?

2. In which district is Parke County?

3. Look at Districts 1 and 5. Why do you think District 1 is made up of fewer counties?

4. In which county do you live? Which is your congressional district?

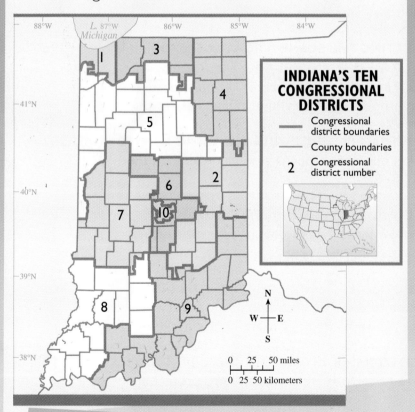

INDIANA'S TEN CONGRESSIONAL DISTRICTS

— Congressional district boundaries
— County boundaries
2 Congressional district number

0   25   50 miles
0   25   50 kilometers

6 TAKE ACTION

CITIZENSHIP

As you have read, citizens of the United States have many rights, such as voting rights and freedom of speech. With these rights come responsibilities. Work with some of your classmates to make a chart like the one pictured. First, list some of the rights that Americans have. Then name some of the responsibilities that come with these rights.

RIGHTS	RESPONSIBILITIES
voting	to learn about candidates and to vote
trial by jury	to serve on juries
freedom of speech	

7 GET CREATIVE

MATH CONNECTION

Voting in elections is one of the most important rights and responsibilities of every American citizen. Poll ten adults to find out whether they voted in the last three presidential elections. Bring your results to class. Then draw a bar graph showing the year of each election along the bottom and the number of adults in your poll who voted each year on the left side. Compare your graph with those of your classmates. Make a class graph by combining all your answers.

LOOKING AHEAD In the next chapter, learn how agriculture, industry, and transportation link Indiana with the world.

LINKS TO THE

Agriculture, manufacturing, and transportation are important industries in Indiana. These industries help connect Indiana with the rest of the nation and the world.

See page 306–307 to find out how science is used in Indiana industry.

CONTENTS

NATION AND THE WORLD

These books tell about resources and technology related to the role of Indiana in the world. Read one that interests you and fill out a book-review form.

READ AND RESEARCH

Energy Resources **by Robin Kerrod** (Thomson Learning, 1994)
This informative book tells about the sources of the world's fuels and about some experimental energy sources. *(nonfiction)*

New Technology: Communications **by Nigel Hawkes**
(Twenty-first Century Books, 1994)
The way we communicate with one another is changing almost daily. Find out about how we are likely to share information in the future. *(nonfiction)*

Ecology **by Steve Pollock** (Dorling Kindersley, 1993)
Learn what ecology is, how scientists study it, and how humans can affect it in either harmful or positive ways. *(nonfiction)*

Using Latitude and Longitude

Lines of latitude and longitude on a map can help you find any place in the world.

UNDERSTAND IT

Suppose someone asked you to find the city of Indianapolis on a world map. It would take a long time if you had to look at all the cities in the world! But what if there were lines and numbers on the map?

Mapmakers draw numbers and lines on maps and globes. Lines of latitude run from east to west all the way around the globe. The equator, which is numbered

0° (zero degrees), is the most important line of latitude. It is located halfway between the North and South Poles.

Lines of longitude run north to south. These lines measure distance from the prime meridian, which is the line of longitude numbered 0°. You can use lines of latitude and longitude to find Indianapolis or any other place on a map or a globe.

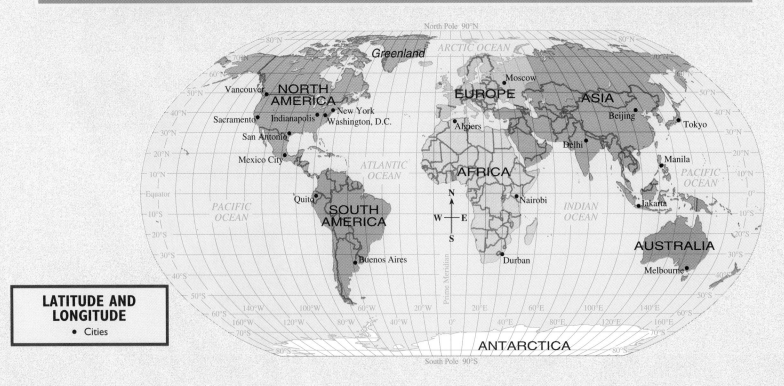

LATITUDE AND LONGITUDE
• Cities

EXPLORE IT

Using the map on page 294, put one finger on the 0° line of latitude (the equator). Follow this line until you reach 85°W longitude. Your finger will be at 0° latitude and 85°W longitude. Then move your finger up until you reach 40°N latitude. Indianapolis is located near this point.

Find the city located at 20°N latitude and near 100°W longitude. Put your finger on the 0° line of latitude. Follow it until you reach the 100°W line of longitude. Then move your finger up to the 20°N line of latitude. Where are you?

TRY IT

Choose three cities on the map on page 294. Write the name of each city on a separate piece of paper. Fold the paper in half. On the outside, write the number of degrees of the lines of latitude and longitude that are closest to the city. For example, you would write 40°N latitude and 120°W longitude for Sacramento, California.

Trade your three papers with a partner. Use the map to find your partner's cities. Then open the folded paper to see if you are correct.

Lines of latitude and longitude help you find places on a map. ▶

SKILL POWER SEARCH *Look through your textbook and study the maps. How do lines of latitude and longitude help you find places?*

Setting the Scene

KEY TERMS
renewable
reservoir
assembly line
export
import

THE CROSSROADS OF AMERICA

FOCUS *Indiana's central location puts it at the crossroads of America. The state sends its many products throughout the United States and the world.*

Indiana in the American Heartland

Indiana is located at the crossroads of America—the place where many roads and highways cross each other. This location makes it easy for goods to be shipped in and out of the state.

Like other midwestern states, Indiana is also part of the American heartland. The heartland is located at the geographical center—or heart—of North America.

In addition, Indiana is located in the area of the United States where the major agricultural belt of the nation overlaps with the major manufacturing belt. The map on this page shows both of these belts.

The agricultural belt includes the towns and farms of the Midwest and Great Plains. The industrial belt includes the cities and factories of the eastern part of the nation. There is also much agriculture and industry outside these major belts.

INDIANA IN THE AGRICULTURAL AND MANUFACTURING BELTS

- Agricultural Belt
- Manufacturing Belt
- Agricultural and Manufacturing Belt

Indiana

0   250   500 miles

0   250   500 kilometers

An Indiana limestone quarry

Indiana Limestone and Other Resources

One of Indiana's most important minerals is limestone. Indiana limestone is a strong, beautiful stone. It has been used to construct many famous buildings throughout the country.

Indiana's lakes and forests are also important resources. These places are home to wildlife. They also provide opportunities for camping and boating.

Indiana's forests provide timber for making furniture. Its lakes and **reservoirs** (REZ ur vwahrz) provide water for drinking and for watering crops.

Soil and Mineral Resources

Both farms and factories use Indiana's natural resources. One of the state's most important resources is its rich, fertile soil. Indiana's soil allows farmers to grow many crops, including corn and soybeans.

Indiana is also rich in minerals, especially coal and limestone. The state's mineral resources are very important to its economy.

Some natural resources are **renewable**. This means that they can be replaced by nature. Trees that have been cut down, for example, can be replanted.

Minerals are nonrenewable resources. Once a mineral is taken from the earth, it cannot be replaced. Hoosiers must use their mineral and other nonrenewable resources wisely so that they will last as long as possible.

 Wildlife like this raccoon and wolf are Indiana resources.

---

 renewable   Able to be replaced

reservoir   A place where water is collected

INDIANA
First in Manufacturing

1st

⭐ raw steel

⭐ mobile homes

⭐ recreational vehicles

⭐ radios and televisions

⭐ truck and bus bodies

⭐ wood office furniture

⭐ elevators and escalators

⭐ refrigerators

Indiana's Products

Indiana's rich resources have helped make the state a leader in manufacturing. Indiana is the largest producer of radios and televisions in the United States. Our state is first in the nation in manufacturing mobile homes and recreational vehicles. It also leads in the production of electrical equipment and steel.

Indiana is one of the top five states in producing medicines and hospital supplies. Large Hoosier companies also make motor vehicle engines and truck and bus bodies.

Indiana ranks eighth in the nation in raising farm crops. Many factories in the state pack and process—or prepare—food.

A pickle factory in northern Indiana turns midwestern cucumbers into pickles. A pretzel factory in southern Indiana is one of the few companies that still twists pretzels by hand rather than by machine.

Other Indiana products include compact discs and musical instruments. Elkhart, Indiana, is often called the musical instrument capital of the country.

Indiana also makes prefabricated (pree FAB rih kayt ed) homes. Prefabricated homes are partly or entirely made in a factory. They are taken by truck to the places where people will live in them.

Connections with the Nation and the World

Indiana businesses work with companies throughout the nation. Car and truck engines, for example, are shipped from Indiana to nearby states. When a new car or truck rolls off an **assembly line** in

 assembly line A process in which each worker in a factory performs a different step or job in putting together a product

298

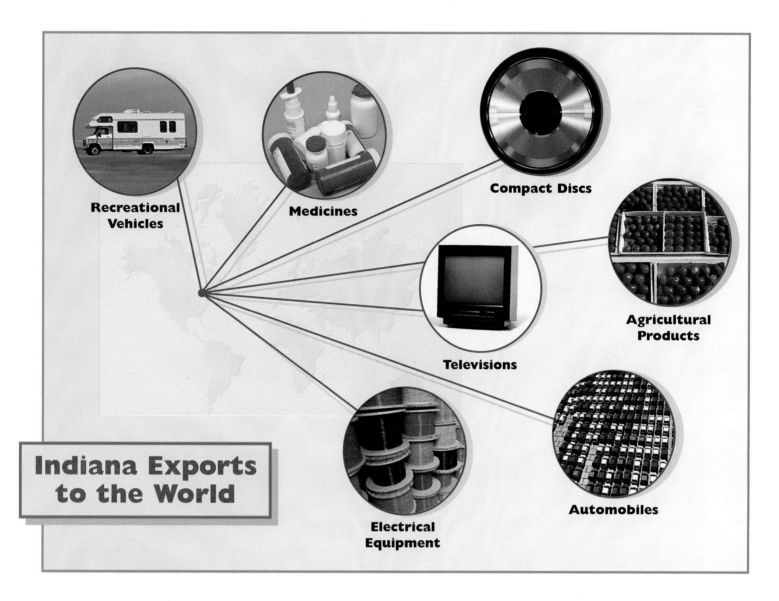

Indiana Exports to the World

Recreational Vehicles

Medicines

Compact Discs

Televisions

Agricultural Products

Electrical Equipment

Automobiles

Michigan, it contains many parts made in Indiana.

Indiana also has many world, or global, connections. Products grown and made in Indiana are *exported* all over the world. Indiana grain feeds people in Africa, Asia, Europe, and South America. Indiana also sells several billion dollars' worth of automobiles, trucks, auto parts, iron, and steel to its neighbors in Canada each year.

Hoosiers also **import** goods from the rest of the country and the world. For example, Indiana imports coke for making iron and steel. Canada supplies Indiana with lumber, wood products, and paper.

 export To send goods out of a country

 import To bring goods into a country

Indiana's Highway System

After the first railroads were built in Indiana in the mid-1800s, the state became a center of transportation. Everyone in the country seemed to pass through Indiana. The state motto became "The Crossroads of America." This motto is still true today.

Since the late 1950s, a network of interstate highways has linked cities across America. Indiana is so centrally located that eight of these highways pass through it. Several interstates circle and pass through Indianapolis.

Many people driving across the country pass through Indiana. Many stop at tourist sites throughout the state.

A Center of Transportation

Indiana is also an important center for the trucking industry. Trucks pass through the state on their way to and from stops all over

INDIANA'S INTERSTATE HIGHWAY SYSTEM
- Interstate highways
- ★ State capital
- • Other cities

the United States and Canada. More than half of the United States, as well as central Canada, is just one day's drive from Indiana.

Indiana is a center for other kinds of transportation, too. Many goods are shipped by train on the railroad lines that cross the state. Other goods are shipped from the state's many airports, including Indianapolis International Airport.

▲ Indianapolis International Airport

PRODUCTS SHIPPED BY WATER

petroleum   iron   coke   steel

On the Great Lakes

lumber   grain   coal   fertilizer

On the Ohio River

Indiana Ports

The first international port in Indiana was opened in 1970 near the town of Portage on Lake Michigan. Today, huge oceangoing ships called freighters carry millions of tons of Indiana steel and other goods to customers throughout the world.

From Lake Michigan, freighters can travel through the Great Lakes to the St. Lawrence Seaway. Then they can sail all the way to the Atlantic Ocean.

Indiana's other international ports are located on the Ohio River. They are Southwind Maritime Centre and Clark Maritime Centre.

Maritime means "having to do with the ocean." Indiana's Ohio River ports connect with the ocean by way of the Mississippi River. Like all shipping centres—or centers—they are busy places.

Many southern Indiana products are shipped on the Ohio River. Most are shipped on large flat-bottomed boats called barges.

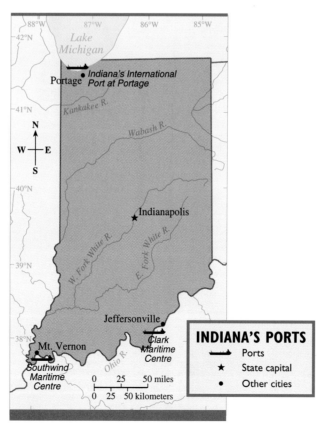

Lake Michigan

Portage • Indiana's International Port at Portage

Kankakee R.

Wabash R.

★ Indianapolis

W. Fork White R.   *E. Fork White R.*

Jeffersonville

Mt. Vernon   Clark Maritime Centre

Southwind Maritime Centre

Ohio R.

INDIANA'S PORTS

→ Ports
★ State capital
• Other cities

0   25   50 miles
0   25   50 kilometers

SHOW WHAT YOU KNOW!

REFOCUS
COMPREHENSION

1. What are two examples of Indiana's global connections?

2. Why is Indiana called "The Crossroads of America"?

THINK ABOUT IT
CRITICAL THINKING

Name two resources, in addition to minerals, that cannot be renewed. Explain your choice.

WRITE ABOUT IT
ACTIVITY

Think of a motto that describes something special about Indiana. Then write a paragraph explaining your choice.

SOUTHWIND MARITIME CENTRE

FOCUS *Southwind Maritime Centre is one of Indiana's major shipping ports. Southwind has helped Indiana grow as an international trading center.*

A Major Indiana Port

Southwind Maritime Centre is located on the Ohio River near the town of Mount Vernon. It is Indiana's largest port on the Ohio.

Companies in Kentucky, Illinois, and Indiana all ship goods in and out of Southwind. Southwind is connected with surrounding areas by train and by the many highways that crisscross the region.

Southwind is located near the country's richest grain- and coal-producing regions. This location makes Southwind one of Indiana's busiest ports.

Barges and a tugboat at Southwind

Storing and Loading Cargo

Many goods are stored at Southwind before they are shipped down the Ohio River. Huge round tanks store millions of gallons of fertilizer. Grain elevators store thousands of **bushels** of grain. Logs awaiting shipment are piled in stacks that seem to reach the sky.

Some cargo arrives at or departs from Southwind in enormous containers. A tall crane lifts these 60-ton giants off and onto the huge barges waiting at docks along the Ohio River. In one hour, other machines can load 25,000 bushels of grain or 4,000 tons of coal onto a barge.

Most barges do not have their own engines. Once a barge is loaded, a powerful tugboat pushes or pulls it down the Ohio River to the Mississippi River.

A Water Superhighway

Sending cargo by water is often cheaper than sending it by truck or train. As a result, many Indiana businesses want to increase shipping on the Ohio River.

These businesses are working to make **navigation** on the Ohio easier by improving the river's system of locks. Then the Ohio can become an even greater water superhighway than it is today.

⭐ *bushel* A measure of volume for grain, fruits, or vegetables

⭐ *navigation* Planning and controlling the course of a ship

SHOW WHAT YOU KNOW!

REFOCUS
COMPREHENSION

1. Why do businesses want to increase shipping on the Ohio River?

2. What Indiana products are shipped out of Southwind?

THINK ABOUT IT
CRITICAL THINKING

Southwind is sometimes called a seaport, or a port that connects with the ocean. Explain how this can be true.

WRITE ABOUT IT
ACTIVITY

Write an entry in your Indiana journal describing what you might see if you visited Southwind.

303

INDIANA'S STONE BELT

FOCUS *Most of Indiana's limestone is quarried in three counties in southern Indiana. This region is known as the stone belt. Limestone from this area is sent to towns and cities throughout the United States and the world.*

STATE CAPITALS AND
INTERSTATE HIGHWAYS

—90— Interstate highways

⊛ National capital

★ State capitals

Indiana's stone belt

Where Is Limestone Shipped?

As the manager of an Indiana company that quarries limestone, you receive orders for limestone from cities around the United States. You arrange for your product to be shipped to these cities.

Cities

Austin, Texas A memorial sculpture and fountain will be created to honor war veterans. The piece will be carved from Indiana limestone.

Boston, Massachusetts A university in the Boston area plans to build a new athletic center. The walls will be constructed of Indiana limestone.

Denver, Colorado A skyscraper will be constructed of Indiana limestone. It will contain twenty-nine floors of office space.

Helena, Montana Limestone from Indiana will be shipped to Helena. The stone will be used to build a new library.

Tallahassee, Florida A three-story shopping mall will be constructed of Indiana limestone.

Washington, D.C. A historical museum covering one city block is being completed in the nation's capital. Most of the structure is made of Indiana limestone.

skyscraper A very tall building

MAP IT

1. You will be invited to attend the dedication of the sculpture in Austin. In which direction will you travel to get there?
2. The limestone is ready to be shipped to Boston. What highway routes will the truck driver travel?
3. Some of the stone for the buildings in Denver and in Helena will be loaded onto the same truck. Where will the driver probably go first? What highway route will he or she travel? In which direction will he or she travel next?
4. A rush order is needed for the Tallahassee construction project. About how many miles is Tallahassee from the stone belt?
5. You decide to visit the new museum in Washington, D.C. In which direction do you travel? What ocean is near this city?

EXPLORE IT

You have received an order for a new government building in Hawaii. Sending the limestone to Hawaii will require two means of transportation. Tell how you might send the limestone to this site.

4

Spotlight

KEY TERMS

component
engineer
biotechnology
satellite
radar

TECHNOLOGY FOR THE FUTURE

FOCUS *Technology helps Hoosiers perform tasks with the touch of a button. In the future, technology will be even more important in people's lives than it is today.*

Technology Today and Tomorrow

Technology is the science of making and using things. Technology is used to improve old tools, machines, and materials and to invent new ones.

Technology helps people fight hunger and disease. It allows industry to produce more goods with less work. It enables people to transport goods all over the world and to lead comfortable lives.

▼ Children learn about computers.

People use the term *high technology*—or *high tech*—to refer to today's complex new technology. High tech uses computers and other electronic equipment.

Many of today's jobs require a knowledge of high technology. Jobs of the future will require even more workers to be high-tech experts.

Using Computers

Computers allow people to gather, display, and understand all kinds of information. Computers solve difficult problems and store large amounts of information. They are becoming smaller, faster, and more powerful all the time.

Today many families have a home computer. People use home computers for everything from keeping track of the money they spend to playing computer games.

Most businesses have at least one and sometimes hundreds of computers. They use their computers to store information about their products, customers, and employees.

Computers are used to help repair automobiles.

Your school may have one or more computers. Schools use computers to teach math, social studies, and many other subjects.

Cars and Computers

Repairing car engines is one job that calls for high technology. Most auto repair shops have computers to diagnose—or find out—what's wrong with a car. People who repair cars must learn how to use these special computers.

The industries that design cars and their **components** also use computers. For example, **engineers** may use computers to design and test engines for cars and trucks.

This technology is called Computer Aided Design, or CAD. It is used to design bridges, buildings, and other products and machines.

Delco Electronic in Kokomo, Indiana, was one of the first companies to use CAD. Delco supplies electronic components, such as car radios, to companies throughout the world.

Growing Better Food

Growing food is an important part of Indiana's economy. Agricultural scientists use a special kind of high technology called **biotechnology** to grow better crops and to make better foods.

Agricultural scientists at Indiana's Purdue University are known throughout the world for their work in biotechnology. They have recently developed a new kind of rice that resists disease better than

component   A part or piece
engineer   A person who uses science and math to design and build things

biotechnology   A branch of science that uses technology to study plants and animals

Scientists use biotechnology to grow better crops, such as these rice plants.

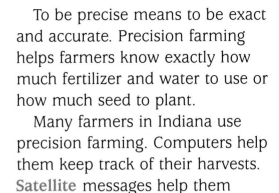

Many farmers use computers to record information about their crops.

other types. It will be used to feed people in many countries around the world.

Precision Farming

Farming is important to Indiana's economy. A technology called precision farming helps Hoosier farmers grow better crops.

To be precise means to be exact and accurate. Precision farming helps farmers know exactly how much fertilizer and water to use or how much seed to plant.

Many farmers in Indiana use precision farming. Computers help them keep track of their harvests. Satellite messages help them locate exactly where they are on their fields.

Today, farmers use shovels to dig up samples of soil. Soon they might use electronic "shovels" instead. These high-tech machines will send radio waves—or radar—deep into the soil to find out whether crops need more water or fertilizer.

Using Medical Technology

Technology has brought huge changes in medicine. A science called radiology (ray dee AHL uh jee) lets doctors look at the inside of the body. Doctors who specialize in radiology are called radiologists.

The first pictures taken by radiologists were X-rays. Today, new technologies allow doctors to see the inside of the body in greater detail than ever before.

This doctor is using an MRI to take a picture of a patient's brain.

satellite An object placed into orbit around the earth in order to gather information
radar Radio waves that are used to gather information

ELI LILLY MANUFACTURING
AND RESEARCH SITES

Countries with an Eli Lilly facility

SHOW WHAT YOU
KNOW!

REFOCUS
COMPREHENSION

1. How does
precision farming
help farmers?

2. What is Computer
Aided Design?

THINK ABOUT IT
CRITICAL THINKING

Describe three
careers that use
computers.

WRITE ABOUT IT
ACTIVITY

Write an entry in
your Indiana journal
that explains the
following statement:
High technology is
important in Indiana
today and will be
important in the
future.

MRI machines, for example, allow
doctors to take pictures of the inside
of the body and diagnose problems
without using X-rays. MRIs are an
important technology because X-rays
can sometimes be harmful to people.

▲ Scientists at work at
Eli Lilly and Company

Eli Lilly and Company

Indiana is a world leader in
producing medicines. The
headquarters of one of the largest
producers of medicines in the
world, Eli Lilly and Company, is
located in Indianapolis.

Eli Lilly and Company relies on
more than 4,000 kinds of
technology to make its medicines.
It uses computers so powerful that
they are called supercomputers.

Eli Lilly and Company has many
global connections. People around
the world feel better or get well
because of the medicines made
by this Indiana company.

Citizenship

KEY TERMS

wetlands
acid rain
erosion
reclaim

PROTECTING THE ENVIRONMENT

FOCUS *Pollution from some industries has harmed Indiana's natural environment. Today people are trying to repair past damage and meet future challenges.*

Challenges to the Environment

Industries are important to Indiana's economy. But industries can hurt the environment. Dangerous materials can find their way into the air, land, and water.

Smoke from steel mills and other factories can cause dirty air. Chemicals from factories and dumps can leak into soil and even into drinking water.

Many people in Indiana work to protect the environment. They also try to repair past damage.

Indiana's Department of Natural Resources (DNR) protects fish, wildlife, parks, and **wetlands** from environmental damage. It also cleans up land damaged by mining.

The state's Department of Environmental Management makes sure that pollution control laws are obeyed. It also works with businesses to prevent pollution.

Transportation 23.8%

Home 16.9%

Business 10.9%

Industry 48.4%

ENERGY USE IN INDIANA

Cleaner Energy

Industries use large amounts of energy to run their machines. In Indiana, almost half of all energy is used by industries.

Some of Indiana's industries burn a great deal of coal to produce energy. Unfortunately, burning some forms of coal is a leading cause of air pollution.

Acid rain results when certain kinds of air pollution combine with moisture in the air. Acid rain is harmful to lakes and wildlife.

acid rain Rain that is full of acids formed in the air when fuels such as coal are burned

Some industries produce air pollution.

wetlands Swamps or marshes, especially in an area reserved for wildlife

coal, they put the soil back. Then they plant trees to prevent **erosion**.

Other coal lies deep within the earth. This coal can only be reached through underground tunnels. In the past miners heaped the soil from the tunnels onto the surrounding earth. This soil contained bits of coal and harmful acids that polluted the land.

Restoring Green Valley

Green Valley, located in western Indiana, was polluted by coal mining beginning in the 1940s. By the 1960s, blackish-gray dirt and coal dust were piled on grass and bushes. Wildlife had moved away and trees had died.

In the 1970s, new laws were passed to clean up Indiana's mining sites. Today, the state's Department of Natural Resources is working to

▲ Green Valley was polluted by coal mining.

Many industries in Indiana are working to stop acid rain. Some have put huge "scrubbers" in their smokestacks to remove polluting chemicals.

Effects of Coal Mining

Mining coal can also harm the environment. Some coal lies near the surface of the earth. Miners remove the soil and dig out the coal. This is called surface mining.

Surface mining used to harm the land because soil was taken away and never replaced. Trees and grass could no longer grow in the area.

Today, mining companies must save the soil when they begin to dig. After they have removed the

 erosion   Loss of soil due to its being washed away by rain or blown away by wind

Indiana Department of ▲ Natural Resources badge

Today the Ohio River is safe for fish and wildlife.

reclaim Green Valley. New soil is being brought in to replace polluted soil. Trees and grass are being planted to prevent erosion. The Department of Natural Resources hopes to have Green Valley and other abandoned mining sites cleaned up by the year 2005.

Restoring Indiana's Rivers

Even in the early 1900s, many of Indiana's rivers and lakes were polluted from sewage and factory waste. The state began cleanup programs in the 1920s.

During the 1940s, Indiana and neighboring states began cleaning up the Ohio River. At that time, the Ohio River had became so polluted that fish could no longer live in it. One goal of the cleanup was to bring back the fish and be sure that they were safe to eat.

As rivers grew cleaner, wildlife came back. Today fishing and boating are major activities on the Ohio River.

Another success story is the river otter. This lively animal disappeared from Indiana's polluted rivers and streams in the early 1940s. During the 1990s, state wildlife officials released hundreds of river otters to new homes in Indiana rivers.

reclaim   Make useable again for growing things

The Superfund Cleanup

Years ago, many industries did not dispose of their harmful wastes carefully. They did not know that these wastes could be dangerous to people's health.

During the 1970s and 1980s, Americans became concerned about the harmful effects of industrial wastes. In 1980 the Federal Environmental Protection Agency (EPA) created the Superfund program. The Superfund provides money to clean up sites that contain harmful industrial wastes.

More than 30 Superfund sites have been identified in Indiana. A Superfund site might be a place where chemicals are stored in tanks that have begun to leak. Or it could be a dump where a factory has thrown away harmful materials.

The Superfund depends on local citizens. They can alert the EPA to a dangerous site and help the agency decide on how to clean it up.

Planting Trees

Planting trees is a good way to help the environment. Trees hold soil in place. They put oxygen into the air we breathe. Trees provide food and shelter for wildlife. That is why several Indiana groups encourage people to plant trees.

One of these groups is the National Arbor Day Foundation. It has given the title *Tree City USA* to many Indiana cities with tree-planting programs, including Fort Wayne, Elkhart, and Lafayette.

▼ Planting trees helps the environment.

SHOW WHAT YOU KNOW!

REFOCUS
COMPREHENSION

1. How are Indiana's industries working to stop air pollution?

2. What are the effects of coal mining on the land? How can the land be restored?

THINK ABOUT IT
CRITICAL THINKING

Describe two ways that you can help improve Indiana's environment.

WRITE ABOUT IT
ACTIVITY

Make a poster encouraging Hoosiers to plant trees. Be sure to explain how tree planting helps the environment.

SUMMING UP

1 DO YOU REMEMBER . . .
COMPREHENSION

1. Name two of Indiana's important natural resources.

2. Describe a route that barges travel from Southwind Maritime Centre to the ocean.

3. What is the main use for limestone from the stone belt?

4. Name three ways that people can use computers in their homes and in their businesses.

5. How do trees help the environment?

2 SKILL POWER
USING LATITUDE AND LONGITUDE

Play a game of "geography bingo" with a group of your classmates. Using a map of the world, one student begins by giving the latitude and longitude of a city somewhere in the world. Members of the group all try to find the city on the map. The first student to call out the correct name of the city chooses the next city and announces its latitude and longitude.

3 WHAT DO YOU THINK?
CRITICAL THINKING

1. What advantage does Indiana's location in the geographical center of the United States give the state?

2. Why is it cheaper to send cargo by barge than by air?

3. Give two reasons to use Indiana limestone in a new building.

4. Why is a knowledge of high technology important to employees of Eli Lilly and Company?

5. Compare Green Valley in the 1950s and 1960s with Green Valley today.

4 SAY IT, WRITE IT, USE IT
VOCABULARY

Write an article in which you follow an Indiana product from a farm or a factory to a market. Use as many vocabulary terms as you can.

acid rain	navigation
assembly line	radar
biotechnology	reclaim
bushel	renewable
component	reservoir
engineer	satellite
erosion	skyscraper
export	wetlands
import	

5 GEOGRAPHY AND YOU
MAP STUDY

Use the map below to answer the following questions.

1. In which directions does Interstate 64 lead?

2. Which interstate highways would you travel to go from Gary to Terre Haute?

3. According to this map, which is the longest interstate highway in Indiana?

4. Which interstate highways would you travel to go from Fort Wayne to South Bend?

INDIANA'S INTERSTATE HIGHWAY SYSTEM

- 65 Interstate highways
- ★ State capital
- • Other cities

6 TAKE ACTION
CITIZENSHIP

In this chapter you read about how the river otter vanished from rivers and streams in Indiana in the early 1940s. Since that time, efforts have been made to clean up the rivers. Find out about other animals in Indiana that are in danger today. Choose one endangered animal and draw a picture of it. Then list some facts about the animal and tell what people can do to help the endangered animal survive.

7 GET CREATIVE
COMPUTER CONNECTION

Create a slogan that encourages people to conserve energy or prevent erosion in Indiana. If possible, use a computer to prepare the final words and images in your slogan. Display your slogan on a bulletin board labeled "Protecting Our Environment."

LOOKING AHEAD
In the next chapter, read about contributions of Hoosiers to the arts, education, and sports.

INDIANA TODAY

As Hoosiers use their talents and abilities to meet today's challenges, they also prepare to shape the future of Indiana, the nation, and the world.

CONTENTS

Find out on page 336 why this girl is waving pennants.

AND TOMORROW

These books tell about some amazing people, places, and events in modern Indiana. Read one that interests you and fill out a book-review form.

READ AND RESEARCH

Out to Win Indy! The Great American Race
by Jay Schleifer (Crestwood House, 1995)
Take your seat behind the wheel at the Indy 500 in this exciting, fact-filled book. *(nonfiction)*
● *You can read a selection from this book on page 332.*

One Giant Leap for Mankind **by Carter Smith III**
(Silver Burdett Company, 1985)
Learn about the Apollo moon landing, the Voyager spacecraft, Hoosier astronaut Gus Grissom, and more! *(nonfiction)*

Sports Great: Larry Bird **by Jack Kavanagh**
(Enslow Publishers, 1992)
Follow Larry Bird's path from schoolboy in French Lick to superstar basketball player with the Celtics in Boston. *(biography)*

Indiana **by Kathleen Thompson** (Raintree
Steck-Vaughn, 1996)
The exciting places and rich traditions of the Hoosier state are all described in this overview. *(nonfiction)*

SKILL POWER

Comparing and Contrasting

Knowing how to compare and contrast can help you better understand the people and places that make Indiana a great state.

UNDERSTAND IT

When you find out how places and things are alike, you are comparing them. In what ways is your school similar to other schools in the area? Is it about the same size as other schools? Do other schools have a cafeteria or lunchroom like the one in your school?

Maybe there are ways in which your school is really different from other schools. Noting differences between two or more things is called contrasting.

Comparing and contrasting ways in which people live and work in different parts of Indiana helps you better understand life in Indiana. For example, how is the job of an Indianapolis worker who makes televisions similar to that of a worker in Terre Haute who makes compact discs? Both of these people produce high-tech goods. In what other ways might their jobs be similar? In what ways might they be different?

EXPLORE IT

Pictures can help you compare and contrast things. In these two pictures, young people are going to school. But the school buildings and the periods in history are different. The picture at the top shows children in an early schoolhouse. The bottom picture shows young people in school today. Compare these two photos. What do you see that is similar about them? What do you see that is different?

318

TRY IT

Is your school like a school in Japan? In some ways it is, but in other ways it is very different. Sometimes it is helpful to make a Venn diagram to show how two things are alike and how they are different.

In the Venn diagram below, the words in the middle show how an American student's school is similar to a Japanese student's school. The words in the two outer sections show differences between the two schools.

You can make a Venn diagram of your own to compare your school with another person's school. Ask an adult to write down things that tell what his or her school was like. Then make a Venn diagram to show how that school was like yours and how it was different.

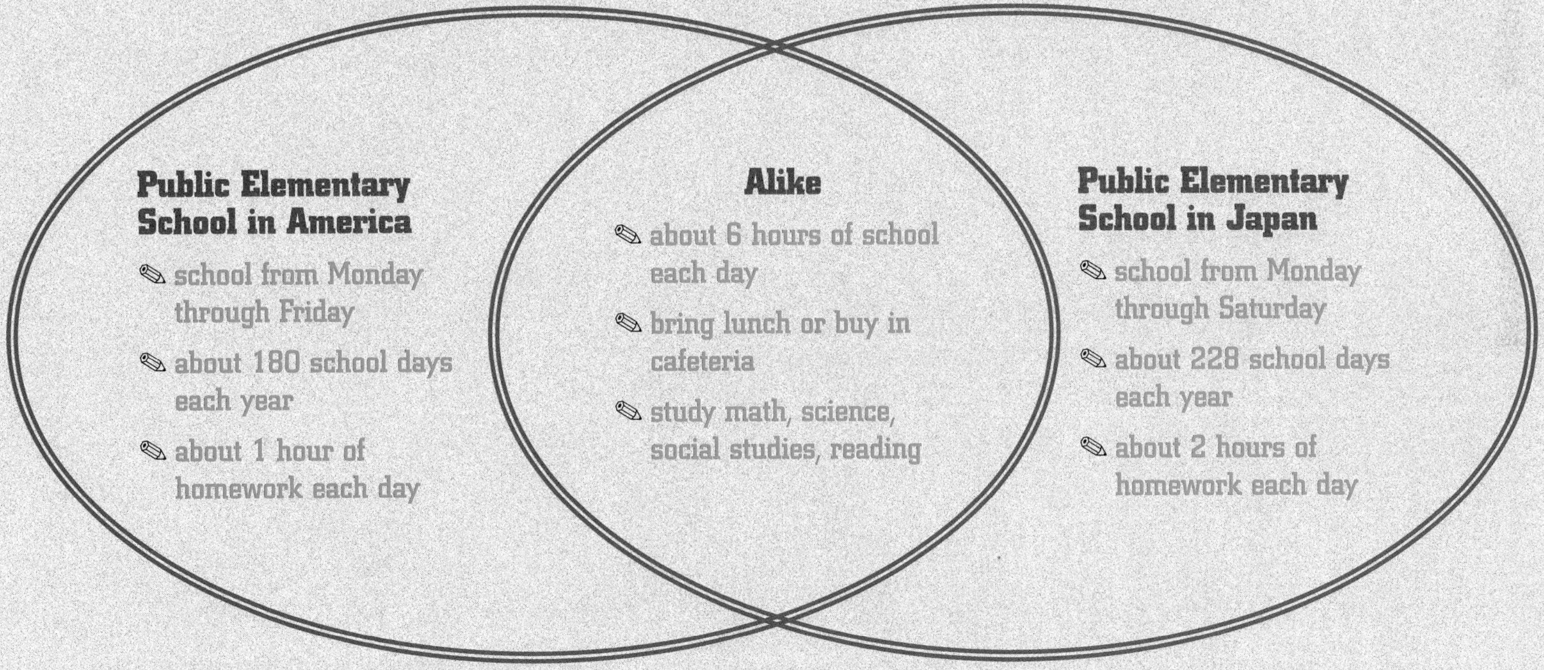

Public Elementary School in America

✎ school from Monday through Friday

✎ about 180 school days each year

✎ about 1 hour of homework each day

Alike

✎ about 6 hours of school each day

✎ bring lunch or buy in cafeteria

✎ study math, science, social studies, reading

Public Elementary School in Japan

✎ school from Monday through Saturday

✎ about 228 school days each year

✎ about 2 hours of homework each day

SKILL POWER SEARCH

Compare and contrast two pictures in this chapter. How are the pictures alike? How are they different?

HOOSIER PRIDE

FOCUS *Indiana is home to people of many backgrounds. The Hoosier state has a long tradition of excellence in education, the arts, and sports.*

One State, Many People

Indiana is a small state in land—but not in people. Of the 50 states, 37 have more land. Yet only 13 have more people than Indiana does. About 5.8 million people call Indiana home. About 2 out of 3 Hoosiers live in cities or towns.

Each year about 50,000 people move into our state. That's enough Hoosiers to fill a medium-sized city.

The chart on this page shows that most of Indiana's counties are growing in population. Many of these new Hoosiers are babies born to Indiana families. But many others are newcomers to our state.

New Hoosiers

Today's immigrants come from places south of the United States, including Mexico, the Caribbean islands, and South America. Others arrive from countries in Asia, such as China, Cambodia, South Korea, and India.

People come to Indiana for many reasons. Our state offers a variety of opportunities. Some people find jobs in Indiana. Others attend the colleges and universities here—and stay on after they graduate. Still others enjoy the lively arts, entertainment, and sports that can be found in the Hoosier state.

Hoosiers follow many religions. In Indiana, you will find Catholics, Baptists, Methodists, Lutherans, Jews, Muslims, Presbyterians, and people of other religions.

INDIANA POPULATION FACTS

From 1990 to 1995, 87 of Indiana's 92 counties grew in population.

Only five Indiana counties have fewer than 10,000 people: Benton, Warren, Switzerland, Union, and Ohio.

Indiana's population today is over 1,000 times bigger than it was 200 years ago.

In 1996, there were 80,835 fourth graders in Indiana schools. Of this total, 72,330 attended public schools.

James Dean

Wes Montgomery

Jane Pauley

Hoosiers in the Arts

Hoosiers are proud of their writers, actors, artists, musicians, composers, and newscasters. And well they should be! Hundreds of Hoosiers have become famous in these fields.

Cole Porter (1891–1964) from Peru, Indiana, is one of America's most famous songwriters. "Night and Day" is perhaps his best-known tune. He also wrote musicals, including *Kiss Me, Kate*.

Hoagy Carmichael (1899–1981) was born in Bloomington. He gained fame with such songs as "Stardust" and "Georgia on My Mind," Georgia's state song.

Paul Dresser (1857–1906) was the brother of novelist Theodore

Cole Porter

Dreiser. He wrote Indiana's state song, "On the Banks of the Wabash, Far Away."

Indiana has been home to many **jazz** musicians. Guitarist John Leslie "Wes" Montgomery (1923–1968) was born in Indianapolis. He made many popular albums. His brothers William Howard "Monk" and Charles "Buddy" also gained fame in the world of jazz. So did Hoosiers Earl "Fox" Walker, J. J. Johnson, and Roger Jones.

Film and Television

Among Hoosier film greats, Marion's James Dean (1931–1955) stands out. Roles in *Giant* and *Rebel Without a Cause* made him a star.

Television journalist Jane Pauley (1950–   ) was born in Indianapolis.

 jazz   A type of American music with strong rhythms that started with black southerners

321

For many years, she hosted "The Today Show," a morning news program.

Writers and Artists

Indiana has been home to hundreds of writers. Jessamyn West (1907–1984) was born in Jennings County. Her best-known novel is *Friendly Persuasion,* the story of a Quaker family during the Civil War period.

More recently, Kurt Vonnegut, Jr. (1922–   ) of Indianapolis has written several best-selling novels, including *Slaughterhouse Five* and *Cat's Cradle.* Marion's Jim Davis created Garfield the Cat. Books of Garfield comics have sold over 60 million copies. Other Hoosier writers who have made important contributions are William E. Wilson, Alexander Thom, Irving Leibowitz, and Jean Shepard.

▲ Books by Indiana writers Beatrice Schenk de Regniers and Phyllis Reynolds Naylor

Many writers for young people also come from Indiana. Phyllis Reynolds Naylor (1933–   ) received the Newbury Medal for her novel *Shiloh.* Other Hoosier writers for children include Beatrice Schenk de Regniers, Eth Clifford, and Nancy Niblack Baxter.

Since pioneer times, many artists have lived and worked in Indiana. Robert Indiana, a modern Hoosier sculptor, was born Robert Clark. He changed his name to honor his Indiana roots. His LOVE sculpture marks the entrance to the Indianapolis Museum of Art. Other well-known Hoosier artists are Mary Beth Edelson and Robert Berkshire.

Hoosiers and Education

Hoosiers have always valued education. Indiana's first constitution promised free public education from elementary school

Robert Indiana's LOVE sculpture stands at the Indianapolis Museum of Art. ▶

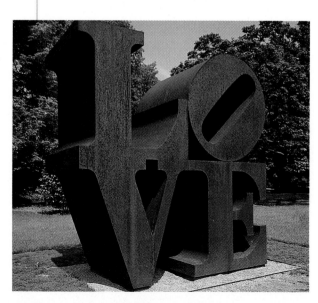

to college. The state built its first colleges in the early 1800s.

Today, about 1 million young people go to Indiana's public schools. In addition, about 250,000 students attend the great colleges of the Hoosier state.

Famous Hoosier Athletes

Cheering on the home team is another old Indiana tradition. Hoosiers have many sports **competitions** to cheer about. There's the famed Indy 500, the greatest car race of all. The Colts and Pacers bring excitement to the state. So do hundreds of college and school teams.

Indiana is a state of great athletes. Hoosiers have won fame in almost every sport. Let's take a look at some of these Hoosier superstars.

Oscar Robertson grew up in Indianapolis. At Crispus Attucks High School, he led the basketball team to two state titles in a row. After starring at the University of Cincinnati, "The Big O" had a great career in the National Basketball Association (NBA). He played with the Cincinnati Royals and the Milwaukee Bucks. Robertson was elected to the Basketball Hall of Fame in 1979.

Larry Bird of French Lick took Indiana State to college basketball's national championship game in 1979. He also led the Boston Celtics to three NBA championships.

Hoosier athletes have earned fame in the Olympics, too. Indiana

University swimmer Mark Spitz took home seven gold medals in the 1972 games. No one person had ever won so many gold medals in a single year.

Wilma Rudolph (1940–1994), a track star, also made Olympic history. In 1960 she became the first American woman to win three gold medals in the same games.

▲ Oscar Robertson (number 43) led Crispus Attucks High School to state championships in 1955 and 1956.

 competition   A contest

Larry Bird

Oscar Robertson

Bobby Knight

In 1982, she adopted Indianapolis as her hometown and founded an organization that helped children through sports.

Baseball is another popular Hoosier sport. In the 1940s and 1950s, the Fort Wayne Daisies played in a professional women's league. One of Indiana's most famous baseball players is Don Mattingly from Evansville. He starred for the New York Yankees in the 1980s and 1990s.

Coaching Legends

It takes a great coach to train a great athlete, and Indiana has had some of the greatest coaches of all. Knute Rockne coached football at the University of Notre Dame in the early 1900s. He is considered one of football's coaching legends.

John Wooden was born in Martinsville. He coached the University of California at Los Angeles to a record ten college basketball championships. Another famous Hoosier coach is Bobby Knight of Indiana University. His basketball teams have won three national championships.

Fort Wayne Daisies professional baseball team in 1945 ▼

Fairs and Festivals

Hoosier celebrations, fairs, and festivals show what Hoosiers value most. They love their heritage, state history, arts, sports, farm products, food—and more. Indiana's biggest celebration is the Indiana State Fair in Indianapolis. Almost every town holds its own special events.

South Bend's annual Ethnic Festival draws 60,000 people. German Hoosiers host many celebrations, such as the Oktoberfests at Terre Haute and Seymour. Vevay has its Swiss Alpine Festival, and Clinton its Little Italy Festival. The Scotland Festival is held in— where else?—Scotland, Indiana! Evansville honors Indiana's first people with Native American Days.

Music Events

Music lovers can get their fill at the Festival of Music in New Harmony. Other music events include Summer with the Symphony in Whiting, the Elkhart Jazz Festival, and the many bluegrass festivals held around the state.

Peru, southwest of Fort Wayne, holds a summer Circus City Festival. At one time, Peru was the winter home of seven circuses. Today Peru honors circus performers at its International Circus Hall of Fame.

▼ Peru, Indiana, claims to be the Circus Capital of the World.

SHOW WHAT YOU KNOW!

REFOCUS
COMPREHENSION

1. What are some reasons people move to Indiana?

2. What did Cole Porter and Wes Montgomery have in common?

THINK ABOUT IT
CRITICAL THINKING

Which of the Hoosier greats from this chapter do you admire most? Explain your choice.

WRITE ABOUT IT
ACTIVITY

Would you like to start a festival? What would it be? Write about it in your Indiana journal.

Spotlight

⭐ **KEY TERMS**

visual artist
gallery
architect
performing artist

A TRADITION IN THE ARTS

FOCUS *Hoosiers are known for excellence in many fields of art, such as painting, architecture, dance, music, and acting.*

Visual Arts

Hoosier artists are known all over the world. Their paintings, photographs, and sculptures can be found in many museums. Their work has influenced the artists of other states and countries, too.

In turn, Indiana museums have always welcomed the works of **visual artists**—painters, sculptors, craftspeople, and photographers.

There are more than 100 craft shops and more than 50 art associations in Indiana. Many towns have a museum or a **gallery**.

The Indianapolis Museum of Art is a well-known regional museum. Inside you can see the works of

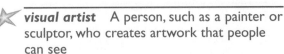

An African mask from the Indianapolis Museum of Art

Indiana artists and collections of Asian and pre-Columbian art.

South Bend and Fort Wayne are home to wonderful art museums, too. Many Indiana colleges also have impressive collections. At Indiana University, for example, you can find a museum that houses more than 35,000 works of art. Notre Dame is also known for its art museum.

Saving the Past

Throughout the Hoosier state, you can find sculptures and buildings from Indiana's past. Concerned citizens make sure old buildings stay in good shape. They also work to keep these buildings from being torn down.

Many Hoosiers also take part in saving Indiana's heritage. Some help with SOS!, a national project to "save outdoor sculpture." Volunteers have identified 1,200 outdoor sculptures in Indiana.

⭐ ***visual artist*** A person, such as a painter or sculptor, who creates artwork that people can see
gallery A place for showing or selling art

Columbus, Indiana

Many Indiana cities have beautiful buildings. Columbus may be the most well known. It contains 50 buildings designed by famous **architects**. Columbus also has many large pieces of sculpture.

The city has saved many old buildings and also built new ones. The first of these projects started in the 1950s. A local business leader donated money for this purpose. Then other groups did the same.

Soon many famous architects wanted to build in Columbus. Because of all these projects, the city has become known as "the Architectural Showplace of America."

⭐ *architect* A person who designs buildings and supervises their construction

Many of Columbus's buildings are unusual. A 192-foot spire rises from the roof of a six-sided church. A seven-ton sculpture decorates a city mall. Some old buildings, such as the courthouse, have been preserved.

Visitors from around the world come to see the city's famous buildings and sculptures. Many Columbus workers now have jobs in the motels and restaurants that serve these visitors.

▲ The Commons

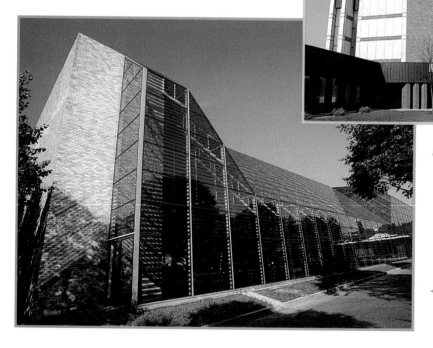

▲ St. Peter's Lutheran Church

Bartholomew County Courthouse ▶

◀ Irwin Union Bank and Trust Company

Twyla Tharp

David Letterman

Janet Jackson

Performing Arts

Hats off to Indiana's performing artists. There's dancer Twyla Tharp from Portland, Indiana. She created dances for stage and movies, including *Hair*. She also started her own dance company. When asked how to create a dance, Twyla answered, "Put yourself in motion."

Many well-known gospel quartets and musical groups have come from Gary. The most famous of these groups was the Jackson Five. Another member of the Jackson family, Janet Jackson, has become a pop music superstar. Her songs are heard by millions worldwide.

Steve McQueen (1930–1980), from Indianapolis, was a famous Hollywood actor. After starting out in TV dramas, McQueen jumped to the movies. He became a star for his roles in *The Great Escape* and *The Magnificent Seven*.

Just about everybody knows David Letterman. One of his first jobs was as a TV weatherman in Indianapolis. He then gained fame as a television talk-show host.

 performing artist   A singer, dancer, actor, or other person who performs for audiences

SHOW WHAT YOU KNOW!

REFOCUS
COMPREHENSION

1. Name three kinds of visual artists.

2. How are performing artists different from visual artists?

THINK ABOUT IT
CRITICAL THINKING

Tell why you think it is or is not worthwhile for a community to invest in beautiful buildings.

WRITE ABOUT IT
ACTIVITY

Choose a performing artist from Indiana. Then write three questions that you would like to ask that person.

Connections

KEY TERMS
intramural
scholarship

LITERATURE
Out to Win Indy

SPORTS IN INDIANA

FOCUS *Whether you play for fun or as a professional, the world of sports gives you many choices. Discover some sports many Hoosiers enjoy.*

▼ High school women run in a track meet.

Indiana Fans

During the basketball season, a kind of fever grips sports fans all over Indiana. This wild excitement is called "Hoosier hysteria."

Basketball is Indiana's number one sport. But Hoosiers get excited about many other sports as well. Marching bands also add to the spirit of excitement and fun.

Hoosiers love their sports teams at every level—professional, college, and school. Indiana's athletes can always count on loyal fans to cheer them on. Maybe that's the secret to Indiana's sports fame across the nation and the world.

School Sports

Every season offers different school sports—football in the fall, basketball in the winter, baseball in the spring. Many high schools also have soccer, tennis, wrestling, and swimming. Some schools have teams in other sports, such as gymnastics and lacrosse.

Every sport holds its own tournaments. **Intramural** sports are played within each school. There are also many tournaments between different schools. Some of these events are small. Others involve large teams and many schools.

The most exciting event in school sports, of course, is the Indiana High School Basketball Tournament in March. School spirit blazes. Large schools and small schools gear up for the games. The movie *Hoosiers* tells one story of this tournament.

Some basketball teams stand out in Indiana sports history.

★ *intramural*   Between members of the same school or college

Skaters compete in the Special Olympics.

Olympics athletes to compete in the World Games. In 1995, 70 Hoosier athletes competed in this event.

College Sports

Sports teams are important to colleges for a number of reasons. Strong teams attract outstanding players. Sports events help to create school spirit. What's more, money from these events helps to fund college **scholarships**. At the same time, training builds athletes' health.

In 1950 at Indiana University, the Little Indy 500 biking race began. At first, it was for men only.

Muncie Central, for instance, has won the state title eight times. Other famous tournament teams include Indianapolis's Crispus Attucks High, Milan Junior-Senior High, Indianapolis Washington High, and East Chicago's Washington High.

Indiana University Little 500

scholarship Gift of money to help a student pay for education

Special Olympics

Every year, about 9,000 Hoosiers with mental handicaps compete in the Indiana Special Olympics. Athletes from age eight and up take part in such sports as basketball, swimming, gymnastics, volleyball, and golf.

Every two years, Indiana sends Special

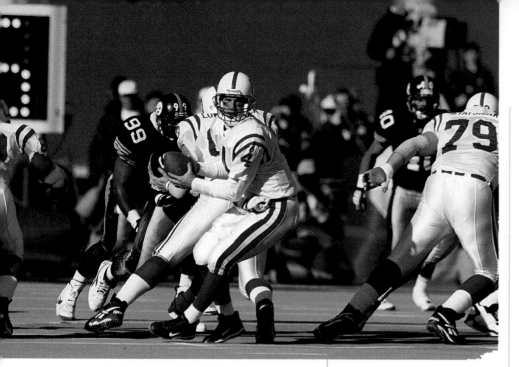

But now men and women compete in separate events. Admission fees go toward college scholarships.

Strong sports programs can be found at large schools like Indiana, Notre Dame, Purdue, and Indiana State. Such programs are also found at smaller schools like Hanover, Wabash, and Butler.

Professional Sports

Indianapolis is home to two professional sports teams. The Indiana Pacers play in the National Basketball Association. The Indianapolis Colts are members of the National Football League.

Indiana also has several minor league teams. Fort Wayne boasts minor league baseball, basketball, and hockey teams.

▲ The Colts provide plenty of excitement for football fans.

Today's race cars are low and sleek. Drivers compete for honor and prizes. ▶

Indy 500

Every May, Indiana hosts the most famous car race in the world—the Indy 500. Racers from all over the world come to the Indianapolis Motor Speedway to compete on the oval track.

The speedway started as a place for car makers to test their cars. The first Indianapolis 500 was run on May 30, 1911. At that time the track was paved with bricks, which gave the speedway its nickname—the Brickyard.

Al Unser, Mario Andretti, and A. J. Foyt are a few names that stand out in Indy 500 history. Another is that of Janet Guthrie, the first woman to qualify.

Out to Win Indy

by Jay Schleifer

Put yourself behind the driver's wheel and whiz along at speeds of more than 200 miles per hour as you read about the Indy 500, the greatest race of them all.

OUT TO WIN

Indy

You slide down into the narrow tunnel of your race car. You ease into the seat and buckle in. Then you lock the removable steering wheel in place. It's a squeeze. There's barely room to grip the wheel. But for the next 3-1/2 hours, this will be your workspace.

Your work is cut out for you. The race you're about to run will be held in tight traffic—wheel to wheel on the narrow track. And you'll be driving at speeds of more than 200 miles per hour (mph).

Around you, over 300,000 fans are screaming their lungs out. Millions more are watching on TV. And all of them are counting down the seconds until the greatest race of them all begins . . .

The Indy 500.

As the cars begin to gather on the track, you know you're about to face the most spectacular, suspenseful racing on any track. You know that the 500 red-hot miles will be riddled with machine breakdowns and heart-wrenching crashes. And at the end of this asphalt rainbow, more than a million dollars in prize money awaits the winner.

Soon the starter will mount the tower and announce the words that kick off this world-famous event:

"Gentlemen, start your engines!" (If a woman is in the race, the starter will begin: "Lady and Gentlemen!" Women don't run in every race, but the first woman raced at Indy in 1977.) . . . You and the rest of the drivers circle as a pack several times. You're going at about 110 mph, and the cars are weaving back and forth across the track, warming up their tires. Then the pace car dives left into the pit lane to get out of the way. Above you, the starter madly waves the green flag, and 33 drivers jam their go-pedals home.

Want to learn more? You can read everything you ever wanted to know about the Indy 500 by checking the book out of your school or public library.

REFOCUS
COMPREHENSION

1. Name some sports that Hoosiers play at school.

2. What are the Special Olympics?

THINK ABOUT IT
CRITICAL THINKING

Why do schools and colleges encourage sports programs?

WRITE ABOUT IT
ACTIVITY

Write an advertisement for the next Indy 500.

GUS GRISSOM

FOCUS *Hoosiers are proud of astronaut Gus Grissom, a native son who gave his life for his country.*

A Space Pioneer

Everybody called him "Gus," but his name was Virgil Ivan Grissom. He was born in 1926 and grew up in a small white house in Mitchell, Indiana. Like many Hoosier boys and girls, Gus dreamed of being a basketball player. But he was too short.

After high school, Gus studied **aeronautics** at Purdue University. In time, Purdue became known as "the mother of astronauts." Gus Grissom was one of the first Purdue astronauts—or space pilots.

After college, Gus joined the Air Force. As a test pilot, he flew planes to check their safety.

In 1958, the U.S. government set up NASA. NASA stands for National Aeronautics and Space Administration. NASA needed astronauts to fly in space. Like the first pioneers, these astronauts would face unknown dangers.

Gus was chosen to join NASA from hundreds of applicants.

As an astronaut, Gus was happy about his size. Maybe he couldn't be a basketball player, but he could easily fit into a space **capsule.** An important part of his work involved testing space capsules to make sure they were safe.

Orbiting the Earth

At last Gus had a chance to fly in space. On July 21, 1961, he soared up 118 miles above Earth. After 15 minutes of flight, his capsule landed in the ocean. But there was trouble. The capsule filled with water and sank. Luckily, Gus escaped.

Despite this setback, Gus didn't give up. He nicknamed his next capsule the *Unsinkable Molly Brown.* On March 23, 1965, Gus orbited Earth three times. When it hit the ocean, *Molly Brown* did not sink.

The next year he was named command pilot of the first Apollo moon flight. His dream of being the first person to walk on the moon seemed near.

aeronautics   The science of making and flying aircraft
capsule   The enclosed part of a spacecraft, which holds the people and instruments

In the early 1960s, the United States began sending rockets into space.

Gus Grissom puts on his space suit.

SHOW WHAT YOU KNOW!

REFOCUS
COMPREHENSION

1. What experience helped Gus Grissom to be chosen as an astronaut?

2. What were the results of Grissom's first two space flights?

THINK ABOUT IT
CRITICAL THINKING

Why is an astronaut's job both exciting and dangerous?

WRITE ABOUT IT
ACTIVITY

Write about why you would or would not like to be an astronaut.

Hoosiers Remember Gus

On January 27, 1967, Gus was testing the space capsule at Cape Canaveral in Florida. He believed it was unsafe. Someone yelled "Fire!" Within 20 seconds, all three astronauts aboard were dead.

The death of Gus Grissom was not in vain. Because of the tragedy, more testing was done to make future spaceships safer. Finally, on July 21, 1969, Neil A. Armstrong walked on the moon. Gus Grissom's sacrifice for his country helped to make this historic event possible.

Indiana built a memorial to Gus Grissom in Spring Mill Park. In it stands the *Unsinkable Molly Brown* and Gus's space suit.

The children of Indiana also gave money to build a monument in his hometown. Their memorial is made of Indiana limestone cut to look like a rocket. It honors Indiana's great patriot in space.

OPPORTUNITIES IN EDUCATION

FOCUS *Indiana's colleges and universities will continue to help shape our state's future.*

INDIANA UNIVERSITIES AND COLLEGES

- ★ State capital
- • Other cities
- ⬜ Public school
- ⬜ Private school

Indiana's Many Colleges

Indiana is a great state for getting a college degree. You might be surprised to learn that almost every Hoosier lives within an hour's drive of a college or a **technical** school.

Indiana University alone has eight **campuses** around the state. Purdue and Indiana State also have several campuses. The map on this page shows many Indiana colleges.

Indiana colleges have a variety of students. Some live on campus. Others live at home, hold jobs, and drive to classes. These students may be older and have their own families. Some are retraining for new jobs. Many come from foreign countries to study here.

Public and Private

Indiana colleges offer variety, too. Some are public colleges. State taxes help support them. Other Hoosier colleges are private.

technical Having to do with useful or industrial skills
campus The grounds and buildings of a school or a college

336

University students take part in lively discussions.

They are not run by the state. Many private schools are operated by churches.

There is also a variety of different programs for students to choose from. At Indiana University, for instance, students study music, archaeology, business, medicine—and 800 other fields. Notre Dame also offers many different programs of study, including business and marketing.

Numerous schools are known for specific programs. DePauw, for example, is known for courses in writing and communications. Ball State trains teachers.

Purdue offers programs in agriculture, engineering, and veterinary medicine, to name a few. More astronauts have graduated from Purdue than from any other university.

Citizens for the Future

Today is not too soon to start thinking about the future. Life is changing quickly in this age of computers and technology. We can only guess what life might be like 50 years from now.

Experts agree, however, that education is an important key to becoming a successful "citizen of the future." Education allows students to unlock opportunities. Hoosiers are lucky to have so many choices available to them.

Indiana University has a well-known opera department.

SHOW WHAT YOU KNOW!

REFOCUS
COMPREHENSION

1. What are technical schools?

2. How are public and private colleges different?

THINK ABOUT IT
CRITICAL THINKING

How does education help to prepare people of all ages for the future?

WRITE ABOUT IT
ACTIVITY

Create a brochure with the title "College Education in Indiana."

SUMMING UP

1 DO YOU REMEMBER . . .
COMPREHENSION

1. Name three things that add to Hoosiers' pride in their home state.

2. Why is Columbus, Indiana, known as the "Architectural Showplace of America"?

3. Name Indiana's professional sports teams.

4. What type of work did Gus Grissom do for the Air Force and for NASA?

5. Which Indiana university has graduated more astronauts than any other university?

2 SKILL POWER
COMPARING AND CONTRASTING

In this chapter you learned that comparing and contrasting can help you understand how things are alike and different. Compare and contrast Gus Grissom, the Indiana hero described in Lesson 4, with either George Rodgers Clark, Abraham Lincoln, or Madame C. J. Walker. Create a Venn diagram like the one on page 319 to show how the two Indiana heroes are alike and how they are different.

3 WHAT DO YOU THINK?
CRITICAL THINKING

1. Which one of the Hoosiers described in this chapter would you want to meet? Why?

2. In what ways do Hoosiers show that they value the arts?

3. Of the sports described in the chapter, which do you enjoy the most? Why?

4. How did Gus Grissom's death affect the space program?

5. Do you agree that education is an important key to becoming a successful citizen of the future? Why?

4 SAY IT, WRITE IT, USE IT
VOCABULARY

Suppose you are writing to a pen pal who wants to know more about Indiana. In the letter, describe your state, using as many vocabulary terms as possible.

aeronautics	intramural
architect	jazz
campus	performing artist
capsule	scholarship
competition	technical
gallery	visual artist

338

5 GEOGRAPHY AND YOU

MAP STUDY

Use the map below to answer the following questions.

1. Name the university located in the northeast corner of Indiana. How do you think it got its name?

2. Which college is located in Richmond?

3. In what direction would you travel from Indianapolis to Vincennes University?

4. Which university is located in Greencastle?

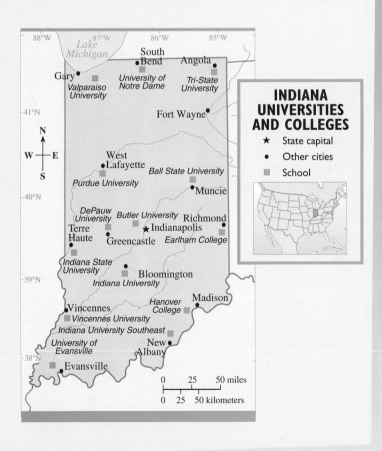

INDIANA UNIVERSITIES AND COLLEGES

★ State capital
• Other cities
■ School

6 TAKE ACTION

CITIZENSHIP

In this chapter you read about the importance of the visual arts to Hoosiers in communities across Indiana. Work with a group of your classmates to think of how you might beautify your school, using one of the visual arts. You might plan to paint a mural to hang on the side of a building or a fence or to create an outdoor sculpture to be placed in a public area. With the help of your teacher, carry out your project and share it with your school community.

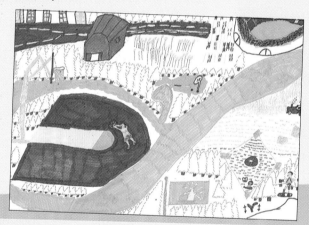

7 GET CREATIVE

LANGUAGE ARTS CONNECTION

As a class, plan and publish a magazine about your city or town. Your magazine can have articles, poems, interviews, reviews, and photographs. The magazine can also describe interesting places to visit or performances, exhibits, or sporting events to attend. Distribute copies of your magazine to other classes and to people in your community.

REFERENCE

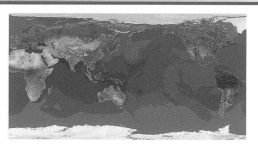

CONTENTS

SECTION

RESEARCH AND REFERENCE

These books will help you learn what makes your own state of Indiana and each of the other 49 states so special. There's even an atlas of the world's natural wonders in the world for you to explore.

Quick Facts About the U.S.A.
by Nancy Hartley (Scholastic, 1995)
Do you know why the motto of Indiana is "the crossroads of America"? Discover many interesting facts about each of our 50 states.

The Children's Atlas of Natural Wonders
by Joyce Pope (The Millbrook Press, 1995)
Take a journey and learn about the geography, geology, and natural history of some of the most spectacular natural wonders in the world.

Kids Learn America: Bringing Geography to Life With People, Places & History
by Patricia Gordon and Reed C. Snow
(Williamson Publishing Co., 1991)
Fun projects and activities help you learn more about the people, places, and events in Indiana and other states.

ARCTIC OCEAN

Greenland
(Den.)

Arctic Circle

Alaska (U.S.)

CANADA

ALEUTIAN IS. (U.S.)

NORTH

AMERICA

UNITED STATES

See inset below

Bermuda (U.K.)

AZORES
(Port.)

ATLANTIC OCEAN

Midway I. (U.S.)

Tropic of Cancer

MEXICO

HAWAII (U.S.)

Caribbean Sea

CAPE VERDE

VENEZUELA

GUYANA
SURINAME

COLOMBIA

French Guiana
(Fr.)

Equator

GALÁPAGOS IS.
(Ecuador)

SOUTH

ECUADOR

AMERICA

PACIFIC OCEAN

WESTERN
SAMOA

BRAZIL

PERU

AMERICAN
SAMOA (U.S.)

FRENCH POLYNESIA
(Fr.)

BOLIVIA

TONGA

PARAGUAY

Pitcairn I. (U.K.)

Tropic of Capricorn

CHILE

URUGUAY

Easter I.
(Chile)

ARGENTINA

N

W   E

S

FALKLAND IS.
(U.K.)

Antarctic Circle

International Date Line

WEST INDIES AND CENTRAL AMERICA

0   150   300 miles

0   150   300 kilometers

UNITED STATES

N

W   E

S

Gulf of Mexico

ATLANTIC OCEAN

B A H A M A S

Tropic of Cancer

TURKS AND
CAICOS IS. (U.K.)

CUBA

Hispaniola

BR. VIRGIN IS.
(U.K.)

MEXICO

CAYMAN
ISLANDS
(U.K.)

GREATER ANTILLES

HAITI

DOMINICAN
REPUBLIC

Puerto Rico
(U.S.)

ANTIGUA
AND BARBUDA

JAMAICA

VIRGIN ISLANDS (U.S.)

ST. KITTS AND NEVIS

Guadeloupe (Fr.)

BELIZE

Caribbean Sea

DOMINICA

GUATEMALA

Martinique (Fr.)

HONDURAS

ST. LUCIA

EL SALVADOR

NICARAGUA

NETH. ANTILLES (Neth.)

ARUBA

ST. VINCENT AND
THE GRENADINES

LESSER ANTILLES

BARBADOS

GRENADA

COSTA
RICA

TRINIDAD
AND
TOBAGO

PANAMA

COLOMBIA

VENEZUELA

North Pole

0° 20°E 40°E 60°E 80°E 100°E 120°E 140°E 160°E

SVALBARD
(Nor.)

See inset below

AND

RUSSIA

EUROPE

ASIA

KAZAKSTAN

MONGOLIA

GEORGIA
ARMENIA
TURKEY
MALTA CYPRUS
TUNISIA

UZBEKISTAN
TURKMENISTAN
KYRGYZSTAN
TAJIKISTAN

N. KOREA
S. KOREA JAPAN

SYRIA AZERBAIJAN
LEBANON IRAQ
ISRAEL
West Bank JORDAN
and Gaza Strip

CHINA

TAIWAN

MOROCCO
ALGERIA

LIBYA

EGYPT

IRAN
KUWAIT
QATAR
BAHRAIN
SAUDI
ARABIA U.A.E.

AFGHANISTAN
PAKISTAN

NEPAL

INDIA

BHUTAN

PACIFIC OCEAN

Hong Kong
Macao (Port.)

AFRICA

MALI NIGER CHAD

ERITREA

SUDAN

YEMEN OMAN

MYANMAR
(BURMA)

LAOS

VIETNAM

*NORTHERN
MARIANA IS.* (U.S.) *Wake I.* (U.S.)

BIA
BURKINA
FASO
BIA
NIGERIA
CAMEROON

DJIBOUTI

BANGLA-
DESH

Guam
(U.S.)

MARSHALL IS.

EA-BISSAU
COTE
D'IVOIRE GHANA
RIA TOGO BENIN
EQUATORIAL
GUINEA GABON CONGO
SAO TOMÉ
AND PRINCIPE
Cabinda
(Angola)

CENTRAL
AFRICAN
REP

ETHIOPIA

SOMALIA

THAILAND

SRI
LANKA

CAMBODIA
BRUNEI
MALAYSIA

PHILIPPINES

PALAU

FEDERATED STATES
OF MICRONESIA

NAURU

ZAIRE UGANDA KENYA
RWANDA
BURUNDI

TANZANIA

MALDIVES

SEYCHELLES

SINGAPORE

I N D O N E S I A

KIRIBATI

PAPUA
NEW GUINEA

TUVALU

SOLOMON IS.

ANGOLA
ZAMBIA
MALAWI

ZIMBABWE

COMOROS

MADAGASCAR
MOZAMBIQUE

Réunion (Fr.)

MAURITIUS

VANUATU

FIJI

NAMIBIA
BOTSWANA

SOUTH
AFRICA
SWAZILAND
LESOTHO

INDIAN OCEAN

New Caledonia (Fr.)

AUSTRALIA

Prime Meridian

WORLD POLITICAL

0   1,000   2,000 miles

0   1,000   2,000 kilometers

NEW
ZEALAND

ANTARCTICA

South Pole

EUROPE

0   200   400 miles

0   400 kilometers

20°E 30°E 40°E

Arctic Circle

N
W   E
S

10°E

60°N

FINLAND

NORWAY

10°W

North Sea

SWEDEN

ESTONIA

RUSSIA

DENMARK

LATVIA

LITHUANIA

50°N

UNITED
KINGDOM

IRELAND

NETHERLANDS

RUSSIA

BELARUS

*ATLANTIC
OCEAN*

GERMANY

BELGIUM
LUX.

POLAND

UKRAINE

CZECH
REP.
SLOVAKIA

LIECH.

FRANCE

AUSTRIA
SWITZ.
SLOVENIA
SAN
MONACO MARINO

HUNGARY

ROMANIA

MOLDOVA

CROATIA
BOSNIA-
HERZ. YUGO

Black Sea

PORTUGAL

ANDORRA

ITALY

BULGARIA

40°N

SPAIN

Corsica (Fr.)
Sardinia (It.)

MACEDONIA
ALBANIA

BALEARIC IS. (Sp.)

GREECE

TURKEY

Gibraltar (U.K.)

Mediterranean Sea

Sicily (It.)

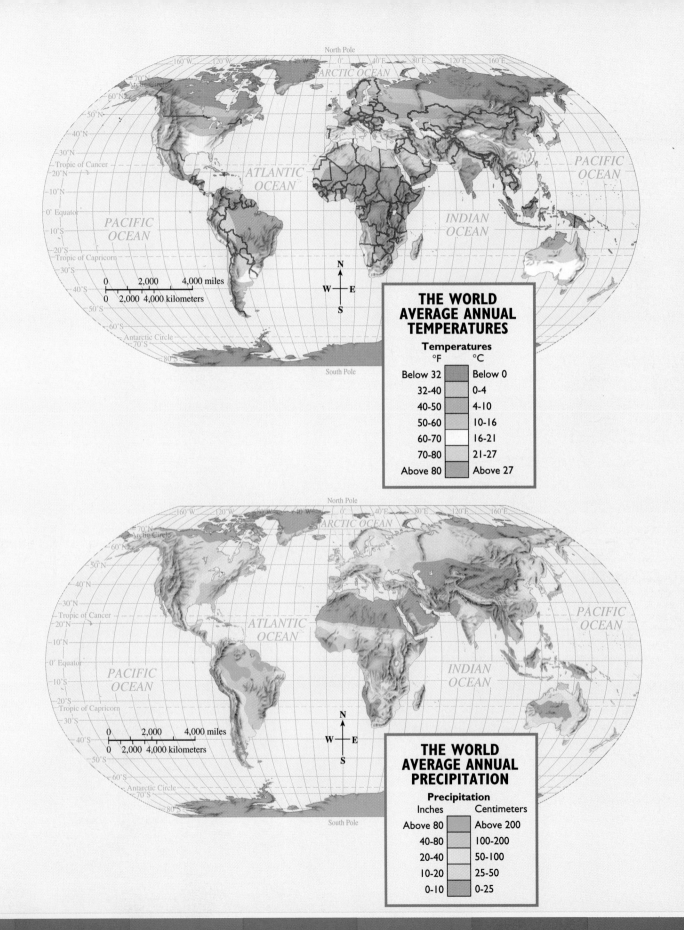

THE WORLD AVERAGE ANNUAL TEMPERATURES

Temperatures

°F		°C
Below 32		Below 0
32–40		0–4
40–50		4–10
50–60		10–16
60–70		16–21
70–80		21–27
Above 80		Above 27

THE WORLD AVERAGE ANNUAL PRECIPITATION

Precipitation

Inches		Centimeters
Above 80		Above 200
40–80		100–200
20–40		50–100
10–20		25–50
0–10		0–25

Desert: almost no rain

Semidesert: some rain

Mediterranean: mild winter; hot, dry summer

Humid subtropical: mild, rainy winter; hot, humid summer

Equatorial: hot and rainy all year

Savanna: hot, with rainy and dry seasons

Marine west coast: mild and rainy

Humid continental: cold, snowy winter; long, warm, humid summer

Subarctic: cold, snowy winter; short, cool summer

Tundra: very cold winter; short, very cool summer

Ice cap: always cold

Mountain: climates vary with height and latitude

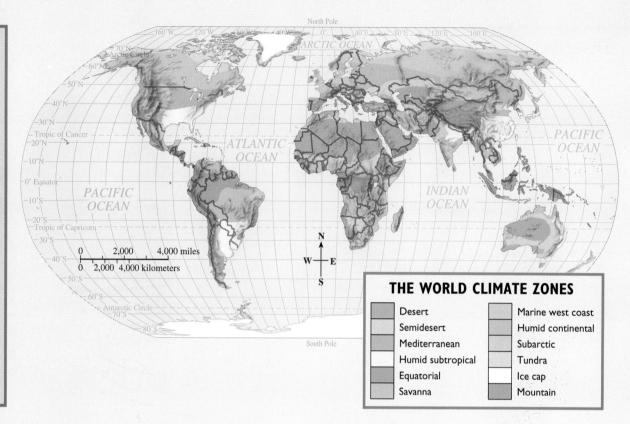

THE WORLD CLIMATE ZONES

- Desert
- Semidesert
- Mediterranean
- Humid subtropical
- Equatorial
- Savanna
- Marine west coast
- Humid continental
- Subarctic
- Tundra
- Ice cap
- Mountain

VEGETATION
DESCRIPTIONS

Rain forest: thick foliage, climbing plants, shrubs

Desert: wiry grass, thorny bushes, cacti

Grassland: grasses, thorny trees

Woodlands and grass: trees that lose their leaves in winter

Scrub or mediterranean: evergreen scrub

Northern forest: cone-bearing trees or shrubs

Tundra or mountain: lichens, mosses

Ice: little vegetation

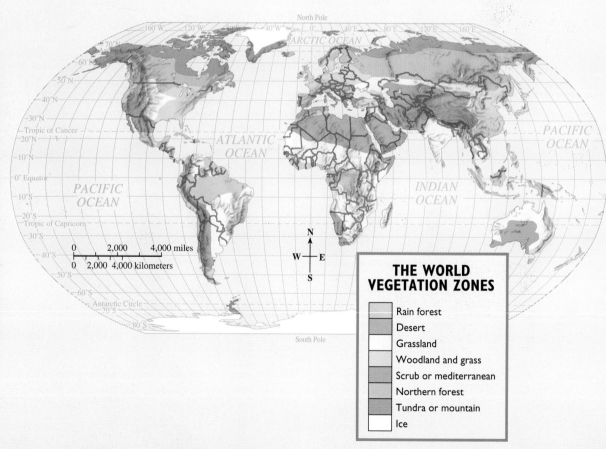

THE WORLD
VEGETATION ZONES

- Rain forest
- Desert
- Grassland
- Woodland and grass
- Scrub or mediterranean
- Northern forest
- Tundra or mountain
- Ice

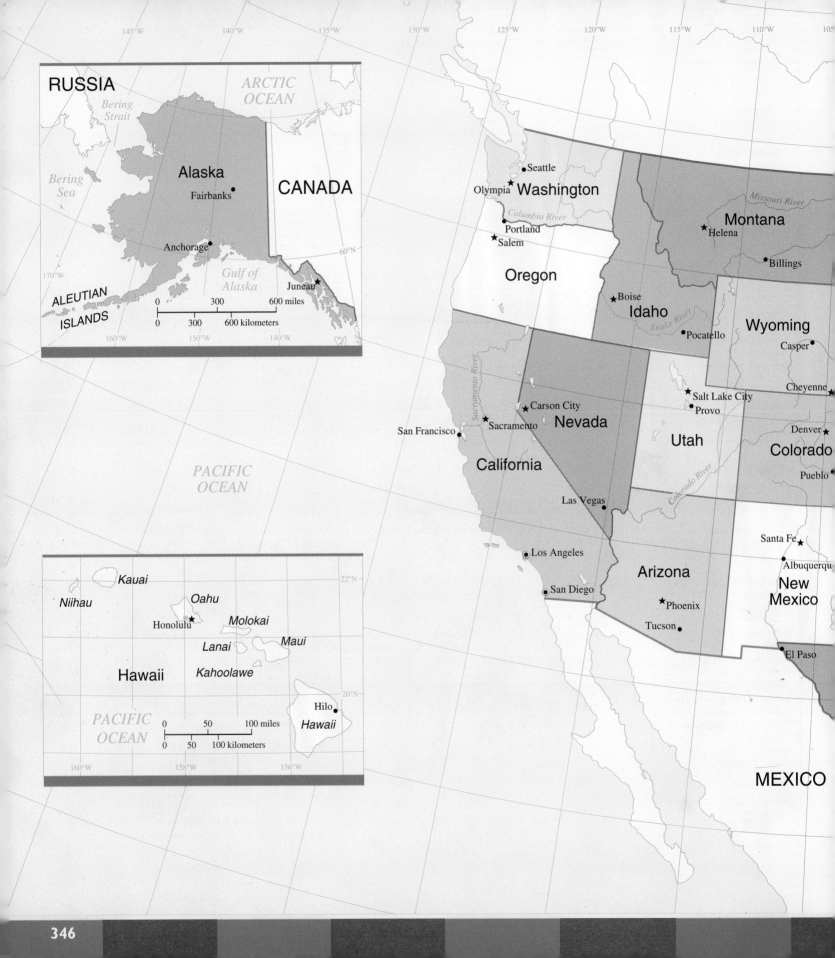

RUSSIA

ARCTIC
OCEAN

*Bering
Strait*

*Bering
Sea*

Alaska

Fairbanks

CANADA

170°W

70°N

60°N

Anchorage

ALEUTIAN

*Gulf of
Alaska*

Juneau

ISLANDS

160°W   150°W   140°W

0   300   600 miles

0   300   600 kilometers

PACIFIC
OCEAN

Kauai

Niihau

Oahu

Honolulu

Molokai

22°N

Lanai

Maui

Hawaii

Kahoolawe

PACIFIC
OCEAN

Hilo

20°N

Hawaii

0   50   100 miles

0   50   100 kilometers

160°W   158°W   156°W

Seattle

Olympia Washington

Columbia River

Montana

Missouri River

Helena

Portland

Salem

Billings

Oregon

Boise

Idaho

Wyoming

Snake River

Pocatello

Casper

San Francisco

Sacramento River

Carson City

Sacramento

Nevada

Salt Lake City

Provo

Cheyenne

Utah

Denver

Colorado

California

Pueblo

Las Vegas

Colorado River

Santa Fe

Los Angeles

Arizona

Albuquerqu

San Diego

New
Mexico

Phoenix

Tucson

El Paso

MEXICO

CANADA

North Dakota
★ Bismarck
• Fargo

Minnesota
Minneapolis • ★ St. Paul

South Dakota
Pierre ★
• Sioux Falls

Wisconsin
Milwaukee •
Madison ★

Michigan

Lake Superior

Lake Michigan

Lansing ★
Detroit ◉

Lake Huron

Lake Ontario

Lake Erie

Cleveland •

St. Lawrence River

Maine

Vermont
Burlington •
Montpelier ★

New Hampshire
Concord ★

Manchester •

Augusta ★
Portland •

Boston ★

Massachusetts

Albany ★
New York
Springfield •

Buffalo •

Hartford •
Bridgeport •

Springfield

Providence ★

Rhode Island

Connecticut

Iowa
Dubuque •
Chicago ◉
Des Moines ★

Fort Wayne •

Ohio
Columbus ★

Pennsylvania
Harrisburg ★
Pittsburgh •

Philadelphia •

Trenton ★
New Jersey

New York City ◉

Nebraska
Omaha •
Lincoln ★

Illinois
Springfield ★

Indiana
Indianapolis ★

Cincinnati •

Wilmington •
Baltimore •

Dover ★
Delaware

Missouri River

Platte River

Kansas City •
Topeka ★
Jefferson City ★

Kansas

St. Louis •

Louisville •

Frankfort ★

West Virginia
Charleston ★

Washington, D.C. ✪
Annapolis ★
Maryland

ATLANTIC OCEAN

Arkansas River

Wichita •

Missouri

Kentucky

Virginia
Richmond ★

Ohio River

Norfolk •

Tulsa •

Oklahoma
★ Oklahoma City

Fort Smith •

Arkansas
★ Little Rock

Memphis •

Nashville ★

Tennessee

North Carolina
Raleigh ★
• Charlotte

Mississippi River

Red River

Greenville •

Mississippi
Jackson ★

Montgomery ★

Alabama
Birmingham •

Atlanta ★

Georgia

South Carolina
• Columbia

Charleston •

UNITED STATES POLITICAL

✪ National capital
★ State capital
◉ Cities with populations over 1 million
• Other cities
─── National boundaries
─── State boundaries

| 0 | 150 | 300 miles |
| 0 | 150 | 300 kilometers |

Texas
Dallas ◉

Louisiana
Baton Rouge ★

Austin ★
Houston ◉
• San Antonio

Mobile •
New Orleans ◉

Savannah •

Tallahassee ★

Rio Grande

Gulf of Mexico

Florida
• Tampa

N
W E
S

• Miami

BAHAMAS

CUBA

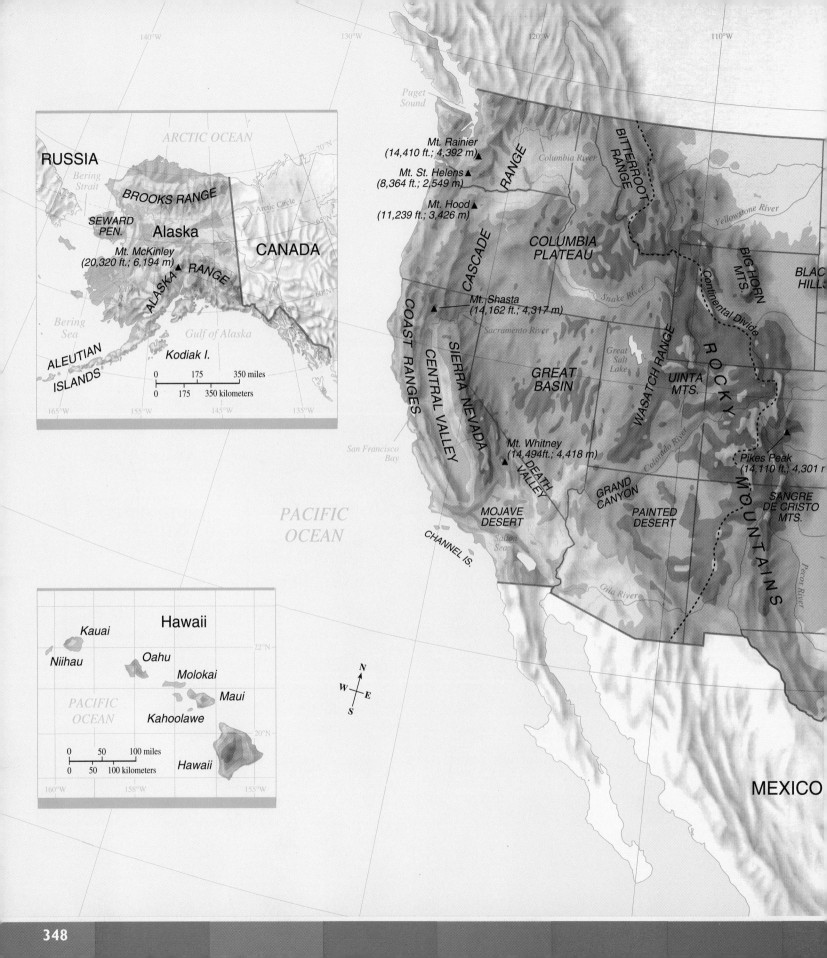

ARCTIC OCEAN

RUSSIA

Bering
Strait

Arctic Circle

BROOKS RANGE

SEWARD
PEN.

Alaska

CANADA

70°N

65°N

Mt. McKinley
(20,320 ft.; 6,194 m)

ALASKA RANGE

60°N

Bering
Sea

Gulf of Alaska

ALEUTIAN
ISLANDS

Kodiak I.

0   175   350 miles

0   175   350 kilometers

165°W   155°W   145°W   135°W

Kauai

Niihau

Hawaii

Oahu

Molokai

PACIFIC
OCEAN

Maui

Kahoolawe

22°N

20°N

0   50   100 miles

0   50   100 kilometers

Hawaii

160°W   158°W   155°W

PACIFIC
OCEAN

N

W   E

S

140°W   130°W   120°W   110°W

Puget
Sound

Mt. Rainier
(14,410 ft.; 4,392 m)

Mt. St. Helens
(8,364 ft.; 2,549 m)

Mt. Hood
(11,239 ft.; 3,426 m)

CASCADE   RANGE

Columbia River

BITTERROOT
RANGE

Yellowstone River

COLUMBIA
PLATEAU

Snake River

Continental Divide

BIG HORN
MTS.

BLACK
HILLS

Mt. Shasta
(14,162 ft.; 4,317 m)

COAST RANGES

CENTRAL VALLEY

SIERRA NEVADA

Sacramento River

GREAT
BASIN

Great Salt
Lake

WASATCH RANGE

UINTA
MTS.

R O C K Y

San Francisco
Bay

Mt. Whitney
(14,494 ft.; 4,418 m)

DEATH
VALLEY

Colorado River

GRAND
CANYON

PAINTED
DESERT

Pikes Peak
(14,110 ft.; 4,301 r

M O U N T A I N S

SANGRE
DE CRISTO
MTS.

MOJAVE
DESERT

Salton
Sea

CHANNEL IS.

Gila River

Pecos River

MEXICO

348

CANADA

MESABI
RANGE

Lake Superior

Lake Huron

Lake Michigan

WHITE
MTS.

Mt. Washington
(6,288 ft.; 1,917 m)

Lake
Ontario

ADIRONDACK
MTS.

St. Lawrence River

CATSKILL
MTS.

Lake Erie

Long I.

G
R
E
A
T

BADLANDS

SAND HILLS

Missouri River

Platte River

P
L
A
I
N
S

CENTRAL PLAINS

Wabash River

ALLEGHENY
PLATEAU

APPALACHIAN MOUNTAINS

Delaware
Bay

ATLANTIC
OCEAN

Chesapeake
Bay

Ohio River

Arkansas River

OZARK
PLATEAU

Cumberland River

CUMBERLAND
PLATEAU

BLUE RIDGE MTS.

Fall Line

ATLANTIC COASTAL PLAIN

Mississippi River

OUACHITA
MOUNTAINS

Mt. Mitchell
(6,684 ft.; 2,037 m)

Santee River

Red River

Atlantic River

LLANO
ESTACADO

EDWARDS
PLATEAU

Colorado River

Sabine River

Brazos River

Pearl River

Alabama River

Apalachicola River

Mobile
Bay

Pensacola
Bay

GULF COASTAL PLAIN

Galveston
Bay

Rio Grande

Gulf of Mexico

Tampa
Bay

Lake
Okeechobee

EVERGLADES

FLORIDA
KEYS

BAHAMAS

CUBA

UNITED STATES PHYSICAL

Elevation

Feet	Meters
Over 13,001	Over 3,001
6,561–13,000	2,001–3,000
3,281–6,560	1,001–2,000
1,641–3,280	501–1,000
661–1,640	201–500
0–660	0–200
Below sea level	Below sea level

▲ Mountain peak

0   150   300 miles

0   150   300 kilometers

INDIANA POLITICAL

- ★ State capital
- ● Major cities
- • Other cities

Lake Michigan

Michigan

Illinois

Ohio

Kentucky

Michigan City
South Bend
Mishawaka
Elkhart
Gary
East Chicago
Hammond

Kankakee R.

St. Joseph R.
Maumee R.
Fort Wayne
St. Marys R.

Wabash R.

Lafayette
Kokomo
Muncie
Anderson
Richmond

Indianapolis

Terre Haute

W. Fork White R.

Bloomington
Columbus

E. Fork White R.

Madison
Ohio R.

Vincennes

Wabash R.
White R.

New Albany

Evansville

Ohio R.

N
W — E
S

0   25   50 miles
0 25   50 kilometers

100°W   95°W   90°W   85°W   80°W

N
W   E
S

CANADA

Lake Superior

ND

Grand Forks •

Red R.

Fargo •

★ Bismarck

Duluth •

MN

45°N

SD

★ Pierre

• Rapid City

Minneapolis •
★
St. Paul

Sioux Falls •

Des Moines R.

Green Bay •

WI

Madison ★

Milwaukee •

Lake Michigan

Lake Huron

MI

Grand
Rapids •

Lansing ★

Detroit •

Lake Erie

Rockford •

Chicago •

Cleveland •

Missouri R.

NE

North Platte R.

Platte R.

Grand
Island •

Omaha •

Cedar
Rapids •

IA

Davenport •

Des
Moines ★

Gary •

Fort
Wayne •

Wabash R.

IL

Illinois R.

Mississippi R.

Springfield ★

IN

Indianapolis ★

OH

Columbus ★

40°N

Lincoln ★

Cincinnati •

Kansas City •

St. Louis •

Kansas R.

Topeka ★
Lawrence •

Jefferson City ★

Ohio R.

KS

Arkansas R.

Wichita •

MO

35°N

0   50   100   150   200 miles

0   100   200 kilometers

**THE MIDWEST AND
GREAT PLAINS REGION**

★ Capital cities

• Other cities

Elevations

Feet	Meters
3,281–6,560	1,001–2,000
1,641–3,280	501–1,000
657–1,640	201–500
0–656	0–200

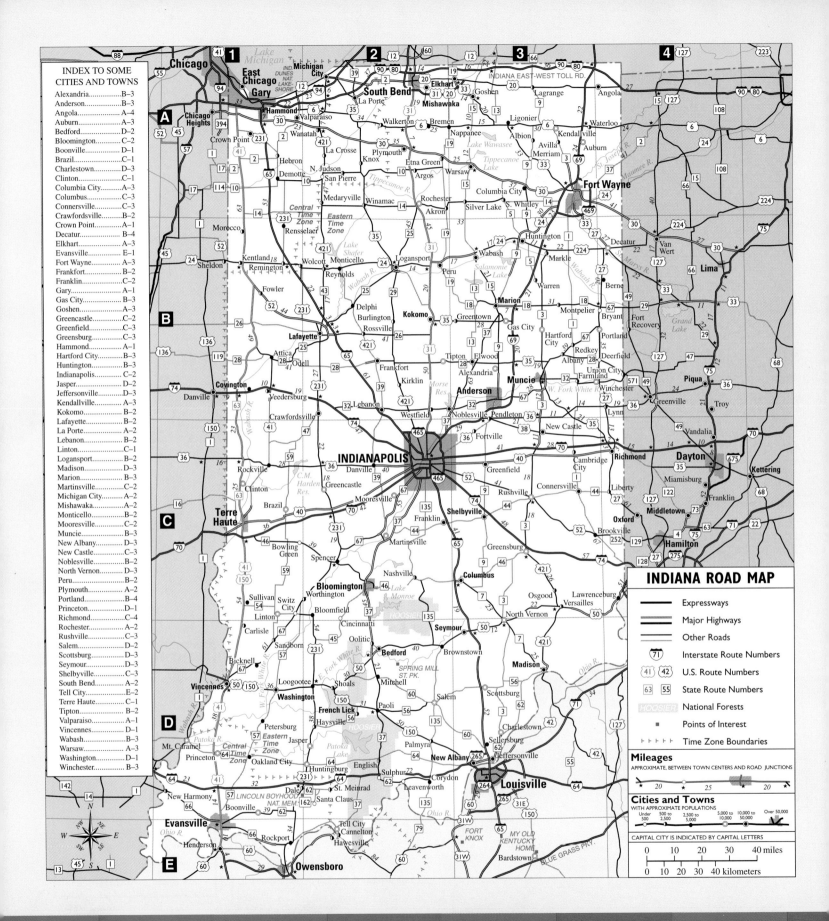

INDIANA ROAD MAP

Legend

— Expressways
═ Major Highways
─ Other Roads
71 Interstate Route Numbers
41 42 U.S. Route Numbers
63 55 State Route Numbers
HOOSIER National Forests
■ Points of Interest
+ + + + + Time Zone Boundaries

Mileages
APPROXIMATE, BETWEEN TOWN CENTERS AND ROAD JUNCTIONS

★ 20 ★ 25 ★ 20 ★

Cities and Towns
WITH APPROXIMATE POPULATIONS

Under 500 | 500 to 2,500 | 2,500 to 5,000 | 5,000 to 10,000 | 10,000 to 50,000 | Over 50,000

CAPITAL CITY IS INDICATED BY CAPITAL LETTERS

0 10 20 30 40 miles
0 10 20 30 40 kilometers

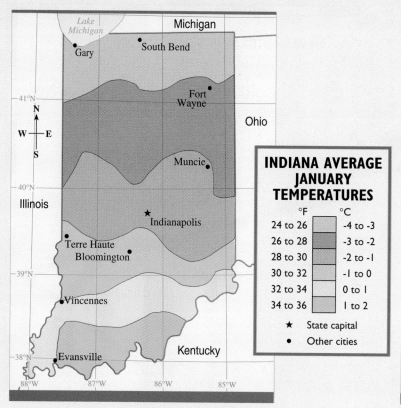

INDIANA AVERAGE JANUARY TEMPERATURES

°F	°C
24 to 26	-4 to -3
26 to 28	-3 to -2
28 to 30	-2 to -1
30 to 32	-1 to 0
32 to 34	0 to 1
34 to 36	1 to 2

★ State capital
● Other cities

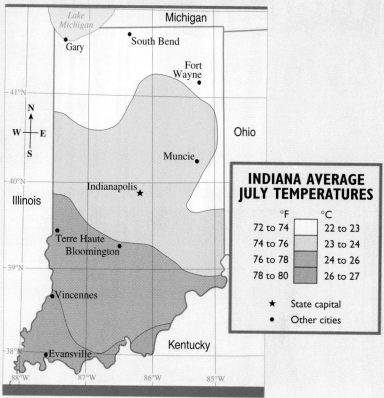

INDIANA AVERAGE JULY TEMPERATURES

°F	°C
72 to 74	22 to 23
74 to 76	23 to 24
76 to 78	24 to 26
78 to 80	26 to 27

★ State capital
● Other cities

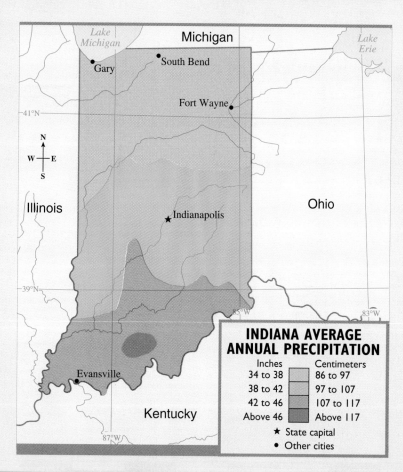

INDIANA AVERAGE ANNUAL PRECIPITATION

Inches	Centimeters
34 to 38	86 to 97
38 to 42	97 to 107
42 to 46	107 to 117
Above 46	Above 117

★ State capital
● Other cities

Indiana
Symbols

Indiana State Seal

Indiana State Flower: Peony

Indiana State Bird:
Cardinal

Indiana State Motto:
The Crossroads of America

Indiana State Flag

Indiana State Tree:
Tulip Tree

Indiana Official River: Wabash River

Indiana

The Hoosier State

Became the 19th state on December 11, 1816

Key

Capital ★Indianapolis

Three largest cities
1. Indianapolis
2. Fort Wayne
3. Evansville

Smallest town
New Amsterdam
Population 30

Geography
+ Highest elevation
Franklin Township
1,257 ft above sea level

- Lowest point
Ohio River in
Posey County
320 ft above sea level

Wabash River

Economy

First in the nation in
 steel
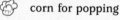 corn for popping

A leading state in
coal mining
turkeys
corn
musical instruments
wheat

Historic Sites
 Vincennes
 Gary
 New Harmony
 South Bend
 Lafayette
 Noblesville

Map labels:
Lake Michigan
MICHIGAN
Gary
South Bend
Ft. Wayne
ILLINOIS
Wabash River
Lafayette
1,257 ft +
OHIO
Noblesville
Speedway
Indianapolis
Oolitic
Vincennes
New Harmony
Evansville
New Amsterdam
KENTUCKY
320 ft
Ohio River

Indianapolis Motor Speedway flag

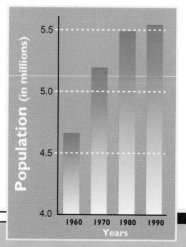

Indiana's blue state flag features a golden torch. The flame stands for liberty and knowledge for everyone. The 19th and largest star, above the torch, represents Indiana, the 19th state.

Fabulous Facts!

- Each year the state makes 40 billion pounds of steel. That is enough to build 20 million automobiles.

- Most of the limestone used to build the Empire State Building, in New York City, came from the Empire Hole, near Oolitic.

- The famous Indianapolis 500 automobile race is held in the town of Speedway every Memorial Day weekend.

Population (in millions)
5.5
5.0
4.5
4.0
1960 1970 1980 1990
Years

Fresh Water Used
1,700 gallons/day/person (average)

Garbage
5,600,000 tons per year

355

Events in Indiana and World History

1763
Pontiac's War

1787
Northwest
Ordinance is passed

▲ Mound builders

1679
La Salle explores
Indiana

1756
French and
Indian War
begins

1779
George Rogers
Clark captures Fort
Sackville

**Indiana
Events**

| 2,000–3,000 years ago | 1600s | 1700s |

**United States
and World
Events**

Written
records
appear

1756
▼ Composer Wolfgang
Amadeus Mozart is
born in Austria

1789
French
Revolution
begins

1607
Jamestown
colony is settled
in Virginia

1630–1650
Taj Mahal is
built in India ▼

1775
American
Revolution
begins

1776
Declaration of
Independence is
signed ▼

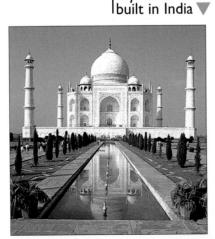

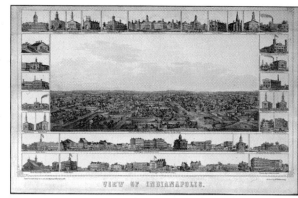

VIEW OF INDIANAPOLIS.

1824
Robert Owen arrives
in New Harmony

1813
Capital of Indiana is
moved to Corydon

1825
Indianapolis becomes
the state capital

1800
Indiana Territory
is established

1811
Harrison's
troops win the
Battle of Tippecanoe

1816
Indiana becomes
the nineteenth
state

1838
Trail of Death

1800s

1815
Napoleon is defeated
at the Battle of
Waterloo

1822
Colony of Liberia
is established
in Africa

1830
Greece becomes
an independent state

1804
Haiti wins
independence
from France

1819
Zulu kingdom
controls south-
eastern Africa

1821
Mexico gains
independence
from Spain

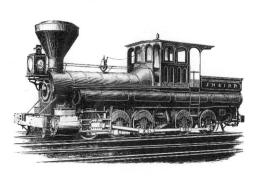

1863 ▲
Morgan's Raid
terrorizes Indiana

1911 ▲
First 500-mile race
is held at Motor Speedway
in Indianapolis

1847 ▲
The Madison-
Indianapolis rail
line is completed

1868
James Oliver of
South Bend invents
a new steel plow

1921
First radio
station in Indiana

**Indiana
Events**

1800s   **1900s**

**United States
and World
Events**

1861–1865
Civil War

1914–1918
World War I

▼ **1920**
American
women get
right to
vote

1845
Potato famine
in Ireland

1881
Pablo Picasso
▼ is born in Spain

1931
Australia wins
independence from
Great Britain

Violin and Guitar, by Pablo Picasso

VIEW OF INDIANAPOLIS.

1824
Robert Owen arrives
in New Harmony

1813
Capital of Indiana is
moved to Corydon

1825
Indianapolis becomes
the state capital

1800
Indiana Territory
is established

1811
Harrison's
troops win the
Battle of Tippecanoe

1816
Indiana becomes
the nineteenth
state

1838
Trail of Death

1800s

1815
Napoleon is defeated
at the Battle of
Waterloo

1830
Greece becomes
an independent state

1822
Colony of Liberia
is established
in Africa

1804
Haiti wins
independence
from France

1819
Zulu kingdom
controls south-
eastern Africa

1821
Mexico gains
independence
from Spain

1863 ▲
Morgan's Raid
terrorizes Indiana

1911 ▲
First 500-mile race
is held at Motor Speedway
in Indianapolis

1847 ▲
The Madison-
Indianapolis rail
line is completed

1868
James Oliver of
South Bend invents
a new steel plow

1921
First radio
station in Indiana

**Indiana
Events**

1800s ◄ ► **1900s**

**United States
and World
Events**

1861–1865
Civil War

1914–1918
World War I

1845
Potato famine
in Ireland

1881
Pablo Picasso
▼ is born in Spain

▼ 1920
American
women get
right to
vote

Violin and Guitar, by Pablo Picasso

1931
Australia wins
independence from
Great Britain

1961
Astronaut Gus
Grissom travels
in space

1986
Larry Bird leads
the Boston Celtics
to third NBA
championship in
the 1980s

1967
Richard Hatcher
is elected mayor
of Gary

1984
First CD is made in
Terre Haute;
the Baltimore Colts
move to Indianapolis

1949
First commercial TV
station in Indiana

1995
Artsgarden is
completed in
Indianapolis

1900s

1939–1945
World War II

1979
Israel and Egypt
sign Camp David
Peace Agreement

1966
Indira Gandhi
becomes the prime
minister of India

1994
Nelson Mandela
becomes president
of South Africa

1995
A peace
agreement is
signed in Bosnia

Indiana

Counties

County Name	County Seat	Population	Population Rank	Area in Square Miles (Square Kilometers)		Rank	Became a County
Adams	Decatur	32,311	47	340	(880)	72	1836
Allen	Fort Wayne	308,503	3	659	(1,706)	1	1824
Bartholomew	Columbus	68,065	23	409	(1,059)	34	1821
Benton	Fowler	9,703	88	407	(1,053)	40	1840
Blackford	Hartford City	14,162	83	166	(429)	89	1839
Boone	Lebanon	41,813	32	423	(1,096)	28	1830
Brown	Nashville	15,098	81	312	(807)	76	1836
Carroll	Delphi	19,505	71	372	(964)	62	1828
Cass	Logansport	38,584	36	414	(1,073)	31	1828
Clark	Jeffersonville	91,826	16	376	(974)	60	1801
Clay	Brazil	26,306	60	360	(933)	70	1825
Clinton	Frankfort	32,594	44	405	(1,049)	41	1830
Crawford	English	10,442	87	307	(795)	79	1818
Daviess	Washington	28,603	53	432	(1,120)	26	1817
Dearborn	Lawrenceburg	44,367	30	307	(795)	79	1803
Decatur	Greensburg	24,998	63	373	(965)	61	1822
De Kalb	Auburn	37,955	38	364	(942)	68	1837
Delaware	Muncie	118,577	11	392	(1,015)	51	1827
Dubois	Jasper	38,732	37	429	(1,112)	27	1818
Elkhart	Goshen	166,994	6	466	(1,207)	16	1830
Fayette	Connersville	26,430	56	215	(558)	87	1817
Floyd	New Albany	70,058	21	150	(388)	91	1819
Fountain	Covington	18,060	77	398	(1,030)	46	1826
Franklin	Brookville	20,957	68	385	(998)	54	1811
Fulton	Rochester	19,922	70	369	(956)	64	1836
Gibson	Princeton	32,165	46	490	(1,268)	13	1813
Grant	Marion	73,720	19	415	(1,075)	30	1831
Greene	Bloomfield	32,696	45	546	(1,414)	4	1821
Hamilton	Noblesville	140,650	9	398	(1,030)	46	1823
Hancock	Greenfield	50,768	25	307	(795)	79	1828
Harrison	Corydon	32,594	48	486	(1,259)	14	1808
Hendricks	Danville	86,620	17	409	(1,059)	34	1824
Henry	New Castle	49,275	26	394	(1,020)	50	1822
Howard	Kokomo	83,763	18	293	(759)	82	1844
Huntington	Huntington	36,807	39	366	(948)	66	1834
Jackson	Brownstown	40,403	35	513	(1,329)	8	1816
Jasper	Rensselaer	27,895	54	561	(1,454)	3	1838
Jay	Portland	21,901	67	384	(995)	56	1836
Jefferson	Madison	30,813	50	363	(939)	69	1811
Jennings	Vernon	26,168	61	378	(980)	59	1817
Johnson	Franklin	101,690	15	321	(832)	75	1823
Knox	Vincennes	40,194	33	520	(1,346)	6	1790

County Name	County Seat	Population	Population Rank	Area in Square Miles (Square Kilometers)		Rank	Became a County
Kosciusko	Warsaw	69,210	22	540	(1,398)	5	1836
Lagrange	Lagrange	31,653	49	380	(984)	58	1832
Lake	Crown Point	482,672	2	501	(1,297)	12	1837
La Porte	La Porte	110,384	13	600	(1,555)	2	1832
Lawrence	Bedford	45,097	28	452	(1,171)	20	1818
Madison	Anderson	132,796	10	453	(1,173)	19	1823
Marion	Indianapolis	817,604	1	396	(1,026)	49	1822
Marshall	Plymouth	44,879	29	444	(1,151)	23	1836
Martin	Shoals	10,545	86	339	(877)	73	1820
Miami	Peru	32,611	42	369	(956)	64	1834
Monroe	Bloomington	115,208	12	385	(996)	54	1818
Montgomery	Crawfordsville	36,090	40	505	(1,308)	10	1823
Morgan	Martinsville	62,115	24	409	(1,060)	34	1822
Newton	Kentland	14,413	82	401	(1,038)	44	1860
Noble	Albion	30,884	34	413	(1,069)	32	1836
Ohio	Rising Sun	5,395	92	87	(226)	92	1844
Orange	Paoli	19,011	75	408	(1,057)	38	1816
Owen	Spencer	19,663	73	386	(1,001)	53	1819
Parke	Rockville	16,094	80	444	(1,149)	23	1821
Perry	Cannelton	19,129	74	382	(989)	57	1814
Pike	Petersburg	12,610	85	341	(883)	71	1817
Porter	Valparaiso	140,487	7	418	(1,083)	29	1836
Posey	Mount Vernon	26,493	58	409	(1,059)	34	1814
Pulaski	Winamac	12,960	84	435	(1,126)	25	1839
Putnam	Greencastle	32,939	43	482	(1,248)	15	1822
Randolph	Winchester	27,377	55	454	(1,175)	18	1818
Ripley	Versailles	26,829	57	447	(1,158)	22	1818
Rush	Rushville	18,456	76	408	(1,057)	38	1822
St. Joseph	South Bend	258,083	4	459	(1,189)	17	1830
Scott	Scottsburg	22,568	66	191	(495)	88	1820
Shelby	Shelbyville	42,809	31	413	(1,070)	32	1822
Spencer	Rockport	20,374	69	400	(1,036)	45	1818
Starke	Knox	22,620	65	309	(801)	77	1850
Steuben	Angola	30,060	51	308	(798)	78	1837
Sullivan	Sullivan	19,879	72	452	(1,171)	20	1817
Switzerland	Vevay	8,222	90	223	(578)	86	1814
Tippecanoe	Lafayette	135,285	8	502	(1,299)	11	1826
Tipton	Tipton	16,463	79	260	(673)	83	1844
Union	Liberty	7,292	91	162	(420)	90	1821
Vanderburgh	Evansville	168,065	5	236	(611)	85	1818
Vermillion	Newport	16,841	78	260	(674)	83	1824
Vigo	Terre Haute	106,622	14	405	(1,049)	42	1818
Wabash	Wabash	34,896	41	398	(1,032)	48	1835
Warren	Williamsport	8,394	89	366	(949)	66	1827
Warrick	Boonville	49,380	27	391	(1,013)	52	1813
Washington	Salem	26,088	62	516	(1,336)	7	1814
Wayne	Richmond	72,802	20	404	(1,046)	43	1811
Wells	Bluffton	26,506	59	370	(959)	63	1837
White	Monticello	24,505	64	506	(1,311)	9	1834
Whitley	Columbia City	29,426	52	336	(870)	74	1838

THE STAR-SPANGLED BANNER

Words by Francis Scott Key

Oh, say! can you see, by the dawn's early light,
What so proudly we hailed at the twilight's last gleaming,
Whose broad stripes and bright stars, through the perilous fight,
O'er the ramparts we watched were so gallantly streaming?
And the rockets' red glare, the bombs bursting in air,
Gave proof through the night that our flag was still there.
Oh, say! does that Star-Spangled Banner yet wave
O'er the land of the free and the home of the brave?

On the shore dimly seen thro' the mists of the deep,
Where the foe's haughty host in dread silence reposes,
What is that which the breeze, o'er the towering steep,
As it fitfully blows, half conceals, half discloses?
Now it catches the gleam of the morning's first beam,
In full glory reflected, now shines on the stream;
'Tis the star-spangled banner: oh, long may it wave
O'er the land of the free and the home of the brave.

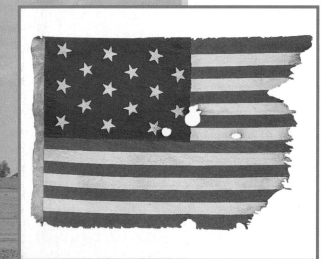

And where is that band who so vauntingly swore
That the havoc of war and the battle's confusion
A home and a country should leave us no more?
Their blood has wash'd out their foul footsteps' pollution.
No refuge could save the hireling and slave
From the terror of flight or the gloom of the grave,
And the star-spangled banner in triumph doth wave
O'er the land of the free and the home of the brave.

Oh, thus be it ever when free men shall stand,
Between their loved homes and the war's desolation;
Blest with vict'ry and peace, may the heav'n-rescued land
Praise the Power that has made and preserved us as a nation.
Then conquer we must, when our cause it is just,
And this be our motto: "In God is our trust";
And the star-spangled banner in triumph shall wave
O'er the land of the free and the home of the brave.

September 14, 1814—A British warship standing off Fort McHenry in the harbor of Baltimore, Maryland, has begun an intense bombardment that will continue through the night. Kept on board when the bombardment started, Francis Scott Key stands at the ship's rail, hoping to catch a glimpse of the fort through the thick smoke. Now, as the sun rises, Key stares in amazement at the proud American flag that continues to wave. He pulls an envelope from his pocket and begins to write, "Oh, say! can you see. . . ."

ON THE BANKS OF THE WABASH, FAR AWAY

Words and music by Paul Dresser

'Round my Indiana homestead wave the cornfields,
In the distance loom the woodlands clear and cool.
Often times my tho'ts revert to scenes of childhood,
Where I first received my lessons—Nature's school.
But one thing there is missing in the picture,
Without her face it seems so incomplete.
I long to see my mother in the doorway,
As she stood there years ago, her boy to greet.

Many years have passed since I strolled by the river,
Arm in arm, with sweetheart Mary by my side,
It was there I tried to tell her that I loved her,
It was there I begged of her to be my bride,
Long years have passed since I strolled thro'
    the churchyard,
She's sleeping there my angel Mary dear.
I loved her but she thought I didn't mean it,
Still I'd give my future were she only here.

Chorus:

Oh, the moonlight's fair tonight along the Wabash,
From the fields there comes the breath of new-
    mown hay.
Through the sycamores the candle lights are gleaming,
On the banks of the Wabash, far away.

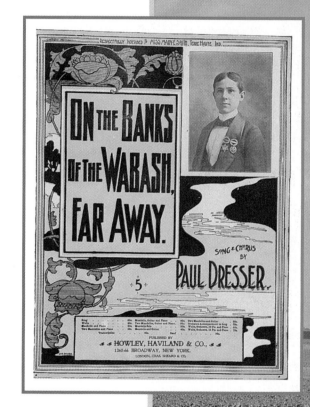

Paul Dresser wrote the words and the music for "On the Banks of the Wabash, Far Away." It became the official state song in 1913. A bound book of Dresser's sheet music, signed by the composer, is kept in the Vigo County Historical Society in Terre Haute.

Indiana

Governors

	Name of Governor	Term		Name of Governor	Term
Territorial Governors	1. William Henry Harrison	1800–1812	23.	Claude Matthews	1893–1897
	2. John Gibson	1812–1813	24.	James A. Mount	1897–1901
	3. Thomas Posey	1813–1816	25.	Winfield T. Durbin	1901–1905
			26.	J. Frank Hanly	1905–1909
State Governors	1. Jonathan Jennings	1816–1822	27.	Thomas R. Marshall	1909–1913
	2. Ratliff Boon	1822	28.	Samuel M. Ralston	1913–1917
	3. William Hendricks	1822–1825	29.	James P. Goodrich	1917–1921
	4. James B. Ray	1825–1831	30.	Warren T. McCray	1921–1924
	5. Noah Noble	1831–1837	31.	Emmett Forest Branch	1924–1925
	6. David Wallace	1837–1840	32.	Ed Jackson	1925–1929
	7. Samuel Bigger	1840–1843	33.	Harry G. Leslie	1929–1933
	8. James Whitcomb	1843–1848	34.	Paul V. McNutt	1933–1937
	9. Paris C. Dunning	1848–1849	35.	M. Clifford Townsend	1937–1941
	10. Joseph A. Wright	1849–1857	36.	Henry F. Schricker	1941–1945
	11. Ashbel P. Willard	1857–1860	37.	Ralph F. Gates	1945–1949
	12. Abram A. Hammond	1860–1861	38.	Henry F. Schricker	1949–1953
	13. Henry Smith Lane	1861	39.	George N. Craig	1953–1957
	14. Oliver P. Morton	1861–1867	40.	Harold W. Handley	1957–1961
	15. Conrad Baker	1867–1873	41.	Matthew E. Welsh	1961–1965
	16. Thomas A. Hendricks	1873–1877	42.	Roger D. Branigin	1965–1969
	17. James D. Williams	1877–1880	43.	Edgar D. Whitcomb	1969–1973
	18. Isaac P. Gray	1880–1881	44.	Dr. Otis R. Bowen	1973–1981
	19. Albert G. Porter	1881–1885	45.	Robert D. Orr	1981–1989
	20. Isaac P. Gray	1885–1889	46.	Evan Bayh	1989–1997
	21. Alvin P. Hovey	1889–1891			
	22. Ira Joy Chase	1891–1893			

Indy 500 Winners

1911	Ray Harroun		1957	Sam Hanks
1912	Joe Dawson		1958	Jimmy Bryan
1913	Jules Goux		1959	Rodger Ward
1914	Rene Thomas		1960	Jim Rathmann
1915	Ralph De Palma		1961	A. J. Foyt
1916	Dario Resta		1962	Rodger Ward
1919	Howdy Wilcox		1963	Parnelli Jones
1920	Gaston Chevrolet		1964	A. J. Foyt
1921	Tommy Milton		1965	Jim Clark
1922	Jimmy Murphy		1966	Graham Hill
1923	Tommy Milton		1967	A. J. Foyt
1924	L. L. Corum and Joe Boyer		1968	Bobby Unser
1925	Peter De Paolo		1969	Mario Andretti
1926	Frank Lockhart		1970	Al Unser
1927	George Souders		1971	Al Unser
1928	Louis Meyer		1972	Mark Donohue
1929	Ray Keech		1973	Gordon Johncock
1930	Billy Arnold		1974	Johnny Rutherford
1931	Louis Schneider		1975	Bobby Unser
1932	Frederick Frame		1976	Johnny Rutherford
1933	Louis Meyer		1977	A. J. Foyt
1934	Bill Cummings		1978	Al Unser
1935	Kelly Petillo		1979	Rick Mears
1936	Louis Meyer		1980	Johnny Rutherford
1937	Wilbur Shaw		1981	Bobby Unser
1938	Floyd Roberts		1982	Gordon Johncock
1939	Wilbur Shaw		1983	Tom Sneva
1940	Wilbur Shaw		1984	Rick Mears
1941	Mauri Rose and Floyd Davis		1985	Danny Sullivan
1946	George Robson		1986	Bobby Rahal
1947	Mauri Rose		1987	Al Unser
1948	Mauri Rose		1988	Rick Mears
1949	William Holland		1989	Emerson Fittipaldi
1950	Johnny Parsons		1990	Arie Luyendyk
1951	Lee Wallard		1991	Rick Mears
1952	Troy Ruttman		1992	Al Unser, Jr.
1953	Bill Vukovich		1993	Emerson Fittipaldi
1954	Bill Vukovich		1994	Al Unser, Jr.
1955	Bob Sweikert		1995	Jacques Villeneuve
1956	Pat Flaherty		1996	Buddy Lazier

Indiana
Festivals and Events

Spencer Apple Butter Festival, Spencer

Fall

Harvest Moon Festival, Whiting

Ethnic Expo Festival, Columbus

Versailles Pumpkin Show, Versailles

Hoosier Storytelling Festival, Indianapolis

Canal Days, Metamora

Feast of the Hunter's Moon, Lafayette

Mississinewa 1812, Marion

Heartland Film Festival, Indianapolis

Valparaiso Popcorn Festival, Valparaiso

Parke County Covered Bridge Festival,
    Rockville

Spencer Apple Butter Festival, Spencer

Winter

WTPI Winter Jazz Festival, Indianapolis

Winterfest, LaPorte

Wawasee Winter Carnival, Syracuse

Lincoln Day Celebration, Lincoln City

Parke County Maple Fair, Rockville

Bluegrass Festival, Columbus

Quilter's Hall of Fame Celebrates
    National Quilting Day, Marion

Jack Frost Jamboree Craft & Art Fair,
    Valparaiso

*Bridgeton Covered Bridge, Parke
County Covered Bridge Festival*

*Ethnic Expo
Festival, Columbus*

4-H Spring Round Up, Evansville

Indiana State Fair, Indianapolis

Spring

4-H Spring Round Up, Evansville

Earthfest, Crown Point

Earth Day at the Zoo, Evansville

International Day Festival, Kokomo

School Days, Rockville

American Indian Council 4th Annual Traditional Pow Wow, Lebanon

Pioneer Days, Evansville

Cabin Days, South Bend

Little 500, Plymouth

Herb Festival, Hope

Spirit of Vincennes Rendezvous, Vincennes

Civil War Days, Hartford City

Summer

Three Rivers Festival, Fort Wayne Civil War Weekend, Lowell

Covington 4th of July Celebration, Covington

Whiting 4th of July Parade and Festival, Whiting

Annual Ethnic Festival, South Bend

City of Lakes Balloonfest, Warsaw

Indiana State Fair, Indianapolis

A Festooned 4th Festival: Crafters'/Artists' Fair & Children's Carnival, Lafayette

Old Settlers Day, Corydon

Indiana Black Expo Summer Celebration, Indianapolis

Thunder in the Field, San Pierre

Commanding Bluff Rendezvous, Bluffton

RCA Tennis Championships, Indianapolis

West Washington Art Fair, South Bend

Marshall County Blueberry Festival, Plymouth

International Culture Festival, Hammond

Swiss Days, Berne

Herb Festival, Hope

GLOSSARY

Some words in this book may be new to you or difficult to pronounce. Those words have been spelled phonetically in parentheses. The syllable that receives stress in a word is shown in small capital letters.

For example: Chicago (shuh KAH goh)

Most phonetic spellings are easy to read. In the following Pronunciation Key, you can see how letters are used to show different sounds.

PRONUNCIATION KEY
---

a	after	(AF tur)	oh	flow	(floh)	ch	chicken	(CHIHK un)
ah	father	(FAH thhur)	oi	boy	(boi)	g	game	(gaym)
ai	care	(kair)	oo	rule	(rool)	ing	coming	(KUM ing)
aw	dog	(dawg)	or	horse	(hors)	j	job	(jahb)
ay	paper	(PAY pur)	ou	cow	(kou)	k	came	(kaym)
						ng	long	(lawng)
e	letter	(LET ur)	yoo	few	(fyoo)	s	city	(SIHT ee)
ee	eat	(eet)	u	taken	(TAYK un)	sh	ship	(shihp)
				matter	(MAT ur)	th	thin	(thihn)
ih	trip	(trihp)	uh	ago	(uh GOH)	thh	feather	(FETHH ur)
eye	idea	(eye DEE uh)				y	yard	(yahrd)
y	hide	(hyd)				z	size	(syz)
ye	lie	(lye)				zh	division	(duh VIHZH un)

A

abolitionist (ab uh LIHSH un ihst) A person who wanted to put an end to slavery. p. 208.

acid rain (AS ihd rayn) Rain that is full of acids formed in the air when fuels such as coal are burned. p. 310.

aeronautics (er oh NAWT iks) The science of making and flying aircraft. p. 334.

ancestor (AN ses tur) A family member from the past. p. 36.

appeal (uh PEEL) A request to have a decision in a law case reviewed by a higher court. p. 280.

archaeologist (ahr kee AHL uh jihst) A scientist who studies ancient times and people. p. 34.

architect (AHR kuh tekt) Person who designs buildings and supervises their construction. p. 327.

artifact (AHRT uh fakt) An object made by humans. p. 32.

artillery (ahr TIHL ur ee) Large guns, such as cannons, that are too heavy to carry. p. 205.

artisan (AHRT uh zun) A person who makes objects using great skill. p. 82.

assembly line (uh SEM blee lyn) A process in which each worker in a factory performs a different step or job in putting together a product. p. 298.

B

bill (bihl) A draft for a possible law. p. 279.

Bill of Rights (bihl uv ryts) A list of citizens' basic rights. p. 272.

biotechnology (bye oh tek NAHL uh jee) A branch of science that uses technology to study plants and animals. p. 307.

bison (BYE sun) The American buffalo. p. 78.

blab school (blab skool) A school where students recite their lessons aloud. p. 156.

blast furnace (blast FUR nus) Enclosed place where heat is produced to melt iron out of iron ore. p. 231.

boycott (BOI kaht) To refuse to buy, use, or sell something. p. 257.

buckskins (BUK skihnz) Deerskin clothing. p. 114.

budget (BUJ iht) A careful plan for spending money. p. 279.

bushel (BUSH ul) A measure of volume for grain, fruits, or vegetables. p. 303.

C

campus (KAM pus) The grounds and buildings of a school or a college. p. 336.

canal (kuh NAL) A waterway that is made by artificial means, as by digging. p. 175.

canyon (KAN yun) A long, narrow valley with high cliffs on each side. p. 260.

capsule (KAP sul) The enclosed part of a spacecraft, which holds the people and instruments. p. 334.

census (SEN sus) An official count of the number of people living in a place. p. 52.

checks and balances (cheks and BAL un sez) A government system that prevents one branch of government from becoming too powerful. p. 274.

civil rights (SIHV ul ryts) The rights of all citizens to life, liberty, property, and equal protection under the law. p. 123.

climate (KLYE mut) The general weather conditions of an area over a long period of time. p. 8.

colony (KAHL uh nee) An area of land settled by people from a distant country and controlled by that country. p. 98.

committee (kum MIHT ee) A group of people chosen to study or do a certain thing. p.259.

competition (kahm puh TIHSH un) A contest. p. 323.

component (kum POH nunt) A part or piece. p. 307.

confederacy (kun FED ur uh see)   A union of people, groups, or states united for a certain purpose. p. 124.

congressional district (kun GRESH uh nul DISH trihkt) A special division of a state from which people elect a representative to Congress. p. 277.

conservation (kahn sur VAY shun) Protecting resources. p. 19.

consolidate (kun SAHL uh dayt) Join together; unite. p. 286.

constitution (kahn stuh TOO shun) A document with the basic laws and rules of a government. p. 127.

cooperative (koh AHP ur uh tihv) Style of living in which members of a community share work, goods, and profits. p. 188.

courthouse (KORT hous) A building with law courts and government offices. p. 58.

culture (KUL chur) The ideas, skills, arts, tools, and way of life of certain people at a certain time. p. 34.

curator (kyoo RAYT ur) A person in charge of a museum. p. 44.

D

depression (dee PRESH un) A time when businesses suffer and people lose their jobs. p. 247.

dialect (DYE uh lekt) Language used only in a certain place or by a certain group of people. p. 237.

dictator (DIHK tayt ur) A ruler who has complete power over a country. p. 248.

discrimination (dih scrihm ih NAY shun) Unfair treatment of a particular person or group. p. 210.

diverse (duh VURS) Different from one another. p. 63.

document (DAHK yoo munt) A written record. p. 32.

E

economy (ih KAHN uh mee) The production and distribution of goods and services. p. 9.

engineer (en juh NEER) A person who uses science and math to design and build things. p. 307.

environment (en VYE run munt) Things that surround us. p. 20.

erosion (ee ROH zhun) Loss of soil due to its being washed away by rain or blown away by wind. p. 311.

exhibit (eg ZIHB iht) A show open to the public. p. 44.

export (eks PORT) To send goods out of a country. p. 299.

F

family tree (FAM uh lee tree) A chart of family members. p. 36.

flatboat (FLAT boht) A flat-bottomed boat. p. 148.

folk tale (fohk tayl) A story passed down by word of mouth. p. 40.

front (frunt) The place where two opposing armies meet. p. 249.

G

gallery (GAL ur ee) A place for showing or selling art. p. 326.

geography (jee AHG ruh fee) The study of the earth and how people use it. p. 7.

glacier (GLAY shur) A huge mass of ice that moves across land until it melts. p. 13.

grant (grant) Something given, such as a piece of land. p. 129.

gristmill (GRIHST mihl) A building with machinery used for grinding grain into flour. p. 150.

H

habitat (HAB ih tat) Native home of a plant or animal. p. 261.

heritage (HER ih tihj) Something handed down from one's ancestors or the past. p. 87.

homespun (HOHM spun) Cloth made at home by spinning and weaving. p. 154.

I

immigrant (IHM uh grunt) Person from one country who moves to another country to live. p. 56.

import (ihm PORT) To bring goods into a country. p. 299.

interstate (IHN tur stayt) Between states. p. 181.

intramural (ihn truh MYOOR ul) Between members of the same school or college. p. 329.

J

jazz (jaz) A type of American music with strong rhythms that started with black southerners. p. 321.

L

labor union (LAY bur YOON yun) A group of workers joined together to work for higher pay and better working conditions. p. 225.

landform (LAND form) A feature of the earth's surface created by nature. p. 12.

landscape (LAND skayp) A picture of an outdoor scene. p. 239.

lean-to (LEEN too) A shelter with a sloping roof. p. 152.

legislature (LEJ ihs lay chur) A group that makes laws. p. 122.

M

majority (muh JOR uh tee) More than half. p. 283.

mansion (MAN shun) A large house. p. 161.

metropolitan (ME troh pahl ih tun) Making up a large city and its suburbs. p. 185.

migration (mye GRAY shun) Movement of people from one region to another. p. 246.

moccasin (MAHK uh sun) A shoe made of soft leather. p. 112.

mound (mound) A heap or bank of earth. p. 79.

N

natural resource (NACH ur ul REE sors) Any useful material from the earth, such as water, oil, or minerals. p. 18.

naturalized citizen (NACH ur ul eyzd SIHT uh zun) A person who was not born here but became a U.S. citizen. p. 272.

navigation (nav uh GAY shun) Planning and controlling the course of a ship. p. 303.

O

oral history (OR ul HIHS tuh ree) Information about the past passed down by word of mouth. p. 40.

ordinance (ORD un uns) An official order or rule. p. 122.

overuse (oh ver YOOS) Too much or too frequent use. p. 261.

P

performing artist (pur FORM ihng AHRT ihst) Singer, dancer, actor, and other person who performs for audiences. p. 328.

petition (puh TIHSH un) A written request to someone in authority signed by a number of people. p. 288.

politics (PAHL ih tihks) The act of taking part in government affairs. p. 288.

popular sovereignty (PAHP yoo lur SAHV run tee) The idea that all political power comes from the people. p. 278.

population (pahp yoo LAY shun) The number of people who live in an area. p. 10.

population density (pahp yoo LAY shun DEN suh tee) The average number of people living in an area. p. 53.

portage (POR tihj) Land route over which boats and supplies are carried from one river or lake to another. p. 111.

prairie (PRER ee) A region of flat, grassy land. p. 162.

precipitation (pree sihp uh TAY shun) Water that falls to the earth as rain, snow, sleet, or hail. p. 8.

prehistoric (pree hihs TOR ihk) Of the time before written history. p. 77.

proclamation (prahk luh MAY shun) An official announcement. p. 103.

public transit (PUB lihk TRANS iht) Transportation available to everyone. p. 223.

R

radar (RAY dahr) Radio waves that are used to gather information. p. 308.

ration (RA shun) To limit the amount of something that a person can get. p. 249.

reaper (REE pur) Machine that cuts crops for harvesting. p. 202.

rebellion (rih BEL yun) A fight or struggle against a government or authority. p. 102.

reclaim (rih KLAHM) Make useable again for growing things. p. 312.

recycle (ree SYE kul) To reuse resources. p. 19.

reform (rih FORM) Correction of faults or evils. p. 203.

refugee (ref yoo JEE) A person who flees from his or her home or country to seek safety. p. 255.

regiment (REJ uh munt) A unit of soldiers made up of ten companies of about 100 soldiers each. p. 206.

region (REE jun) A part of the earth's surface that has common characteristics. p. 7.

renewable (rih NOO uh bul) Able to be replaced. p. 297.

repeal (rih PEEL) Put an end to, withdraw. p. 206.

research (REE surch) Careful study to find out facts about a subject. p. 31.

reservoir (REZ ur vwahr) A place where water is collected. p. 297.

resist (rih ZIHST) To fight or work against; oppose. p. 130.

restore (rih STOR) To make like new. p. 162.

root cellar (root SEL ur) An underground storage room. p. 112.

rural (ROOR ul) Having to do with the countryside. p. 54.

S

sapling (SAP lihng) A young tree. p. 89.

satellite (SAT ul eyt) An object placed into orbit around the earth in order to gather information. p. 308.

scholarship (SKAHL ur shihp) Gift of money to help a student pay for education. p. 330.

secede (sih SEED) Break away from an organization or nation. p. 198.

segregation (seg ruh GAY shun) The practice of separating people of different races. p. 257.

separation of powers (sep uh RAY shun uv POU urz) A way of dividing the powers of government among its branches. p. 275.

service industry (SUR vihs IHN dus tree) A business that employs people who help others. p. 64.

shard (shahrd) A broken piece of pottery. p. 83.

sheriff (SHER ihf) The chief county law officer. p. 284.

silt (sihlt) Small pieces of soil left by water or wind. p. 16

skyscraper (SKYE skray pur) A very tall building. p. 305.

slave (slayv) A person owned by another person. p. 157.

smelt (smelt) To melt in order to separate the pure metal from the waste substances. p. 231.

squatter (SKWAHT ur) A person who settles on land he or she does not own. p. 146.

stockade (stah KAYD) A wall of tall stakes built around a place for defense. p. 85.

strike (stryk) To refuse to work until certain demands, such as higher pay, are met. p. 225.

suburb (SUB urb) A town on the outskirts of a city. p. 54.

suffrage (SUF rihj) The right to vote. p. 256.

surrender (suh REN dur) To give up. p. 107.

survey (sur VAY) To measure the size, shape, boundaries, or other features of an area. p. 23.

T

tax (taks) Money paid to the government. p. 103.

technical (TEK nih kul) Having to do with useful or industrial skills. p. 336.

telecommunications (tel ih kuh myoo nih KAY shunz) The exchange of information by computer, telephone, and satellite. p. 67.

temperance (TEM pur uns) Drinking little or no alcohol. p. 211.

territory (TER uh tor ee) Land ruled by a nation or state. p. 122.

textile (TEKS tyl) A fabric made by weaving. p. 175.

threshing machine (THRESH ihng muh SHEEN) Machine that cuts and separates grain. p. 202.

till (tihl) Soil made of clay, sand, gravel, and other materials left by a glacier. p. 14.

town square (toun skwer) A park or green in the center of a town. p. 58.

township (TOUN shihp) Division of land six-miles square. p. 146.

trace (trays) A natural trail created by animal hooves over time. p. 180.

trading post (TRAYD ihng pohst) A store where goods are bought, sold, and traded. p. 100.

treaty (TREET ee) An agreement between nations. p. 103.

tribute (TRIHB yoot) Something given or done to show thanks or respect. p. 235.

U

urban (UR bun) Having to do with cities. p. 54.

V

vegetation (vej uh TAY shun) Plant life. p. 22.

veto (VEE toh) To reject a proposed law. p. 280.

visual artist (VIHZH oo ul AHRT ihst) A person, such as a painter or sculptor, who creates artwork that people can see. p. 326.

W

war bond (wor bahnd) A certificate sold by the government to raise money. p. 253.

wetlands (WET landz) Swamps or marshes, especially in an area reserved for wildlife. p. 310.

wigwam (WIHG wahm) A round, bark-covered house. p. 88.

ACKNOWLEDGMENTS

Grateful acknowledgment is made to the following publishers, authors, and agents for their permission to reprint copyrighted material. Every effort has been made to locate all copyright proprietors; any errors or omissions in copyright notice are inadvertent and will be corrected in future printings as they are discovered.

Excerpt and cover art from *Allen Jay and the Underground Railroad* by Marlene Targ Brill. Text copyright © 1993 by Marlene Targ Brill. Illustrations copyright © 1993 by Carolrhoda Books, Inc. Used by permission of the publisher. All rights reserved.

Excerpt and cover art from *A Clearing in the Forest* by Joanne Landers Henry. Text copyright © 1992 by Joanne Landers Henry. Reprinted by permission of Simon & Schuster Books for Young Readers.

Excerpt and cover art from *The Floating House* by Scott Russell Sanders, illustrated by Helen Cogancherry. Text copyright © 1995 by Scott Russell Sanders. Illustrations copyright © 1995 by Helen Cogancherry. Reprinted by permission of Atheneum Books for Young Readers, an imprint of Simon & Schuster.

Excerpt and cover art from *If You Grew Up with Abraham Lincoln* by Ann McGovern, illustrated by George Ulrich. Text copyright © 1966 by Ann McGovern. Illustrations copyright © 1992 by Scholastic. Reprinted by permission of the publisher.

Excerpt and cover art from *Johnny Appleseed* by Steven Kellogg. Copyright © 1988 by Steven Kellogg. Used by permission of Morrow Junior Books, a division of William Morrow & Company, Inc.

Cover art from *May I Bring a Friend?* by Beatrice Schenk de Regniers, illustrated by Beni Montresor. Illustrations copyright © 1964 by Beni Montresor. Published by Atheneum Books for Young Readers, an imprint of Simon & Schuster.

Excerpt and cover art from *Out to Win Indy!* by Jay Schleifer. Copyright © 1995 by Silver Burdett Press. Published by Crestwood House, an imprint of Silver Burdett Press, Simon & Schuster Elementary. Used by permission

Cover art from *Shiloh* by Phyllis Reynolds Naylor, jacket illustration by Lynne Dennis. Illustration copyright © 1991 by Lynne Dennis. Published by Atheneum Books for Young Readers, an imprint of Simon & Schuster.

CREDITS

Front Cover *Design, Art Direction, and Production* Design Five, NYC; *Photo* Dana Sigall. Photos: top to bottom, left to right: © Dede Gilman/Unicorn Stock Photos. © Martha McBride/Unicorn Stock Photos. © Andre Jenny/N E Stock Photos. © Indy 500 Photos, IMS photo by Jim Fennig. © Cheryl A. Ertelt/N E Stock Photos. © Andre Jenny/N E Stock Photos. © J.C. Allen & Son. © Michael Shedlock/N E Stock Photos. © Dick Keen/Unicorn Stock Photos.

Maps Mapping Specialists Limited

All photographs by Silver Burdett Ginn (SBG) unless otherwise noted.

Photographs 1: *bkgd:* Tom Stack & Associates. *t.l.* © Michael Shedlock/N E Stock Photos. *t.r.* © Richard Fields. *m.r.* Indiana Historical Society, neg. KCT 202. 2: Parker/Boon Productions for SBG. 2–3: © Michael Shedlock/N E Stock Photos. 4: © Robin Rudd/Unicorn Stock Photos. 6: *t.r.* © Mike Bowman/Ski Paoli Peaks. *m.r.* © Pete Helfrich/Evansville Convention and Visitors Bureau. *b.r.* © Richard Fields. 9: *t.r.* © Ted Rose/Unicorn Stock Photos. *b.r.* Courtesy Carpenter Manufacturing, Richmond, IN. 10: Bureau of the Census. 13: © William J. Jahoda/Photo Researchers. 14: © Cathlyn Melloan/Tony Stone Images. 15: © Michael Shedlock/N E Stock Photos. 16: © Alex S. MacLean/Landslides. 17: © Richard Fields. 18–19: © Peter Pearson/Tony Stone Images. 20: © Richard Fields. 22: © Sam Scott. 23: *t.l.* © Bob Daemmrich. *b.r.* © Michael Newman/PhotoEdit. 25: © Peter Beck/The Stock Market. 26: Parker/Boon Productions for SBG. 26–27: Indiana Historical Society, neg. KCT 197 and 198. 28: Indiana Historical Society, neg. KCT 203. 29: *t.r.* Indiana Historical Society, neg. KCT 202. *m.* Indiana Historical Society, neg. KC7 201. 31: *t.l.* © Richard Fields. *m.* Courtesy Office of Army Public Affairs. 32: *t.l.* Indiana Historical Society, neg. KCT 200. *b.l.* © Charles H. Phillips. 33: *t.r.* Indiana Historical Society, neg. KCT 199. *m.l.* © David Young-Wolff/PhotoEdit. *b.r.* © Baseball Hall of Fame. 34: © Richard Fields. 35: © Darryl Jones. 36: Indiana State Archives. 37: *t.l.* Indiana Historical Society, neg. KCT 197 and 198. *b.* © Richard Fields. 38: *t.l.* © Cathy Melloan/Tony Stone Images. *t.r.* Photo courtesy Richard Day. 39: *t.* © James P. Rowan. *b.l.* Courtesy Nancy Wolfe, Indiana Junior Historical Society. 40: © Rhoda Sidney/PhotoEdit. 41: © Richard Fields. 45: *t.* © Eiteljorg Museum of American Indians and Western Art. *b.* Indianapolis Motor Speedway Hall of Fame Museum/Steve Ellis, photographer. 48: Parker/Boon Productions for SBG. 48–49: © Mark Lewis/Tony Stone Images. 52: © Robert Daemmrich/Tony Stone Images. 56: *m.t.* © Trevor Wood/Tony Stone Images. *t.l.* © Thompson & Thompson/Tony Stone Images. *t.r.* © Don Smetzer/Tony Stone Images. *m.l.* © Chris Bayley/Tony Stone Images. *m.r.* © Chris Everard/Tony Stone Images. *b.l.* © John Kelly/Tony Stone Images. 57: © Phil McCarten/PhotoEdit. 58: © Cathlyn Melloan/Tony Stone Images. 59: *t.l.* © Richard Fields. *b.* Studebaker National Museum, South Bend, IN. 60: *t.l.* © Cheryl A. Ertelt/N E Stock Photos. 60–61: *m.b.* © Andre Jenny/Unicorn Stock Photos. 61: *m.t.* © Richard Fields. *t.r.* Photograph courtesy The Children's Museum of Indianapolis. 64: © Richard Fields. 66: *t.l.* © Richard Fields. *t.r.* © Richard Fields. *m.l.* Photo courtesy Gettelfinger Popcorn Co. 67: *m.t.* © Don Hamerman/N E Stock Photos. *m.b.* The Selmer Company/L.P., Elkhart, IN. *t.l.* © John Nation/Falls of the Ohio State Park. 70: © Delta Queen Steamboat Company. 71: *m.t.* © Filson Club Historical Society. *t.r.* From the collections of the Henry Ford Museum and Greenfield Village. *m.r.* Library of Congress. 72: Parker/Boon Productions for SBG. 72–73: 1995 The Detroit Institute of Arts, Robert Hensleigh, photographer/Collection of Cranbrook Institute of Science. 75: © Myrleen Ferguson/PhotoEdit. 79: *t.l.* Courtesy of the Glenn A. Black Laboratory, Indiana University. *b.l.* Courtesy Ball State University, Archaeological Research Management Service, Charles A. Smith. 82: *m.t.* Courtesy Ball State University, Archaeological Research Management Service, Charles A. Smith. *m.b.* Courtesy of the Glenn A. Black Laboratory, Indiana University. 83: Courtesy of the Glenn A. Black Laboratory, Indiana University. 85: *t.* © James P. Rowan. *b.* Courtesy of the Glenn A. Black Laboratory, Indiana University. 87: Courtesy of the Glenn A. Black Laboratory, Indiana University. 89: 1995 The Detroit Institute of Arts, Robert Hensleigh, photographer/Collection of Cranbrook Institute of Science. 91: © Carissa Mongosa. 94: Parker/Boon Productions for SBG. 94–95: © Richard Fields. 96: © Richard Fields. 98: *m.* © Detroit Institute of Arts, Founders Society Purchase. *b.r.* Courtesy Gerald Peters Gallery, Santa Fe, NM. 100: *b.r.* Courtesy, Richard Day. *m.b.* Danbury Scott-Fanton Museum. 102: Anne S.K. Brown Military Collection, John Hay Library, Brown

University. 103: The Bettmann Archive. 106: © Filson Club Historical Society. 108: Photo courtesy George Rogers Clark, NHP. 109: *m.b.* © James P. Rowan. *t.l.* Photo courtesy George Rogers Clark, NHP. 114 © James P. Rowan. 115: © James P. Rowan. 118: Parker/Boon Productions for SBG. 118–119: Photo courtesy Conner Prairie. 120: © Spencer Grant/Liaison International. 121: © David Young-Wolff/PhotoEdit. 123: George Harvey 1801–1878 *Spring—Burning Fallen Leaves,* circa 1840, watercolor, 35.2 x 26.2, 46.49 Dick S. Ramsay Fund, The Brooklyn Museum. 124: The Granger Collection. 125: *m.b.* The Granger Collection. *t.* Chicago Historical Society. 126: *t.l.* The Field Museum, Neg #A93851.1c, Chicago, photographer John Weinstein. *m.l.* Royal Ontario Museum. *b.r.* © James P. Rowan. 130: Smithsonian Institution, neg. 794. 131: *t.* Courtesy The Henry Francis du Pont Winterthur Museum. *b.r.* Indiana Historical Bureau. 132: Tecumseh Belt, Department of Canadian Heritage: Fort Malden National Historic Site. 133: The Granger Collection. 142: Parker/Boon Productions for SBG. 142–143: © Richard Fields. 146–147: © Alex Maclean/Landslides. 148: *t.l.* The Granger Collection. *b.* From the collections of the Henry Ford Museum and Greenfield Village. 149: *t.l.* Courtesy Peabody Essex Museum, Salem, Mass./Mark Sexton. *b.r.* Photo courtesy Conner Prairie. 152: *t.r.* © Andre Jenny/N E Stock Photos. *l.* © Old Sturbridge Village. 154: *t.l.* Photo courtesy Sage Historic Costume Collection, Bloomington, IN. *b.r.* From the collections of the Henry Ford Museum and Greenfield Village. 155: Abby Aldrich Folk Art Center, Williamsburg, VA. 156: Illinois State Historical Society. 157: *t.* Indiana Historical Society, Photo M567, neg. No C5306. *b.* Photo courtesy Illinois Historic Preservation Agency. 158–159: © Shelburne Museum, photo by Ken Burris. 160: Photo courtesy Delta Queen Steamboat Company. 161: *t.* © James P. Rowan. *m.* © Richard Fields. *b.* © Richard Fields. 162: *m.t.* © Mary Stadtfield/Unicorn Stock Photos. *t.l.* Photo courtesy Conner Prairie. *r.* Photo courtesy Conner Prairie. 163: *m.b.* © Old Sturbridge Village. *t.l.* Photo courtesy Conner Prairie. *m.m.* © Old Sturbridge Village. 166: Library of Congress. 166–167: Tom Stack & Associates. 167: *t.* © Keith Wood/Tony Stone Images. *r.* © UPI/Corbis-Bettmann. 168: Parker/Boon Productions for SBG. 168–169: H.G. Colyer Collection, Altoona Railroaders Memorial Museum. 170: © Tommy Dodson/Unicorn Stock Photos. 171: *t.* © Hans Schlapfer/Tony Stone Images. *b.* © Peter Pearson/Tony Stone Images. 172: Indiana Historical Society. 173: Indiana Historical Society. 175: Indiana State Library. 176: *m.t.* Photo/Film Courtesy of Old Economy Village, Pennsylvania Historical and Museum Commission, 1996. *t.r.* Indiana Historical Society. *b.* Collection of the New-York Historical Society. 177: George Winter, Tippecanoe County Historical Association. 178: Photo courtesy American Antiquarian Society. 179: Erie Canal Museum, Syracuse, NY. 180: Indiana State Library. 181: *t.r.* Courtesy of the Decorative and Industrial Arts Collection, Chicago Historical Society. *b.r.* © James P. Rowan. 182: Indiana Historical Society, neg. no. C6522. 183: The Bettmann Archive. 184–185: © Andre Jenny/N E Stock Photos. 186–187: © Richard Fields. 188: Karl Bodmer, *View of New Harmony* Joslyn Art Museum, Omaha, Nebraska; Gift of the Enron Art Foundation. 189: © Tom Ebenhoh/Black Star. 190: © L.L.T. Rhodes/Tony Stone Images. 191: © Jim Steinberg/Photo Researchers. 194: Parker/Boon Productions for SBG. 194–195: Indiana Historical Society, neg. no. C5203. 198: John Hay Library, Brown University, photographed by John Miller. 200: *t.l.* Indiana Historical Society/Bass Photo Collection, neg. 101242F. *m.* Indiana Historical Society, neg. no. C4363. 201: *t.* Picture Research Consultants/Collection of William Gladstone. *b.* Indiana Historical Society. 202: Indiana Historical Society, neg. no. C4715. 203: *m.m.* © Charles H. Phillips. *m.t.* President Benjamin Harrison Home. 205: *t.* © Filson Club Historical Society. 206: *t.r.* Lewis Historical

Collection, Vincennes University. *m.l.* Courtesy Indiana War Memorial, Indianapolis; Photo by Tom Pierson. 207: *t.* Stamatelos Brothers from *Echoes of Glory: Arms and Equipment of the Union.* Photograph by Larry Sherer © 1991 Time-Life Books Inc. *t.* (knife, fork, spoon) Christopher Nelson from *Echoes of Glory: Arms and Equipment of the Union.* Photograph by Larry Sherer © 1991 Time-Life Books Inc. 209: *t.l.* Cincinnati Art Museum, Subscription Fund Purchase. *t.r.* Indiana State Library. 210: *t.* Photo courtesy Abe Roth, Goshen, IN. *b.* © Charles H. Phillips. 211: *t.l.* Courtesy Schlesinger Library, Radcliffe College. *b.r.* Picture Research Consultants, Inc. 218: Parker/Boon Productions for SBG. 218–219: © Alan S. Orling/Black Star. 221: Photo courtesy Patricia Hall. 222: *t.r.* Courtesy Burndy Library, MIT. *b.l.* Indiana State Archives. 223: Courtesy National Historical Fire Foundation/Hall of Flame Museum. 224: *t.r.* Courtesy The Ball Corporation. *m.* © Charles H. Phillips. 225: *m.t.* Photo by Lewis Hine. *b.* Brown Brothers. 226: *t.l.* The Bettmann Archive. *t.r.* Courtesy Crawfordsville, IN. Public Library. 227: Indiana Historical Society/Bretzman Collection, neg. no. C2643. 228: *m.t.* Culver Pictures, Inc. *b.l.* Courtesy Purdue University. *b.r.* Calumet Regional Archives, Indiana University N.W. 229: *l.* Indiana Historical Society. *r.* © Margo Taussig Pinkerton/N E Stock Photos. 233: Indiana Historical Society. 234: Indiana Historical Society. 235: *t.l.* Courtesy Madame Walker Urban Life Center, Indianapolis. *t.r.* © Darryl Jones. 236: *t.r.* Indiana Historical Society/Lester C. Negley, Bass Photo Collection 207580F. *m.m.* Courtesy The Lilly Library, Indiana University, Bloomington, IN. 237: *t.* From the Collection of the Indiana State Museum and Historic Sites. *m.r.* Indiana State Library. 238: *t.* © 1935 RKO Pictures, Inc. Used by Permission of Turner Entertainment Co. All Rights Reserved. *b.r.* Ada Walter Shulz, *Pet Duck,* 1928, Oil on Canvas, 30 x 21. Courtesy Jay and Ellen Carter. 239: *t.* T.C. Steele, *Selma in the Garden.* c.1910, from the Collection of the Indiana State Museum and Historic Sites. *b.* © Dale Bernstein. 242: Parker/Boon Productions for SBG. 242–243: Culver Pictures, Inc. 246: Culver Pictures, Inc. 247: © Darryl Jones. 248: *t.l.* Courtesy University of Southern Indiana, Special Collections. *m.r.* Indiana State Library. *b.l.* Indiana Military Museum, Vincennes, photos by Kim Charles Ferrill. 249: *t.* Margaret Bourke-White, Life Magazine © Time, Inc. *b.* Courtesy The Indiana War Memorial. 250: © Dennis Brack/Black Star. 252: Cornell Capa, LIFE Magazine, © Time Inc., set # 38217. 253: *t.l.* The Bettmann Archive. *m.m.* Jim R. Osborne. *b.r.* Culver Pictures, Inc. 255: *m.b.* Collection of Michael Barson/Picture Research Consultants, Inc. *m.m.* Jim R. Osborne, © Hammond, Inc., Maplewood, NJ, license #12,283. 256: *m.b.* Culver Pictures, Inc. *t.l.* Indiana State Library. *m.r.* © Charles H. Phillips. 257: *m.t.* © Andy Sacks/Tony Stone Images. *t.l.* © Jane Bernard/Black Star. *b.* © Flip Schulke/Black Star. 258: *t.r.* The Bettmann Archive. *m.r.* Courtesy Dolly Millendar/Gary Historic Society. 259: *m.l.* Indiana State Library. *m.r.* Indiana Historical Society/Bass Photo Collection. 260: *m.b.* © James P. Rowan. *m.t.* © Michael Shedlock/N E Stock Photos. *t.l.* © Andre Jenny/N E Stock Photos. *b.l.* © James P. Rowan. *b.r.* © James P. Rowan. 261: *t.l.* © Richard Fields. 262: *m.b.* The Bettmann Archive. *t.r.* The Bettmann Archive. *m.l.* Courtesy WSBT Radio, South Bend, IN. 263: *t.* Tom Sobolik/Black Star. *b.l.* © Phil Degginger/Tony Stone Images. 265: © Bob Daemmrich. 266: William S. Nawrocki/Nawrocki Stock Photo. 267: *t.* Indiana Department of Commerce. *b.* © Rick Graves/Tony Stone Images. 268: Parker/Boon Productions for SBG. 268–269: © Don Mason/The Stock Market. 270: Indiana State Library. 272: © Ron Dye/Photo Dyenamics. 273: © David Frazier/Tony Stone Images. 274: Courtesy Supreme Court Historical Society. 275: *t.* Phoebe Bell/Folio. *b.* Michael Melford/The Image Bank. 276: *m.l.* Courtesy Indiana Democratic Party. *b.l.* Courtesy U.S. Senate. 278: © Richard Fields. 280: *t.l.* © Andre Jenny/N E Stock Photos.